Alpha 94

Literacy and Cultural Development Strategies in Rural Areas

Edited by
Jean-Paul Hautecoeur

Prepared by the Unesco Institute for Education
with the assistance of the
Ministry of Education & Science Government of Quebec,
the National Literacy Secretariat Department
of Human Resources Development Government of Canada
and the Ministry of Education & Science Government of Spain

CULTURE CONCEPTS
Publishers
Toronto, Canada

ALPHA 94 © 1994 jointly by Culture Concepts Inc. and Unesco Institute for Education

UIE ISBN 92 820 1067 8
Culture Concepts ISBN 0-921472-12-9

The Unesco Institute for Education, Hamburg, is a legally independent entity. While the programs of the Institute are established along the lines laid down by the General Conference of Unesco, the publications of the Institute are issued under its sole responsibility; Unesco is not responsible for their contents. The points of view, selection of facts and opinions expressed are those of the authors and do not necessarily coincide with the official positions of the Unesco Institute for Education, Hamburg. The designations employed and the presentation of the material in this publication do not imply the expression of any opinion whatsoever on the part of the Unesco Secretariat concerning the legal status of any country or territory, or its authorities, or concerning the delimitations of the frontiers of any country or territory.

The opinions expressed, facts selected and points of view expressed by the authors do not necessarily represent those of the publisher. Nor does the publisher claim any responsibility for the accuracy of referencs and sources provided by the authors.

CANADIAN CATALOGUING IN PUBLICATION DATA
Main entry under title:

Alpha 94: literacy & cultural development
   strategies in rural areas

Translation of: Alpha 94 : strategies d'alphabétisation et de la developpement culturel en milieu rural.
Co-published by Unesco Institute for Education.
Includes bibliographical references.
ISBN 0-921472-12-9

1. Literacy programs. 2. Rural development. 3. Rural conditions.
4. Rural development projects. 5. Communication in rural development.
I. Hautecoeur, Jean-Paul, 1943-.
II. Unesco Institute for Education. III. Title:
Literacy & cultural development strategies in rural areas.

LC149.A513 1994   302.2'244   C94-932534-1

Cover photograph «VELO», 1993
   by André Mathieu, sculptor

Book Cover Design by Robert MacDonald, MediaClones Inc.
Typesetting: Accurate Typesetting Limited
Printed & Bound in Canada

Unesco Institute for Education
B.P. 131023
20110 Hamburg
Germany

Culture Concepts Inc.
5 Darlingbrook Crescent
Toronto Canada M9A 3H4
Phone: 416-231-1692   Fax: 416-237-1832

CONTENTS

NORTH & SOUTH AMERICA

Previous titles in collection:

ALPHA 90 Current Research in Literacy
ALPHA 92 Literacy Strategies in the Community Movement

Orders to:

Unesco Institute for Education, Publication Unit   B. P. 131023, 2011 Hamburg,   Germany

PREFACE

Jean-Paul Hautecoeur
Unesco Institute for Education

LITERACY AND CULTURAL DEVELOPMENT STRATEGIES IN RURAL AREAS

ALPHA 94, is the third publication in the Unesco Institute for Education's Literacy Strategies in Industrialized Countries program.[1] The objectives of this action research program, coordinated by the Hamburg Institute, are to promote international intellectual cooperation in the field of adult literacy education, to support experimental socio-educational practices, and to disseminate its findings at the international level. The projects all run for two years. They are made possible by support from government agencies and non-governmental organizations, and by the participation of numerous researchers.

Through literacy issues, this book investigates the response of groups, local communities and organizations to the crises ravaging rural communities in many regions of industrialized countries. We examine the cultural initiatives being launched by these groups at the periphery of major systems of communications in their struggle to resist exclusion and exodus; the role educational activities, facilities and personnel are playing in comprehensive integrated development operations in outlying regions, often independently of national institutions and policies; and the function that local communities assign to educational activities and cultural research in their efforts to recreate vital, attractive and locally-controlled environments in places which have suffered major dislocations.

Aims

At the regional seminars held at the beginning of the study, the project was presented to the researchers in the following terms:

> This project aims at renewing literacy issues in rural areas from the perspective of cultural development integrated into community-based activities of local/regional development. In three Northern regions of the world, dynamic experiments in cultural action are to be implemented which explicitly link individual basic education and a collective change in the conditions of local life, and relate the technique of the written word to either the development of communication channels or an exchange between rural areas "with problems". Another goal is to make known and to upgrade

these experiences in local development as well as to establish an international network of research and action in a field which joins three phenomena: popular education, cultural action and local development.

This action research project is intended to be inductive and pragmatic. The starting point is the **local community**: its context, history, discourse, experience, plans, knowledge. On this basis, we probe the realities of **rural societies**, attentive to the particularities of local speech, and we strive to discover common situations, comparable forms of knowledge, transferable experiments. Periods of lonely labour were interrupted by seminars where we tried to differentiate situations and points of view, and to reassess our experiences. The 21 articles in this volume are the result of this mostly individual, partly collective effort. The articles are largely "peripheral", as are rural communities, but they are tied together by a common concern with literacy.

OUR PURPOSE & THEORETICAL UNDERPINNINGS

Our purpose was to renew the literacy problematic through a local, rural pluricultural perspective which admits regional and ethnic **differences**, brings them into focus, makes them known. One departure is this project's rejection of central authorized assessments of language skills and therefore our refusal to apply national or international standards to language use, skill assessment, statistical measurement of illiteracy rates in different populations, and so forth. In this respect, we are continuing along the path marked out by the previous studies in this series and our stance is consistent with the international position which emerged from a recent Unesco seminar.[2]

Our cultural understanding of literacy leads us to situate the written word within the social problematic of **communication**, rather than within the context of theories of reading/writing instruction. Our purpose is to investigate the processes of communication, the state of development of the means of communication, how they are used by groups, the meanings of their messages, etc. including literacy strategies which address the serious problems of loss of information, meaning and value in human interchanges. A second departure is therefore this project's rejection of all linguistic/scholastic approaches to literacy (reading, writing, arithmetic), which has led us to examine literacy in all aspects of the community's existence, not just in educational programs. This is why our title links literacy and cultural action.

Consequently, we are interested in **collective** aspects of literacy: on the one hand, the relationship between social role and language skills, the division of labour and relations of solidarity in human interchanges, the distribution of skills in the community; on the other hand, relations of oppression and the effects of colonization. Our third departure is that we have refused to isolate individual skills from the cultural context in which they are practised and from which they derive their meaning.

Our methodology and policy lead us to support cultural action strategies based on committed, dialogic **participatory intervention** by outside workers (group leaders, researchers, educators, etc.) in rural localities. In this respect, we must distance ourselves both from mass culture and from systemic educational programs or any other "mechanism" planned from the outside for rural "clienteles".

These are the theoretical underpinnings — the "four deviations" as they might say in China — which have guided our work. At the outset, the field of study was to embrace the four points of the compass, starting from Hamburg: south (southern Europe), east (central and eastern Europe), west (North America) and north (Arctic regions in the U.S. and Russia). In the end, rural societies in three major geopolitical regions were explored by participants from sixteen countries: southern Europe (Spain, Portugal, Italy, Greece, France, Belgium and the U.K.), central Europe (the Czech Republic, Slovakia, Slovenia, Bulgaria, Romania, Hungary), North America (Canada, the U.S.), with two deliberate detours, to Canada's Northwest Territories and Chile. Thus, we did deal with the Far North after all. The inclusion of Chile, which is further off the track, was doubly significant for us: Chile represents the newly industrialized countries of the south, and it also refers us to the popular education experiments in Latin America which helped to stimulate our interest in literacy (and echoes of which can be found in a number of the chapters in this volume).

Each of the three geopolitical regions had a particular significance for this study. In rural areas of the European Community, devastation of the countryside and mass demonstrations by farmers have ebbed under the Common Agriculture Policy (CAP), and a search for comprehensive solutions to the problems of these areas and their remaining communities has begun. In this context, southern Europe, which is the most rural region, has waged a vigorous resistance to underdevelopment and seen innovations which have been in keeping with both local cultures and the demands of post-modernity.

In the early 1990s, central Europe is, first and foremost, post-Communist Europe. On the one hand, rural societies had been subjected to collectivization and even the eradication of villages and displacement of populations (primarily but not exclusively in Romania, as the Hungarian contribution shows). On the other hand, the Communist regimes had safeguarded and supported local popular cultures (or at least those customs which were compatible with scientific socialism), provided rural areas with cultural facilities which had no counterparts in the West, and in some countries tolerated the development of a private subsistence economy. It was of great interest to us to discover how rural communities had "survived" under the dictatorial regimes, and how they are now enlisting this heritage to confront the new radical crisis of "liberalization" to reorganize their own survival.

North America has also suffered the full brunt of economic liberalization and the application of the productivist model to rural regions, with their dramatic social consequences. On the basis of my experience in Quebec, I saw the history of peripheral rural regions as the history of bankrupt regional development policies; the impoverishment of vast zones; the organized resistance by local communities, regions and farmers' unions; and the search for alternative models of development.[3]

This search for different literacy education practices — ones which break with the dominant "fight against illiteracy" model, with its scholastic solutions and individualistic, rehabilitative "psychological" approaches — also has counterparts in the United States, notably at the University of Tennessee and Kansas State University.[4] In Canada, a 1991 conference on rural literacy yielded orientations close to our own: "In the view of conference participants, rural literacy must be seen in relation to the development of threatened communities .... New cultural policies accompanied by the development of communication infrastructures and support for local experiments could maintain a balance between rural and urban areas."[5]

While it was not possible to include Siberian minorities in this study, we did attend to minority issues in each of the three major geopolitical regions. They receive prominent treatment in the North American contributions, with two chapters on the "First Nations" in Canada and one on migrant workers in the United States. Western European minorities are discussed in the contributions from the U.K. and Belgium; unfortunately, it was impossible to include an article on a popular theatre experiment with immigrants in France in this volume. In central Europe, the "Gypsy question" is dealt with in the Hungarian paper.

Intercultural issues were the subject of lively discussion at a conference held in Bratislava in October 1992 with the support of Comenius University, the Institute of Culture, and the Gypsy Cultural Association of Bratislava. We promised at Bratislave to give readers of *ALPHA 94* two sides of the "Gypsy question" (from the majority and minority points of view). We also undertook to make known the state of fear in which Gypsy minorities in central Europe subsist due to the frequency of attacks by extreme right-wing fringe groups. The message got through; the texts did not.[6]

Of the 16 countries which were involved in the study, 12 remain, represented by the 38 authors and 23 articles. Unfortunately, we could not include in this volume papers on the projects in Bulgaria, Slovenia, Slovakia and France (Foyers ruraux and Missions locales rurales). The number of texts from Spain is due to both the quality of the contributions and a deliberate choice on our part. We had decided to select a southern European country where different approaches to literacy and cultural action have been tried and where rural issues are contentious. It was Spain which hosted the first regional conference at El Escorial in April 1992, and then the wrap-up conference in Salamanca in April 1993.

Most of the contributors met at the end of the study at the Salamanca conference,[7] to pool the results of our separate efforts, experiences and projects with a view to critiquing them and discussing local and international action research strategies for the future. We devoted a large part of our time to the first stage — sharing results — and too little to the second. Nevertheless, most of the contributors will discover the work of the others, in a language they understand, only when the book is published in French, Spanish and English. The seminar did serve purposes other than the dry work of reporting findings The conclusions which emerged from this meeting are summarized in the conclusion to this volume.

This massive and exciting project received support from many individuals and organizations. On behalf of all the contributors and the Unesco Institute for Education, I wish to express my gratitude to the following organizations: the Quebec Department of Education, particularly the Basic Adult Education Directorate, the Communications Directorate, and the External Relations Directorate; the Canadian Government's National Literacy Secretariat; the Canadian Commission for Unesco; the Spanish Department of Education and Science's Subdirectorate for Continuing Education; the Salamanca "Diputación," especially its Department of Culture; the University of Salamanca's Directorate of International Relations; the Germán Sánchez Ruipérez Foundation and the Peñaranda Cultural Centre; the Santa Maria Foundation in Madrid; in Bratislava, Slovakia, Comenius University and its Andragogy Department, the Institute of Culture and the Gypsy Cultural Association.

We also received assistance for the production of this book from the Center for Literacy Studies at the University of Tennessee, Cáritas Española, Alpha Consultants in Toronto, the Maison de la culture in Marche-en-Famenne, Belgium, and the Groupe permanent de lutte contre l'illetrisme in France. For the huge task of translation, we thank the National Literacy Secretariat in Ottawa and the Linguistic Services Department of the Quebec Department of Education.

Notes & References

1. The first two were ALPHA 90, produced in cooperation with the European Network for Research, Action and Training in Basic Adult Education, and *ALPHA 92 - Literacy Strategies in the Community Movement*. Both were published in English and French and distributed by the Unesco Institute for Education. *ALPHA 92* is also available in Spanish from the Institute and from the Department of Education and Science, Subdirectorate for Continuing Education, Madrid, Spain.

2. See the Introduction to *ALPHA 92* and *The Future of Literacy and the Literacy of the Future*, Report of the Seminar on Adult Literacy in Industrialized Countries, Unesco Institute for Education, December 4-7, 1991 (UIE Reports No. 9). Strong support for minorities was also evident at the Ottawa international conference on "Rural Literacy" (May 1991), where aboriginal participants from Canada and the former Soviet Union set the tone. *See Rural Literacy*, Proceedings of the Conference, Toronto, Alpha Consultants, 1992.

3. For example, while this study was in preparation, the États généraux du monde rural (Rural Estates General) was held in Quebec; two important books were published: *Deux Québec dans un*, Social Affairs Council (Boucherville: Gaëtan Morin/Government of Quebec, 1989); Bernard Vachon, ed., *Le Québec rural dans tous ses états* (Montréal: Boréal, 1991); and an international conference bearing directly on the literacy problematic, *Rural Literacy* (op. cit.) was held in Ottawa.

4. The Center for Literacy Studies at the University of Tennessee and the Rural Clearinghouse for Lifelong Education and Development at Kansas State University. In the conclusion to *Literacy in Rural America* (Manhattan: Kansas State University, 1992) G. Bailey, P. Daisey, S.C. Maes and J.D. Spears of the Rural Clearinghouse argue for an overhaul of literacy policies in rural areas:

   "For the most part, rural literacy programs remain more aligned with formal education than with nonformal or community-based efforts. Although those programs show extraordinary creativity in stretching limited resources and adapting to the logistical barriers posed by rural environments, few exploit *strategies that build on local culture and empower the local people*. In that sense, *rural literacy programs have generally not been integrated into efforts to strengthen or revitalize the communities of which they are a part*" (p. 57, emphasis added).

5. *Rural Literacy*, op. cit. (Summary Report and Recommendations, p. 4).

6. See Olivia Oliveira, S. Nova and G. Coelho, "Community Development Project Among the Gypsies of Sáo Gregorio" (Portugal), *ALPHA 92*, op. cit., pp. 119-164.

7. The proceedings of the three regional preparatory seminars and the wrap-up seminar for *ALPHA 94* are available upon request from Jean-Paul Hautecoeur, Unesco Institute for Education, Hamburg.

Opening Reflections:
LITERACY IN RURAL AREAS — ORIENTATIONS FOR ACTION RESEARCH

Jean-Paul Hautecoeur
Unesco Institute for Education

THREE INITIAL QUESTIONS

The theme of this study — **literacy in rural areas** — immediately suggests an assertion rather than a question. At least three types of arguments immediately militate in favour of educational intervention in rural areas.

The First Argument

The first is spontaneous, even reflexive: the association of rural areas with illiteracy, or its modern version, functional illiteracy, is still a widely-held cliché. *Homo rusticus* is seen as being by his very nature the opposite of *homo academicus*. From the point of view of the tourist or the poet or the ecologist, rural people must be preserved for their picturesqueness, their homely frankness, their simple common sense. But from the "progressive" standpoint, they are an anachronistic minority who need to be retrained. We are told that rural populations must "evolve". Static, burdensome (because heavily subsidized by the rest of society), they would gain in mobility and autonomy if they could be trained "up to standard" as they say in France. They would understand better why the local school and the local post office have to be closed, and the farms, and the co-ops. It seems that the battle against functional illiteracy must be won for the sake of modernity.

A Second Argument

A second argument takes the first further but reaches an analogous conclusion. Its style, however, is more technocratic. Its proponents start from the same premise, the crisis in rural life, but instead of accepting the negative consequences for local populations, as though the disappearance of their

7

communities were inevitable, they look for local and regional solutions. The politicians and the planners have changed their tune since rural residents started their protests, and since the appearance of a trend toward repopulation of small towns in many regions.

In Europe, reform of the Common Agricultural Policy (CAP) would tend to halt the exodus to the cities and lead to specialization of regional economic vocations.[1] One of the key buzzwords is "structural reconversion" of regional economies. This implies a change in outlook, skills and essential services, with retraining required for the entire active population. It would be selective retraining: vocational or professional for the few and reintegration, basic education or "functional literacy education" (to use the North American expression) for the many, to adapt them to new working conditions, new methods of territorial management, even (in some cases) new forms of social assistance.

The objective is no longer simply to teach rural people to read and write, or to improve an obsolete school background. Rather it is to teach them to adapt to plans for making unproductive land productive (at best) or if this is impossible at least the site of subsidized projects. The search for formulas tailored to fit training needs would constitute an acceptable project.

A Third Argument

The third argument is more technical: training in rural areas ought to be tailored to local needs, since we know from experience that monolithic, centralized programs work poorly in the country. Traditional educational services are often difficult of access, decentralization is expensive, qualified personnel are few and far between, "motivation" cannot be taken for granted, programs are not well adapted to local realities.

For marketers of training programs (and training is one of the rare growth sectors in this period of recession), experimenting with training strategies adapted to rural areas carries the promise of both improving supply and finding new ways to stimulate demand. So here again the argument is in favour of educational intervention in rural areas, even though the rural population itself seems to be a marginal concern. The expectation is that this intervention will be an opportunity to test new communication technologies, to observe distance education and independent learning in operation, to produce new training tools.[2] The out-of-date rural life is to be a stimulus to modernity, and vice versa!

These three complementary schools of thought, favourable to educational intervention in rural areas, have at least two things in common: they see rural life very much from the outside, as anomic, or at least problematical, and they have a prejudice in favour of training that amounts to blind faith in its magic ability to solve a wide range of critical, even desperate, problems.

Our Action Research Perspective

Our study of literacy and cultural action in rural areas will take an opposite approach to that of the three positions described above (which fail to conceal a patronizing, authoritarian attitude to rural residents). It will make a clear distinction between its approach and that of "anti-illiteracy campaigns" and training programs externally imposed (which exist primarily to serve the agencies and professionals that provide them). Three broad questions will orient our action research perspective:

1. In what terms do the local people themselves pose the questions of shortfall, development, cultural change, preservation and revitalization of cultural heritage (in the anthropological sense)? Are such questions asked at all? How large does regional "illiteracy" loom in the thinking of rural communities and residents?

   The important thing here is to construct an interpretation of the rural world that takes into account first and foremost its own reading of its own reality, that finds out what it knows, that accepts its word as legitimate, and above all that considers its plans as the shared goal of outside research and local action. If these conditions were met, a joint process of research and action can be constructed, without the parasitical intervention of a questionnaire and a questioner.

   This is the basis for the study's entirely positive attitude to the facts, questions and practices of "literacy" in rural areas. It will seek to determine in what terms and with what means communities communicate inside their immediate environment but also in a broader context. It will not measure literacy levels or estimate the extent of functional illiteracy in rural populations. Let us leave that to the social sciences and the merchandisers of teaching aids.

2. The second question is implicit in the first. It is heuristic. How are we to apprehend literacy facts and issues in rural areas if not in the specialized terms of individuals' linguistic competence or school performance results?

   The usual handling of literacy questions is normative: it reflects the ideological standards of the school or organization that defines them (a social service, a business, a vocational training program, a charitable organization, etc.). **The aim of our study will be to situate literacy questions within a broader cultural environment, to phrase them as problems of communication and social organization rather than a social pathology**. We will try to understand them in terms of their social and territorial context, their local history and their cultural/ intercultural community. In short, their daily life.

   So the problems facing us are conceptual and methodological. A way must be found to enlarge the scope of the questions (to include cultural and sociocultural factors) without losing sight of their object (literacy) or undermining their ability to generate action (cultural action strategies).

3. The main question concerns action. What plans have local individuals, groups and communities formulated to resist the destructuring of their community? What cultural strategies have they implemented to try to recreate their accustomed environment? What changes in their interactions have they made to transform marginalization (which may be self-imposed), exile, subsistence and even death (or suicide) into new forms of co-operation, education, production, interaction? With what results?

   If we are not to lose sight of practical literacy strategies, we must avoid parcelling them out into self-sufficient activities, unrelated to the context where they appeared and the ends for which they were designed. Political, economic and social organization initiatives are not independent of the cultural dynamics that make them possible, legitimize them or reject them. In the same way, educational initiatives cannot be restricted to segmented training programs.

From a categorized vision of educational or cultural action we move on to a territorial vision, necessarily focused on the community and not the individual or the category. We must define the concept of "rural area" and of "literacy programs": two open, experimental realities that professionals, whether they belong to the community or not, cannot hope to construct by themselves. This is the aim of our study. Once its terms have been defined, we will go on to explain the "method", more appropriately referred to as the "action-research process".

LITERACY

The Meaning of "Literacy"

Usually what is meant by literacy education is the process of giving adults a basic education, which means that at a minimum, "literate" adults can read, write and count. Literacy is evaluated as an individual skill, corresponding to external criteria, generally based on school norms. In many countries the focus on this skill has given rise to universal basic education programs, which are generally unrelated to the sociocultural contexts in which they operate.

Literacy education is also identified as a socio-educational service designed for "problem" individuals or groups. Massive campaigns have been mounted to "fight illiteracy". At a time of growing marginalization of unemployment, illiteracy is the object of training policies designed to reintegrate people both socially and vocationally.

There are many other accepted meanings of this concept,[3] but most often it is defined as an educational intervention aimed at making up psycho-social shortcomings. **We want to apprehend the facts of literacy differently**. A terminological difficulty in French, which also exists in certain other languages, does create difficulties, however.

In French the word "illettrisme" [functional illiteracy] has been introduced to designate (and create) a fact of modern life in postindustrial areas more accurately than did the older term "analphabétisme" [illiteracy].[4] But there is no word in French that can be considered the positive counterpart in French for "illettrisme": "lettrisme" designates a particular literary school, and "lettré" used to mean someone erudite or cultivated but is now old-fashioned.

To convey the idea of familiarity with the written language and its usages, and more generally the means of communication in this postindustrial era, we have only the English term "literacy", which we translate into French as "alphabétisme". The English word has the advantage of more cultural connotations than the French (which is too narrowly concerned with language) and also of evoking a very abundant corpus of multidisciplinary knowledge, going far beyond the purely pedagogical. Based on a British tradition in the humanities, we model our understanding of the facts of literacy, exemplified by Jack Goody and Richard Hoggart in particular, to name just the best known.[5]

In short, literacy is everything to do with the written word. "Functional" literacy may be understood as the ability to cope solely with the reading and writing demanded in everyday situations or in certain specialized contexts, but it is an expression with so many meanings that in this study it will be avoided. In our computerized society, the concept of literacy must necessarily include the use of communication technologies, but it must also mean access to information and to the means of making use of it. These uses cannot be separated from the sociopolitical context of which they are a part.

Four Important Variables

What major variables are common to the complex facts of literacy education within their social environment? We will examine at least four in this study: the infrastructure of the means of communication, the written culture, the social organization and cultural policies (including education).

Every region has its own unique blend of means of communication that make up its infrastructural and technological environment: roads, telephone service, postal service, radio stations, television stations, newspapers, libraries, schools, cultural industries, theatres, resource centres, etc. Outlying rural areas are the least well equipped in means of communication. When these are present, are they used? What comes into the area? What form does communication take: unidirectional? consumption only? with feedback? How do messages circulate in the small town or village? using what medium? in what language? how often? Who is "out of the loop"?

It is definitely important to know the structures, intensities, directions and subjects of information exchange, the zones of silence, the broken networks, if we are to understand a territory's scope of literacy education, its potential for expression and information, its independence, its risk of isolation. For example, it is significant that the threat of closing a post office in a village can provoke a bigger and louder protest from the residents than the closure of a mine or a fish-processing plant. The establishment of a radio station in the minority language can be decisive in setting a linguistic minority, apparently threatened with assimilation, and on the road to literacy and social organization.[6]

Without adequate means of communication in rural areas, without schools, services or cultural industries, a rural population risks forced emigration or loss of literacy.[7] But a shortage of cultural infrastructures and facilities does not always have destabilizing consequences. Cut off from these resources a community may in fact stiffen its resistance and initiate its own cultural activities, sometimes underground if the context is one of prohibitions and repression: hedge school, clandestine printing press, "bush telegraph", etc.[8]

The need and desire for self-expression, information and human interchange via the written word refer to a **written culture**. Among individuals (some or all), this culture takes the form not only of technical skill in processing information but above all of a cultural *habitus*[9] of interaction with the written word. This cultural *habitus* presupposes that the written word is recognized and looked on favourably by the user's society. It also presupposes a need to communicate at a distance in everyday life. Jack Goody would consider distance, as opposed to the immediacy of oral communication, the distinguishing characteristic of the *habitus* of written communication, since it opens the way to the systematic assembling, classifying, analysis and critical review, transformation and controlled transmission of information. In an outlying village the written culture and access to modern means of communication are supposed to open the local territory to the larger world, an essential condition for gaining access to the "supermarket" of goods and messages and for participating in its exchanges.

Is becoming literate (i.e. changing over to a written culture) enough to transform the networks by which information passes between the centre and the periphery? Does it enable the periphery to play an active role in those networks? Most important, does it transform deserted regions into populated, vital, attractive places? Surely not. The inevitable shift that literacy education entails, which is also a shift of subjectivity, presupposes the reversal of that once-powerful tendency (external but also internalized) to wipe clean the slate of oral culture (beliefs, habits, knowledge, heritage), as though a break with the past were the only way to achieve modernity or social mobility.

School and official one-size-fits-all literacy education have long been the vehicle of acculturation for children in rural areas and for minorities. Being unable to read and write has often equalled discreditation, humiliation and exclusion for communities that sought to preserve their cultural heritage and identity.[10]

This written culture, composed of a cultural *habitus* of interaction with the written word and the use of modern means of communication, can be a fact for a minority or for the majority. It fits within a **social organization** that may facilitate access to the written word or may on the contrary restrict it. It also has an economic value on a market that may be either limited or universal (academic culture, popular culture).

In every community there is a division of labour in which specialized communication roles are attributed to certain individuals and certain groups. The result is that not everyone needs to achieve the same level of skill in communicating. Equally, because of the uneven distribution of intellectual capacity, access to information may be well controlled, though initiation to the written culture often depends more on an individual's place in society than on intelligence or level of formal education.

This means that certain events that affect the social organization of a small town or village can be more decisive for cultural dynamism than the introduction of a literacy program. For example, the departure or arrival of professionals who can change the community's socioprofessional make-up; plans to construct a dam, which provoke widespread opposition, a new community organization, popular education initiatives; the arrival of a large group of outsiders, which sparks questions of identity and rights and can change communication practices; the taking-root of a theatre company that bases its cultural action on local history and appeals to the local population to participate, and so on.

The last factor in local cultural development involves **policy**. At the national level, policies supporting local cultural initiatives, decentralization of cultural production and of research centres, enhancement (symbolic/economic) of regional heritage, assistance for local umbrella organizations, etc., can have a stimulating effect on local organizations and the development of sociocultural services and facilities.[11] In a context of liberalism and withdrawal of the central government from local management, local organizations will have no choice but to strengthen their communication, solidarity and co-operation networks to create powerful synergies and transform traditional decision-making methods. In the context of authoritarian regimes where cultural production and dissemination is limited to ideological education, existing local cultural facilities and organizations may be powerless to reach the local population.[12] According to César Birzea, the fall of the totalitarian Communist regimes can be attributed in part to their anomalous policy of literacy. Birzea states that the top priority now must be revitalization of social participation and the promotion of critical thought.[13]

WHAT ABOUT THE ECONOMY?

The **state of the economy** — local, national, international — will determine the overall context within which the variables listed above take effect. It is ineluctably a factor in the acquisition or loss of literacy, as has been observable over the most recent economic crisis bedeviling the industrialized nations. The increasing dichotomy between society's insiders and society's outcasts underlies policies on education and training, as has often been demonstrated. But an additional consequence of the general pauperization is that governments have cut investment in many areas of culture and education. In certain cases (and rural areas are often the first victims) they have eliminated altogether what used to be considered essential services: school buses, schools, post offices, cultural centres, libraries, etc.[14] This phenomenon has led people to describe many regional economies, and even entire national economies in the case of Eastern Europe, as being "assimilated into the Third World".

Quebec, for example, had at the start of the recession and the disquieting climb of unemployment, a new continuing education act guaranteeing to all adults free access to basic education programs in all regions. Several years later, although the economy had not recovered and the unemployment rose, the government tied these basic education services to guaranteed minimum income social benefits, making them virtually subject to a quota system.

Although an economic crisis favours growth in the training and education sector, it leads to cuts in other cultural services and facilities. This makes it difficult to define the impact of the economy on the acquisition or loss of literacy among rural populations.

Hence the importance of local studies that explore factors affecting cultural development to find an explanation for the emergence of voluntary cultural actions and their ability to modify the communication practices of individuals within the community. Educational activities must also be situated within this broader context so that their territorial effects, if any, can be taken into account. In educational circles the tendency is quite the reverse: toward separating and isolating the microsystem's various components (program, pedagogy, teacher training, etc.) in order to explain the results, which are themselves defined on the basis of the system's own logic, its "sub-culture".

A Plurality of Codes

In current usage, "literacy education" means learning to decipher a code, and "literacy" means using the code. "Literacy" also includes the approved or forbidden ways in which the code is used, within a single — usually national — cultural corpus whose boundaries are defined by customs, rules and a whole network of cultural institutions. In national enquiries into adult literacy, the assumption is that literacy is part of a single-track progression of skills and can be measured by tests based on a collective, shared context.

The ideological assumption that the one context and one school is the same or appropriate for everybody, camouflages the reality of a strongly heterogeneous cultural environment, where there is a plurality not only of messages and communication strategies but also of codes themselves.

The whole thrust of this study is to pinpoint literacy education practices that reflect diversity, complexity, and even conflicting cultural background to show how bridges may be created between differing cultural entities instead of the enforcement of linguistic unity or presentation as a means of access to "normality".

There are situations where the written code and the oral code (or codes, in situations of bilingualism or multilingualism) bear no resemblance at all. Sometimes the oral code and the written code exist side by side; sometimes each rejects the other; sometimes they mix. Literacy education can be regarded as one possible way of linking the two codes, rather than representing a seamless passage from the oral to the written in the same language. For example, among the aboriginal peoples of Canada, literacy education can aim at transferring the second or third language learned by mandatory attendance at a French or English school into the oral vernacular once the children return to their home community.

But the processes of communication are more complex still. We do not use just two codes, the oral and the written. Visual signs, symbols of status or power, rituals, appeals to paralinguistic codes, all crop up in the messages we transmit, and in any form of expression psychoanalysts strive to reconstruct hidden language, the unconscious (whether individual or collective), which one can learn to decode through analysis. **Literacy may be considered as the semiotic process of playing with the codes to deconstruct and reconstruct meanings and strategies of communication.** It is a game that is not reserved for specialists. In the pragmatic perspective of everyday communication, each participant learns a certain number of the rules of the game and applies them. Trying to modify the rules or introduce new ones is the objective of cultural intervention.

What we are looking for, then, is evidence of experiments in literacy education that allow for this plurality of codes and media in the facts of communication: the spoken word, of course, theatre, gesture, dance, music, combinations of these. We are interested in these codes and media not as art forms but as channels of communication and interchange in real and open sociocultural contexts, to open, transform and reconstruct.[15]

Ideological Plurality

We have referred to the plurality of media seeking this plurality in both the message and the meaning. If the meaning of a message can be decoded within the same linguistic context with the aid of dictionaries, then the message has a common meaning. There is then, a consensus of meaning based upon a common cultural background from which the individual inherits vocabulary, values, taboos and obligations, and ways of saying, listening and understanding. Literacy education (basic education) is also viewed as the imparting of these collective meanings, blended with the concept of identity or national cultural heritage.[16]

This common meaning is less a reflection of popular wisdom which would result in agreement by atavistic intuition than it is a reflection of a dominant ideology, strengthened by the legitimacy granted to it by the social groups that are its advocates and by the institutions which impart and give value to this ideology (among others national education institutions which more often than not control private education), the mass media and in some countries, the Church or the single governing party. In this kind of unitary system, or in one that has become unitary because of the minimization, integration and outright eradication of different/dissident/antagonistic cultural expressions, there is no other choice but to conform or to be excluded, to be welcomed or to remain/become illiterate. This is the dual logic of the associative ideology of a common meaning.

Many rural literacy initiatives also tend to embrace these common meanings. They do so for the sake of the local community, source of a unitary territorial ideology; or for the sake of progress, or for the global village of planetary communications in a universal market. These ideologies share external imposition of values and meanings and converge on the same emancipatory, mythical destiny.

Our attention is focused on the search for traces of literacy initiatives which fall somewhere between the ideological associations. We are looking for linkages between cultures and codes, for possible linkages to be explored between languages, peoples, groups, territories, generations, knowledge and multiple experiences. Territory, history, identity and local culture are, as we know, hybrid or crossbreed forms, "chaotic stabilities" intersected by contradictory currents, by fragments of history.[17]

In our research, we attempt to achieve intercultural contracts aimed at temporarily restoring order to chaos, while staving off the re-emergence of the unitary myth or the monopoly of one group.

A CRITICISM OF LITERACY EDUCATION

To conclude these orientations, it is useful to focus again on the **critical function**. Awareness and political commitment to cultural action on the part of those on the fringes remains an integral component of literacy education that cannot easily be circumvented. The strong impetus given by Paulo Freire remains current, even though as the end of the century approaches, we have retreated somewhat from his revolutionary messianisms.

Functional literacy implies a minimum level of initiation, or initiation for survival purposes, to the ordinary written communication process used in everyday life. From a technical standpoint, it implies the mastery of a more or less specialized code of communication. In a neutral, undemanding and well-meaning way, functional literacy is the ability to manipulate several basic tools in a familiar context with a view to "functioning at a minimum level".

For a foreigner who is excluded, outclassed or merely rural, making the transition to a higher level of literacy is not an easy experience. Not everyone can proceed through these doors, some of which may be closed. Some conditions associated with the process are unacceptable: having to leave one's identity at the door, or leaning to live elsewhere when what one really wants is to live in one's own village. Some steps cannot be avoided, such as literacy courses for eligibility to social welfare.

The ideology associated with literacy education is marked by generous positivism coupled with redeeming progressivism. This ideology is regularly embraced by economic liberalism in the quest for manpower training, for mobility and autonomy in the management of computerized environments. It is courted by public welfare services contending with the growing burden of unemployed workers. It is also embraced by public and associative continuing education networks which need to hold on to their markets.

This ideology is regularly shaken by alarmist reports on the rise of illiteracy, with the negative consequences this implies in terms of culture and national language, health, morality and public safety (a characteristically North American problem). It is still embraced by government organizations seeking to "optimize" communications with the public through an "easy language" and by private enterprises wishing to market their services more effectively and reduce their losses.

All of which proves just how diverse and divergent the aims of literacy education actually are. There appears to be a consensus of public opinion on the extent of illiteracy and its dangers, on the need for literacy programs and on the urgent need to ensure minimum literacy training for everyone. We have moved rapidly from proclamations of universal literacy entitelement to the recognition of the need for illiteracy eradication and universal literacy training.

This explains our reluctance to associate ourselves with mass communication mechanisms and our desire to focus on independent actions, on the goals identified by local communities. This also explains our global view of local cultural action, quite different from sectoral training activities that target specific groups quite aside from local/regional cultures.

ACTION RESEARCH

We view our research activities involving literacy education as an integral part of the literacy and cultural action process, and as continuing education initiatives. This series of activities and initiatives in which a great many individuals and agencies are involved can be grouped into three categories: research focused on the quest for knowledge; action focused on social change; and education focused on an initiation to new relationships. These functions are not separate, but rather complementary and integrated.

This is the reason why we speak of literacy education strategies, rather than of methodology as is done in scientific field. We speak of taking a realistic, pragmatic approach to action research where the goal, as on the battlefield, is to win. We must reflect upon and organize cultural action by working with those involved in the field and by considering all of the parameters, relying on science as policy, on intuition and on art. The strategies must be reinvented and revised for each context. The approach to the game is never the same, unlike medieval tournaments where strict rules were the order of the day, or the traditional education context which consists of controlling the largest possible number of parameters in order to apply a method with little variation.

In terms of local action, research becomes another means of communication and feedback through writings, seminars, publications and distance interactions. Research involves examining, explaining and comparing local practices, informing others about them and forging a network of exchanges and solidarity. The aim is to impart to those outside this network the knowledge, experiences, projects and claims which seem to lack legitimacy and therefore are not well communicated.

The act of writing about experiences is preferably carried out by the person or community involved. The research function is situated within the general timeframe of cultural action. If an outsider takes on the task of analyzing, evaluating and serving as a historiographer, he or she will have to be receptive to the participation of the community and of other actors.

Dialogue, not scientific isolation or "safe" education, is critical to building knowledge that can be reinvested into daily action by local practitioners. It involves experimental know-how, clarifying, evaluating, criticizing and fine-tuning it, in keeping with a process of a democratic exchange of ideas. By popular education, we mean the "maieutic" (the teasing out of ideas through questions and reflection) practice of engaging in discourse. The role of the "midwife" philosopher is not assigned to a sage or outside expert, it is shared and developed by the community.

What is sought is not recognized ability and strict adherence to a code of ethics associated with a discipline and a professional association, but rather a range of disciplines, writings, positions and experiences. That which partners have in common are the problems experienced within the same community and within similar regions, and the search for solutions through effective strategies for action.

We have said that this process of cultural action research is rooted in the communities and is based on voluntary association. We have also said that research is possible only with the participation of persons who have some practical knowledge of the local cultural action. Continuing education must rely on action taken in response to specific situations and on dialogue between the various partners who are seeking a solution to common problems. The outcome of this effort is a common "cultural capital" which can be called "literacy education", a process of collective cultural development where the important things are not measured according to each individual's instrumental ability, but rather according to their participation in the process and the results obtained: an improvement in local living conditions.

This then is the primary objective of action research initiatives conducted on an international scale with a view to strengthening solidarity networks, universalizing investigations, searches and resulting in local victories.

THE RURAL CONCEPT

To conclude this paper on the directions and focus of this reseach process, we would like to define what is meant by "rural" and why we wish to concentrate on the rural environment. To start with, we can adopt a socio-cultural understanding of the 'rurality' as it is currently defined, for example, by Bruno in Quebec. Instead of defining the rural world negatively by what it lacks in comparison to the urban world, Bruno provides a positive view: "the rural space as a particular use of space and social life..." And further:

"More than a distinct bio-physical environment, the contemporary rurality presents three specific attributes. First, a human, ecological, cultural and historical patrimony of high value, which is also a certain way of life.Second, an intimate knowledge of the land, the territory, which creates an identity. Lastly, a strong community spirit or solidarity which builds a society of mutual knowledge."[19]

UNDERSTANDING THE MEANING OF "RURAL"

The rural environment is often perceived as a series of bucolic images set against a backdrop of economic crisis, conservation projects and ecological disasters, an idyllic place to take a vacation in contrast to the urban environment. The image is also one of regional cultures and languages threatened by the culture of the masses, by the aging of the population, or by a "cultural drain". The old cliché of the illiterate, rural peasant invariably springs to mind.

In my research on earlier literacy education initiatives in rural areas,[20] I discovered almost invariably that these peripheral areas presented many problems when it came to implementing literacy programs.

On the one hand, research showed that the population was generally under-educated and read very little (with the exception of regional or local newspapers.[21] On the other hand, expanding cultural and continuing education services in rural areas was found to be a difficult and costly process. The rural environment was often described as a barrier to the extension of basic education services. Consequently, it was also an environment in which services better geared to local needs could be tested. The goal, however, remained the provision of educational programs. And in order to import specialized services, the application methods or mechanisms had to be developed at the local level.

My next encounter with the issue of literacy education in rural areas was my participation in an international conference on this subject.[22] The main conclusions drawn from this conference included that literacy aducation and the rural environment had become separate entities, and a so-called global approach to various local issues helped to recreate a kind of unity in rural development actions. Moreover, literacy education and the rural environment had joined together once again (at least ideologically) in the will to launch a rural, quasi-corporate rural literacy movement, with technologies forming part of the overall package.

This conference enriched my understanding of the rural environment by introducing me to concepts such as multi and intercultural, local community-based development and an holistic approach to literary issues dissociated from educational systems. It confirmed the need to set aside any kind of sectarian or corporate vision of literacy education and to focus on local development (or the resistance to under-development) in terms of **cultural/intercultural action,**[23] which obviously includes the need for popular education initiatives. Issues such as rediscovering, expressing, creating and sharing **identities** are fundamental to organizations which provide or facilitate cultural initiatives in rural areas.

The concept of **peripheral societies** (instead of rural environments) was also discussed during this conference. This concept provides a global perspective to rural issues and their connection with the centres (decision-making, production, distribution, attraction...), just as communications and exchanges are also largely associated with literacy education issues.

The advantage of assuming a peripheral position in a geographic, economic, sociopolitical, demographic and cultural perspective is that it furthers our understanding of the rural environment above all as part of a system of relationships or linkages. It also helps to prevent blind adherence to no less important notions of **locality, territory and identity**. The latter are relative differences, subjective notions, moving cultural realities and ideological forms, rather than essential entities that have merged together.

Our understanding of literacy issues in a rural environment is closely linked to the concept of peripheral societies. Rural communities are situated on the fringes of communication processes. They face the threat of exclusion. Very little, if anything, is invested in these rural communities. Communities which not long ago were self-sufficient have become dependent societies, even in matters of religion: churches that have been closed down, televised mass, religious holidays celebrated in the cities instead of in the villages, messianic cults operating by way of disinformation and the withholding of literacy... (it would be useful to assemble monographs on these types of cultural actions which seal the disastrous fate of numerous rural communities).

However, some rural populations have resisted dependency by reinforcing local and regional organizations, utilizing grants for investment purposes and by establishing voluntary policies respecting industrial redeployment, cultural or tourist attractions, etc. Associations set out on a mission to reintegrate and develop rural populations,[23] sometimes working in co-operation with government and the private sector. A great many cultural initiatives are aimed at establishing new exchange networks with the peripheral societies and setting up small cultural production enterprises. One important movement, operating under the ecological banner, is helping to recreate viable, even attractive spaces in areas which not long ago were condemned. An accurate description of this phenomenon is provided in the following excerpt of a paper published not long after the États généraux du monde rural.

> Underlying the coalition and solidarity movement in rural areas in the slow emergence of an innovative spirit with which to counter the forces of marginalization, exclusion and extinction.
>
> After being deserted for more than a century as industrialization and urbanization took hold, the rural environment is being called upon to play the role of host to the development of a post-industrial, even post-economic society.[25]

The geopolitical aspect of this issue still needs to be examined in order to distinguish more clearly between the peripheral regions. We will attempt to do just this in the following pages.

Why the Rural Areas

Our initial motivation is heuristic. We wanted to examine literacy education within a social context and within a physical/technical environment (this refers to Marx's mode of capitalistic production: the relationship of the technical means of production to the society) according to the concept (borrowed from J. Goody[5]) of communication relations. The rural environment appears to lend itself well to such an approach. Hypothetically, factors such as distance, isolation and lack of equipment are critical; states of crisis and radical social change also justified the interest shown in cultural and educational actions, since the latter were supposed to better represent current history and invent, at least in the mind and in words, collective solutions to these states of anomia.

The rural environment seemed particularly well suited for studying community literacy strategies, using a global or holistic or integrated local development approach. The village, the parish and the local community have relatively independent histories that justify a priori taking a global approach to the local territory. The goal was to discover the local territory through experimentation with new linkages and through the expression of new messages or suggestion of new ways of living life at this rural level, with more autonomy and greater participation and effectiveness.

Our second motivation was to discover the possible utopian dimension to the rural environment. Cultural action, literacy and popular education programs must, if they are to break new ground[26] and blend the old with the new, move from the realm of reality to that of desire, if only to represent more dramatically the desolation felt by many moribund populations.[27] They must seek out with renewed vigour, an all-encompassing alternative to isolation, to programmed waste, to despair and to anthropocentric nihilism as well as to nostalgic ways of restoring original values and glory.[28]

The rural environment can offer better living conditions, housing and creative work for the post-modern era, given its isolation from the periphery of major movements and the general hubbub. To do this, the rural environment must be recreated. It is not enough to pretend to resuscitate them. Old identities will have to come to terms with ideas, issues and newly arrived people in order to invent new territories, ones that are far more fluid and adaptable than the old ones that died off because they were closed to the outside world.

This undertaking will involve radical changes to the old order, to foundations, to social organizations, and to power structures. Above all, it will involve a mental metamorphosis (which will be accomplished with the help of technologies, of course, and which will generate a new pedagogy). These changes can be perceived as literacy education action which today we identify with local cultural/intercultural action. This vision of literacy education is not "functional", but necessarily creative.

A third reason for the search for alternate but current literacy education practices in rural areas, is of a moral nature. Once we would have called it "progressive", or "socialist" or even political. Now, we speak of technological and cultural literacy education geared to national heritage. Or we speak of remedial education, of qualifying training, of standardization, of minority integration, etc. This is the discourse of public agencies and of promoters of massive literacy campaigns.

> Of all living creatures, is there anything so dangerous today, as an example of his peers and to the whole world, than the arrogant adult male who has, as they say, succeeded in the competitive world? We sometimes catch a glimpse of this terrifying creature, briefcase in hand, in airports.
>
> Michelle Serres[29]

We have chosen peripheral areas as the focus of our action research because they are perceived as "obstacles" to cultural standardization, because they present "alarming rate of illiteracy" and unemployment, because at times, the majority of people residing in these areas rely permanently on social assistance, because increasingly they attract similar people excluded from the cities as a result of irreversible "structural mutations", as well as similar people from the South, who not so long ago were for the most part rural people.

> Clearly, the most philosophically essential, if not urgent, questions are as follows: which language do the most disadvantaged speak? How will the weakest escape certain death?
>
> When I speak of weakest, I am also referring to intellectual weakness. How is it that in this era when science has triumphed, technology prevails and truths are widely proclaimed by the media, education has been allowed to decline to such an extent, that cultures have collapsed and ignorance and illiteracy have been allowed to flourish?
>
> Once again, we are left to deal with pain and sorrow on a broad scale..."
>
> Michel Serres[29]

The search for solutions to the most important questions falls to the peripheries, the gathering point for hybrid researchers on a quest to find an "environment" that no longer exists, one which they will necessarily have to invent using their different languages and broad knowledge. That is what we hope to achieve through action research in the Third World of northern countries. Changes will only occur under the banner of resistance, solidarity, imagination and creativity.

Notes & References

1. *Le Monde des Débats, no. 2, November 1992.*

2. *Literacy in Rural Communities* — proceedings of the international conference held in Ottawa, May 10-13, 1991. Alpha-Consultants, Toronto, 1992.

3. Hautecoeur, Jean-Paul. "L'analphabétisme: Quel sens? Quelles actions? Quels résultats?", *Alpha 92*, Ministry of Education/UNESCO Institute for Education, Quebec City/Hambourg, 1992.

4. Vélis, Jean-Pierre. *La France illettrée*, Paris, Seuil, 1988.

5. Goody, Jack. *The Domestication of the Savage Mind* (French edition published by Les

Editions de Minuit, Paris, 1979).

Hoggart, Richard. *The Uses of Literacy* (French edition published by Les Editions de Minuit, Paris, 1970).

6. Bertola, Marc and Patricia Pardel. "Les Indiens d'Equateur prennent la voie des ondes", *Le Monde diplomatique*, November 1992.

7. Carrasco, Joaquin Garcia and Javier Valbuena. "Functional Literacy Programs: Intervention in the School and the Community", *Illiteracy in the European Community*, De Lier, Academisch Bocken Centrum, 1992.

8. Birzea, César, "Literacy and Development in Eastern European Countries: the Case of Romania", *International Conference: Attaining Functional Literacy*, Tilburg University, October 10-12, 1991.

9. Bourdieu, Pierre. *Ce que parler veut dire*, Paris Fayard, 1982.

10. Wagner, Serge. *Analphabétisme de minorité et alphabétisation d'affirmation nationale*, Ministry of Education, Toronto, 1990.

11. Bihr, Alain. "Le mirage des politiques de développement local"; Carraud, Michel. "Décentralisation du pouvoir sans contrôle des citoyens"; *Le Monde diplomatique*, November 1992.

12. CIRAT, "Chartre pour un projet associatif", *Alpha 92*, op. cit.

13. Birzea, César, op. cit. See also: Kunst-Gnamus, Olga. "Literacy at the Threshold of the 21st Century", *Literacy and Basic Education on the Eve of the 21st Century*, Council of Europe, Strasbourg, 1992.

14. In the United States, some bankrupt rural municipalies are obliged to stop transporting children to school by bus for several months a year. In Quebec, the residents of the village of Saint-Clément in the Lower Saint Lawrence region fought off the closure of their post office for 60 days, until an injunction forced them to stop their demonstrations.

15. A member of an intercultural theatre group described the experience this way: "Now I can talk, I can hold a conversation. Before I used to go off in all directions, now I'm in control, I can stand back... Apart from being part of the working world again, I regained my dignity, because I was doing something without failing, I moved beyond the initial misery and agitated rebellion." Bellet, Alain. "La riposte des exclus", *Le Monde diplomatique*, December 1991.

16. Ferdman, Bernardo. "Literacy and cultural identity", *Harvard Educational Review*, Vol. 60, no. 2, 1980.

17. Serres, Michel. *Éclaircissements - Entretiens avec Bruno Latour*, Paris, François Bourin, 1992.

18. *The Future of Literacy and the Literacy of the Future*, Report of the Seminar on Adult Literacy in Industrialized Countries, UNESCO Institute for Education, Hamburg, 4-7 December 1991 (UIE Reports, no. 9, 1992).

19. Bruno, Jean. Declin ou renaisance: l'agriculture et la ruralite au Canada a la croises des chemins, Federation canadienne de l'agriculture, Ottawa, 1994. (a free and shortened translation by Jean-Paul Hautecoeur)

20. In particular, several British experiments have been the focus of ALBSU reports, namely: *Mendip project, Dorset Adult Literacy and Numeracy Scheme, Adult Education in Powys, Somerset Report*. For example, here is the conclusion of the Powys report: "The provision of an effective basic education service to adults in rural areas present[s] considerable difficulties and the experience of the special development project in Powys would suggest that there is no one method to overcome the difficulties. However, by a considerable investment of time and resources; adopting a variety of approaches; establishing personal contracts [sic] and developing an accessible support system, it is possible to provide an effective provision" (p. 40), *Adult Basic Education in Powys*, ALBSU, Kingsbourne House, 229-231, High Holborn, London WC1C7DA, U.K. 1985.

21. *Les pratiques culturelles individuelles et collectives en milieu rural*, Fédération nationale des associations familiales rurales, Paris, 1989;
Pompougnac, Jean-Claude. *La lecture en milieu rural*, Bibliothéque publique d'information,

Centre Georges Pompidou, Paris, 1992.

22. *Literacy in Rural Communities* — proceedings of the international conference held in Ottawa, May 10-13, 1991. Alpha-Consultants, Toronto, 1992.

23. "Awareness of the cultural dimension becomes a determining component of rural integration and development policies... Rural local missions participate in this general movement in various ways: by giving a voice to people in trouble, by providing support to local radio stations or to the written press, or by organizing formal consultation initiatives with young people." *Solidarité et développement rural*, Union nationale des missions locales rurales, 71 rue Saint-Dominique, 75007 Paris, France, 1991.

24. For example, the Fédération nationale des foyers ruraux de France, Caritas in Spain, Solidarité rurale in Québec, etc.

25. Vachon, Bernard. *Le Québec rural dans tous ses états*, under the direction of B. Vachon, Boréal, Montréal, 1991 (Introduction, p. 14).

26. In France, the Fédédation des foyers ruraux du Vaucluse, working in co-operation with children of immigrants living in several villages, produced a play on the theme of crossing borders: *Passages-Suds en Luberon*, Fédération des foyers ruraux du Vaucluse, BP 15, 84141, Mont Favet, Cedex, France, 1992.

27. Perrier, Olivier. This dramatic author and popular theatre producer in a small village in central France described his work in Hérisson in the following words: "If we want to think about Hérisson's future, we should consider opening a national cemetery here, because we have the space for it. We would build a nice romantic cemetery, easily accessible from the highway, better even than Père Lachaise! Moreover, it would mean work for all the unemployed people in the area. Work building coffins, doing maintenance... We could even develop the aesthetic quality of death. The only business currently making a go of it in Hérisson is the hospice... What we need to do is consider the best possible way of experiencing grief and making it our purpose in life". Scène de deuil — Conversation with Olivier Perrier, *Le Monde des débats*, November 1992.

28. Felix Gattari calls this kind of research "ecosophy". "*Danger does have the power to genuinely fascinate... Above all, the emphasis should be on rediscovering collective co-operation with a view to developing innovative practices. If we do not change our way of thinking and enter a postmedia era, there will be no durable effect on the environment. However, if we do not change the material and social environment, there will be no change in our way of thinking. We are faced with a circular argument, which brings us to postulate the need for "ecosophy", an approach that blends environmental ecology with social ecology and mental ecology.*" "Pour une refondation des pratiques sociales", *Le Monde diplomatique*, October 1992.

29. Serres, Michel. *Éclaircissements*, op. cit., (p. 273).

Chapter 1
RURAL SPAIN

Purificación Marcos
Cáritas Española, Madrid

RURAL SPAIN

Rural Spain is made up of diverse regions, lands and villages whose resources, climates and terrain influence the local way of life.

It is clear that lifestyles and socio-cultural conditions are different in the mountains and the plain, in Galicia and Andalusia and Estremadura. Despite this diversity, rural communities are in the majority in Spain, and have a shared sense of marginalization. The rural is defined in contrast to the urban, as something different, marginal. The National Statistical Institute defines rural zones in terms of population, as "districts with fewer than 2,000 inhabitants, in which 3,151,149 Spaniards live".

Changes in the Agricultural Sector

For centuries, agriculture has been the leading source of employment and income in rural regions. But now the situation has changed, and while agriculture is still an essential component, it is no longer the only one. In 1980, it accounted for more than 17% of jobs, but by 1991 this had declined to a little over 10% and is expected to decline further.

There is therefore an alarming unemployment rate among rural populations, for most Spanish farmers are not in a position to operate under the Common Agricultural Policy (CAP) competitive policies. Because of these policies, many small farms have been abandoned, and early retirement for farmers aged 55 and over has left vast rural areas dependent on subsidies, with the major economic and social consequences that this entails.

The poor cultural and occupational qualifications of rural inhabitants block access to the job market and place them in an inferior position in relation to the inhabitants of urban and semi-urban areas, where educational and vocational training opportunities are greater.

Agriculture's relative loss of importance has changed the rural economy. The agricultural sector is currently undergoing a major restructuring aimed at paving the way towards other economic activities (mixed activities, crop diversification, etc.).

Changes are not occurring at the same speed or in the same way in all regions

- Rural areas which are close to urban areas and have industry and services: these areas have mixed economies (crop and fruit-growing areas of southern Spain and the Ebro Valley, part of the Cordillera Cantabrica, etc.). Their agricultural practices are being modernized and greatly intensified, often at the expense of the environment. The rural economy is diversifying.

- Rural areas with medium-sized communities and few activities and services: latifundia (estates) using labourers and seasonal workers predominate (Andalusia and Estremadura).

- Areas dominated by family farms belonging to small and medium-sized property-owners (the entire interior, the dryland farming regions of the Ebro Valley and Estremadura). These regions have experienced a massive exodus of men and women to the cities. Confronted by structural obstacles, young men and women are deserting their villages, leaving behind an aging population and a decrease and decline in services.

- Mountainous sierra areas: rural decline and depopulation are very evident.

Two problems which affect all of rural Spain are the agricultural sector's structural lag and the inhabitants' low level of personal and occupational qualifications. However, restructuring is affecting not only agriculture but also education, health, social services, etc.

With the increasing rural/agricultural split, rural territory is seen as a social space, a recreational site, as well as a source of water, food, etc. This new view leads us to consider new ways of life and work embracing many possibilities and capable of developing and exploiting all of the region's resources in order to achieve a better quality of life.

COMPENSATORY MEASURES FOR NEW ACTION POLICIES

The European Economic Community (EEC), member countries, autonomous communities and municipal councils have introduced a series of aid programs to counter the negative effects resulting from the reconversion of the economy.

Joint financing of infrastructures from structural funds has, however, been accorded greater importance than economic cohesion, and planned sectorial actions have an economic rather than social content. There is a considerable difference between the role of the structural funds as such and that of practical programs such as Leader and Habitat.

The first of these initiatives is the Leader program (which addresses relations among rural economic development activities). Its goals are:

- "to create a network of social action groups to promote rural development, using information and communication technologies, and with considerable evaluative leeway to allow delegated management of global subsidies;"
- "to implement innovative solutions which could serve as a model for all rural regions by establishing optimal integration between different sectorial measures."

The EEC's **Habitat directive** was designed to extend subsidies to areas which submit concrete projects for the conservation of native species. The regions selected for the Leader program may be eligible for the Habitat directive, depending on their natural resources.

The EEC has also proposed **accompanying measures** to support the new Common Agricultural Policy reform. Their implementation and results will depend in large part on the government's policy in this respect. These accompanying measures may change the conception of rural society and the inhabitants' way of life. Rural society is more than agriculture, but agriculture must remain a part of rural society.

The CAP's production-related content has been expanded and now includes the defense and protection of the environment, the reforestation of agricultural lands and early retirement. These three lines of action are important for rural areas, as indeed they are for society as a whole. They are aimed at harmonizing pricing and market policies, environmental policy, and attempts to enhance the competitiveness of small and medium-sized farms. They are also aimed at improving market equilibrium by stabilizing farm incomes while tackling the difficult task of conserving the environment.

These funds and subsidies address the social effects of economic reconversion, especially in the regions and groups most affected by exclusion.

Given the social situation in southern Spain (Andalusia and Estremadura), the old Community Employment program has been reconverted on the basis of the Rural Employment Plan (PER). The new system is built on three components:

- unemployment benefits equalling 75% of the intervocational minimum wage, granted for 180 days per year, for workers who pay into a special agricultural plan during at least 60 days of work;
- a Rural Employment Plan (PER) designed to channel public funds for the creation of rural employment;
- a vocational training plan adapted for rural use.

The PER is now directing all its efforts towards obtaining public funds. This plan has become an essential tool in ensuring income stability. Workers are thus turning to the Municipal Council (the employer). But as this resource is proving to be insufficient, they must moonlight or be content with an irregular income (agricultural income, unemployment allowances) to secure their subsistence.

This situation has led to a shift in the discourse of agricultural trade unions:

"From the fight for land to obtaining and negotiating the PER."

"From agrarian reform to the improvement of a certain number of properties."

Protest leaders have become managers of associations or cooperatives. Similarly, in the case of family farms, the farm union has attempted to maintain a certain level of productivity through price protection and by obtaining public funds for income support. The struggle is also being waged in the agribusiness field, which is in the process of becoming the country's leading sector and is experiencing an increasing influx of multinationals and foreign capital.

In short, unionism must make a number of transitions: from a pricing policy to a structural policy; from a price maintenance policy to defending the region and promoting its potential; from sectorial view to a comprehensive vision; from an autonomous communities perspective to a state which coordinates with European and international bodies; to training in various environmental and job-creation areas.

GLOBAL ACTION

Most initiatives are aimed at offsetting the social effects of the reconversion. These initiatives derive support from a number of agencies.

Government Departments

Department of Agriculture, Fish & Food

Through its various agencies, this department provides production support and assistance, calling upon associational principles: rural community development, advice, promotion. It offers financial support for local projects such as programs for youth associations and rural employment, integrated development organization plans in mountain zones; joint agrarian action in disadvantaged zones and land use planning councils.

Department of Labour & Social Security

This department's programs include: local employment initiatives; training and recruiting local development agents; funding workshop schools and trades centres: using traditional trades for environmentally useful projects and the national vocational education plan.

The Department of Social Affairs, through basic social services, is setting up:

information centres on services and resources; support for home aid based on the rural solidarity which characterizes the rural environment; a network of facilities to meet social needs; general and specific social service centres (residences, integration, social relations); and assistance and subsidies for community organizations in difficulty.

The Department of Education & Science has initiated:

a community development, education and continuing education plan (non-traditional education); preschool at home provided as compensatory education; various experiments during the 1985-86 school year in 44 rural schools located in different provinces and autonomous communities. At present, 83 schools are participating in the Rural School project; a socio-cultural activities and com-munity development plan in some disadvantaged rural areas.

The Department of Public Works and Urban Planning has launched a rural housing rehabilitation plan.

Social movements, grassroots organizations, the church

The following collectives have developed and launched initiatives to coun-teract the social effects of what is known as modernity: solidarity action collectives, Estremadura rural community action, trade unions, rural Chris-tian adult and youth movements, the Southern Mission, Cáritas, rural pastoral work teams in the various autonomous communities, environmental and peace movements, cultural associations, Rural School teachers' collectives, the youth movement.

Livestock breeders and farmers (in Castile, Galicia, Aragon, Estremadura, etc.) are mobilizing against the EEC milk production quotas in these many ways: labourers are demanding work instead of hand-outs; people are fighting for the Rural School and for quality schools in rural areas; people are mobilizing against the loss of farmland to shooting ranges, nuclear dumping grounds, golf courses, etc.; people are demanding job creation and local initiative projects; home care is provided through women's associations to give senior citizens a better quality of life in their homes or in their villages; women's education projects; activities to defend heritage and regional identity are organized. The rural platform has become an instrument to co-ordinate activities in rural areas: protest actions, solidarity actions to change the way of life (capitalism, consum-erism) — and channel the potential for change in rural society in an organized and practical manner.

Creating means of communication

Distributing the news has become a regional networking tool which serves to promote knowledge and maintain regional identity. Experiments include newspapers, newsletters and magazines, published and distributed by organizations from the rural environment (cultural associations, the Church, unions): *Sementera, Gritos en la Sierra, El Trigarral, El Valle, Mundo Rural, Militante, Agricultura Familiar, Tierra y Libertad, Semilla.*

Clearly, considerable efforts are being made to become aware of the problems and potential of rural areas.

Campaigns

Campaigns are being waged to address concrete problems with the aim of raising awareness of social conditions and also to mobilize local communities and involve them in solving their problems. These campaigns have been launched which are aimed at all sectors of the rural population with these slogans: *There's a lot to do in your village — participate!... Not a single rural child without schooling: for a quality school in each village... Labourers' living and working conditions... Alone, we can do nothing; together we can do anything.*

Horizontal networks to share experiences & develop joint actions

Such networks have had the clear advantage of making local initiatives widely known. Every one has heard of *Tierra de Campos, Preescolar na Casa, Cooperativa El Bosque, Guayente, Montaña Palentina, Sierra Sur, Valle Alcudia, Aldeas Montes Norte, Sierra de Yeste — Nerpio.* The wish to avoid isolation in all its forms underlies all these experiments. The needs of rural populations are the basis for the experiments and initiatives launched in the areas most affected by the crisis. These needs revolve around: job creation (especially for women and young people); improving infrastructures and community facilities in order to provide every one with acceptable living conditions and participation in matters of concern to the entire community including the school, the union, the municipal council, etc.

A number of social projects based on these needs and on the development of local human and physical resources are now being planned.

HOW WILL ACTION BE TAKEN?

The actions listed above are based on continuing education and encompass all the fields in which rural men and women, children and senior citizens are active. They also take place in a specific social environment which in fact they seek to transform.

The actions always involve specific problems. Becoming aware of these problems represents the first step in an educational process. The situations are examined from the standpoint of their social, political and economic context, past and present, so as to be able to find appropriate solutions. Educational spaces are created with the aim of developing a social culture characterized by: support for forms of association; education: personal education (information, expression, developing independence); group education (co-operation, solidarity) and vocational training.

Education rooted in action and designed for action in which the content is life itself, work and social conflicts. Through debate, people learn to listen, to speak, to plan and to participate.

It promotes civic values, solidarity, loyalty and so on, which enable people to work together: for a pacifist society reconciled with nature; for a fair distribution of wealth; for an ethical life; for democracy and freedom.

Participation in the social life of the community is encouraged: municipal council, school, nursing homes, festivities, etc.: by identifying the causes of the inhabitants' reluctant to participate; by establishing concrete operational objectives; by raising public consciousness about the importance of active participation in community affairs.

In primary groups, solidarity takes the form of self-organization. Without organization, it is difficult to progress horizontally; hence the importance of social education: to create groups; to encourage and support social movements; to strengthen service networks and cooperation.

Organized social cooperation is conducive to encounter, debate, tasking and task evaluation. It is the crucible of new social co-operation projects, of useful projects for the community. The linking together of all these small groups, the forging of community spirit, the co-ordination of individual efforts: these are the essential tasks today.

There is an effort to develop economic spaces encompassing various sectors of production and the services which support them, by harnessing resources and traditions: to transform the population's social needs into mobilization and job creation; to develop and market quality products, and ensure that raw materials are processed at point of origin; to support cottage industries based on co-operative labour: clay, woodworking, tapestry, etc.

Participation must be considered the essential factor underlying all these initiatives for personal and group development. Participation must proceed from the bottom up, from the inside out, so as to allow people to: reflect, express their opinions, act; actualize liberating relationships; act freely and autonomously; become active agents-subjects of their own development and self-realization; decide for themselves what they want to do and how they want to do it; examine and develop their own understanding of the events, facts and situations which affect them, locally, regionally and nationally.

The educational process is built on interrelations between: problems, behaviours and values; socio-economic structures, groups and social movements and social problems and conditions. An understanding of the action in progress involves a specific pedagogical method under which the way the action is carried out becomes fundamental. It is therefore an inductive approach: non-competitive; based on solidarity: mutual aid, co-operation in shared tasks; active (non-directive), in which the individual and the group are protagonists. The facilitator motivates, serves as a catalyst for ideas and concerns, drives the process "with" and "from within" the group itself; joint study and participatory action; it does not use abstract preconceived schemes to interpret reality. It proceeds from the simple to the complex, from the particular to the universal.

Action is in itself an educational method. What is apprehended cannot be lived until it has been assimilated into individual and collective experience. The process works by starting from a specific real-life fact and then narrating and discussing events the group has experienced. These are compared with other similar events in order to elicit further group involvement. Together, the group analyzes the causes and considers the potential consequences for the community. Through this process, attitudes that emerge in discussion are also evaluated. Finally, with extra materials brought in to add to the discussions, the group determines actions to be taken and committments are made, both on personal and collective levels.

The action-reflection-action process leads participants to confront their real-life experiences and program activities dynamically and evaluate them on an on-going basis, propelling a new transformative action.

Another way to proceed: examine: critical reading of reality beyond what we see and hear; judge: critical judgement of facts related to questions and values; act: in the light of the facts analyzed.

Some popular techniques that further aid these processes include relaxation exercises, techniques to promote verbal expression, interpersonal communication, self-evaluation, respect for others; small group exercises: brainstorming on topics of interest, reality techniques, debates, interviews, large group exercises, etc.

EVALUATION

Evaluation indicators and time-spans must be established for action initiatives and on-going evaluations must be performed. They should not consist simply of listing what has been done, but also and primarily of analyzing the progress made and determining what should be corrected. A proper evaluation provides a basis which makes it possible to go forward. An evaluation is an invitation to reflect on the road travelled and the distance that remains to be covered.

Any experiment is bound to fail if it does not inspire more experiments. No service, social movement or institution is capable of changing rural existence by itself. All of them must be willing to work with the people in place. Breaking the isolation of individuals and groups living in rural Spain, and going beyond narrow corporate and group interests, are priorities.

All social movements are in transition from voluntary activism and protest actions towards a certain professionalism. It seems clear that sensitization and involvement in the search for solutions to community problems are greater in localities which have already experienced community organizing.

In short, real co-ordinating processes must be launched, both horizontally and vertically, and the sectorial outlook must be replaced by a regional outlook, in which local development is accomplished on the basis of joint planning, joint execution and joint evaluation of all available means — governmental, private, trade union and community-based.

Notes & References

Aganzo, Andrés, *Presente y Futuro del Mundo Rural Español*, Cáritas Española, Rural community development plan.

Desarrollo y Futuro de la Politica Agraria Común (PAC) (Commission of the European Communities proposal) Brussels/Strasbourg, July 9, 1991.

Marcos, Purificación, *La Mujer Rural*, Cáritas Española, Rural community development plan, Madrid: January 1992.

"El Futuro del Mundo Rural", *Documentación Social*, No. 87, April/June 1992. *Revista de Estudios Sociales y Sociología Aplicada*, Cáritas Española.

"Métodos de Intervención Social", *Documentación Social*, No. 81, October/December 1990. Cáritas Española.

Documentation for Cáritas Española's Programa de Animación Comunitaria Rural.

Documentation compiled and systematized by Cáritas Española's Rural community development plan.

On Cáritas' activities in Spain and its publications see: MEMORIA 1991 Cáritas Española, General catalogue of Cáritas Española publications, 1992.

Memoria 1991 Cáritas Espagñola
General catalogue of Cáritas Espagñola publications, 1992

Chapter 2
TWELVE YEARS OF SOCIOCULTURAL ACTION IN THE LAS VILLAS AREA

Quintín Garciá González
Rural continuing Education Centre
Las Villas, Salamanca, Spain

LAS VILLAS RURAL CONTINUING EDUCATION CENTRE

The Rural Continuing Education Centre (CREPA) is a nongovernmental cultural organization run by volunteers from local villages. Its initial purpose was to promote social and cultural initiatives in the Las Villas area of Salamanca, Spain. Educators, school teachers, psychologists, sociocultural group leaders, priests, adult education teachers, doctors, social workers and other professionals work with CREPA. The organization was essentially founded by citizens — young workers and students, housewives, farmers, old people, recreational councellors — who have continued over the years to form the backbone of the organization and manage its programs.

Our idea of sociocultural action in adult education is based on direct participation by target groups at all stages: analyzing the situation in our villages in general and by sector, organizing activities, planning and implementing measures proposed by different groups, evaluation, etc. A team of community workers dedicated almost exclusively to organizational tasks has also been involved in the program.

Over the last 12 years, CREPA has worked closely with a number of social, educational and cultural movements at both the national and provincial levels (Cáritas, Rural Schools, provincial cultural organizations, Christian Rural Movement, the General Council of Salamanca's Cultural Program); all of whom agreed with us on the need to defend and enhance rural life in Spain. We continue to cultivate these relationships, even though we must recognize that for the past few years pro-rural social and cultural movements have been losing steam and that we are losing intensity, zeal and the ability to mobilize people, due no doubt to the general process of impoverishment in the countryside and the grim outlook for the future.

Description of Area

The Las Villas area is located in the province of Salamanca, which is part of the Autonomous Community of Castilla-León. It is located off the Madrid-Salamanca highway, some 20-30 kilometers from Salamanca. There are 10 villages in Las Villas and some of our activities were carried out in all 10 (such as community work with farmers), but most programs were implemented in six only: Babilafuente (population 1,002), Cordovilla (150), Moriñigo (153), Villoria (1,396), Villoruela (1,081) and Francos (320).

For the new program, the village of Cordovilla has been replaced by Francos. It is interesting to note that Francos is a village which has not seen any cultural activity over the past 15-20 years, at least not of a sustained type. We will thus be able to compare and evaluate the response rate in relation to other villages with longstanding cultural traditions and saturation level exposure to the program.

With the exception of Francos, which was founded 40 years ago, the villages experienced a large wave of emigration in the 1960s. Today, the drain has been almost entirely stemmed. Few people are leaving and when they do, it is for temporary work in the hotel business, domestic service in the city, or it is graduates who are seeking work elsewhere. The population is however declining gradually due to an imbalance between births and deaths. In the three villages with more than 1,000 inhabitants, the proportion of children and young people is well above the average for rural populations in Salamanca province.

Las Villas is an irrigated agricultural area with mostly small and medium-sized farms. It suffers from the general problems of farming in Castilla-León. There is little livestock. Villoruela is an exception, for its economy is based on wickerwork.

Two Preliminary Questions

Literacy Education, Basic Education, Adult Education, Popular Education or Sociocultural Action?

I do not intend to examine the subtleties of what these terms mean to different educational experts and schools of thought. In this practical study, I will briefly define the meaning we ascribe to these terms.

Each of these terms has its own history and has been used to designate different educational and social approaches. I believe, however, that most people working with adults now use them to refer to similar contents and goals.

This convergence is probably a result of the declarations of UNESCO conferences (such as the International Conference on Adult Education, Paris, 1985), the agreements reached at international meetings of experts (for example, the Latin American Technical Consultation on Functional Illiteracy, Salamanca, Spain, 1988) and the official policies of each country (such as the White Paper on Adult Education, Department of Education and Science, Madrid, 1986).

We usually use the term **sociocultural action** because it embraces cultural, educational, social, vocational, economic and political objectives in their entirety. In material intended for the public, however, we prefer to use the terms **adult education, basic education** or **popular culture** because we feel they are more readily understood. But for us, each of these terms represents, in the final analysis, a response to the material, individual, family, social, economic and political needs of village inhabitants.

Is Sociocultural Action Still Relevant?

After 12 years of activity in the Las Villas area, the sociocultural group leaders asked themselves bluntly, before embarking on a new project, whether sociocultural action was still a valid means for improving living conditions and individual and community life for these villagers in particular and rural Spain in general.

Our experience of the past 12 years has left us with contradictory impressions and feelings. On the one hand, we have seen that activities carried out in the villages had a mobilizing effect on some segments of the population and bolstered some associations that serve to enrich individual and social life. On the other hand, we have also observed that a large portion of the population has not participated in these forums, or at best only sporadically and then preferably in recreational activities; and that organizing efforts, including all activities and all partial goals, wear out over the years, become elitist (leading to the formation of self-enclosed groups), and in the end lose all influence over the population as a whole.

Certainly the most disappointing conclusion, however, was that **sociocultural action** is an extremely limited tool, notwithstanding the theorizing and fashionable definitions, the expectations and goals that activists may set themselves. Its basic limitation is that major political (economic, social, cultural) decisions affecting rural regions are at odds with the aims of sociocultural action. The state of neglect endured by rural populations and their organizations renders us powerless against governments and national and international institutions whose decisions in most cases — official rhetoric aside — run counter to the interests of rural citizens.

Given the situation, with little to show after 12 years of work and deteriorating living conditions in the countryside following implementation of the Common Agricultural Policy (CAP), what can we do? We believe only two attitudes are possible:

- **Submit and survive** as best we can, accepting that only the individuals and regions capable of adapting to the new conditions brought on by membership in the EEC will escape unscathed.
- **Assume an active attitude** and work for change in rural living conditions by uncovering the causes of rural problems and seeking solutions which are within the grasp of rural populations.

In 1992-93, CREPA launched a new sociocultural action program that stems from the second attitude. The program's goals are to attain individual maturity, to change individualistic attitudes and to organize cultural, social and economic initiatives designed to improve the quality of rural life.

With a certain disenchantment, we began by asking ourselves questions about the validity of sociocultural action. We see around us other educational groups and even public institutions involved in adult education, changing their strategies, discarding education and culture as a means of mobilizing citizens and instead, are channelling their efforts, wherever possible, almost exclusively into economic projects. Despite the dissatisfactions and limitations we have discussed, our answer to the question is yes, although undoubtedly we shall have to set less ambitious goals. In the absence of other more effective sociopolitical instruments, sociocultural action remains a very useful tool to foster the creation and growth of attitudes (support for trade unions, cooperatives, etc.) and may indeed be the only tool available to villagers to try to better their lives.

COMPREHENSIVE SOCIOCULTURAL ACTION PLAN

In the Las Villas area, sociocultural activities began, at least in an organized way, in 1981 with the arrival of a group of Dominican priests. Their presence aroused expectations among individuals and groups in the villages, who then devised a **comprehensive sociocultural action plan**.

The initial aims were:

- to raise awareness of the situation in the villages and examine the causes;
- to break with the assigned roles performed by men and women in rural regions (working and producing); to discover other vital needs;
- to develop the habit of meeting, discussing, making decisions on a community basis; to prepare citizens for participation; to encourage a civic spirited attitude towards the interests of the tribe or family clan;
- to prompt people to organize on the basis of common interests;
- to consider continuing education as every individual's right and duty.

Even these initial goals required a long educational process, for they demanded changes in deeply entrenched mental and social structures. Later, we would progress to more ambitious objectives: reforming production and distribution systems, setting up a viable cooperative, creating strong and representative agricultural unions, achieving active participation by rural citizens in all the institutions that affect their lives, providing appropriate vocational training, distributing agricultural information on an ongoing basis, creating new sources of employment and wealth, upgrading and modernizing social services and social and cultural facilities.

Phase One: Creating Centres & Schools

We began working simultaneously with two segments of the population where there was a demand by creating Cultural Centres for young people and Parenting Schools for parents. The Cultural Centres are open to everyone but attract primarily youths. They were used as a base for outreach to other segments of the population: children, women, the elderly, farmers. The centres flourished for three to four years before falling into stagnation and crisis (see Evaluation). The Parenting Schools consist of weekly or biweekly meetings, depending on the village (using the ECCA method). Over the years, most of these schools have become Parent Associations linked to the local elementary school or high school.

Leisure time educational activities are organized for children and teens on a weekly basis; summer schools and summer camps are set up during the summer. For the elderly, we have set up separate organizations and created places where they can meet and socialize.

Phase Two: The Founding Of CREPA (1983)

Once the Cultural Centres and Parenting Schools had realized their potential for organizing and conducting activities, participation gradually began to decline due to conflicts between different groups, loss of interest, burn-out in the first generation of active members, etc. It became clear that activities would have to be more specifically targeted in order to reach more people. General meetings were not having a sufficient mobilizing effect. We needed new methods and themes. Holding broad-based assemblies with spontaneous participation tended to leave by the wayside, those people with a weak cultural and participatory background.

The Rural Continuing Education Centre (CREPA) therefore decided to get involved in the following activities:

- awareness-raising and information campaigns: postering in public places, distributing pamphlets to households;
- women's section: general culture, specific training courses;

- farmer's section: Rural Week, the "Las Villas" cooperative;
- the college certificate: before and after;
- senior citizens' section: Seniors Week, recreational activities, lectures;
- work-study programs, workshops to enhance occupational skills and create jobs.

Phase Three: Cooperation Between CREPA & the Salamanca General Council

CREPA has been involved to varying degrees in the Adult Education Program sponsored by the General Council since the program's creation. The program was initially managed by officials at the province's cultural centres. At first, the General Council funded CREPA chapters. Later, it provided villages with a cultural coordinator. In the beginning, the CREPA program was followed for the most part. There was adequate coordination and allocation of duties. Later, territories and duties were divided between the coordinators and CREPA cultural agents, leading to a growing split and lack of coordination.

The General Council also slashed the number of coordinators and funding, causing a cultural development void in some areas which CREPA is not in a position to fill.

The Approach

It must be based on people's real circumstances: groups express their interests, and activities are planned on that basis.

It must be truly transformative: cultural dissemination is not enough. Prevailing conditions in each segment of the population must be changed. This is why segmental associations have been created.

It must be integrated: the approach must address the whole person in all his or her facets including education, personal life, family life, social and economic life.

It must address all segments of the population: not only adults, with whom possibilities are severely limited by the difficulty of changing attitudes and habits; not only children and youths, for family influences will draw them into traditional attitudes and lifestyles when they grow up.

It must be progressive, permanent and planned: it must be compatible with the pace of life in rural areas, which is slow, to be sure, but never stops; there is a risk of starting actions and then dropping them; activities must be analyzed, planned and reviewed.

Public Attitudes

Adult males: unreceptive, individualistic, fundamentally pessimistic. Accepted social role: work. Normal daily cycle: work, family, TV, bar.

Women: very receptive; more socially sensitive due to their work, their use of time, being alone at home, yearning for liberation.

Young people: easier to make progress but difficult to keep them involved.

The elderly, children, teens: these segments of the population are relatively receptive and open to initiatives of all kinds.

Problems

In addition to public resistance and related difficulties, a number of external factors must be noted:

- premises not set up at the beginning, lacking furniture and heating for the long winter;
- infighting among cliques and political factions (an unfortunate effect of the political party system in small towns). Many activities have been blocked by divisions of this kind;
- lack of funds for any larger-scale project such as the creation of vocational workshops for unemployed youths;
- lack of coordination with public institutions, such as the National Employment Agency, the Department of Agriculture, etc.

General Evaluation

The first days of sociocultural activities in the Las Villas area in the fall of 1987 were held under the slogan "What is happening today in our villages?" The intention was to conduct an in-depth review of the sociocultural action program with the active participation of all segments of the population. The main topics of discussion were the specific needs of each segment, examination of the program to date, objectives attained and not attained, the level of mobilization and participation in each segment of the population, defining new objectives and new action strategies.

The general conclusions were:

- villages were mobilized through the creation of associations and the organization of activities. The response and the level of participation varied according to the segment of the population and the village. The initial objectives were mostly attained;
- but the majority of villages were not reached due to citizens' lack of motivation and lack of ability to relate, and due also to the use of inappropriate planning and methods;
- participants were painfully aware of the limitations of sociocultural action as an instrument for changing the village way of life. They saw it as a valid tool, but insufficient. It is dependant on other social, political and cultural bodies, which impose their agendas;
- the results of economic development projects were particularly wanting: the bag cooperative for unemployed youths survived for a few years and failed due to unfair demands by the concessionaire; the Las Villas regional cooperative failed

to recruit enough members to set up its own facilities; a long series of meetings for the handicrafts cooperative in Villoruela came to naught due to the existence of opposing interests; the ceramics workshop did not survive; the Villoria protected agriculture cooperative foundered as soon as it tried to expand, due to lack of capital; the vocational workshops and greenhouse work-study programs did not yield results in the job market.

After this review was completed, there was a lack of will to attempt new approaches with the adult segments (although the work with children and teens continued), associations continued but proved largely inadequate in planning and participation. Because of the change in the social climate (a decline in social motivation and awareness), scepticism existed about the effectiveness of the existing arenas to really mobilize large segments of the population. There was weariness due to the fact that the burden or organizational work always fell on the same people year after year, and there was even an intensification of the work-family-TV-bar cycle and amusements on the weekend. There was also a lack of facilitators: many volunteers left and the professionals practically disappeared.

A NEW SITUATION IN OUR VILLAGES

For some years, rural Spain has been experiencing major changes, and it is likely that these will intensify in the years to come. The villages in the Las Villas area have not been spared these transformations; the changes must therefore be considered as the point of departure for any cultural or educational action.

Economic Situation

The two leading economic sectors in the Las Villas area are agriculture (in all villages) and wickerwork (in Villoruela only). These two sectors are currently experiencing a crisis, leaving the region under a cloud of uncertainty.

Agriculture is experiencing ill effects from Spain's membership in the Common Market. European surpluses have hit the area's traditional products hard: beet production has fallen, grain prices have dropped, all control has been lost over potato marketing, corn and sunflower production is suffering from uncertainty, etc. Farmers don't know what to grow anymore. An irrigation system has been set up in the area, but it in itself is no guarantee for the future.

The prevailing type of farming is not appropriate for achieving the level of competitiveness that European and international markets demand: most farms are small or medium-sized and the machinery is often absolute. Farmers are not actively involved in agricultural organizations, cooperatives or unions which could improve the viability of their operations and defend their rights against the administration. The only farming association in the area has very low participation.

The consequences of market pressure for reconversion have been swift in coming: lower revenues for most farmers, indebtedness, unemployment, discouragement, powerlessness. Farmers have not yet begun to leave the land, but some have started taking subsidies to let their land lie fallow rather than planting and working it.

Wickerwork is currently experiencing one of its most serious crises ever. The sector had grown without interruption for 25 years, breeding boundless enthusiasm and a steady rise in the standard of living in Villoruela, although it was at the price of long working hours for the whole family. Unbridled production and optimism in the sector masked two problems, namely the need for training and organization to secure the cottage industry's future. Nobody thought to specialize in design or marketing; in addition, overproduction led to a loss of interest in the quality of traditional products. The market was left to wholesalers, who set the prices of the raw materials and the finished product. The laws of the European and international markets opened the floodgates to higher quality, lower priced imports from the Far East (China, Thailand, Hong Kong, Indonesia), destroying the markets for our goods.

Here too the consequences were fast in coming: many people abandoned wickerwork totally or partly as soon as they had the opportunity to do so (over 40 workers left the sector last year), for family storerooms were overflowing with chairs for lack of buyers, prices were falling, disenchantment and pessimism were setting in, and the industry did not succeed in reorganizing (it may already be too late).

The small **industrial sector** which had long existed in the area has been wiped out over the past ten years. It had consisted of two brickyards and a flour mill, all located in Babilafuente. They had been the livelihood of many families in the village; now, they have been turned into a landfill site or repossessed by a realty company.

To be sure, the **services sector** is not huge, but the shops, bars, repair shops, etc. do support quite a number of families. Masonry was booming in recent years but it can be expected to enter a crisis as well, at least in the villages. The drop in earnings in other sectors — agriculture, crafts, — will inevitably affect the entire services sector.

Political & Social Situation

Democracy has come slowly to our villages. Formal democracy was accepted, to be sure, but there is no real political consciousness. The rate of membership in political parties is very low, disenchantment with the political process is growing, political and administrative institutions — regional, provincial and national — lack credibility, especially when it comes to defending rural interests. The municipal councils tend to be close to the people, whether or not specific policies enjoy public support. Local representatives of political parties are overly dependent on the party leadership in the county seats, whose political power can decide the fate of projects submitted by the villages.

With respect to politics in the sense of citizen participation, the villages of the Las Villas area have changed significantly in the past ten years. An extensive network of participatory arenas has been created: children's movements, youth groups, cultural centres, women's associations, parents' associations, golden age groups, which have contributed, albeit with varying degrees of skill, to refashioning the social fabric and forging a new civic spirit.

The general social climate has also changed. The widespread optimism and high expectations of years past have given way to adjustments in some cases, weariness in others. While participation has declined, some small groups in our villages still have hope and are the symbol of a new way of life, remaining committed to being players at a time when the decisions are being made far from rural regions.

Mainstream Culture, Critical Culture

It has become commonplace to say that rural regions are gradually losing their own culture, that the villages have been invaded and colonized by the dominant urban culture. New modes of production, more travel — especially in villages located near the city — the return of emigrants to visit or to live permanently, and the influence of the media have all created a crisis for the traditional village way of life.

This observation should not lead us to cast urban culture and rural culture, town and country in mutual opposition. Our society's dynamism is gradually breaking down traditional barriers of place and carrying us towards a universal planetary way of life. The culture which now dominates all of society — including our villages — is a culture of **consumerism, individualism** and **competition**. Under a veil of **democratic values** (freedom, equal opportunity, participation, pluralism, etc.), it seeks to justify and perpetuate a profoundly antidemocratic economic and social system. This culture has invaded and attacked rural culture as it has other cultures (black culture, aboriginal culture, etc.), despising and destroying anything that is different. It seeks to standardize tastes, interests, practices, feelings, anything of interest to the market.

This culture may be seen as the ideological weapon of the world economic system which has divided humanity into two groups: master and slave, rich and poor, "developed" and "underdeveloped". Its goal is not personal fulfilment but simply to keep people adapted to the system. The concepts of **humanity** and **humanization** (justice, solidarity, austerity, critical spirit, creativity, personality, etc.) have been permanently devalued, even if these terms are presented as desirable goals in educational and political programs. Moreover, this dominant culture is now assuming new tones: **individualistic narcissism** and **disillusionment** are helping to turn people away from political concerns and enclose them in the petty pleasures of daily life. This is undoubtedly the best way to ensure nothing changes.

Let us not be deluded: it is this culture which interests decision-makers and the holders of power. It is this culture with which the media bombards us daily and which holds sway in the schools in a somewhat moderated form; and this is the culture in which so many people, including villagers, lay their hopes for success and a better life.

There remains however another culture in our society and in our villages which may be called utopian-critical culture, culture of solidarity, popular culture (people's culture) which serves to mobilize individuals and groups to build future worlds as yet unknown. It uses a specific language: consciousness-raising, awareness; **Seeing**: evaluating, assessing, critiquing, denouncing; **judging**: creating, planning, building, joint action, transformation; **acting**. It does not judge people or things in terms of their economic profitability but on the basis of what they are and what they mean. This is the foundation for actions which spring from dedication and conviction, to reclaim and support home-grown art and culture and daily social interaction among citizens (get-togethers, parties, etc.). This type of culture is still alive in our villages, though it is slowly waning.

A NEW SOCIOCULTURAL PROJECT

A group of people, including some from the old CREPA team and some newcomers, felt there was an urgent need for consciousness-raising to overcome the crisis of community organizing of recent years and help citizens respond to the current crisis in our villages in an active and critical way.

During the evaluation, we found that most citizens never attend cultural events or participate in civic forums, municipal councils, political parties, trade unions. We estimate that this is true for 80% of inhabitants in all age brackets; the figures are higher still for those aged over 50. We consider this to be a relative failure, for one of the objectives of the former plan had been to reach all, or at least most, village inhabitants. We could only conclude that the old plan was inappropriate. The results suggest that we must consider adopting different methods and contents for the program so as to adapt it to the real circumstances of the majority of the population.

Evaluation of Functional Illiteracy in Our Villages

After 12 years of ongoing contact with a given population, one comes to know its specific characteristics. Our plan was to conduct a more in-depth study of pockets of functional illiteracy: to locate, assess, describe, and analyze their causes. After this study, a new, realistic and viable educational project was to be set up to address the 80% of the non-participating population whom we identify as functionally illiterate.

The project team conducted a qualitative study of three age groups: youths, the middle-aged and pensioners, by means of questionnaires and meetings. The following general profile emerged:

- little or no participation in CREPA programs. This fact reflects lack of interest, lack of motivation and interpersonal difficulties; clearly, it is also an indication that the methods and contents were inadequate;
- poor attitudes and practices with respect to associations;
- low level of education: elementary school in the case of adults, college certificate in the case of young people and the middle-aged;
- little or no reading and writing in everyday life;
- inadequate and uniform use of community media, almost no exercise of the right to information and free speech;
- low self-esteem in terms of culture and education, resulting in insecurity, embarrassment and social blocks;
- inadequate vocational preparation for current job or for career goal;
- little knowledge of, use of and satisfaction with the practical skills demanded by modern life (dealing with bureaucracy, banking, handling household appliances or machinery in the workplace, voting, etc.);
- outdated skills and knowledge in basic areas: nutrition, hygiene, health, medicine, environmental education, etc.;
- inadequate preparation for assuming family responsibilities and living together.

Main Concerns

The three target groups reported their concerns, apprehensions, problems, specific group and individual situations:

1. young people: labour rights, unionization; vocational information; the difficulty of finding a job in the villages; family and relationships; leisure and entertainment; use of community media; village organizing, etc.;

2. the middle-aged: family (parents and children); their children's future; education; health instruction; community media; public affairs education; general culture; the grim prospects for agriculture; individualism; the failure of cooperatives, etc.;

3. the elderly: family; relations among the generations; social change; community media; social organization in the village; social and economic rights; hygiene and preventive medicine, etc.

The results will serve to help develop a new sociocultural action strategy.

These fundamental concerns represent areas of interest which can serve as a basis for a **Basic education and sociocultural action** program designed to provide citizens with the training and information they need, and to support the search for solutions to villagers' daily problems. **This brings us back to the fundamental principle that genuine adult education must proceed from the participants' own experiences and real-life situations**.

New Methodology

How could we reach the entire population? We could not repeat the old formula, even with a new content. We therefore drew up a three-part sociocultural action plan.

1.   Outreach cards

Where are the people who never accept repeated invitations and never participate in any activity in any program? They're at home! Home and family are therefore the logical site for the new program to target, but the problem was finding a way to contact each family. The only viable solution was to send them written material (cards) simply presented with colours, illustrations and uncrowded layout, with accessible content (basic, linear) and using plain, simple, familiar language.

We then had to decide on the content, basing our ideas on the positive results from written material used in the Santibáñez de Béjar project (see "A cultural empowerment process in rural areas" by Joaquin Carasco).

For the preliminary stages, we set up a pilot team (10 people of different backgrounds) on which to test response to the frequency of card delivery. The response has been very positive. We have decided to reduce the number of cards and spread out the delivery.

The new schedule calls for the CREPA program to be spread over three consecutive school years. The following frequency is considered feasible and acceptable for the entire population: two cards sent to every home every 15 days throughout the school year. Segmental cards will be distributed only to the segments of the population in question and at the times considered appropriate.

The immediate objectives of the cards will be:

- to convey information and raise topics for discussion by individuals and families; to broaden people's knowledge; to present concrete problems;
- to create reading habits;
- to encourage writing (which is increasingly neglected by adults) by leaving spaces for comments and soliciting answers to questionnaires.

2.   Neighbourhood meetings & segmental meetings

The study revealed poor attitudes and practices with respect to associations and a trend towards cocooning due to lack of interest, lack of motivation and interpersonal problems. How could we address this situation at the educational level?

We felt that meetings at a neighbourhood level were indispensable to try to break the daily cycle of work-family-TV-bar (on the weekends), which has been reinforced by the modern way of life. But another attempt to organize meetings by inviting the whole village proved to have negative results in the past. This division into neighbourhoods has two advantages:

- it capitalizes on a traditional, deeply-entrenched sense of identification of the neighbourhood before the village. This feeling stems from personal and family relationships and from daily physical proximity, which inspires trust;
- it enables us to organize smaller meetings, facilitating participation and avoiding stage-fright for the people with the worst cultural inferiority complexes.

The division is based on results of other events of recent years in which participation has been high: religious activities, neighbourhood efforts to solve common problems, holiday celebrations, recreation activities.

These neighbourhood meetings will be held at the rate of one meeting every 15 days throughout the school year, to follow up on the two cards distributed to homes the previous week. Segmental meetings are planned only for appropriate groups — farmers, young people, the elderly — who are less likely to attend the neighbourhood meetings. The segmental meetings will be village-wide as there is no problem of too many participants.

The meetings are intended to be an arena where everyone can speak, where people can discuss the content of the cards and the questionnaires. This method is the most appropriate for adults, as it encourages participation and follows up on a process of information distribution and reflection, especially with a moderator, to aid discussion in groups where people are not used to speaking.

Given the simple content of the cards, the discussion can be expected to yield a more in-depth treatment of the issues based on each participant's experience. In some cases, additional documentation may be introduced.

3.   Practical services

Adult education must prompt changes in individual attitudes. Sociocultural action must spark a process of transformation and lead to improved services and living conditions in the villages. The purpose of this third stage of the CREPA program is therefore to seek solutions to the problems which have been uncovered and to pursue the initiatives proposed during the group discussion of issues.

Without replacing the organizations and associations in which the 20% of the population are already involved, the goal is to secure steady participation by the 80% of the population which is not currently involved in the institutions and associations that form the social backbone of our villages. One of the cards — *information on institutions* — was intended precisely to arouse a desire for information and a willingness to participate in the various groups.

A FIRST GENERAL ASSESSMENT
OF THE CURRENT PROGRAM

The program includes an on-going assessment mechanism and uses family group leaders. When the questionnaires are distributed every two weeks, the group leaders, through their conversations with the families, evaluate the degree of acceptance and follow-up of the program. This makes it possible to gradually make corrections in the procedure for preparing the questionnaires, the schedule for meetings and so on. To this end, family group leaders are offered a wide range of on-going assessment material.

Here are the most significant data available at the present time.

Home distribution of questionnaires

The program was accepted by 95% of the families in various villages and municipalities. This shows that there was initially great interest in it. Approximately 80% of the common questionnaires were read by the women in the families. Among the men, the rate was only about 30% (the response rate was 80% for the sectoral questionnaire for farmers). Children of age in the families generally showed little interest. As for comprehension of the questionnaires, no one indicated any problem. This is significant, since the need for informal language was one of the serious challenges of the program.

The rate of response for the section of the questionnaire in which a personal answer, in writing, was required was very low: 5% to 10%. This major objective in basic education is not being achieved.

Meetings in neighbourhoods & sectors

In the first quarter, before the Christmas holiday, the rate of participation was about 40%. After Christmas, it dropped by almost half: the meetings were held at a late hour (after a day of work), making it difficult for adults and mothers with small children to attend; the very cold weather in the Castillian winter; the poorly equipped premises, people forgetting to attend, the fact that such gatherings were not customary, the participatory style of the meetings, which resembled a "tertulia", a small get-together in the back room of a café, which was to the liking of those who participated regularly. There was massive participation in the farmers' sectoral domain.

Creation of services of practical use

The lack of economic means and the complexity of the program made it impossible to set up some of the social platforms initially envisaged, such as the family orientation workshop and the labour market orientation workshop for young people, which required greater specialization. The remainder of the "yes" domains were supplemented by the following practical activities: information campaigns on nutrition, support for newspapers or magazines in two municipalies, implementation of the sub-program entitled "A Library in Our Home" (1630 books in constant circulation, from family to family); support for zonal demands (the fight to keep the train that was to be eliminated), promotion and advice for the agricultural marketing cooperative, "Las Villas del Tormes", to which 97 farmers now belong; organization and management of a course for recreational coaches; management of the psychotechnical workshop at the regional institute.

In the initial phase, i.e. until Christmas, there was a very high degree of participation. Then it declined in the winter months, and picked up somewhat in the spring.

It may be too much to ask adults to pay constant attention during a complete course from October to June. This requires encouragement and development of the sectoral domains, which, because of the specific nature of the subjects, motivate participants more. An attempt has been made in the course to compensate for this loss of interest through the implementation of a sub-program entitled "A Library in Our Homes".

There was the same type of resistance — indifference, reading and writing problems, a lack of motivation to leave their homes to attend meetings, a lack of continuity, particularly in sectors with greater functional illiteracy. Experience has shown that it is increasingly difficult to break the very firmly rooted, vital circle of home-family-television-bar, which persists in some sectors of the population.

Hence, the objectives of the program have been achieved, but only partially. Since the program is so broad and complex, and is being implemented in various villages, some phases and aspects have more impact than others, depending on the village and the sector of the population.

This is also only the first year of the program, which must be developed before the degree to which its objectives have been achieved can be assessed in detail. At the present time, and with the necessary corrections that are gradually becoming apparent (a less extensive schedule, a greater role for the sectoral domains), we believe that the program is a valid tool for encouraging the cultural and socioeconomic mobilization of the zone and, ultimately, for improving the quality of lif of all those living in the villages and municipalities.

Chapter 3
"PREESCOLAR NA CASA" TEACHING PARENTS TO TEACH CHILDREN

Ermitas Fernández
Cáritas, Galicia
Spain

"Preescolar na Casa" (preschool at home) is an educational program in rural Galicia aimed at teaching parents to teach children by getting them directly involved in the education of their own children. "Preescolar na Casa" is organized in the home by the parents and families for children aged 0-6. It capitalizes on real-life experiences, daily activities and the local environment.

Parents cannot provide this type of education without help from professionals, who discuss, elaborate and systematize, and without materials specially designed by these professionals. The process is based on a program of regular meetings.

GALICIA

Galicia, one of Spain's 17 autonomous communities, is located at the northwest tip of the peninsula. It has its own government and parliament.

Population

Of all the autonomous communities, Galicia has suffered the greatest loss of population. Between 1981 and 1991, its population fell from 2,811,912 to 2,709,743, a drop of 3.6%. The population loss has been primarily in the hinterland. The population is tending to concentrate in the Vigo-La Coruña corridor, at the expense of the Lugo-Orense corridor, leading to not only a demographic but also an economic and social imbalance between the coast and the interior.

Seventy percent of the population lives in rural areas. The population is aging rapidly; there are now more deaths than births in Galicia. In 1990, the region lost 5,534 inhabitants. Fifteen percent of the population is over 65, as much as 20% in Lugo and Orense provinces.

The population is scattered. Galicia has 31,984 population clusters, half of all the communities in Spain, although it covers only 5.8% of Spain's area and contains only 7.1% of its population. Despite their dispersal, these population centres fit into a hierarchy which goes from the village and the parish up to the region.

The parish is the basic historic, economic, social and cultural unit of Galician society, but paradoxically it has no legal status. In this system, the village, the parish, the region and "a vila" (where there is one) form a web; the commune, as it exists in the rest of the country, is therefore a purely artificial construct.

Economy

Galicia has little industry. Only 14.6% of the population is employed in the industrial sector (compared with the national average of 21.7%). There is no Galician industrial model based on a regional economic development strategy. There are however a number of industries exploiting our resources for foreign interests. Galicia has no home-grown entrepreneurial class, with only a few exceptions in the garment industry (Inditex) and food (Coren, Pescanova). There is no entrepreneurial "culture" in Galicia, which makes it difficult to create the indigenous developmental dynamic.

The economy remains primarily agricultural. Thirty percent of the labour force works on small farms, compared with the national average of 11%. These farms are very fragmented (15 plots of an average 0.4 hectares per farm) and 70% have less than 5 hectares of land. The leading activity is livestock production. Few of these farms can be said to be prospering.

Society

Traditional agricultural society has left its imprint on our character and way of life. This society was built on community. Individuals existed through the group — home, family, parish, neighbours — breeding a deep sense of solidarity and mutual aid and giving rise to a close-knit community.

Economic modernization and the resulting crisis in traditional agricultural society have not produced in Galicia a coherent transformation adapted to local realities and accepted by the population. A capitalist economy was introduced into a precapitalist system, fragmenting traditional social structures and ushering in profound social and cultural change. However, there is widespread resistance to change. Galician society is today divided between rurality, which we all bear within us, and the gradual spread of modernity.

So it is that while supermarkets are invading our cities, village markets still continue to exist, although their numbers are shrinking. The introduction of new services in rural areas is sparking rivalry but at the same time, neighbourhood support systems remain strong. In the past, political bosses served as intermediaries between town and country, between peasants and the bureaucracy. Today, they have adopted more "democratic" methods: services rendered are no longer paid for in kind but with votes. Despite the rise of the nuclear family, the decline in the birth rate and the exodus of young people to the cities, families continue to be close-knit patriarchal units.

Language

Galician is closely related to Portuguese. As it is not a recognized language and does represent a cornerstone of our cultural identity, the use and defense of Galician is often seen as a political act. The majority of citizens consider themselves Galician rather than Spanish or European, and 39% consider themselves very or quite nationalist.

The overwhelming majority of Galicians understand Galician (94%) and speak it (87%). Fewer people use it daily (50%). In rural areas Galician is the common language, but in the towns of La Coruña, Ferrol and Vigo, Castilian dominates. Moreover, Galician is primarily a spoken language: only 35% of Galicians can write it and 50% read it.

Poverty

Thirty-four percent of Galicia's population derives its livelihood from agriculture. The peasants live in grinding poverty. With small farms and small herds, long delayed and poorly applied modernization, an aging farm population (35% of farm operators are over 65), widespread functional illiteracy (80% of farm operators did not go to school) and the departure of young people, the situation has deteriorated to the point where farm families now survive on the pensions of the elderly, the little money that emigrants send home, and extra income from odd jobs.

Fishermen are probably the most exploited group. Their living and working conditions are harsh. According to a recent survey, 50% of Galicians who fish off the Canary-Sahara bank work 18 hours a day and the accident rate is 92%; 34% will abandon the trade to work on shore, even for less money. Family problems, alcoholism and drugs abuse are rampant. Young sailers are often drawn into the drug trade.

In 1976-77, Galicia lost 30% of its jobs due to the decline of the industrial sector (compared with a national average of 19%). Galicia's unemployment rate is 15%, of which 57% are women. According to a trade union survey, 60% of Galician women are single mothers living a precarious existence. Fifty-three percent of farm workers are women, the bulk of whom work with their husbands and, in a patriarchal society, have no decision-making power.

Between 1950 and 1970, Galicia suffered a net loss of 466,510 people through migration. Most emigrants, who left illegally, came from farm families. Just as today North Africans cross the Straits of Gibraltar in skiffs, large numbers of Galicians once crossed the Bidassoa hidden in trucks. Almost half of Galicia's population lives outside Galicia's borders, for we consider emigrants to be part of the Community still.

It is true that some of those who emigrated to other parts of Europe have worked their way up by dint of effort and sacrifice and are now living well; some emigrants have made their fortune in America; but it is also true that many emigrants have come back to their native land, defeated by the economic crisis and preferring life at home to a life of uprootedness and insecurity, and many others live in abject poverty with no social safety net.

In 1989, 20% of Galicia's population received social security. There are almost as many recipients as there are workers paying premiums — one recipient per 1.36 farms. Galicians earn not only less than the national average, but less than any of the other autonomous communities. Of all the autonomous communities, Galicia has the largest number of public assistance recipients.

Education

Education is cut off from the local community. The dispersal of the population makes it difficult to adapt educational programs to local conditions and communications and service infrastructures are largely inadequate.

There is a 40% failure rate in the schools (higher in rural areas). Many students have learning difficulties and many have to repeat grades. Rural families are doing little to improve their education and that of their children, due either to indifference or because they do not think they are capable of it, even though they are well aware of the demands of modern society and want to help their children succeed.

"PREESCOLAR NA CASA"

History

Given the situation we have described, the need for action to raise education levels is clear. But in Galicia, any action of this type must secure the participation of parents as educators from the first years of the child's life. When parents (father and mother) become involved in educating themselves and their children, the educational level of both parents and children is bound to increase significantly.

There was an urgent need for a solution. At first, there were protests (letters, press releases, reports, study sessions, etc.), but it soon became clear that this approach was insufficient. As it was impossible to quickly reach children in rural areas, a program was developed to help them by other means, for children cannot wait.

The project was intended for all rural families with children under the age of 6 not yet attending school. The purpose was to reach parents to raise their own level of education and help them participate in the education of their children.

The project began in 1977 in four communities where pooled work and education experiments had already been conducted. At the same time, a questionnaire containing three questions was sent to all parish priests in Galicia. These questions were basic to the viability of the project:

- How many children aged 3-5 are there in your parish not attending kindergarten?
- Would you be willing to organize a meeting with the parents of these children?
- Would you be prepared to support a school readiness program addressed to the parents of preschool children?

The survey results indicated that a program of this type was possible and a project was therefore submitted to the Department of National Education, which assigned three school teachers. Parents were then invited to meetings at which we explained why we wanted them to work with their children: the need for a good education in this day and age, the importance of the first years of life in the educational process, the decisive role of parents in the education of their children. We conducted a field test to determine whether parents would be able to contribute effectively to the education of their children.

In most cases, the weekly meetings with the parents and children were led by volunteers, mostly school teachers or priests. They worked with the team of three school teachers, who established the guidelines and organized the meetings. This phase lasted two years. Though the project had a number of failings (weak content, divergence from original objectives, lack of preparation, inadequate follow-up, etc.), we continued to consider the idea valid.

The program was later expanded in quantitative terms with an increase from three full-time teachers to 11, also assigned by the Department of National Education, and a reduction in the number of volunteers. It now has 22 counsellors assigned by the Department of Education of the "Xunta de Galicia," assisted by four volunteers and 19 aides paid by the Department of Social Affairs of the "Xunta de Galicia" and six municipal councils. At the same time, there was also a qualitative improvement. The program was overhauled, its underlying principles and objectives redefined, and the preparation of the counsellors and direct follow-up revised.

Theoretical Foundations

The creation of the "Preescolar na Casa" program sprang from its initiators' conviction that lack of knowledge breeds backwardness, dependence, marginalization and injustice. The more knowledge and skills citizens possess, the greater their chances of enjoying freedom, prosperity and justice.

Research in infant psychology indicates that the first years of life are decisive (see for example B.S. Bloom, *Human Characteristics*) and that culture and knowledge are the fruits of an educational process which must begin in a systematic way before the age of 6, for the ability to develop intellectual abilities and emotional balance declines with age. We believe that if preschool education is lacking, the inevitable result will be slow progress in school.

Parents play a determining role in the educational process. As emotional maturity and intellectual progress are conditioned by the educational atmosphere in the home and by child-rearing practices in the first years of life, and as a good teacher-student relationship helps promote and motivate learning, parental support is always essential to preschool children.

Presently, the preschool education children receive in the home is inadequate and unsuitable, for parents are unaware of their own potential as educators and of the needs and abilities of young children. Indeed, they often labour under serious misconceptions about child-rearing. The education children receive in the schools is also inadequate, for in most cases it is neither adapted nor complemented in the home. Children who live far from school must rise at dawn, contend with tiring travel to and from school, rowdy recesses, etc., without the support of their parents. All this can make them insecure. Moreover, most children go to schools which make no concession to either their language or their cultural background.

Children cannot wait for solutions to be forthcoming, for they obviously cannot stop growing up. Our experience has confirmed that parents are able to adapt and to acquire the skills and knowledge they need to educate their preschool children. We have listened to many mothers report intellectually stimulating conversations with their children and their children's reactions to discovery-oriented activities.

Objectives

The central objective is to prepare parents to create a conducive educational environment in the home and help them choose activities to support their children's physical, psychomotor, intellectual, creative, emotional, social and moral development.

The general goals are the following:

• make sure that everyone has the education they need for full enjoyment of

culture and knowledge;
- improve preschool education in rural areas and reduce the school failure rate;
- rear physically and psychologically healthy children who are intellectually alert and emotionally balanced;

- encourage parents to continue participating in their children's education after they start attending school;

- make sure parents look after non-academic areas of education.

For these goals to be achieved, the father and mother must be:
- aware of the importance of education in the first years of life and of the role that family and school can play at this age;
- aware of a child's psychological, physiological, intellectual, emotional and motor development needs, of educational possibilities and the most appropriate actions and attitudes;
- prepared to work on their children's education in a thoughtful, systematic and steady way.

Principles of Action

- proceed from family educational skills;
- promote activities which are practical in a rural environment;
- create and discover educational situations in everyday life;
- make sure both parents and children acquire some inherently important skills;
- work to modify some traditional child-rearing practices;
- encourage creativity in the family soas to develop creative capacities in the child;
- evaluate the educational process (development of skills, knowledge and attitudes, family structure, etc.) on an ongoing basis;
- work to ensure that children fulfil their potential;
- always remember that nothing is insignificant: children absorb everything;
- bear in mind that child-rearing is based on a symbiotic family relationship.

IMPLEMENTATION

The families of 2,658 boys and girls aged 0-6 are now involved in the program. They are divided into 659 work groups and come from 266 communes (out of Galicia's total of 313 communes), although the program does not cover all parts of Galicia.

Meetings with Parents & Children

Invitations

A general assembly is planned with all families, but given conditions of isolation and lack of transportation, the invitation is tailored as much as possible to the specific situation of each village and each family. We distinguish between regions and families who are already familiar with "Preescolar na Casa" and those who know little or nothing about it. In regions where people know about the program, one meeting is held for quite a large area and all the parents in the villages within a reasonable radius are invited, taking into account available means of transportation.

The purpose of this first meeting is to get the parents involved in the organizing process. They themselves will decide who will attend the meetings and where they will meet in the course of the year. In this way, they assume some responsibility from the outset.

In some cases, the counsellor sends out the invitations himself based on information on the families provided by the municipal council or parish priest. In other cases, the invitations are sent out by a resource person, who is not directly involved in the program but serves as a backer and helper. Usually, the resource person is a priest or someone who knows the region and its people well. Today, parents who have taken the "Preescolar na Casa" program in the past often serve in this capacity, taking it upon themselves to motivate other parents and encourage them to attend the meetings.

In the case of regions where people are unfamiliar with the "Preescolar na Casa" program, the counsellor goes to homes in the community and encourages parents to take the program if he observes a need, thus establishing a relationship and opening lines of communication. The visits to people's homes also help us to determine which families are the most underprivileged and which have the fewest options. We therefore try to visit all the parents, if we can, to invite them to a group meeting, which is also important so the parents themselves can decide who will attend the meetings and where they will be held.

The meetings

Once the group has been formed and the site chosen, meetings are held with the parents and the children every two weeks. As a rule, all the parents undertake at the beginning to complete the program. A meeting usually takes at least two hours. It usually includes the following parts:

1) Call to order. Discussion of progress during the previous two weeks. All participants express their points of view. Children present activities done at home; emphasis on the creativity of the parents and children and on everyday activities; comments.

b) One or more activities conducted with the participation of parents. All types of materials are used, but preference is given to materials which are locally available to everyone. Great importance is also attached to play, songs, etc. All these activities are designed to demonstrate what can be done at home and stimulate the creativity of the parents. The purpose of the meeting is to motivate, explain, encourage, guide, prompt reflection, seek the best approach in each case. But the real work starts after the meeting and continues until the following meeting.

3.   Presentation of the program for the next two weeks. Brainstorming to come up with activities related to the theme for the next two weeks, and to the activities already planned in the material given to the families.

4.   While the children play, the adults discuss a practical question related to child-rearing. The question may be prompted by their experiences or by a magazine, book, etc. (e.g. children's drawings, play and playthings, bed-wetting, bladder control, jealousy, etc.).

Parents show lively interest and attend regularly, even though some have to travel long distances to do so.

Counsellors

The counsellors, chosen for their familiarity with rural Galicia (and their ability to adapt to it), are knowledgeable about education and practice it in keeping with the spirit of the program. They are school teachers on loan, paid employees, or in some cases volunteers.

The training they receive includes: training tailored to help them work with adults; theoretical, but geared to facilitating practice; not only pedagogical, but broad and integrated with respect to rural society; tailored to the specific characteristics of the work in question.

It is designed to turn out counsellors who are:

* sensitive to the situation in rural Galicia;
* able to foster in people an awareness of their own values: language, sense of community, wholesome living, etc.;
* informed or interested in becoming informed about problems in rural Galicia;
* able to establish good relations with the families so they can base their approach on socialand family life, not just scholastics;
* able to use simple language and stay close to the people;
* open, tolerant, understanding, able to understand local realities, always willing to learn;
* willing to take a back seat to the parents;
* enthusiastic and able to infect others with their enthusiasm;
* and, of course, knowledgeable about child-rearing.

Information & Training

The "Preescolar na Casa" program puts out a monthly 12-page publication called The Magazine for the parents of children aged 0-6 (circulation, 3,500). It deals with the program's activities, with issues related to pre-school children, the goals their education ought to pursue, ways to use the natural and social environment to stimulate children, etc. It also deals with health and nutrition and includes suggestions for activities, games, stories, hobbies, etc.

The program produces two half-hour radio programs each week for parents, children and the general public. These programs are intended to support the work of the counsellors and promote communication between adults and children, educational activities, and play. They also provide information on all questions related to early childhood education as well as songs, stories, riddles, games, comments and interviews related to education.

We also produce in association with Galician Television a weekly half-hour television program for parents including suggestions for activities.

The library was created to meet the training needs of the counsellors. It has a section on child-rearing for parents. The counsellors have found that parents from rural areas, especially the younger ones, want to read and do read the books they can get their hands on.

The program has also published booklets for parents on various subjects: play and playthings, children and drawing, songs, etc. Last but not least, the library has a well-stocked children's section; these books are lent to parents at the meetings so they can read them to their children and show them the illustrations.

The counsellors are convinced of the vital importance of spontaneous play for children, and hence of toys which encourage play. Despite everything, toys are often indispensable. Consequently, the material distributed to the families includes toy-making suggestions. The program also has other types of toys for the children to play with during the meetings. One of the goals is to teach the parents to appreciate the importance of play for children.

EVALUATION

Successes

After years out of school and uninterested in education, the parents in the program start learning again, not only about child-rearing but about all aspects of their lives. The discussions lead the parents to gradual involvement in joint actions. They start to support community efforts which eventually influence the family and the entire neighbourhood: struggles, protests, the fight for a higher standard of living or better quality of life.

The meetings are valuable for promoting participation, dialogue and spontaneous communication, for such opportunities are often lacking in rural regions.

The observed results include:

- enhanced self-esteem and self-acceptance;

- a positive influence on family life with improved participation by all;
- better use of local resources;
- closer observation of their children's progress and more encouragement.

The parents become educators, whose process progresses from schooling in the home to general education, and from part-time education to ongoing education. Demand is growing. Many parents are taking the initiative and approaching the program coordinators. Supply has been supplanted by demand. What was originally conceived of as an extension to school has become a self-sufficient entity. The children's interest and enthusiasm serves to motivate the parents.

The children display improved communication skills, spontaneity, confidence, self-esteem and independence. They are not shy to ask questions. They trade stories and share toys more willingly. The program has also given rise to broader cultural development experiments. Beyond the borders of Galicia, a number of similar programs have been launched, usually bearing the same name.

Problems

Parents underestimate the educational potential of the home and overestimate the role of the school system. They do not realize their own capacities and the value of the local environment. Parents often fail to realize the importance of the first years of life. They connect childhood development with school; education therefore begins too late. Parents participate in the program for only a short time. They start late and drop it as soon as the child enters school.

The educators change frequently, due to the hard and untypical working conditions and transfers, which means that the counsellors often lack experience and specific training for the program. We find we have an inadequate background in adult education; this has proven to be a handicap. Human and financial resources are limited.

REFLECTIONS

Rural areas have enormous needs, but there are also opportunities for development. People want to improve their living conditions, even if they do not always know how to go about it. They are capable of joining forces, working together, creating bonds of solidarity. The results of the project lead us to conclude that the following factors are essential for the success of an adult education program in a rural environment. The educators must:

- know about existing needs and be able to predict future needs;
- identify the basic factors influencing people's lives;
- organize simple activities whose results can be evaluated in the short-term;
- be able to draw conclusions from the results which can be applied elsewhere;
- define objectives, delve into issues, review and assess the approach;
- foresee potential difficulties caused by the personalities of the participants or by the conditions under which the activities are conducted;
- select activities on the basis of the program's general objectives and spirit.

Illiteracy is not only the inability to read and write; it is a person's inability to understand what is happening all around, and what he or she is doing; to grasp the causes of problems and find appropriate, fundamentally effective, long-term solutions. This type of illiteracy is common in rural areas, where people have a poor understanding of the changes brought on by progress. Rural regions also lack a vision of the future and fail to realize the importance of education in order to adapt to the complexities of modern life.

But these problems are not unique to rural environments. The educators who go to work in the countryside are also beset by them. They are ill-prepared for innovative educational approaches in which citizens are called upon to play an active role, and they reduce education to the schools, dismissing educational efforts conducted outside the walls of the institution.

The experience of "Preescolar na Casa" and other similar programs has demonstrated that with proper guidance, rural populations are perfectly capable of participating in an innovative educational project and achieving good results. There are educators who are aware of their own limitations and are striving to improve their skills to meet the specific needs of citizens in rural areas.

There is also hope for the ability of educational institutions to adapt, insofar as they are putting up no resistance to the innovative experiments springing up in so many places, For the results tend to be positive and the costs are low.

Broadening the Scope of Education

The Ancares region of Lugo province is a mountainous beekeeping area. A teacher in the "Preescolar na Casa" program organized and led a beekeeping training project for youths and adults in the region to help them boost honey production. A training program funded by the Spanish government and the European Social Fund was therefore set up under the supervision of two technicians to promote the transition from cottage industry to modern production. From this project there emerged a honey producers' cooperative whose purpose was to train new beekeepers and market the honey.

This experience demonstrated to local citizens that they could improve their economic and social lot without leaving home. The project led to the creation of a sheep and goat farm and produced improved crop yields through the use of better methods and the end result was better knowledge of agricultural production and marketing techniques, and at the psychological level a greater inclination to stay in the region and increased awareness of the possibilities of collective action.

This experiment also yielded a new community development project on which three people — a community organizer, a psychologist and an agrologist — worked full time under the supervision of "Preescolar na Casa" counsellors. It was funded by Cáritas Española, the local municipal council and the government of the Autonomous Community.

The project's main results were:

- a study of local inhabitants' most pressing needs and how they could be satisfied in the short term;
- extensive and detailed information on all public and private assistance programs for which local citizens could be eligible (subsidies, bursaries, technical assistance, etc.);
- a home care service for elderly people in need who have no family and do not want to leave their homes and communities.

The Ancares regional development project is now entirely locally managed and staffed; a number of local community organizers are involved. Local development projects have also been launched in other parts of Galicia in cooperation with the "Preescolar na Casa" program, in some cases organized by people who had been involved in "Preescolar na Casa."

Chapter 4
A CULTURAL EMPOWERMENT PROCESS IN RURAL AREAS

Joaquín Garciá Carrasco
University of Salamanca
Spain

IDEOLOGICAL FRAMEWORK

In cultural empowerment initiatives, being aware of the determining variables upon which we intend to act, is no less important than defining the social objective we are targeting. If, for example, we believe that illiteracy depends solely on a set of perceptual and motor skills,[1] we shall consider it eradicated when all members of the community have learned to read and write, something which good teachers can bring about in a short period. However, we shall then be surprised to find that in our rural areas, adults who have become illiterate by losing their reading skills outnumber those who never had any. We shall also be surprised that although at the outset so many people recognize the need for basic education, in many instances a very high percentage drop out in the early stages. Lastly, less expert interveners, and others who do not put themselves in that category, cannot understand how in certain communities a simple announcement that they are going to intervene in basic adult education does not bring them into contact reliably with the potential clientele.

To understand the problem of illiteracy among adults in rural areas we must grasp the following:

- Illiteracy is a **social problem** which affects social mechanisms and relationships, when community development reaches a level of complexity at which written culture becomes essential or significantly useful. A proposal to teach literacy is socially valuable because of its mediating or instrumental nature in improving quality of life or to bring into circulation social goods and services which can only be accessed, enjoyed or maintained by those who can read and write.

It follows that the meaning of illiteracy refers to social expectations and social relations within a particular sociological environment.

- The ability to read and write remains purely instrumental in value if the cultural values with which the population identifies, or which the structure of production or the flow of goods and services allows, are not values which must necessarily be conveyed by **written communications** systems. These include the value of up-to-date news, of knowing the state of the social and political system, the pleasure of enjoying artistic creation, enthusiasm for social involvement, the absolute necessity of long-distance communications, the extension of the social and production relations systems beyond the area which can be covered by oral communications, the transformation of the dissemination of knowledge and culture into an industry, the organization of cultural demand in the market and so forth.

- Motivation to develop reading and writing skills is generated by changes in **social expectations**. Thus the decision to take part in cultural dissemination centres must be associated with projects to improve quality of life or provide vocational retraining.

- The ability to read and write becomes a cultural component in a sociological environment, or for a person, if it plays a **functional role** in relation to positioning of the individual or collective personality in accordance with economic objectives, production relations, social organization, aesthetic values and so forth.

- The dependence of the level of writing skills on the state of the social system leads us to believe that, at least in our rural areas, we should **constantly increase the connection between cultural empowerment programs and comprehensive development programs** in those areas, for we are convinced that the development of the quality of social productivity is hampered both by failure to bring about change in social attitudes through failure to accept necessarily linked cultural and cognitive progress and by failure to transform the relations within the community associated with changes in production systems and production relations.

THE SANTIBÉÑEZ DE BÉJAR PROJECT (PROVINCE OF SALAMANCA)

This project stems from the Program to prevent and combat illiteracy promoted by the Commission of the European Communities in co-operation with member states. It ran for two years, from October 1988 to October 1990, in Santibáñez de Béjar, a small village in the province of Salamanca with an independent economy (almost the entire population works and lives in the same place). The reason for calling this project preventive is that we did not concentrate on direct promotion of literacy in the strict sense of literacy campaigns, but we did emphasize creating circumstances to increase the social role of written mediation in the communications system of the human group we studied. That is precisely why the project was not aimed specifically at any one population group or age bracket.

The project sought to mobilize the village's entire network of social institutions. Since all these institutions embody complex social projects, maximizing their effects stimulates the cultural empowerment necessary for the process of becoming literate. Reading by decoding the written word is transformed into a component of a more comprehensive social phenomenon encompassing the decodification of the community's system of relations and transactions: a process of active awareness and existential ability to "read".

We interviewed all social interveners, not in order to determine the internal validity of the work they were doing but to discover the communications systems they established within their institutions and in relation with other institutions and social interveners in the community. Even more importantly, we interviewed to determine the impact of written communications on such interaction mechanisms. Our observations informed us of the following qualitative facts:

- The school constitutes an information and communications centre relying heavily on reading and writing but has little communication with students' families. Such contact as does take place is through oral communications and qualitative assessments, and the materials used by students contain no elements that could be used in interactions between parents and students. Parents themselves recognize the gap and the difference between what their children study and their own areas of information. The written contents of school material are a real locus of non-communication between parents and students. The only piece of writing which is addressed specifically to parents is the report card.

- The municipal council conducts its sessions and debates with direct involvement of local representatives. Debates are oral and there is very little written communication with the locality. This includes municipal announcements which are delivered orally in the form of proclamations by the peace officer and "town crier", who shouts them in the streets.

- The physician communicates orally with his patients. Instructions for administering medication are given in brief notes about dosages, and there is not the faintest hope that patients will read the instructions accompanying their medication. Furthermore, the printed directions enclosed with medications are not written in a language consumers can understand. Their codes of expression are clearly established to inform only the physicians who prescribe them, not the patients who take them.

- Essentially, the priest communicates with the population orally. The people of the village reinforce their beliefs through oral communications rather than reading.

- The social worker learns about people's needs orally, and they give their impressions in the same way regarding the services they need.

- The impact of social communications media is small. The very few copies of provincial newspapers which come into the village go to the bars, where those who wish have an opportunity to consult them and read the news.

National news is primarily carried by television and radio. There is a municipal library but no adult names appear on book borrowing cards. It is used by children at the request of teachers. The main qualitative assessment of the communications of members of the community is that this is fundamentally an oral culture.

DESCRIPTION OF INTERVENTION INITIATIVE

Definition of the Model

This project fitted into the context of community intervention. It sought to involve all the elements intervening in a community with the objective of changing those elements which supported its socio-cultural and educational level and its characteristics. The aim was to change the structure of the systems of relationships in the community, so that the measures which we attempted to take would continue through their own momentum without the need for outside assistance.

We consider the introduction of the measures advocated by this project to be a rational problem-solving strategy. Consequently, before taking any action, we defined the problem clearly, drew up a list of potential solutions, discussed and analyzed them with all participating interveners and developed those solutions which promised to be most effective. Finally, we assessed the effects of the actions and initiatives we had taken. This strategy was common to the entire project and specific to each of its components or actions. This in turn implied that the type of description model selected was "incremental".

This model of successive increments implicitly entailed a structural change in the community which we endeavoured to bring about by replacing the set of conditioning factors retaining the socio-cultural and educational levels with a new system of relationships which would be functional in terms of the community's needs. We consider the condition usually called functional illiteracy as not just an individual problem but a social one. Acquiring and maintaining basic culture depends on individual skills and on socio-cultural forces.

Actions

Initiatives began at the same time as interveners studied the state in which local institutions carried out their tasks from the point of view of communications. While local structures operated in a really complex way, very old communications mechanisms were maintained which did not correspond to or promote written communications: word of mouth ("you tell X and have him tell it to Y" and so forth), and the town crier, a peace officer whose duties include proclaiming in the streets the most urgent notices of public interest and who reported directly to the mayor.

The school, for its part, justifiably confined its action to the enrolled children. No influence on the cultural behaviour of adults was evident, not even on students' parents. The starting point was:

- initial availability of the teaching team to take part in the initiative, although they were committed to defending their own role, their own administrative status, the quality of the existing situation, and the transfer of responsibility for constraints to the administration;

- resistance by teachers to outside interveners becoming involved in consultations on educational action;

- fatalism regarding lack of co-ordination between teaching activity and other institutional activities in the locality.

The attitude had spread through the village that each social leader (physician, priest, teacher, mayor and so forth) should defend his task and function from the other social roles as a means of maintaining quality in the social action they undertook. They worked together only in acts of social representation.

During the closing ceremony for the project on 21 March 1991, the same social leaders declared publicly that the benefits they had derived from two years of activities in the village included the gratification of working together and the enrichment of having increased the flow of communications between institutions and social representatives. These experiences confirmed to us that **literacy taken as an integral process of social intervention** proves that the real meaning lies in the forms of collective communication it achieves.

It also proves that the need for literacy is not only political, or vocational, it is also, given today's historical and social context, communicative. Quality of life throughout the animal kingdom is quality of communications in all directions in accordance with each organism's possibilities and potential for communication. Humans are essentially social animals, and the deepest deterioration of the human psyche is always related to failure to communicate. Becoming alienated means not communicating, being alienated means not being in communication, being impoverished in some way means suffering from lack of communication: not being in contact with the flow of goods and social services, not being able to cross the border, not speaking the other person's language, not understanding other people's feelings, suffering from a diminution of one or more sensory organs and so forth.

These criterion were used to draw up the socio-cultural intervention plan, and these various general objectives were chosen:

- to increase the circulation of paper naturally, and essentially in relation to the life of the population;
- to improve the public character of social actions and make more villagers actually aware of them and involved in them;
- to induce "cultural spillovers" or new initiatives in the village which would increase the flow of communications as a temporary experimental stimulant of the population's own cultural life: new impetus for the local library, adult evenings and so forth.

The population became aware of the last point and many commented on what would happen when the outside interveners left, which would mean that the cultural events would no longer depend on initiatives by individuals.

Development of Information Sheets for the Entire Population

These sheets, developed by the institutions and by the municipality's social interveners, provide more information about significant aspects of the social reality in which villagers live. They contribute to open communication between the population and the institutions, in addition to promoting reading and communication within the family and in the population. The principle of "circulation of paper" containing items on the interests of the group in which it circulates was established. Members of the community are aware of the source of the information and recognize the meaning of its content. These sheets are written by the physician to circulate health suggestions based on what he observes in his consultations, by the mayor to communicate general or specific agreements reached at municipal council meetings, or by the social workers regarding new pension payments for retirees. The volume of written information of community interest increased significantly during the experiment.

- The physician wrote easy-to-understand health information sheets about diseases most common at the time or representing risk, or presented certain health habits which could reduce the incidence of injuries or disease. He ensured that these reached every home by having the peace officer go from door to door. Even though the content of these sheets was designed for adults, teachers were informed of their content, referred to them in their activities and encouraged discussions at home on those topics. As we observed, communication was organized around written information.

- Teachers at the Education Centre notified families at regular intervals coinciding, for example, with examination periods, to explain when they would take place, what they meant, what qualitative performance levels their children might attain, what might result from a negative evaluation, how important it was to catch up and so forth.

- The conclusions and proclamations of Municipal Council sessions, previously announced as public functions, were changed to written records which circulated through the population, explaining the decisions taken by representatives and informing villagers about scheduled public events. At the end of the project period, the entire village displayed solidarity as regards the state of the road, regardless of political affiliation or voting expectations, even though the next municipal elections were close.

Support for Continuing Education of Professionals

The Santibáñez de Béjar cultural project is making possible national and international exchanges, attendance at conferences, contribution of technical materials and so forth which support training for professionals and enhance their intervention in the community. Thus the simple act of resituating the work of each professional, and especially teachers, in a perspective of community and co-operative interest leads to more thinking about what is being done. Because all those responsible for social functions bear the program focus in their work and hold critical meetings about it, this has a formative role.

The experiment's international stature, co-operation with the university and the co-operation and patronage of national administrative institutions gave the extra motivation to make social interveners more aware that interventions as a systematic object of study plays a role in improving their quality. Those who were initially resistant to the critique now fear that this research process will fall behind. The improvement and potential generated by new literacy communications systems demand higher quality interventions from social interveners.

The apparent conflict between the intervention methods of educators at the education centres and socio-cultural facilitators warrants special attention. Notwithstanding, there is great opportunity for sharing experiences.

Beyond the conflict, communications must be established because the basic principles governing intervention in adult education, whose specific nature seems to be represented by the facilitators, are the same as those which govern the more innovative educational practices in the schools. Simply organizing "cultural events" (lecture series, conferences, films, recreational activities and free time) does not in itself constitute learning of these principles or applying them.

Such basic principles of any pedagogical intervention corresponding to open, democratic social ideals can be summed up in the following points:

1. The expression and cultivation of individuality within group identity must take precedence over contents and processes that are based solely on previous precedents. Individualizing the rate of progress by means of self-teaching materials are a big step forward. In an activity with adults, there can be many individualizing elements whereby progress is made toward the community's shared cultural objectives.

2. Free activity must take precedence over external discipline. The adult educator must avoid clinging to his or her own childhood models of education and reproducing methods of authoirty identification. Situations created in adult education, unless adequate vocational training is given, can reactivate processes of affirming the authority-submission-education role of childhood. It is curious that new adult educators who have little training and no experience begin by proposing an activity plan including lectures, courses... activity cycles with no protagonists' participation.

3. Learning through experience, which we also call significant learning, must take precedence over rote learning. In schools we often observe that problem-solving, activities, application of rules and description based on observation prevail, rather than learning concepts and memorizing laws and principles. The poverty of the environment in which the most culturally disadvantaged people live is matched by the poverty of the spaces and institutions through which they later attempt to make up for lost time. We do not understand why adults should not have the same hands-on approach as children enjoy to learn the same concepts. Experimenting is a characteristic of the species, of human learning.

    We believe that the elements for reflective experimenting among adults is in their own technical and productive surroundings. From the bicycle to the coffee mill, from the pet to the electrical plant, from the telephone to the television, from the pump to the bell tower, opportunities for experiential learning abound. A great substitute for live experiments is viewing scientific films. Good collections of these can easily be obtained by resource centres at a moderate price. We are not speaking here of cultural "events" but of learning developed out of culture (daily life). National and regional television networks and production centres have an important role to play in this area. Adult education, together with school teaching, is an untouched market for lowering the cost of producing this type of cultural goods. Today we rented a "Western" film at a shopping centre for ninety pesetas, the cost of a drink.

    Education and learning from experience again raises the question of adequate training for adult educators that creates awareness of their own past formative educational experience.. They should be aware of their own past formative experiences, which may have been very deficient, and knowing this, they should prevent the same thing from happening for their adult students by encouraging them to bring their own rural experiences: cheesemaking, baking, tinsmithing, farming, mechanics and so forth as part of the adult educative experience. Teacher training schools are geared entirely to children, and the school is a major creator of childhood experience.

    The adult, however, resembles the educator with complete cycles of experience. It is not unusual for a young bachelor adult educator to have to present contents dealing with man-woman relationships to adults, or to explain a topic relating to soil behaviour in food production without being able to distinguish young wheat plants from barley plants. There is a need to professionalize various adult education tasks and to create an adult pedagogical career providing suitable compensation, status and economic power, as in other careers. So long as the adult educator is a migratory bird, professionally we cannot make a deep commitment toadult education experience.

4.   Learning skills considered effective for pursuing goals which are really of vital interest to adults must take precedence over acquiring skills which are called formative in themselves.

5.   Using every available opportunity for learning from daily life experience (culture) must take precedence over learning which refers to situations that might only potentially or hypothetically arise. We heard a provincial official responsible for culture criticize village women because the majority of them called for dressmaking courses. Perhaps he thought it would be better to give them logarithms and supernovas.

6.   A dynamic and flexible educational construct must supersede once and for all the presentation of a static, closed world order. Otherwise, older men and women will shut themselves away in their inner microcosms or small isolated groups, and will remain non-communicating misfits, closed to new ideas which bring a better quality of life. The role of women in rural areas, their external conditioning, clothing, decoration and equipment of the house, outings and trips, the use of leisure time, kinds and types of recreation are all examples of static phenomena. An educated man is not necessarily educated once and for all.

All these principles are abstract and purely philosophical. There is no alternative but to apply them and to learn about the consequences of applying them. The main elements which modulates the above principles is the actual experience of adults engaged in the learning process.

Parents' Night

On the basis of the principles outlined above, we set up what we called "Adults' Night".

This initiative was designed to create an opportunity to discuss and debate topics selected by participants themselves. An average of 45 people gathered each month to talk about relationships between parents and children, men and women, families and school, and other interesting subjects ranging from nerves to wine.

This initiative began with the initial understanding that adults would choose specific themes on which they would communicate. The usual term for this is "parents' schools". We observed that this name was misunderstood by children (who supposed that their parents would go to school and be taught the same things as they themselves studied at school). To avoid any misunderstanding, we called it "Adults' Night". The average age of those attending was over thirty, and most were married.

The areas covered during these evenings expanded as participants became more personally involved. This does not mean that they corresponded to interesting topical themes or culturally and ideologically elevated subjects. In our opinion, the evenings were at their most intense when the last three topics were discussed:

- "Nerves": not the physiology of the nervous system — although it may appear later that this also is of interest, but "nervous disorders". A surprising number of people, on one side or another, felt compelled to talk about insomnia, anxiety and depression. We also spoke about appropriate medication and its use. Broadly speaking, health and matters relating to the body and vital functions are subjects with a great capacity for cultural motivation.

- "Wine" was another topic of great interest. Because the level of communication achieved in the evening was very high at that time, this topic was treated from many angles. Interesting aspects of wine range from oenological aspects (its origin, its history, production circumstances, the origin of its colour and types, its taste and an explanation of winemaking vocabulary) through dietary considerations (method of consumption, affinity with other foods) to health (positive and negative effects of drinking wine, including psychological effects on behaviour) and finally to the question of dependence and alcoholism. Parents added the question of introducing children and young people to drinking wine. We also included the bar as a business and a social centre. This demonstrated the usefulness of taking topics of communication which relate to people's everyday behaviour. Several families brought quality wines to taste.

- The third typical and highly motivating topic was a presentation of the various social services existing in the locality and a description of the social worker's role. Special emphasis was placed on seniors. In villages, this information is especially important because a number of these services have their intervention centre in another village and provide service to the surrounding area on demand.

Adults' Night plays a very important role in raising awareness about problems which could then be solved by print mass communications media or by books from the municipal library.

Each Adults' Night initiative was prepared according to a set of objectives:

a)   General criterion

All training initiatives aimed at adults, whether or not they have a curriculum, must simultaneously meet two conditions: respond to a concrete need, respecting the contents of interest expressed by the people at a given time; and secondly, take the central core of the information requested or the skills which they seek to pass on as the organizing principles of a cultural project which goes beyond the confines of immediate interests. By this means, identifying and meeting a need will be converted into the pivot and hinge of a movement toward cultural empowerment, and lead to an improvement in the quality of village life. This broadens the base on which to build potential social and vocational reorientations and the enjoyment of cultural goods which seemed inaccessible.

Initially, we should not be concerned because the topics which villagers seem to insist on most are activities and affairs directly relating to their lifestyle or immediately useful matters. People's real motivation must always be taken as the starting point for any activity of broad scope.

b) Complementary criteria

On every occasion, the co-ordinator must pursue three basic cultural objectives, tailoring his treatment to the specific object which gives shape to the demand expressed. Unless these three objectives are met, the basic direction is lost.

1. Situate the affair in a broad social field, within which it has its true historical, social and cultural meaning;

2. improve each participant's vocabulary and ability to express himself or herself, with the conviction that limitations to expression are indicators of social limitations;

3. have a direct or indirect impact on the network of social relations between people in the village. Deficiencies in the structure of social relations cause limitations in the potential for cultural action and hinder initiatives which promote improvement in the quality of life.

These three design channels must convey contents which are as attractive as the actual interests from which the demand for the course stems. Co-ordinators must be able to arouse people's curiosity and sustain their cultural enrichment project, even when the benefits are not direct and they are not utilitarian in character from other standpoints. The economic weakness of villages are exacerbated by distance from cultural pleasures.

Such commitments require co-ordinators to prepare adequate material — which their university preparation enabled them to do — and to intervene directly in courses, complementing the work of monitors. This material may extend its influence to nearby villages, providing for co-operation and contact between co-ordinators, and draw on the skills developed by all co-ordinators during their university training period, improving their teaching ability.

Adult men and women in our villages have a poor opinion of their intellectual abilities and do not use the knowledge they have because of limitations on their ability to express themselves.

The disadvantage of what we have just proposed, knowing that nothing is easy, is that the co-ordinator's school experience does not exactly foreshadow what he must do with adults. A person who has been immersed for a long time in a violent environment learns to be violent and learns ways of being so. A person who has been in school for a long time learns to teach: he learns what to teach and how to teach it, but always in adult education, teaching begins with the experiences of the adults.

All this may not coincide either with the adult's capacity for wonder or with historically possible action. There is no use complaining. We go to the villages to facilitate, not to complain.

If any adult drew up a list of subjects needed to penetrate the reality of their environment in order to transform it, the number of experts required would render it unfeasible to offer a reasonable rural intervention program (domestic electricity, tractor mechanics, farming techniques, dressmaking, health and so forth). What institution trains this type of teachers? What teacher is able to decide on the crop variety best suited to the present state of the market? Hence the difficulty of training an "empowerer" or "cultural facilitator", because we cannot choose between the two essential poles of activity, communicator and co-ordinator, to respond to their obvious need to find solutions, together with training and instructing skills considered necessary for adults in rural areas. Do we need an educator or a vocational trainer?

This difficulty reveals the real problem of what urban areas have and rural areas do not. Cities possess a broad network of institutions and services of all types. There is a network of informal and non-formal institutions and education services: books, newsstands, cinemas, theatres, lectures, school centres, libraries and universities with a standing offer of cultural "menus". In villages, we seek to remedy the poverty of cultural resources through the initiative and activity of a man who is called a "cultural facilitator". I cannot help thinking about the mystique of the project. It seems to indicate that we hope that in one fell swoop, men will be rescued from the rural quagmire and set free and women will be culturally liberated thanks to some attention from a man.

The radical cure for cultural impoverishment in a human space will only be effected by creating human conditions which will bring about the material changes to give all groups equal access to social and cultural resources regardless of geographic location. Moving country people to the cities changes nothing, because they bring their limitations to the suburbs. It is unrealistic to establish urban environments in a village because many cultural resources can travel. The essential point is to create in the village a system of cultural preferences which induces people to seek resources which satisfy them.

Information Centre

A computer system was used to develop a shared data base for all village institutions and associations (town hall, school, physician, priest and social worker) to gain a better knowledge of human and material resources, services provided by each institution, follow-up of these services and evaluation of the intervention. This data base provides one institution's reports and supplies information to prepare written circulars with summaries of interest to readers.

In addition to the shared data base, we developed specific programs for each institution in order to facilitate the work of professionals in the municipality.

We hope that making data from each institution available to all the rest will improve the circulation of information. In democratic countries, management of public activity and progress in participation is measured by the ease of access to all information required for decision-making.

EVALUATION

The objective of evaluation was to collect large volumes of information which would enable us at the end of the two years to assess the relative effectiveness of the actions and initiatives undertaken.

Our first survey in June 1989 covered 100 people in the population. At the end of the project we administered another questionnaire to determine the effectiveness of the measures we had developed. We also conducted a qualitative evaluation with all institutions and social interveners in the municipality. Obviously, what was evaluated was neither the technique used nor the ingenuity of the socio-cultural information officers, but rather the enormous potential of existing social institutions to improve the cultural situation of a community, provided that they change their methods of action, the structure of their services and their handling of situations.

We are aware that the effect produced is largely invisible. It is also true that we were going against the flow, that many people in the village were not directly affected and, by the same token, the effect may be short-lived. But this is typical of educational processes. In each generation we must start afresh, steering between the shoals of overprotection and abandonment. In due course, we shall have some data on the effects produced and some indicators with which to determine which of the things that have happened is definitely being transformed into the heritage of the community.

We developed a questionnaire which sought to investigate four specific areas: (1) implementation of the project; (2) basic cultural attitudes in the population; (3) basic cultural level; and (4) initial attitudes toward initiatives and interventions and their ultimate effects. We established two evaluation points: the progress achieved between the end of 1989 and the end of 1990, the time period in which the intervention was carried out. The same questionnaire was administered two years later; we consider that the minimum period for demonstrating the persistence of an effect is two years. The 100 subjects in the stratified random sample (of whom 88 responded) were selected from those over 16 (first year after leaving school). As for the characteristics of the population, 57.5% consisted of retirees and homemakers.

Regarding the results of the first administration, immediately after the intervention ended, we shall relate only the following:

- Extent of influence of information sheets: 77% of respondents replied that they had read the medical sheets, 67% the material from the town hall information source and 50% those produced by the social worker. This corroborated the findings of the other adult intervention officers that health issues initially held greater potential for impact on the adult population.

- The population expressed that culture improves quality of life (92%) but only 70% believed that the project conferred real benefits. The frequency of rejection of the project in all aspects relating to attitudes contained in the questionnaire fluctuated between 10% to 30%.

According to data from the surveys, 50% of the population "never reads anything", which is the starting point, while 95% admits to watching television regularly. For social information, 75% prefer radio and 77% prefer television over any type of written source.

A positive attitude toward all the social interveners (adult educators) involved in the project was ultimately registered by 100% of the sample. As noted earlier, the level of rejection of the initiatives was very low, and the attitudes aroused by the project must be considered totally favourable. It remains to be determined whether two years later, initiatives are being maintained, level of voluntary reading in addition to reading the information sheets has risen, the level of reading of the print media has risen, and whether requests for books have increased at the municipal library and so forth.

At present, because of the significant increase in the circulation of paper, the town crier has become a "distributor" of written material to the population.

Researchers' main findings are:

a) According to observation in the field, deterioration in reading and writing skills occurs because, in these population centres, the dominant culture, the dominant communications and the dominant information sources continue to be oral.

b) Having an effect on these realities requires transforming the communications mechanisms used by local information sources. This means more written involvement by agents and interveners (writing reports, demanding services, preparing information documents, social action which gives rise to writing and develops it) increasing the need for reading for villagers to be exposed to the news.

c) Increasing written management of productive activities (from control by local government to control of production in family businesses) by expanding access to computer information services increases participation in the social system (strict control over production and the cost/benefit ratio, tax returns, reports on the local macroeconomy, economic justification of business association and so forth). This all leads toward social organization in which the movement to written communication becomes a necessary requirement.

d) In the present social communications, outside school, there is only a minimal need for reading and writing skills in day-to-day life. It follows that this type of program must be classified as impeding general functional illiteracy.

REFLECTIONS

After the contact with the population described in the experiment, we can assert that the basic cultural problem in developed countries is not well described by the terms "illiteracy" or "functional illiteracy". By the same token, intervention measures are not well described by the concept of literacy training or functional literacy training. In any theoretical analysis and any description of experience, the condition of being illiterate is one characteristic of a major problem and reading and writing skills are a tool for addressing it. That major problem is **communication** and **cultural policies**.

UNESCO Director General D. Federico Mayor Zaragoza published an article on 13 December 1992 in the newspaper *La Gaceta de Salamanca* containing this observation:

> This alarming situation is occurring at a time when all countries, whether developed or developing, understand the vital importance of relying on an educated population. By "educated" we mean not only able to read, write and express their wishes but also steeped in the values of tolerance, respect and understanding which are the foundation of peace and co-operation between nations.

Clearly, the concept of an "educated population" refers to a literate population in the fullest sense of the term. There are, however, connotations in its definition which go beyond reading and writing skills, which are propagated by initiatives directly addressing the processes of communication and which require attitudes parallel to or independent of those skills. **The place which the concept of literacy has occupied in the past must now be occupied by the concepts of cultural empowerment, basic education and cultural policy. The real problem is not confined to whether or not a person knows how to read or write, but lies in all the rest.**

Note & Reference

1.   Joaquín Carrasco and Javier Valbuena, "Alphabétisation fonctionnelle: intervention dans l'école et dans la communauté", *Illiteracy in the European Community* (Academisch Boeken Centrum, postbus 1322678 25 De Lier, The Netherlands, 1992).

Chapter 5
NEW CULTURAL DEVELOPMENT OPTIONS

Hilario Hernández Sánchez
Germán Sánchez Ruipérez Foundation
Sociocultural Development Centre,
Peñaranda, Spain

THE PEÑARANDA CULTURAL CENTRE

The Germán Sánchez Ruipérez Foundation Sociocultural Development Centre in Peñaranda de Bracamonte launched its activities some three years ago. Peñaranda is a municipality of 6,500 people located 40 km east of Salamanca; its economy is based on light industry and services to the predominantly agricultural surrounding area. The Centre was therefore designed as an additional, cultural service in a situation common to the entire Castilian plateau, where manifestations of traditional culture have gradually disappeared as a result of the socioeconomic changes of the past few decades. Modern sociocultural facilities are still quite rare in the rural environment and the population's cultural habits and needs remain rudimentary.

The Germán Sánchez Ruipérez Foundation Centre's three years of operation have made it a unique experiment in the rural Spanish setting, not only because it has constituted an unusual and innovative endeavour for a private foundation, but especially because of the high level of acceptance and use its action plans and services have achieved among the population.

This Centre was initially conceived as a public service facility that would operate in conjunction with other institutions in the same environment. A prior sociological study on the cultural habits and demands of Peñaranda de Bracamonte and its vicinity[1] served as the basis for the design of the building and for the action plans intended to meet these needs and to change habits as part of an individual and community cultural development process. The Centre currently focuses on three areas of service: **the library and support for reading; education; cultural dissemination**. These three areas are closely linked in planning and execution but have developed and been consolidated at very different rates.

The *Library* (which is the town's public library) was designed as an active and dynamic environment which could house the various technologies involved in the contemporary transmission of human knowledge; its development has been based on a three-way relationship among the functions assigned to a public library (education, information, recreation), information media (print, audio-visual, computers, etc.) and the sectors of the population which make up the user community. By the spring of 1992, 37% of the Peñaranda population were users, three times the Spanish average for public library use.[2]

The education component was structured around diversified services targeting three priorities: gaps in education, some of which are already chronic in the rural environment (music, languages, information technology, etc.) and which at this time can be considered a form of discrimination against rural populations; informally-structured training sessions and workshops designed to allow the use of free time for creativity and personal enrichment; and finally, training programs to develop occupational qualifications.

The third area, cultural dissemination, involves regular programming of art exhibits designed primarily to popularize culture and develop the community's cultural identity. In the first ones, particular attention was paid to artists from Peñaranda and the surrounding area. Theatre programs are also organized. This is probably the area in which the development of a regular audience and revival of long-lapsed cultural habits are most difficult to achieve. The third area also organizes music programs (jazz to classical), movies (after providing for commercial programming, there is a focus on specific themes or population sectors), and finally, activities related to festivities and events.

STABILITY AND INTEGRATION OF ACTION PLANS

We should point out a number of principles which have been key in the development of the project to date. First, having a high-quality building and facilities suitable for today's world is part of an explicit commitment to considering people in rural areas as first-class citizens, with the immediately observable result of enhanced community self-esteem. Furthermore, services and action plans have been developed based on the criteria of stability and dynamism. In rural Spain, cultural projects and activities too often appear and disappear without a trace, compromising the very credibility of initiatives of this sort in the eyes of a population group that in fact needs, above all, grounds for confidence in the future. If the aim is to positively alter certain forms of social behaviour where cultural habits are concerned, the continuity and stability of any actions undertaken are essential. Not only do rural areas need cultural programs designed to stimulate and galvanize, but these programs must also aim to create cultural infrastructures capable of supporting a number of services without which any population, rural or urban, would have difficulty developing reading habits and the practice of producing and consuming culture.

But stable does not mean static. On the contrary, stability and dynamism are two sides of the same coin, the fruits of project analysis and self-evaluation, the capacity to innovate and adapt to new realities, and a requisite minimal level of professional rigour are complimentary and interdependent qualities.

The Centre's current areas of activity — the library, education and cultural dissemination — are closely linked in planning and execution. These services represent a comprehensive and integrated program. As a result, management of these services is also performed in an integrated fashion. In practical terms, this means that each area not only obeys its own dynamic but also serves the action plans in the other areas. Moreover, while interdisciplinary problems continue to arise, each sphere contributes its specific potentialities to solve such problems on the basis of a common theme and objective. The building's design, with its open spaces, facilitates this approach, so that users can gradually and systematically move from one service to another, from one interest to another.

The project thus consists of a cultural centre in which the library is the cornerstone and the basis of the design. This approach is obviously far from original. The UNESCO Manifesto on public libraries sets out, in theory at least, the relationship that should ideally exist between cultural practices and the library. But such a theory is only rarely applied in practice, in Spain at least. Cultural policies and library policies generally take different paths, as though they had nothing to do with each other. Examples where libraries are transformed into cultural centres or cultural projects are based on libraries, are unfortunately, rare.

Cooperation and joint action with institutions and organizations in our field of action are also among the Centre's basic principles. Indeed, the bulk of the Centre's activities and services are developed to some extent in collaboration with other organizations. This is perhaps easier to achieve in a small rural community than in large urban centres. It also allows for more cost-effective use of resources and a better match between plans and real needs. There are various means of implementing such a policy.

First, agreements have been reached with institutions responsible for cultural matters, such as the Peñaranda municipal council, the Salamanca general council and the regional government. For example, the Centre's library is the municipal public library, whose staff and acquisitions budget are provided partly by the municipal council. Ongoing co-operation with educational institutions and cultural associations to develop and implement action plans has helped ensure that plans are effectively tailored to the needs of the people. Some of our actions have the secondary aim of enriching the community's associative fabric by consolidating associations and interest groups. This was the case, for example, with the Peñaranda photography society and the folklore association, which sprang from training sessions and workshops on these subjects.

THE CULTURAL DEVELOPMENT COMMISSION: A COOPERATIVE STRUCTURE

The most obvious and meaningful expression of the policy of cooperation and joint action is the Cultural Development Commission, created by the Peñaranda municipal council a year prior to the Centre's opening. This project is therefore not an initiative of the Foundation alone but one to which a number of community institutions have contributed. Within the Commission, the municipal council, the regional continuing education centre and the Foundation work alongside social representatives and citizens in planning and evaluating training activities. All organizations and institutions that can offer suggestions and viewpoints (educational institutions, parent and student groups, cultural associations, unions, etc.) take an active part in developing education programs in Peñaranda and subsequently evaluating them. The actual implementation of these programs is then overseen by the municipal council's department of culture, the continuing education centre or the Foundation Centre, depending on their nature and possibilities. In addition to optimizing the use of available resources, the existence of a body of this type has advantages in terms of enhancing the process of reflection by fostering diversity of ideas, so that the services offered can best be adapted to the needs of the various sectors of the population.

Two other comments should be made with respect to the Cultural Development Commission. First, there has been some dispute over its operations because of a certain lack of operational capacity and the low level of co-operation it receives from the community. The fact that the Commission's status is poorly defined is at the root of these criticisms. The Commission is split between its role as a co-ordinating organ, hence as an executive body, and as an advisory body, which involves other sectors of the community in studying and assessing action plans and projects and then takes part in decision-making. A solution to this contradiction remains to be found, especially (and this is a second topic for reflection) if one wants either to expand the Commission's field of activities or to establish similar bodies in other areas (the library, cultural dissemination, festivals, etc.). The experience to date has clearly been a positive one; it may therefore be considered a means of integrating institutions and people, a means of promoting participation and enriching social and cultural activity in the community. Consequently, it does not seem logical to restrict this approach to educational programs alone.

PROFESSIONALIZATION OF CULTURAL MANAGEMENT

Finally, among the action criteria structuring the orientation of Peñaranda's

Sociocultural Development Centre, we must mention the pursuit of professionalism for the Centre staff working as managers of a number of cultural services for a particular environment. One can say that cultural services developed over the past decade in Spain have generally lacked qualified professionals (except in a few specific sectors). In addition to the variety of requirements and the different management systems in use, there is very often a diversity of strategies and methodologies and, even more seriously, an uncertainty with respect to the professional status of "cultural managers". This situation has resulted in the predominant use of volunteers and self-taught employees, and a general lack of training and information systems to enable cultural workers to optimize their efforts and available resources. Fortunately, the situation is beginning to improve. With the experience which has been obtained and the introduction of new management and planning systems, efforts to secure rigour and professionalism are now starting to bear fruit.

In this regard, the Peñaranda Centre has benefited from its relationship with a group of private firms, which has introduced new managerial and administrative techniques, different from earlier approaches better suited to public administrations or relatively unstructured volunteer associations. But these facts cannot be assessed in terms of results and efficiency alone. In speaking of the world of cultural communication, where the border between cultural industries and the public sector is often ill-defined, a logical and desirable attitude is needed.

THE PUBLIC LIBRARY: A NEW CHALLENGE

Analysis of the Peñaranda experiment prompts a number of comments, which could be formulated on a general level. But in the context of this research study, two aspects should be emphasized: the role that public libraries can and should play in rural communities today, and the need to overcome the isolation and lack of communication generally associated with experiments of this type wherever they are conducted.

For centuries, human culture and knowledge were transmitted primarily through the written word, while rural communities preserved a strong oral tradition. Today, the situation has changed radically. With the spread of new information technologies, it is now possible to have access not only to books and newspapers but also to cassettes, compact disks and a variety of telematic services which are interrelated. Their information content tends to be complementary, bringing to bear different approaches or viewpoints on the same issue or focusing on their own specific fields. But the fact remains that they are far from common or usual in the rural environment.

In general, new communication technologies continue to exhibit a slower, less extensive and more fragmentary penetration in rural areas. This observation is equally valid for radio and television broadcasting and the print media.

Consequently, the public library, the only community cultural facility in many rural localities, must take up the challenge of providing its users with the latest information media. Today, the value of a public library can no longer be gauged solely in terms of its capacity to store and disseminate human knowledge, but primarily in terms of its skill in appropriating and transmitting this knowledge, wherever it may be found, regardless of its particular medium. This involves more than merely expansion of the range of information produced by society.

The essential issue is not one of quantity. It is important that a person entering a library can choose from a multitude of possibilities appropriate to his or her knowledge, education and cultural tastes. This is important because of the change which can be effected in the relationship between the individual and the various information media and technologies. People can learn how to master the various information technologies and use them rationally, critically and freely. This is indeed the challenge for libraries in rural areas: to enable the communities they serve to know and use the many communication techniques available in the contemporary world; to become perhaps the only possible environment, where men and women, children and adults can find the various information media and technologies, assembled and harmonized on the basis of their complementarity, which can foster individual and collective growth. It may thus be possible to combat what might be termed a new form of illiteracy, seen in sectors of the population which are deprived of access to communication technologies (starting with books), and are limited to technologies such as audio-visual technologies that are essentially oriented toward passive recreation and entertainment.

The challenges of literacy in rural Western European environments clearly involves far more than written language skills as traditionally defined. In other words, literacy in Europe should be defined in terms of two kinds of media: the traditional media of the text and the image (book, audiovisual) on the one hand, and informatics and telematics, on the other. Failing this, we may soon see a new "class distinction" between an elite with unlimited access to the new information media and a very large sector of the population condemned to another kind of illiteracy. The media accessible to the population as a whole are those which, are primarily directed toward recreation and entertainment, where the audiovisual component predominates. Needless to say, this new type of illiteracy affects especially the rural environment where the penetration of new information technologies is significantly fragmentary and slow by comparison with urban areas.[3]

On another point, it is clear that cultural development projects in the rural European environment are quite varied and indeed radically different in nature. It is increasingly urgent that the lack of stable information and exchange networks, the absence of research projects to help identify the most appropriate solutions, and the lack of educational structures to develop and update the professional skills of project staff be remedied at the level of daily practices. Information, research and professionalization: these three elements are the key to progress in a society based on change, whose rural regions cannot be reduced to mere monuments to the past.

FROM THE EXCEPTION TO THE RULE

This examination of the Peñaranda Sociocultural Development Centre's principles naturally raises the following question: is this an exceptional project which cannot be generalized to other places and other players? Do the positive results of this project in fact derive from a combination of circumstances that would be hard to reproduce? Do they demand an exceptional allocation of resources? Or do they, on the contrary, have practical application as a model and reference for the development of cultural services in rural Spain?

Each community has specific needs which must be met with equally specific solutions. But although, on the whole, the Peñaranda Centre can in no way claim to represent a model to be imitated, it nonetheless has a moral obligation: to publicize its experience, to complete its action plans, and to serve as a reference point with regard to infrastructures and facilities, services, management systems and cooperative approaches. Those aspects of the Peñaranda experience that can best be generalized have for the most part already been cited. The most obvious generalizations are perhaps also the most universal, in that they may prove to be valid in both urban and rural areas. This is the case for the role the public library can and should play at present: the integrated approach to action plans and services, particularly integration of the library with other services, and the cooperative policy.

Within this working perspective, the Centre will nevertheless have to strive harder in the years ahead to remedy problems hampering the dissemination of its experiences. First of all, it will have to implement assessment and planning systems for cultural services in order to rigorously evaluate the work it has accomplished and anticipate future needs. It is essential that a number of cultural information and reference services as well as cultural management training programs be set up in the rural environment, to facilitate the dissemination and communication of experiences and to allow the Centre to offer services extending beyond its immediate territorial area. Finally, new methods of cultural cooperation will have to be implemented and strengthened, especially those with a potential to bring together the initiatives of both public and private institutions. Ultimately, one of the most interesting elements in the Peñaranda experience lies in the participation of a private foundation in an area which, in Spain, seemed to be reserved for the public sector, and also in the explicit desire to work cooperatively.

Notes & References

1.   The results of this research study were published in 1984 under the title [Translation] *Basis for*

the creation of a cultural centre in Peñaranda de Bracamonte. Éditions Tecnos.

2.   In Spain, 11% of people aged 6 and older use libraries. The figure is lower in communities of under 50,000 people. [Translation] *Survey of cultural behaviour in Spain*. Ministry of Culture, Madrid, 1986.

3.   Recently published data on cultural equipment in Spanish homes are quite significant: the levels are highest in localities of more than 20,000 people and decline with declining community size. Levels in localities of less than 20,000 people are in every case below the national average. Cf. [Translation] *Spaniards' [cultural] equipment, habits and consumption*. Ministry of Culture, 1991.

Chapter 6
FROM LITERACY ACTIVITIES TO ENTREPRENEURSHIP IN SIETE PILAS

Antonio Chacón, Ángel Polo
Adult Education Centre
Siete Pilas, Spain

THE SIERRA DE RONDA REGION

The area in which this adult education project was conducted lies within the Sierra de Ronda region and has a population of approximately 8,000. It occupies a narrow strip between the Genal and Guadiaro valleys, sprinkled with small villages of 500 to 1,000 inhabitants and small scattered houses. Access to the area is difficult due to the mountainous terrain and the lack of adequate roads. The economy is based primarily on small family farms and providing unskilled labour to the Costa del Sol.

Over the past seven years, rural Spain (and especially Andalusia) has undergone radical changes as a result of EEC (European Economic Council) social and economic policies. The community development project which has been in operation in the area since 1980 has therefore been subject to constant change, to which we have tried to adapt our project by modifying it as required.

PHASE 1: TO STIMULATE THROUGH LITERACY & CULTURAL DEVELOPMENT

The Siete Pilas rural community development project grew out of the Sierra Education Program sponsored by the Malaga General Council. In 1980, a group of young teachers were sent to five villages in the Sierra de Ronda region — Algatocin, Benalauria, Atajate, Salitre, Siete Pilas — to provide adult education. The basic idea was to try to stimulate a socially and economically very depressed area through literacy and cultural development. The centres set up in the first four villages disappeared one after the other, but the Siete Pilas centre has grown steadily stronger, becoming a driving force for the development of an area of the Genal valley over the years.

The project coordinators (the authors) decided at the outset that they would have to live with the local people to understand their way of life and way of thinking. The goal was to create a school which would influence the behaviour of youths and adults and help them realize their full potential. The two teachers therefore rented a house in the Siete Pilas area (without electricity or running water, like all the other houses in the commune) and set about making direct contact with kids who had failed in the formal education system and whose relations with their parents were difficult. These first meetings revealed the following facts:

- people in the area learn by imitation (due in large part to their location in a small rural community);

- people had almost no capacity for abstraction (it was found only in a few set phrases and expressions);

- their written and oral expression was very under-developed (and compensated for by strong and complex emotionality);

- they viewed the unknown and anything new with complete distrust (they simply passed on unchanged the values inherited from their forefathers, never venturing outside the framework of preestablished ideas);

- their thinking was wholly practical.

The only way to persuade young people to attend the school at first was to make them realize that they might be able to earn a school certificate, which was of practical value. During this initial period, the teachers gradually fell in with the pace of local life, and they did so in the best possible way, through work. They worked the land without pay, helping the people plough, sow, reap, etc. Thus, when information meetings on the planned school were announced, parents attended with little resistance because their fear of the unknown (the teachers in this case) had gradually faded.

After the Siete Pilas Adult Education Centre began operating, the contacts made during these first meetings (which were held first in individual homes and then in the school with everyone invited) were put to use to launch an educational process aimed at meeting the needs of the local population:

- for young people seeking a school certificate, creating a participation-based school oriented towards use of intelligence rather than rote learning; a school aimed at rounded education and at ending the individualism typical of isolated regions;

- for adults, holding meetings on a continuous basis to discuss their problems and help them find solutions (e.g. lack of water and electricity, poor roads, random distribution of work days by the rural employment plan, etc.).

A hog barn measuring 6 m by 3 m was renovated for the preparatory classes for the school certificate. Youths aged 15 to 20 received 10 hours of instruction a day based primarily on the ideas of Lorenzo Milani's Barbiana school and Francisco Gutiérrez's "productive pedagogy". The method was founded on four elements:

- developing command of language (expression and comprehension) through detailed and analytic readings of texts of interest and anthologies; based on the individual ideas contributed by each student, a detailed and accurate synthesis is produced;

- promoting a comprehensive understanding of history capable of grasping the mechanisms governing social change, focusing in particular on the present day through analysis of texts and documents and through critical readings of the newspapers;

- developing logical and mathematical thinking by solving problems with practical applications;

- studying specific problems of the area to identify a specific issue, which is then given a wider application to other fields through objective and critical readings, with a view to drawing conclusions.

In the first two years, students reacted positively to this type of non-traditional education without tests, which was jointly and progressively developed by students and teacher. However, the school gradually came to appear inadequate:

- the school shifted from participatory education gradually towards "instrumental education" due to a lack of specific and valid reference points for the youths (such as a work activity);

- solidarity was conveyed through teaching — i.e. on the basis of theory — without creating concrete situations in which the spirit of solidarity could be applied.

On the adult education side, the meetings got over 30 people (out of a population of 250) involved in discussing problems affecting the Siete Pilas commune. They served to establish priorities (installing electricity, improving roads, information on the distribution of work days, etc.) and gave participants an opportunity to express their opinions. The fact that the teachers had worked side-by-side with the participants in the fields and were running a school to help their children obtain their school certificates directly contributed to the success of the meetings. But the meetings and the school for youths failed to mobilize participants. Once a week for over a year, rural problems were discussed and potential solutions were put forward. But when it came to using pressure tactics to fight for rights, people seemed to back off.

PHASE 2: ADDING VOCATIONAL TRAINING

In Phase 2, an effort was made to add vocational training to general education, to make the school an instrument of integration. The mornings were now devoted to Phase 1 and the afternoons to Phase 2. This was an attempt to take two factors into account: the need to expand the educational experience through a vocational activity in order to broaden the youths' horizons in this respect and parents' expectations for more practical schooling, given that the youths were spending the whole day in class and had deserted the fields.

Parents were ready to make do without their children's labour as long as the school could offer alternative work. (It must not be forgotten that the youths had previously spent 10 hours a day working with their parents and were now spending 10 hours in school).

Given the total lack of means and unfamiliarity with the world of work, the school turned, as it had to in a rural area, to the only local agent who could exert any influence on vocational training at this level, the district agricultural engineer. Two inhabitants of the commune made tracts of land available and the group of youths, together with the teachers and the agricultural engineer, planted a row of saffron and a row of anise. (It seemed clear that an agricultural activity had to be chosen, given that the youths' work experience was limited to working in the fields. However, we felt that for this very reason the experiment was doomed to failure, for neither the parents nor the youths were prepared to give it their full support, the parents because they had not accepted their children leaving the family farm to work in other fields, and the youths because they wanted to do work unrelated to agriculture or livestock.)

As was to be expected, the experiment was a resounding failure as a work project, but it did enable the school to redirect its educational approach. The school's dynamic changed radically, because general education was now based on the work activities, allowing the youths to apply their knowledge outside school for the first time (they had to solve practical problems related to their work, thus promoting the development of logical/mathematical thinking). Solidarity education entered a second phase, for the requirement to divide the small production profit made solidarity among the youths a practical issue, not a theoretical matter. And finally, the educational process was based for the first time on social factors. During this period, the teachers tried to reverse the typical rural attitude to work, to replace "we want to do something, let's turn to the paternalism of the state" by "we are doing something, let's apply for grants to support our effort".

In the meetings with adults, the teachers tried to make progress and arrive at practical decisions to resolve the electricity issue. It was decided to form a committee to pressure the Town Council. However, not one of the members turned up on the appointed day. Clearly, there was a gap between the theory of the meetings (where everyone participated) and the practical implementation of decisions (where no one was willing to accept responsibility).

The most negative aspect of this situation was that, in the end, it became irreversible. From this point on, the meetings started to become less frequent and attendance declined. After two years of meetings, the teachers conducting the project decided it was time to take practical action on the electricity front. This clear failure points to three conclusions:

1. lack of information and distrust are so deeply rooted among these people (due to their very hard lives) that it will take years to obtain positive results;

2. fear of the unknown leads them to value their small properties immensely, and they will not risklosing them for anything;

3. the teachers did not adopt the right approach.

PHASE 3: LINKING EDUCATION & WORK

By 1985, it seemed that the school had succeeded in inculcating some sense of solidarity and enterprise in the youths. It now seemed possible to link education more and more closely to work. At this stage the school was split into two groups to meet the youths' needs. One group came in the morning for a session focused on practical education. The afternoon was set aside for meetings of a group of students working on launching a cooperative.

The choice of work activity was based on the following factors:

a) Characteristics: easy to learn, small investment required, use of local resources.

b) Group composition: five youths who had obtained a school certificate at the Centre were made directly responsible for starting up the project and working on it; indirectly, all of the eight students attending the school worked on production twice a week on a volunteer basis.

c) Organization: the activity was organized around the two teachers. One essentially assumed responsibility for educating the youths and the other for coordinating all work-related activities intended to complement the education.

Beekeeping was chosen as the co-op's activity not only because it meets the above criteria but also and especially because it is an old local tradition in the Sierra de Ronda.

As money was needed to set up the co-op, the two teachers guaranteed a 1.5 million peseta loan to acquire equipment. The decision to provide the guarantee had a very positive effect on the youths (both the school population and the members of the future co-op); the teachers' willingness to assume responsibility generated enthusiasm about the school's new role. With the possibility of an integrated education meeting, the following description began to emerge:

•   **Instrumental**: the creation of the cooperative prompted the members of the newly-created association to consolidate and enlarge their linguistic knowledge (in the afternoon, they read and analyzed the Andalusian Cooperatives Act under the guidance of a teacher in order to understand it and be able to draft the cooperative's statutes and by-laws).

- **Based on Solidarity**: the youths attending the school only in the morning helped the association members in the afternoon on a volunteer basis in order to cut production costs and facilitate market access for the work team. The association members worked on the project knowing they would not receive any income in the short term.

- **Empowering**: At the future co-op's afternoon meetings with one of the teachers, it was clear that the people involved in the project were relying only on their own labour and resources.

The time had come to raise funds. This responsibility fell to the teacher who was serving as coordinator of work-related activities. All aid received by the group from that time forth was considered a complement — a necessary complement, to be sure, but a complement nevertheless. The money was not being raised in order to start up a work project with a group of youths, in which case it would have been state paternalism and the aid received would not have been appreciated; grants were rather being sought to consolidate a project which the youths had themselves launched with the teachers.

A Cordoba foundation funded the acquisition of 100 complete beehives, and a continuing education association in Madrid provided a general purpose machine with which the youths could start to manufacture their first hives for sale. At this time, one of the teachers set about organizing six-month work-study programs in carpentry for the students. This project was approved and the students travelled to Ronda daily to improve their skills. To make up for their absence, the remaining students at the school increased their participation in the project and began working every afternoon on a volunteer basis. This dynamic meant a radical change in the educational process, which shifted towards teaching the principles of cooperative management. From this point on, the work project guided the activities of the school.

Meanwhile, the meetings and work with adults ended in 1986. There were two reasons for this relative failure. As the teachers were increasingly involved in their work with the youths, they found it very difficult to attend meetings regularly; and it is possible that the orientation of the meetings did not meet the participants' expectations.

The situation deteriorated at the end of the year, when the members of the work project and the teachers barricaded themselves inside the Town Hall to draw the attention of municipal officials to the need for premises for their activities. Most of the inhabitants of the village were against this initiative by the students and the participants in the meetings refused to support them. This lack of commitment on the part of the adults led the teachers to focus all their efforts on the school's new education/production dynamic, in the hope that they would eventually have an effect on they older members of the community through the youths.

PHASE 4: COMBINING PRODUCTION & EDUCATION

From the outset, this phase had to confront a specific problematic which continues to define the situation to this day — how to combine production and education.

On the one hand, the occupational qualifications of the youths had to be enhanced and the new carpentry workshop for making the beehives had to be better equipped; on the other hand, the youths had to be given a minimum salary to encourage them to continue, for they were beginning to grow discouraged after two years of work. The solution was not easy to find; if we decided to boost production, it could only be at the expense of the group's vocational education, which in the long term would weaken its competitiveness and sap its cooperative spirit; if we decided to emphasize the work-study programs, the number of hours allocated to production would have to be reduced and with it the chances of obtaining a decent salary. This problem was aggravated by a crash in the prices of apiculture-related products due to a disease which struck over 50% of honey bees. The market collapsed and the work team had to consider a hasty conversion. The youths knew how to use carpentry equipment, having manufactured beehives, and they had a small but adequate infrastructure with which they could try to gradually penetrate the professional woodworking market.

The time had therefore come to consider a project to help finance the new work activity, taking into consideration three priority needs:

- developing specialized vocational skills for the youths, by means of an 800-hour work-study program in carpentry/cabinet-making;
- organizing a work-study program in bricklaying to met the need for new buildings;
- adapting the school program to this new activity.

Aid was received in 1987; a European Social Fund-financed work-study program provided enough support to allow gradual consolidation of the work project. The core carpentry workshop team (which already had eight members) combined training in the trade (mornings) with production (afternoons); meanwhile, financing was obtained for materials over a period of nearly seven months, thus providing the first regular revenues, as costs were subsidized. The group met weekly with a teacher in order to complement its education by performing mathematical calculations to set selling prices, and by studying the operation of cooperatives, the last step in order to prepare the group's constitution.

A bricklaying work team was formed at the same time, also as a European Social Fund-financed work-study program. Preliminary meetings were held among all the participants in the project and the new group, and a joint decision was made to build a shed to house the future cooperative. During this time, the group of youths attending the school continued the program established at the end of Phase 2: instrumental education in the morning tailored to the work to be done, and volunteer work in the afternoon, either in the carpentry workshop or the bricklaying workshop.

PHASE 5: INCREASING SALES

The progressive increase in sales and the need to handle any subsidies which might be received in an appropriate manner raised two important questions: legally registering the cooperative (initially under the trusteeship of one of the teachers) in order to secure legal status for the work activity; and creating an association with representation from all the groups involved in the experiment for the purpose of operating the projects and managing subsidies.

The time had come to find resources to consolidate the work team's participation in the work force. The Siete Pilas Adult Education Centre began working to forge relationships with local social actors. Together, the participants in the experiment, led by the teachers, analyzed the upheaval under way in rural Spain and the myriad of subsidies and programs developed by the EEC and the Spanish government to help rural citizens adapt. Each group involved in the project met once a week with one of the teachers to examine these issues in detail.

The APISUR work cooperative was legally founded with five members in late 1987. The group split in two at this time: the members of the co-op now spent all their time on structural carpentry while the others — a group of eight youths plus the students attending the school — continued the work-study program. They had a Trades Centre (during the 1988-89 period, courtesy of Cáritas Española) where they could learn a another skill of a different type than the co-op, so as not to saturate the structural carpentry market. This new group devoted itself primarily to manufacturing rustic furniture. One of the teachers taught a course on drafting specifications and estimates and cooperative management two afternoons per week. The Trades Centre made it possible to create a bricklaying module, which continued to work on the facilities needed for the Adult Education Centre's work-study activities. After the Trades Centre, two sheds measuring 350 m² were built to house the two carpentry work teams.

It became clear that the project had shifted from a school offering instrumental education to a centre providing mainly work-study programs and instruction in cooperative management. At the same time as the Trades Centre was being set up, and following a number of meetings with all the participants in the experiment, the decision was made to set up a non-profit organization, the Guadiro Socioeconomic Initiatives Centre (CISE). This organization was created in order to settle the problem of the ownership of the immovable property built at the initiative of the Adult Education Centre. The purpose of the Association is to manage projects as they are set up and to advise the youths in all matters, especially the creation of viable work projects.

During the 1988-89 period, a group of nine youths continued to attend the school in the morning; in the afternoon, the entire group went to the furniture workshop. Equipment had to be acquired for this new group. One of the teachers and the district agricultural engineer landed a 2,500,000 peseta order for beehives. The work team built the bodies and the students from the school assembled the frames in the afternoon. With funding from the Trades Centre for the materials and volunteer labour by the students in the school, a large profit was realized which was allocated to the purchase of basic furniture manufacturing equipment.

The APISUR co-op also consolidated its position during this period, due essentially to the addition of two 30-year-old carpenters to the group, who gave the co-op a professionalism which had previously been lacking. It was at this point that one of the most important steps in the entire experiment was decided upon: each self-sufficient work team was required to contribute 5% of its sales to a solidarity fund for youths in the region (solidarity through production). APISUR made its first contribution in January 1990 and the furniture manufacturing work team did so in 1991.

PHASE 6: FROM HERE TO THE FUTURE

This phase extends into the present. The current objectives are to:

- consolidate the work teams and hence the youths' participation in the work force;
- develop solidarity in the work environment;
- adapt theoretical instruction to the work situation (the school as it had been conceived disappeared);
- set up new mechanisms to create a number of CISE;
- strengthen links with local social agents.

The following two examples bear witness to these orientations:

1. In late 1989, a project to manufacture Moresque tiles and clay tiles was set up. This project was no longer launched from the same starting point as the first project but instead was built on specific components based on the Centre's past experience. This included the 5% contribution to the solidarity fund; support from the CISE for accounting, taxes, work and the market, rather than from one of the teachers acting as liaison agent; and financing from the European Social Fund for the tile kiln, managed through the CISE.

2. During this phase, the Centre set about contacting local social agents through CISE. In 1990, the "Valle del Guadiaro" workshop/school project was conceived. It involved seven villages in the region and was sponsored in conjunction with the seven town councils. In 1991, the LEADER project (a community initiative co-ordinated by CISE) was launched in the Sierra de Ronda region.

This overture to the outside world brought the project into contact with local socioeconomic realities and EEC economic directives. In accordance with local needs and EEC orientations, all economic activity generated by the project was clearly oriented towards manufacturing a number of high-quality, closely interrelated handicraft products, so that a purchaser of one of our products is a potential customer for all the others. This approach facilitates sales by concentrating efforts on a single market rather than three different ones, thereby realizing savings on marketing and advertising. For example, a person who is having a country-house built can be offered hardwood structural carpentry hand-finished in virgin wax, as well as unique old pine rustic furniture decorated with encrustations or hand-carved designs and hand-made clay tiles with original designs.

The training is adapted to the work activities and is based on two ideas:

1.   ongoing practical education:

- one hour per day of instrumental education (design specifications and calculation of estimates);
- attending exhibitions either as exhibitors or as visitors;
- weekly meetings for each group with the teachers to monitor activities, examine new initiatives, provide information on EEC socioeconomic directives for rural regions;
- follow-up on work-study programs organized by the Andalusian Federation of Cooperatives (currently, a basic program in business management);
- joint initiatives to create projects that qualify for subsidies;

2.   ongoing education in solidarity:

- production co-ops contribute 5% of sales to support other work projects for young people;
- members of marginal social groups are included on work teams (e.g. a mentally handicapped person in the Tiles work team, an ex-addict in the Structural Carpentry co-op);
- a housing co-op has been created which is now building nine homes for the members of the three work teams;
- establishment of an information centre on alternative community service. Of approximately 30 youths who have taken part in the experiment, eight declared themselves to be conscientious objectors, which is consistent with the philosophy of Milani schools, which aim to develop critical thinking and a participatory spirit capable of involving all people at all levels in strengthening the local social fabric.

REFLECTIONS

The community-based experiment conducted in Siete Pilas by the Adult Education Centre initially aimed to promote cultural development by providing literacy education and also by stimulating the social fabric through the development of an educational process embracing as many aspects as possible and based in all cases on instrumental education. Twelve years later, the goal remains the same — to stimulate the social fabric — but the methods and bases have changed, and elements which were not considered essential at the outset have been added.

The educational process, which initially focused on cultural development, is now focused on work. Today, the type of theoretical training given is determined by the practical training, and the objectives have been reversed. Initially, all the activities considered were subordinated to instrumental education required to obtain a school certificate. Today, the school's orientation is based on the work activities, and youths must adapt to the work, which is chosen on the basis of its viability and EEC socioeconomic directives for rural regions.

The original school set up has disappeared because it was unable to adapt to a rapidly changing rural environment. Imparting knowledge for a school certificate has been relegated to a secondary position. Instead, youths are learning a set of practical skills directly related to the work they will do, while participating in solidarity education. Social commitment has changed from a theoretical goal to a practical reality.

The work with adults (aged 40 and over) has gradually been abandoned. The negative results of that experiment and the emphasis in the school on work made continuity in the meetings with adults impossible. Communication with the adults did improve to some extent, but only because of the successes with the work teams for youths. It may be up to the youths to continue, as far as they are able, the work the teachers had begun in the meetings with parents.

The project's shortcomings are that the teaching methodology and evaluation methods used in this "training through work" lack systematization, and basic education has been neglected. Today, the project initiators can be seen as promoters of work teams for youths, advisors on cooperatives, developers of projects at the regional level, teachers responsible for work-study programs in cooperative management, seekers of subsidies, specialists in socioeconomic realities, etc. However, their essential role is unchanged.

Note & Reference

1.   Corzo, José Luis and Julio Lancho, "Adult Education: Literacy for the Masses" in Jean-Paul Hautecoeur, ed., *ALPHA 92* (Hamburg: Unesco Institute for Education, 1992).

Chapter 7
LITERACY EDUCATION
& CULTURAL DEVELOPMENT
IN REGUENGOS DE MONZARAZ

Maria Da Graça Abreu
Joaquina Maria Margalha
Sothern Regional School Directorate
Évora, Portugal

HISTORY OF THE INTERIOR REGIONS OF PORTUGAL

In the rural regions of the Portuguese interior, weak industrial growth, low population density, the dominance of the primary sector and migrations have all contributed to a rise in the illiteracy rate. If we examine the history of education in this country, we observe that despite the 1835 law on compulsory education, the level of schooling has remained quite low, a situation caused in some measure by the concentration of educational facilities in urban centres, at the expense of rural areas.

Here where an essentially oral tradition and a subsistence economy using antiquated methods have always predominated, reading and writing are not fundamental needs. Children, even those of school age, are indispensable to production, due to the population's low standard of living.

After 1974, firmer political will combined with more grassroots involvement raised the level of motivation and provided the population with opportunities for improvement through literacy campaigns. But these campaigns had the limited aim of "stamping out" illiteracy, and actions were removed from cultural, social and economic context. Studies have confirmed that although people suffer from a certain lack of stimulation due to slim prospects for life changes, they do want, rather than learning to read and write or earning a diploma, to realize deeper aspirations, improve their occupational situation, better their station in life, or find employment.

It was therefore necessary to restructure the adult education programs to include more than reading and writing. To meet the population's expressed needs, attempts were made to expand the programs' scope to tap community resources and develop a **comprehensive local development program** based on empowering people through community development achieved on a basis of respect for local culture. From such principles was born the Reguengos de Monsaraz adult education project.

DEVELOPING A LITERACY STRATEGY

If adult education activities had to be restructured to meet explicit and implicit needs of the population, then the project would have to meet people's expectations for improved living conditions. These integrated activities were designed to contribute to local development, encourage attitudinal change and foster more active and aware participation in community life. Improving educational levels and occupational situations would also promote personal development and awareness of the individual's present situation and societal relationship.

At the beginning, the project was entrusted to a limited group, including the commune coordinator and a Level 1 elementary school teacher. Their tasks consisted of taking stock of the situation and defining action strategies, and making the contacts needed to set up the program. Four Level 2 elementary school teachers and five volunteers, received grants. The team organized direct activities during the courses and established ties with the community, and the group's composition changed from year to year, according to the project's needs and priorities.

In the second year, three teachers were added to the team, owing to the increasing initiatives. The original team had been composed of commune residents, who had a certain knowledge of the environment in which they were going to work, but they had to broaden this knowledge in order to effectively implement a three-phase project comprising: 1) study of the community and survey of needs and resources, 2) defining action strategies, 3) evaluation.

STUDY OF COMMUNITY

Economic Activities

Reguengos de Monsaraz is a commune of 11,000 inhabitants, located in a rural region of the Portuguese interior where Latifundios (large estates) dominate land distribution in the commune. The population consequently suffers from a lack of economic self-sufficiency, reflected in its social organization. Private initiative is therefore rare.

Here there are a few small industrial concerns, mainly tied to agriculture and a lack of initiative on the part of potential entrepreneurs, despite strong demand for the region's products. The labour force is unskilled, and experience is passed down from father to son. Family businesses prevail, with the exception of the Reguengos de Monsaraz farm cooperative, a wine growers' association whose members receive training directly related to their activities (courses in vine and olive tree pruning, grafting, etc.). The agricultural sector, important as it is, uses unskilled labour and offers only seasonal work, resulting in high unemployment during part of the year, especially among women and young people. Animal husbandry and grape and olive-growing are the main activities. Produce is sold through the agricultural cooperative.

Service industries constitute the most specialized sector. The commune seat has a network of services which enable residents to achieve a higher level of development at the expense of neighbouring localities, thereby leading to migration from these villages.

Tourism is starting to interest many people. Thanks to the region's rich historic heritage and tourist lodgings vocation, there is real potential in this sector, bolstered by the renovation of country houses. The growth of the tourist industry could create, in the short or medium term, jobs that would require the training of a specialized labour force.

Sociocultural Context

The region has health and educational facilities, libraries, small and medium-sized businesses, local governments and associations. But schools offering elementary levels 2 and 3 (Grades 5 to 9) are found only in the commune, contributing to a high drop-out rate among students who must leave home very early in the morning and return extremely late due to the poor transportation system. Cultural, social and humanitarian organizations confine themselves to organizing some recreational activities. These could prove useful in organizing real cultural events. But a general lack of public interest, economic difficulties, changing interests and recreational activities (discotheques, pubs, urban centres and models, television), low level of education in the community, etc. severely limits any local associations.

The dominance of the primary sector and stagnation of industrial growth, which is related to low population density and the isolation of rural regions, have resulted in low motivation for pursuing an education, since schooling offers no assurance of improved living conditions. The result has been a high illiteracy rate — approximately 30% in 1980 — and a low level of education. The local population therefore lacked the habit of reading and writing and their culture essentially belonged to the oral tradition. Rural work, which had once been family-based, was now done by groups of workers — ranchos — working in a spirit of fraternity. Working hard in a harsh climate, the ranchos lightened their labours with songs and legends (modas), which recounted everyday occurrences or historical events. With the advent of mechanized farm labour, these traditions gradually declined. Today, they exist only in the memory of the oldest citizens.

ASSESSMENT OF NEEDS

The study of the community identified many deficiencies such as an absence of skilled labour in the agricultural, industrial service sectors (the latter being significant, considering the potential for tourism in the region); low level of schooling and still a very large number of people without schooling; reading habits are rare, as are educational aspirations; associations and other local resources are underutilized; local bodies are not sufficiently committed to education; incentives to stay in the region are insufficient. Recreation should be used creatively to develop communication skills and build knowledge; and the region's rich cultural heritage is not being exploited.

The same situation may be observed in many neighbouring communes reflecting social realities in a peripheral, depressed region of the interior which is losing its population — a region where the population suffers from numerous problems: backwardness, lack of a socioeconomic dynamic, passivity and a reluctance to take risks, aging. The project's challenge — and it was a big one — was to confront all of these deficiencies experienced by the population.

COMMUNITY ACTION STRATEGIES

Based on the survey of needs in the region, we were able to diagnose the situation and define the types of actions and their objectives. These included: raising the adult population's level of education and skills; stimulating an interest in reading; improving social life by reviving traditions and enhancing leisure activities; and interesting and involving various organizations in adult education, seen as indispensable for community development.

Raising Adult Population's Educational Level & Skills

Motivation had to be related to people's life experience and acquired knowledge, respect their cultural traditions and aim always to develop the whole person by promoting active participation in the social, economic and cultural development of the community.

Our first priority was to revamp the Level 1 literacy course. This course had been taught in a rather routine manner with undue reliance on "school-like" adult education methods which make little reference to participants' daily lives, attracted few students and had a high drop-out rate. All efforts therefore had to be concentrated on fostering a change in attitude to respect the culture, acquired knowledge and life experience of the students, enabling them to identify with the organized activities.

Finding innovative ways to arouse curiosity we met with the Dorval Cultural Centre and together planned the activities to be offered. Since theatre is a dying tradition but is generally well-received, we decided to take the Dorval Centre's black light puppet theatre right into the classroom, enlisting a community educator who was also a member of the theatre group. To "bring our characters to life," we studied the attitudes, dress, customs, language and interests of the population. Then we made puppets representing a typical family of the region, with its problems, experiences, behaviour and attitudes. (see excerpt at end of chapter)

This innovative technique lent an element of novelty and surprise to our program. The students' response to the characters was so positive that they began to call them by name. During performances, they entered into a very frank and natural dialogue with the characters, expressing their doubts, opinions and feelings. In this way, the classes became pleasant settings for social interaction which were at once conducive to literacy education.[1]

Increasing participation required us to set up additional activities. We now had at our disposal a means to convey diverse and enriching messages and to encourage even the most underprivileged participants to explore new horizons. But how could we reach the whole community, arouse curiosity and involve the public?

The method we chose was black light theatre, a technique which uses figures similar to those of puppet theatre but larger. Ultraviolet rays make the colours appear fluorescent and neutralize black. The effect is spectacular. At first, we used characters inspired by popular poetry, but they subsequently evolved to reflect themes of general interest, such as alcoholism, health, etc.

The black light performances took place in the halls of associations that had suitable facilities.[2] We invited organizations with specific goals (National Consumer Protection Institute, Anti-Tuberculosis Service, athletic teams, Southern Hydro-Electric Directorate, health centres, etc.) to take part in meetings where problems were discussed and participants could ask questions. These activities gave us an opportunity to highlight the idea that adult education is not simply a matter of setting up courses leading to a diploma, but must be viewed in a broader context, that of educating individuals to be informed and active participants in community affairs. It was therefore necessary to create activities which would meet their real needs and interests, Level 2 elementary school classes (Grade 6)[3] and introductory vocational courses.

Attendance among the young was high and we organized six additional courses in six localities in the commune, as part of a process of decentralization. These classes had usually been held in the commune seat and were therefore inaccessible to many young people, due to the inadequate transportation system.

FOCUSING ON REAL EMPLOYMENT

As our initial study indicated, the labour force was still largely unskilled. The creation of the European Social Fund educational development program for Portugal (PRODEP) gave us the opportunity to promote vocational training, focusing on fields that offered real employment or occupational improvement prospects and corresponded to participants' expressed aspirations.

We were able to demonstrate that some fields are directly related to these needs than others and thus offer better employment or job creation opportunities. In other cases, courses not leading directly to employment prospects served as a first step and guide towards subsequent education and qualifications.

With the help of official local bodies — local authorities, associations, business leaders — a number of courses were set up: weaving, introduction to ceramic painting, introduction to electricity, agricultural mechanics, gardening, etc. The courses combined two aspects: 1) technical and practical training, and 2) general instruction at elementary school levels 1 and 2. At the end of the course, students received two certificates: an academic diploma and a Level 1 vocational training certificate.

The implementation of community integrated adult education programs where the entire population actively participates. The involvement and commitment of existing local organizations, which can act as catalysts, is indispensable. All of our actions have therefore been implemented through partnerships to obtain the direct, integrated support of some local bodies, enabling us to raise consciousness and change attitudes among some others, whose participation had generally been quite limited.

Stimulating Interest in Reading

Another obvious problem was the lack of reading habits. Almost all the localities in the commune had underutilized public libraries, perhaps related to the fact that they were located in schools, where they were inaccessible to the majority of the population. They also lacked adequate operating resources, and did not attract the students at the schools because their books were unsuitable for the age level.

In these localities, we joined forces with the Juntas de Freguesia and other associations who made a commitment to revitalizing the libraries and expanding their collections. After the libraries moved to new facilities, consultation and loans increased sharply. To boost the libraries, special events were also planned: book fairs, poetry contests, creative use of library space, reading activities. Plans are also being made to award study grants to library facilitators, who will require adequate training. However, this will not be enough to stimulate reading. Even if the books are captivating, informative and educational, their subjects are often removed from the daily life of the community who need to read about subjects close to their cultural roots, making reading more pleasurable and encouraging the revival of traditions. In this connection, a booklet on the region's traditional cooking has already been published. Another book is forthcoming on prayers and incantations (folk medicine), and a third on local sayings.

DEVELOPING SOCIAL LIFE BY BUILDING ON TRADITIONS & LEISURE ACTIVITIES

In a community which tends to neglect and downgrade their cultural tradition, adult education must reclaim traditions to defend and preserve it. Social pressures and rudimentary media messages are rapidly leading to cultural uniformity.

Education must endow people with the ability to optimize contact with other cultures especially in the areas of science, technology and leisure activities while preserving their own cultures. There should be an integration between contemporary and traditional cultures, enriching individuals and the entire social life.

To preserve local culture, our first step was to draw up a detailed record of the region's dying traditions on the basis of the adult education activities. As these traditions are transmitted orally for the most part, and since young and old do not spend their leisure time in the same way, we deemed it useful to attempt to bring the two age groups closer together so as to reclaim, revive and disseminate their cultural heritage.

The young people obtained information from friends and relatives, making audio recordings and videotapes, and assembling photographs and other documents to support activities. The experience of organizing provided them with a high degree of self-sufficiency and a sense of initiative, creating more direct ties between institutions and the young people's community. We cite the following examples: two competitions of traditional games, Hygiene and Cleanliness Week, sensitizing the community to water purification problems, various compilations, such as one of the region's culinary traditions, which yielded a booklet and a history and sociocultural survey of S. Pedro do Corbal (a locality in the commune).

ENCOURAGING & INVOLVING LOCAL INSTITUTIONS IN ADULT EDUCATION: A PREREQUISITE FOR COMMUNITY DEVELOPMENT

Adult education can never be removed from its cultural, social and economic context. It is therefore indispensable to the development of the community that local bodies be involved in and committed to the educational process. These bodies however, did not make a sufficient commitment. Local authorities had other priorities; associations lacked the material and human resources; educational and medical institutions were more concerned with solving immediate
problems.

For this reason, the project team attempted from the outset to establish close ties with partners in the community. But our contacts, which we had hoped would be regular, turned out to be sporadic, but the progress made has caused some of these bodies to rethink their positions and we are now seeing a certain change in attitudes towards adult education.

The first phase of a historical and cultural heritage development project has just begun. It is a joint effort by our team and the Association for the Defense of the Interests of Monsaraz. (We should point out that the commune's medieval architecture is a major tourist attraction.) As the name suggests, the aim of this project is to conduct a study of the community's historic and cultural heritage, to upgrade the local population's knowledge. The study should enable the inhabitants of Monsaraz to supply accurate information to the many visitors who flock to the region year round.

There are also plans for community literacy work. An activities grant has already been awarded to a library facilitator, who also received appropriate training. In addition, a small community library is currently being set up. Working with us on this project are a teacher who is on loan and two monitors from a practical Level 1 elementary course in which students collect information on traditions and produce texts based on their research. In a later phase, literacy activities will be organized and structured based on identified public needs and interests.

Since the launch of this project in 1987, we have seen that the progress is based on associations' understanding of and committment to the community. Such support ensures the success of literacy campaigns.

REFLECTIONS

After analyzing the community's needs, we evaluated the action strategies we had adopted to raise citizens' level of education since 1987. After increasing steadily, the courses began to decline after the fourth year. We believe we have been successful in responding to the community's educational needs and, as these needs were progressively met, the number of courses were reduced accordingly. The situation has continued and we now have to organize courses at elementary Level 3 (Grade 9).

Our assessment is less positive regarding our attempts to sensitize and involve local bodies. Despite dozens of initiatives realized during these years, we recognized that the literacy campaign in the Reguengos de Monsaraz commune did not evolve as we had hoped. Sporadic and isolated public, private, and associations' participation resulted in the lack of a joint strategy developed with all the institutions. A recent assessment has led to the conclusion that the action strategy must be revised in order to strike a better balance between the energy invested and results obtained. Results have not always been proportionate to the effort.

We must modify our approach and we have thus begun a series of meetings with numerous associations in order to undertake a new phase of the project together to set up a task force to develop a joint action strategy to realize in practice the potential and synergy we detected and helped create. But carrying out these measures requires a high degree of co-operation. Local development can be achieved only if all available resources, including governmental, private and community resources, are involved in planning, implementing and evaluating our actions.

EXCERPT FROM THE PUPPET THEATRE

- (Manuel Antonio and Joao go fishing)

JOAO:	I'm telling you, if I had a bigger fishing rod, that one wouldn't have gotten away!
MANUEL ANTONIO:	You just like anything modern! Look what I caught — no sweat!
JOAO:	Well you'd better be careful. You're taking a lot of risks. You know it's illegal to use nets.
MANUEL ANTONIO:	So it's illegal! There aren't any fish! If I didn't do it this way, what would I catch? In my day, all you had to do was put your hands in the water and you'd catch tons of fish. And they didn't smell of oil like they do today!
JOAO:	What do you want, Dad? That's the price of progress. If we want factories, we have to pay the price.
MANUEL ANTONIO:	Well, the price is too high! They're factories, they're wine presses; they're not pollution. In my day, we put the net in the water and we had a nice nap in the shade of the bay-tree. Today there aren't even any bay-trees!
JOAO:	But it isn't just the factories. Don't forget the pig pen by the stream. Where does the waste go? In the stream! So there you have it!
MANUEL ANTONIO:	Okay, okay! Go call your mother and tell her I'd like to know what's doing with lunch.
JOAO:	Okay, Dad.

- (Exit Joao. Enter Chica Rosa)

MANUEL ANTONIO:	So! Now it's my suckling pigs that are mucking up the stream!
CHICA ROSA:	What?
MANUEL ANTONIO:	You want to know? Our son Joao says our suckling pigs down there in the pen are polluting the stream. I can't believe I'm hearing that from him! I might expect that from our daughter. But not Joao! Next thing he'll be saying the river's running dry because I'm using it to water my crops!
CHICA ROSA:	Come on, don't let it get to you. He's been to school. He thinks he knows more than the "old folk."
MANUEL ANTONIO:	Who's old? My whole life I got by with what my father taught me and he was "old" too!
CHICA ROSA:	Let's go eat. Everybody's waiting for us. Come on: today for once Joao's eating with us.

- (Exeunt)

MANUEL ANTONIO:	Let's go. So it's my little porkers that are mucking up the stream! That's a good one!

Notes & References

1. **Literacy education**: process of developing self-sufficiency and taking an active role in the community by achieving a critical understanding of oneself and reality through the enhancement of knowledge, values and skills; and the process of developing the required skills for reading, writing and language.

2. Performances of the puppet theatre and black light theatre were used only sporadically to avoid monotony and loss of novelty. We did continue to work with the Dorval Cultural Centre on other types of actions. We subsequently set up a drama course, creating a theatre group for the Centre. Age limits were imposed because it was impossible to accept all who wished to enroll. A second drama course without any age limit served to consolidate the already-existing theatre group which staged many performances during festivals and other cultural events.

3. Starting with Grade 4, students have a long trip to the school. They must leave very early in the morning and return home late at night. This is one of the most common reasons for dropping out.

Chapter 8
ANSWERS
TO EDUCATION PROBLEMS
IN RURAL ITALY

Paolo Federighi
University of Florence
Giovanni Parlavecchia
Castelfiorentino Commune
Italy

THE LIBRARY IN CASTELFIORENTINO:
NO LONGER THE DOMAIN OF A PRIVILEGED FEW

Castelfiorentino is a town with a population of about 20,000 located in the heart of Tuscany, around 50 km from Florence, Pisa and Siena. The surrounding countryside is dotted by poultry, pig and sheep farms as well as some 40 vineyards. Several major industries, in particular clothing, shoes and furniture, thrive in this region, generating business for 600 firms. Tourism is also expanding.

Since the mid-1980s, the Tuscany regional government, the University of Florence (adult education department) and the Commune of Castelfiorentino participated in a joint project aimed at narrowing the ever-widening gap between different segments of the population with regard to education and culture, focusing on the role of the most important public infrastructure in Castelfiorentino, the library. The Tuscany regional government has redefined and broadened the role of the library in society, identified the conditions needed to increase access, and tried to determine how the present services could be adapted to meet new needs.

The University of Florence, for its part, has been interested in studying and implementing strategies that would enable libraries like the one in Castelfiorentino to modify and expand their clientele by attracting groups that are unaccustomed to using these facilties, such as workers, young people, house-wives, the elderly, and so forth.[1]

As for the Commune of Castelfiorentino, it has helped to focus these research activities on the educational needs of society and to devise ways of adapting its own cultural structures to satisfy a new type of clientele. The ultimate goal is to cope with a situation where 60% of the town's population has not completed elementary school.

One of the major initiatives of this joint project was a conference held in Castelfiorentino on education, culture and information. Participants were asked to consider an action plan entitled "The Library and the Public", where the library is the primary link in a local information system, playing a more active role in adult education. The conference focused on the measures that should be taken to effect future changes, and was designed to achieve two main objectives: first, to determine what organizational structures would enable the population of Castelfiorentino to meet their needs; and second, to identify which factors create effective organizational structures. When people play a more active role in the learning process, they assure that precedence will be given to their own needs rather than to those expressed by others.

Upgrading adults' education should not be the concern of libraries alone. The people themselves must want to learn and be informed, while other services must strive to modify existing attitudes and behaviour. It is only then that we will see an increase in the number of adults enrolled in night school to earn a secondary school leaving certificate, and libraries will be able to fulfil their function to the fullest.

The conference paved the way for future action by defining concrete measures that would enable the library of Castelfiorentino to respond to the educational needs of the population as a whole, and highlighted the crucial role played by education in ensuring that adults lead a full, meaningful life.

The Action Plan

"Public" libraries are usually the "private" domain of students and the well-educated. Improved access to information in private, working and social life has produced more opportunities for reading and fostered the use of books, newspapers, radio and television.

It was important to adopt an organized participatory approach to bring about changes in adult education, to promote the social role of cultural structures and to identify the kind of information people needed.

Although the average level of schooling in Italian society has improved, it has not kept pace with developments in science and communication. Consequently, people are increasingly out of touch with the various channels of information and more and more passive with regard to the mass media, and our already low levels of instruction have fallen even further behind those of other European countries we like to consider our equals. Most people who lack education take their situation personally and experience feelings of "psychological submission" and "social subordination".[2]

Population is not a homogeneous entity and to explore the possibility of establishing a relationship between people and books we have to divide the population into several different categories. The simplistic, two-fold classification, i.e. those who read and those who do not read, is totally inadequate, since it holds people solely responsible for the frequency with which they read.[3] We have to face the fact that cultural resources are **unequally distributed** in Italy. By acknowledging this reality, we will better understand the conditions which promote or preclude public participation.

Dictionaries often define the library as a "place where books are kept." Readers are not taken into account. Tullio De Mauro has proposed another definition, that is, a "place where books are lent or consulted." Once again, however, the emphasis is placed on the building or room where the books themselves are stored; the readers' needs are secondary. Readers are conspicuously absent from the history of Italian libraries, a phenomenon that can be attributed to the notion that people do not have to read. This attitude has had a harmful effect on the lower classes of Italian society. The government has not created an efficient public library system, but an "Italian" system where people have not been encouraged to read and where public libraries have become the "private" domain of a privileged few.

To date, librarians have studied the needs of those who already use libraries, but have not considered those who never set foot in these institutions. Nor have they considered the paradox that those most in need of information usually ask for less, while those who are least in need, ask for more and obtain more. The public library is a product of educational policies. As in Anglo-Saxon countries, it is extremely important that people view their library as a repository of written knowledge that belongs to all citizens. The absence of a broad-based ideology where the community identifies with its library explains the absence of ordinary citizens in the library's clientele historically.[4]

Libraries play an essential role in the process set in motion the moment books are written for they are responsible for distributing these works to the public. Instead of waiting for "customers" to arrive, shouldn't they seek them out and try to understand what they need? And if, as De Sanctis and Federighi have written,[5] learning to read is not merely a spontaneous phenomenon of childhood and adolescence but the result of real opportunities provided by a person's family and social background, shouldn't public libraries join forces with other political and social structures to eliminate the discrepancies that prevent many people from entering libraries?

The ideal library can preserve a collection of books, contribute to the intellectual development of all people, and ensure book distribution according to needs. Also important, is the encouragement of self expression through written culture and the transmission of this to those acting as receivers and spectators.[6]

Implementation of the Action Plan

Our first task was to pave the way for the proposed changes by studying the sociological make-up of the population of Castelfiorentino, their reading habits, education, and cultural situation. New library services were then introduced.

Creation of a Local Information System

The following steps have been taken to set up a local information system in Castelfiorentino:

- Space has been acquired at the local radio and television station and placed at the disposal of thetown's various associations.

- Permission has been obtained to broadcast a program on educational, cultural, recreational and sporting events.

- Citizens have started up a local newspaper. Introductory journalism courses and training sessions are offered to the general public.

- Air time has been granted by the local radio network for discussing local problems and providing information on the action plan *The Library and the Public*.

- A telephone information service has been set up and air time granted by the local television network.

In addition, the Italian pensioners' trade union helped to set up a telephone information service on work and health in the library. People can phone in to ask questions, make suggestions, and lodge complaints about municipal services, such as health care. Answers are given during a program broadcast on the local television network: *Dalla parte del cittadino* (The People's Point of View).

Satellite Service Points

We have not only studied and implemented ways of responding more effectively to the real needs of the library's new clientele but also increased the number of places where people can find, read and borrow books. This has involved setting up a number of satellite service points, with the town library serving as the main outlet making it possible to bring books to those living outside the downtown core or who are less likely to use the public library because of their social situation. The system could not have been implemented without the help of university students and cultural operators.

In Beauty Salons

The owners of certain beauty salons in Castelfiorentino received information on the library's action plan as well as training on how to present books and magazines to their customers. It is extremely important to clearly explain the purpose of satellite service points to the owners since this enables them to more effectively fulfil their role as "intermediaries" between the library and the public. When setting up the system in a beauty parlour, it is important to select a clearly visible and accessible place for displaying the reading material, to arouse the customer's curiosity.

Beauty salons were chosen in the downtown area, the suburbs, and the outskirts of the town. A total of 16 are now involved in the project, receiving some 30 to 50 books every 30 to 40 days. Salon owners are constantly urged to assure that their books are properly displayed, to compile a data bank, to gather criticisms and suggestions and, above all, to make more of an effort to shape customer preferences, since they are the ones who transmit information from one customer to another.

In Recreational and Cultural Centres

Setting up satellite service points where people can borrow books were chosen for this purpose since they serve as meeting places for the inhabitants of Castelfiorentino's suburbs, namely, Cambiano, Castelnuovo d'Elsa and Petrazzi. The opening of these service points has been anxiously awaited by many people, most of whom have never set foot in the town library. They now have access on a daily basis to books dealing with a wide range of popular subjects.

A continuous supply of books is renewed regularly to respond to specific requests or ensure sufficient variety. It is mainly men who use these facilities, although women, mostly housewives or homeworkers, also visit them. to pursue specific interests or look for answers to everyday problems. Many users specify that reading is not one of their hobbies and that they are merely looking for a specific piece of information. The ultimate challenge is to persuade people to read, to discuss and to be more critical in their appraisal.

The comments made by a pensioner are very significant in this regard. In his opinion, the library has brought to Castelnuovo, one of the suburbs of Castelfiorentino, the only form of culture the population can ever have. He thanked the service point for providing him with reading material, saying that people can never know enough in life, that knowledge is everything.

In Hospitals

Satellite service points set up in hospitals offer people with physical or psychological problems an opportunity to read and thus make better use of their time by developing interests they often ignore in daily life. We also hoped to prevent the other service points established during the project from being perceived as "self-service" centres catering only to the healthy, a situation that would have perpetuated the kind of discrepancies of our present multi-tiered society. The relationship between users and service point operators is crucial, helping users to understand that reading is essential to satisfying their cultural needs and pursuing their everyday interests.

In the UNICOOP Supermarket

As agreed by the members of this consumers' cooperative, customers may borrow books exploring a wide range of subjects as well as other material dealing with problems discussed by INFOCOOP, a touch-sensitive display system providing information on food, diet, etc. A section of the store, known as the Ecological Isle, is also used for providing customers with information on environmental issues and inviting them to make use of a selective, waste disposal system for paper, glass, cans, batteries, medicine, clothing, plastics, and so forth.

In Schools

An analysis of the relationship between reading and the media provided the point of departure for this part of the project. Our objective was to show how the public library could be an effective tool for demonstrating that language and images cannot be dissociated from one another, for encouraging people to study the questions raised by images in greater depth, and to provide a better understanding of the messages relayed by the media since books usually analyze these questions in more detail.

Prior to setting up service points in schools, students' parents were surveyed through questionnaires, meetings and guided tours to identify problems that might have an impact on their children's education both in and out of school. The goal was to bring our project to the attention of a wider audience and to help parents realize that reading is not a sporadic or boring activity restricted to personal or school libraries and finally, that the public library offers services geared to the needs of everyone.

The students are now making full use of the service points and many adults and parents are now visiting a public reading facility, for the first time in their life. Some are even playing a role in managing the outlets.

Other Service Points

Other more "traditional" measures have been taken to promote the new image of Castelfiorentino's public library. For example, satellite service points where people can read and borrow books have been set up in parks, the favourite meeting place of elderly people. In addition, the standard practice of interrupting library service during the summer has been abandoned because many people stay in town. The library's opening hours have a direct impact on the effectiveness of its services. A "book-at-home" program offers the elderly or those having difficulty getting around, even if only temporarily, the opportunity to order books from the library by telephone.

Over the past few years, we have worked to establish a new kind of public library, similar to that defined by Filippo De Sanctis shortly before his death. We continue to pursue this objective. De Sanctis described the public library as the cultural and educational heritage of all people and specified that it should contribute to the intellectual development of the population as a whole by offering coherent, regular services; helping people to overcome difficult situations by assuring they have access to books and other reading material; promoting communication through written culture; and ensuring the preservation of books, which are the universal heritage of civilization and the historic memory of mankind.

BASIC APPROACHES

One of the crucial problems in Italy is the lack of a public adult education system. Over the years a broad consensus has emerged on the need to establish such a system. One of the objectives of the Castelfiorentino project is to make the educational tools available to a large public, and to ensure consistency through administration at the local level. This administrative function is fulfilled by the communes which, in conjunction with the associations, determine the educational and cultural environment of local communities. This tendency to establish local systems is especially strong in rural areas, in part because of the need to use all accessible resources and to make all existing resources available to everyone.

Strategic Hypotheses

This project examines the approaches used to solve current problems. It has a utopian aspect to it, with the possibility of immediately putting in place a framework that can regulate the entire education system and overcome existing differences between various educational and cultural systems and between locations where educational activities are conducted and those where they are not. Such a system has the potential to be directed and controlled by the very public for which it is designed.

The reasons for adopting this approach are not purely idealistic, however. Italy's educational and cultural system cannot be transformed by half-measures, only a global approach can yield solutions to today's problems. The problems of adult education, library development, local economic development and so on cannot be addressed separately. This hypothesis of reorganization of the education system, serving as a starting point, does not specifically entail the establishment of networks, co-ordination mechanisms or "bridges" between the various sectors. The elimination of barriers between different stages in life and between various infrastructures and institutions constitutes an objective, but not a unifying end, serving as a landmark on the road toward a new educational environment.

Instead, the key to this approach may lie in increasing the current capacity of the public to adapt to the transformation of the local education system, the pace of which will be determined by the public itself.

A second working hypothesis, which is based on other projects in Italy, deals with involving younger students in the development of adult education, especially in rural areas, because of the lack of resources and infrastructures. This hypothesis is based on the possibility of developing socially productive school curricula for solving societal problems with relevancy. Acquiring and using scientific tools can yield immediate opportunities for assessing, validating or invalidating the objectives, methods and tools selected. This is thus a working hypothesis, which sees young people not as part of the problem, but rather as a resource for changing education conditions.

The third hypothesis deals with making cultural institutions accessible to the entire population. Libraries are a good illustration of the situation in rural areas, where they are often the only cultural institutions. Problems with their operation are much more serious in areas where the population is scattered throughout numerous small villages and there is a lack of practical means of communication, funding for culture is limited, and there are no cultural and library networks that have even the potential of meeting the population's reading requirements.

Innovative ways must be found of distributing cultural products (such as books), so that the large number of people who currently do not frequent cultural institutions can benefit. A critical analysis must be made to eliminate the factors which limit book distribution and prevent these institutions from truly serving the public.

Measures

The principal measures that characterize the success of projects such as the one in Castelfiorentino typically fall into one of the following categories:

- contextual measures, making it possible and feasible to intervene in the area of adult education and which determine the outcomes;

- measures that ensure the operation and implementation of the education system;

- development measures, which seek to foster conditions allowing for a permanent place for adults in the various branches of the educational and cultural system.

Contextual Measures

Contextual measures, which determine the direction, content and feasibility of educational intervention, fall into one of the following three categories:

1. The planning process, which defines the objectives of educational and cultural programs; the available resources, the methods to use, the action to be taken and the procedures to follow.

Planning is an essential stage in adult education (we are referring here to local policies on adult education, and not to didactic planning) where decisive choices are made. Because this is a relatively new field, this task is often assigned to technocrats. For example, here are some of the crucial choices that must be made and the action that must be taken include determining

- the target clientele and the type of problems that need to be solved;

- the educational objectives to be achieved;

- division of responsibilities among the different institutions and parties involved (associations, businesses, unions, communes and so on);

- the extent of the resources available and what action is feasible;

- the preliminary elements (locations, players and so on);

- what methods are feasible (in light of the required resources);

- how the project should be managed and the role of the various local educational bodies.

2. The definition of the subject of the education program, meaning the clientele on whose behalf the interventions are made.

Using specific measures to define the target clientele makes it possible to define the training objectives of the educational and cultural activities more effectively. It should be stressed that no activities have universal application, and that the methods and structure selected determine the target clientele. For example, deciding to focus on workers in a given production sector would have obvious consequences for activity planning. In addition, defining the target clientele makes possible the determination of conditions under which they will participate and, eventually define and plan measures to make educa-tion more accessible, in conjunction with cultural institutions, schools, businesses and so on.

Defining the primary subject of the education program makes possible public organization and management mechanisms to implement forms of "educational negotiation" at the individual and group level, so that the public can participate directly in the management of activities.

3. The scope of application and the resources available for training activities. These measures involve:

• First, the scope of the planned educational project. Specifically, this refers to the links to be established between the workplace and the educational institutions (not through practice, but rather through research projects, for example) and among the various cultural institutions involved in the project (ranging from databanks to museums). After all, is it possible to acquire real information without databanks, libraries and museums, and without arts-oriented educational activities, which are so important in an economic context in which the arts and tourism sectors play such a large role?

This also refers to the use of basic services in support of the interventions, in particular the following services, indispensable to the Italian project: public information; assistance and orientation; academic initiation; training and research for teachers; documentation;

• second, planning the labour-market entry of each participant in the education project and ensuring that these persons become real clients of the local education system. This point will be examined in greater detail later on.

Implementation of Activities

To understand the effects that a systematic approach can have on activities and helping participants, it is useful to examine the basic stages of implementation that include the pre-course stage consisting of public information and orientation activities and having the participants adopt the role of subject of the project. A social incentive to education is reflected in the measures to make education opportunities more accessible to workers and small business people; to involve local organizations and leaders in the public information process and to develop future education opportunities; and tailoring of activities and programs to the participants' needs and skills. Educational practices based essentially on the teacher/student relationship result only from an approach that is devoid of context and does not make use of local resources. This approach, seeks to situate education within the context of individual learning problems, lack of skills in the local economy; and participants' opportunities for educational and occupational activities dictates that the educational environment extend well beyond the walls of the classrooms or workshops of the educational institution or vocational training centre. It requires that education be linked to ongoing social and economic changes and be based on research methods rather than top-down, non-interactive communication techniques.

Development Measures

The social demand for a basic education involves more than just obtaining a diploma. While a diploma is certainly a legitimate goal, it cannot provide sufficient motivation for completing studies at this level.

The demand for training must be seen as an attempt to reintegrate the educational and cultural system on a permanent basis. Otherwise, the individual and public investment in time and money would be wasted. We feel that action is required in the following three areas:

1. assessing the skills acquired during training by comparing them with the requirements for local socio-economic development. Developing assessment tools to identify training problems faced by participants who have completed courses and informal educational activities would prove invaluable for replanning and restructuring the project and would have tremendous advantages for all concerned;

2. preparing the public, to give them access to new training opportunities (not only by adapting existing eligibility requirements, but also by adapting local infrastructures to the educational requirements of the new clientele). This refers to various educational and cultural institutions in cities and, for secondary school graduates, to universities;

3. making students accountable for participation in organized community life. This aspect is often neglected in the course follow-up stage, but for both strategic and practical reasons, developing abilities and opportunities for participating in organized community life is often the key to preparing people for management, teamwork and innovation. To mention only one of the many functions of such participation, one might ask who is better positioned and has more flexibility to meet urgent needs for information than associations? Who should be given the responsibility of anticipating institutional responses?

Public Organization & Development of Adult Education Research

Although the working hypotheses focus on the future and how to implement potential projects, the model that is best suited to meet the objectives and yield the desired results is one which examines and creates a virtual future. The basic methods thus consist of research. However, methods that make research a sequential process, by separating "before" (the research) from "after" (the transformation, which is generally not a logical result), are not productive. "After", meaning the changes that one wants to bring about and the desire to make those changes, also determines "before", meaning the research methods that are used. The processes of stagnation or development of the subject matter have already begun, evolving negatively or positively, in response to the action or inaction of the parties involved. For this reason, at all levels of our work, the key to success lies in the ability of the education system's new clientele to recognize the power it has to control and direct these processes.

Enlightened minds often plan "stellar" projects that nevertheless turn out to be "astronomical" flops. Research must therefore always be grounded in educational realities, and designed to give the end users of projects the conscious ability to control and change the educational process. The issue is thus one of organizing scientifically the process of skill development and consolidation among the new clientele of the education system, in order to redefine collectively the system's objectives and relationships with workers, the unemployed, cultural institutions, governments and, ultimately, the realities of everyday life.

With this in mind, the methods used are designed to foster a social framework for the desire and need for change, and to provide solutions to institutional, financial, educational and other problems.

Notes & References

Bibliography

Cirri, D., Federighi, P. *Verso un 2000 educativo* [Toward an educational 21st century], Primo rapporto di ricerca [First research report], Prato, 1991.

De Sanctis, Filippo M. *Verso un 2000 educativo*, Prato, 1988.

Orefice, P., Sarracino, V. *Ente locale et formazione* [Local organization and training], Naples, Liguori, 1988.

Parlavecchia, G., Tarchiani, G. *Nuovo pubblico et biblioteca* [The new public and libraries], Milan, La bibliografica, 1991.

Scaglioso, C., Catelli, G. *Educazione permanente e realtà locali* [Continuing education and local realities], Milan, Angeli, 1985.

Operatori culturali nei paesi dell'arco alpino [Cultural bodies of countries in the Alpine chain], Bolzano, Bolzano autonomous region, 1992.

1.   Filippo De Sanctis and Paolo Federighi, *Pubblico e biblioteca*, Rome: Bulzoni, 1981, p. 150.

2.   Filippo De Sanctis, *Verso un duemila educativo*, Università degli studi di Firenzi/Comune di Prato, 1988, p. 15.

3.   Filippo De Sanctis, op. cit, p.23.

4.   Armando Petrucci, *Per un centro studi a sostegno metodologico degli operatori dei servizi bibliotecari*, in *Verso una biblioteca del pubblico*, Milan: Bibliografica, 1991, p. 38-46.

5.   Op. cit., p. 63.

6.   Paolo Federighi, *Per lo sviluppo dei rapporti tra "nuovo" pubblico e biblioteco*, in *Verso una biblioteca del pubblico*, op. cit., p. 31.

Chapter 9
THE VELVENDOS WOMEN'S AGRICULTURAL AND CRAFT CO-OPERATIVE

Gella Vornava Skoura, Dimitris Vergidis,
Georgia Sariyannidou, Sophia Avgitidou
Greece

VELVENDOS HISTORICAL BACKGROUND

In 1984, researchers from Athens and from the department of Kozani conducted participative research financed by the European Social Fund and the
prefecture of the department of Kozani in western Macedonia. The study was a
lead up to some form of integrated action.[1] The objective was to develop the
social sector of the economy through community action, with special emphasis
on training and literacy as actions encompassing all aspects of writing and
playing a pivotal support role with regard to the proposed initiatives.

The establishment of an agro-industrial women's co-operative to produce and
standardize local agricultural products such as traditional preservative-free
jams, preserves and cakes[2] was the realization of proposals put forward by
certain members of the cultural association of Velvendos, a town of about 4,000
people located at the foot of Mount Olympus and 20 km from the capital of the
department. The town has a rich tradition of community involvement, as
illustrated by the founding in 1958 of SEPOP, a fruit and vegetable processing
and marketing co-operative. SEPOP is one of only a handful of Greek co-
operatives to ensure excellent incomes for members and the only one of the 182
co-operatives in the department to have its very own product processing and
storage facilities. Furthermore, this co-operative has marketing centres outside
Velvendos, notably in Kozani and in Athens and exports products to other
European markets.

However, it should be noted that because of legislation in force until 1983,
women were prohibited from joining agricultural co-operatives or from owning

their own farm, unless they were widowed and single. They were relegated to a marginal role in terms of social interaction. Accordingly, one must bear in mind the times when examining the projects undertaken by the Velvendos cultural association, as described below.

Despite a number of problems,[3] the Velvendos agricultural and craft co-operatives were formed in 1985 through the combined efforts of 75 mostly young women representing all social classes in the town of Velvendos. The choice of name for the co-operative was by no means fortuitous. It reflects the concerns of women about moving away from traditional activities such as embroidery and weaving and turning to activities tied to product processing and the cottage industry sector. Only gradually and with experience did the activities of the co-operative evolve to coincide with the initially stated objectives.

The purpose of this study is to describe the sociocultural experiences born of this community involvement and to draw a connection with the resulting focus on literacy within the cultural context of Velvendos. Our study is based on a series of interviews with 18 of the 140 co-operative members , with five managers (the president, former president and three members of the board of directors) and with various local officials such as the mayor, the president of SEPOP and political party representatives. In addition, articles about the co-operative written by the local press, particularly during the critical consolidation phase from 1985 to 1987, provided added information.

LOCAL SITUATION

With a total population of 150,000, the department of Kozani reflects, on a smaller scale, the major characteristics of the prevailing economic and social situation throughout Greece. The level of economic growth in the country has been uneven, leading to a significant exodus from the countryside and to a wave of emigration, with all of the attendant negative consequences on local development. The department of Kozani is home to a large industrial zone, but activities are limited primarily to mining (lignite, asbestos, chromium, marble). The rate of growth of the primary sector is poor, primarily because of the limited number of irrigated areas and the small size and the partioned nature of farms.

Despite the rapid decline in rural populations, both in Kozani and throughout the country and even in remote regions far away from rural tourist areas where population levels have remained steady, the town of Velvendos has managed to keep most of its residents from leaving, in spite of frequent severe unemployment problems. This was apparent from comments made by the mayor of Velvendos. "About ten young people from Velvendos have emigrated over the past two years to the United States and Germany in order to find work."[4]

The primary employment demographics in Velvendos are as follows:

- residents of working age generally remain in the town, with the exception of those between the ages of 20 and 29. A significant number of people in the latter category leave the community for a certain period of time, either to do their military service or to study in the city. However, most of them return to live and work in Velvendos or in the surrounding region;

- with respect to employment according to age bracket, residents over the age of 50 are generally employed in the primary sector, whereas young people are mainly employed in the tertiary sector and, to a lesser extent, the secondary sector (public electric utility company, construction sector, public works).

The fact that the natives of Velvendos have, to a very large extent, chosen to remain in their community is quite exceptional and can be attributed to a series of local community initiatives and to the resulting social interaction.

Concerning the level of formal schooling, we unfortunately do not have sufficient data on the adult population of Velvendos. Statistics for the 1980s show that student enrolment levels are down — because of the declining birth rate, a phenomenon occurring throughout the country[5] — at the primary level (by more than 30 per cent) as well as at the pre-primary level. It is only at the secondary school level that enrolment has increased, primarily in the general program. Virtually all students (90 per cent) continue on to secondary school.

The majority of girls, having completed the "gymnase" (first cycle), enrol in the general program, where they account for nearly 60 per cent of the enrolment, as compared to 45 per cent at the "gymnase" level (owing to the clearly higher number of boys than girls in the 10 to 14 age bracket). Boys, on the other hand, tend to continue on in the technical and professional program.

A community based education centre has been established in Velvendos where adult classes attended primarily by women are given in sewing and stitching, machine embroidery, typing and foreign languages. During the 1980s, senior officials with the general secretariat responsible for public education had remarked that the excessive number of such classes made it somewhat difficult to establish a link between community based education on the one hand and genuine needs and local development on the other hand.[6] The centre's activities gradually evolved and by 1992, journalism seminars and a computer course were being offered in co-operation with the cultural association, and specialized training programs were instituted in Velvendos by the Agricultural Training Centre and by the OAED (manpower employment agency).

The Velvendos cultural association, active since 1964, plays an especially important role In literacy. It is responsible for the local monthly publication *To Velvendo* and oversees a number of institutions such as the lending library, the museum of archeology and folklore, the band, the film club and a number of other activities organized in conjunction with the community based education centre. Members of the centre spearheaded the drive to establish the women's agricultural and craft co-operative.

Given the sociocultural context of Velvendos, we must emphasize that until quite recently, women played only a marginal role in the decision-making process. they were not among the founding members of any of the local organizations representing major political parties. As we discovered during interviews with local representatives of the Communist, Socialist and neo-liberal parties, only a very small number of women participate in local political activities or in broader political movements.

The comments of the interviewed women belonging to the agricultural and craft co-operative reflect a generally positive attitude toward the cultural and social context in Velvendos and genuine optimism about the future:

> "Overall I am satisfied because I belong to the cultural association and to the women's co-operative. Some "illiterate" women feel insecure and lack self-confidence because of their lack of education. Others, however, while illiterate, still manage to make their mark."
>
> (Unemployed graduate)

> "There are no special problems here. Of course, we do not have the same range of cultural activities as the large urban centres. There is no theatre, no cultural institutions such as the Palais de la musique in Athens. However, the Velvendos cultural association is quite active."
>
> (Library employee)

THE VELVENDOS AGRICULTURAL & CRAFT CO-OPERATIVE

When it was initially established, the co-operative had two main objectives:

- to provide an opportunity to raise family income levels by employing women to perform various tasks within the co-operative;

- and to create a social climate for women within the co-operative by involving them in a range of areas such as communication, information, decision making and production, giving them an opportunity to acquire new skills and gain more self-confidence.

In accordance with the co-operative's bylaws, special emphasis was placed on crafts involving the use of wool, cotton, silk and so forth. The first products produced by the co-operative were embroidered and traditional woven items. However, it proved difficult to sell these products because the markets were already saturated with similar goods. This became apparent when the co-operative took part in a pan-hellenic craft fair on the Isle of Rhodes. After the fair, the president of the co-operative declared after the fair that the outcome for co-operatives in general had not been very encouraging.

Following a general assembly meeting, the members of the co-operative decided to move in a new direction and to focus on activities which thus far had been only of secondary importance, although mentioned in the initial proposal. The co-operative decided to use local farm products to produce preservative-free jams, preserves, syrup cakes, etc. Preparing and preserving unprocessed goods is considered part of the traditional knowledge held by women. However, mass (large-scale) production, standardization and marketing go beyond the traditional skills of women farmers. They represented a transition from traditional female know-how to industrial methods of marketing preservative-free food products.

This transition was successful. Production increased in four years (1986-1990) from 5,000 to 11,000 jars, while membership more than doubled from 75 to 180 people, finally levelling off at 140 members. As far as expanding production is concerned, an investment of 60 million drachma is projected for the construction of facilities on land granted by the township of Velvendos and for the acquisition of needed equipment. Once these expansion plans were submitted to the appropriate authorities for approval, a grant representing 43 per cent of the total investment was secured from the State, along with a loan corresponding to 34 per cent of the investment made by the Farm Bank.[7] Members agreed to one-third of the payments received to the cooperative in conjunction with subsidized seminars they were attending.[8]

However, this success in terms of economic performance does not appear to have resulted thus far in any appreciable improvement in income levels, as we discovered during from the interviews conducted with co-operative members. They appear to have acquired more self-confidence and believe in the positive role the co-operative has to play in their future well-being and they look to the results achieved by the co-operative from a cultural and interpersonal standpoint. Many of them had comments such as the following to make:

> "The most positive aspect is the people whom I have had the opportunity of meeting through the co-operative. Such encounters would otherwise not have been possible."

To understand their attitude clearly, we must examine how the women's co-operative is structured and how it operates.

The Structure

The women who took the initiative of establishing this co-operative worked hard to ensure the broadest possible involvement. They adopted a relatively flexible policy respecting decision-making, calling for input from all members.

The co-operative is headed by a five-member board of directors with a three-year mandate. Various committees operate at the same time and oversee activities such as weaving, embroidery and processing. All members are free to take part in the proceedings and decisions of these committees. Each committee meets on a regular basis to pass along information received from the board of directors pertaining to specific issues and to make the necessary decisions. The general assembly, which is comprised of all members, is the supreme decision-making body of the co-operative.

Owing to cramped quarters and the limited number of work stations, the women work on a rotating basis in groups of ten, formed by alphabetical order. They have learned to work as a group, no longer on the basis of ties with family members or neighbours, but in keeping with collective rules and have been able to forge new relationships, an extremely important point in a rural, and according to these women, somewhat closed society.

The co-operative focused on three goals, with the ultimate aim being the mobilization of its members:

1.   The co-operative sought support from local institutions and agencies such as city hall, SEPOP, the cultural association and the community based education centre.

2.   The co-operative has endeavoured to establish through every means possible ties with all agencies capable of lending it support and contributing to its development.

3.   Officials responsible for the co-operative have conducted a series of information visits with a view to participating in fairs and exhibits taking place in other regions of Greece.

From the outset, the women's co-operative has benefited from all of the existing experience at the local level and adopted a collective and flexible decision-making structure. It sought information from other co-operatives, specialized agencies and experts in an effort to secure the necessary funding for its investment projects — funding which it now has — and the technical assistance needed to ensure optimum production, qualitatively as well as quantitatively.

This structure allowed the co-operative to diagnose problems it was experiencing with the marketing of its traditional woven and embroidered items and prompted restructuring adjustments and restructuring its production activities. As can be seen, the structure of the co-operative, its integration into the community and its ties to a broad range of public agencies concerned about development are all factors which, when combined, explain why the co-operative has become an important thread in the socioeconomic fabric of the community and why it has been able to analyze its problems and plan its future growth.

Communications

The women's co-operative has not restricted its activities to product production and marketing. It has also become involved on a social level. A column written by the co-operative appears in the local monthly publication *To Velvendo*. The column showcases the achievements of Greek women and portrays them in a new light contrasting with the previous image of the traditional homemaker.

Following are several excerpts from these columns which provide a general idea of the dynamic cultural climate generated by the co-operative from its activities. From the outset, the co-operative gave a new social and cultural direction to women's lives, which was not exclusively on the accumulation or consumption of cultural products.

"Today's Greek woman is trying to shape her personality, to debunk all of the myths, to confront institutions and to overcome secular prejudices encountered in her way.

She is fighting to change those institutions that degrade women and to ensure a new standard of living for all, men and women alike." (August 1986).

This column also serves as a vehicle for promoting new values such as the financial independence of women and their active participation in society and in politics:

"Working outside the home gives women real financial independence, enables them to participate in the social and political life of the country and to become involved with institutions responsible for making decisions that directly affect women." (June 1986).

In addition, the co-operative's column gives women of science in Velvendos a forum for discussing their particular areas of expertise. In one such article, Mrs. D.P., a chemist and nutrition expert, analyzed the composition of food products and chemical processing (June 1986).

What matters is not so much promoting a new image of women through the local media as it is developing new attitudes and ways of doing things on a community level. As noted in the column:

"One of the reasons that led us to set up a co-operative was to give women an opportunity to get out of the home, considered their exclusive and sole domain, to become involved in participative activities which until then had been unfamiliar to them and to interact and communicate on a daily basis with other women." (May 1986).

The co-operative puts a new face on women and familiarizes the community with the values, attitudes and practices it espouses. The local newspaper is not just any publication. It is the only source of information about events taking place in Velvendos for the town's population as well as for all natives of the community now living either in major urban centres or abroad. Promoting a new image of women also helps the voice of women to be heard in the community, through the written word which still carries a certain measure of prestige in rural regions:

"We are trying through this column in the local newspaper to make the presence of the women's craft co-operative known in Velvendos and to share with readers issues that concern us both as individuals living in this society and as women who, because of our sex and the way society is structured, face unique problems." (May 1986)

In addition to writing this local newspaper column, the women of the co-operative have been invited to air their views on television and to discuss their activities. This is a clear indication of just how important their work is viewed on the local as well as on the national level:

"In addition to presenting their crafts on television, the women shared their experiences as members of the co-operative and discussed the training they had received." (January 1986).

Social Changes

These different activities, as well as all aspects of the production process, did lead to a certain number of conflicts, disagreements and hesitations.

"When the women of the co-operative are mobilized, they begin to reflect upon the entire economic structure of Velvendos. This mobilization is responsible for the small advances that have been made by women in terms of actively participating in public life and in local organizations, movements and cultural associations. This involvement has without question resulted in problems and conflicts, both within the co-operative and within the community in general. These problems will, however, lead to concrete development proposals." (October 1987)

Promoting new values and roles for women and guiding them through their transition from traditional to modern, naturally results in problems and conflicts between members of the co-operative and the community. However, women are not the only ones to evolve as a result of changing values and attitudes. The entire community is affected, with all of the conflict and dithering associated with changing traditional social roles in a small agricultural society.

The women's co-operative appears to have succeeded in gaining recognition as an important component of Velvendos' social evolution. After the co-operative had been in operation for several years, the mayor made reference to it when proposing solutions to some of the community's most pressing problems:

"To keep the people from leaving, I feel we must take steps to ensure that the co-operatives (the agricultural co-operative and the women's agricultural and craft co-operative) provide or continue to provide opportunities, through market studies, the introduction of new initiatives or alternative approaches." (February 1993)

Educational Initiatives

The co-operative has developed professional training, development strategies and policies geared to helping members acquire the knowledge and know-how they need to perform their new tasks. A collaborative relationship was forged with public educational institutions and local authorities to develop a structure for training and educating as many co-operative members as possible. Training programs are advertised in the local newspaper and the public can obtain information about this critical aspect of the activities of the women's co-operative.

"Tuesday July 1 marks the beginning of a training program where the main focus will be on the processing of farms products, fruits and vegetables; 30 members of the agricultural and craft co-operative will attend the course as trainees for a period of nine months during which they will be remunerated..." (June 1986).

"The weaving unit is proceeding normally with its training program. The quality of our goods has already improved markedly..." (October 1985).

"Until now, the focus of training activities has been on improving and specializing techniques as well as on various issues pertaining to co-operatives in general, marketing and so forth..." (May 1986).

"A seminar on fruit processing organized by the department's agricultural office at the instigation of our co-operative (ei0.8), the manufacturing of preservative-free processed goods such as preserves, jams, liqueurs, etc." (October 1985).

"At the children's agricultural library, a 20-day seminar was held on the subject of co-operatives and issues such as the principles of rural economics, rural sociology, etc." (March 1985).

The announcements published by women of the co-operative in the local newspaper show that they give special importance to education and professional development with a view to improving product quality.

Finally, according to the president of the co-operative:

"Close to 90 women received training in technical areas and virtually all of the women attended seminars on marketing, co-operatives and so forth. Thus, opportunities do exist, both in terms of staff and abilities. The trick is to know how to organize and to ensure that all members have the desire to work and some community spirit."[9]

REFLECTIONS

As a result of the participative initiatives described in this paper, we can confidently state that the Velvendos women's co-operative has fostered a dynamic cultural spirit which has helped to broaden the written communication network and enhanced the learning process for the population of Velvendos.

The co-operative's contribution is clearly evidenced by the following:

- the development in Velvendos of oral and written communication as well as the underlying processes;

- the change in the cultural status of women (values, attitudes, roles, etc.) as a result of the development of communication processes and the diversification of social relationships on the local level;

- the development on the local level of education and professional development strategies and policies for women;

- the fostering of the participation of the women of Velvendos in modern culture;

- the recognition of the traditional know-how of women within the context of the co-operative and the dynamic involvement of women both socially and politically;

- the preservation and promotion of local heritage and traditions through the production of traditional local products.

Therefore, it is clear that the women of the co-operative have contributed to the educational and professional development of members. They were not content to rely solely on the knowledge they already had, but rather devised a training and education strategy with a specific goal to enhance the operation of the co-operative and improve product quality. Consequently, in addition to promoting new ideas, attitudes, values and practices associated with women's modern role in society, the co-operative created appropriate conditions for the personal growth of its members by providing a productive, commercial, educational and cultural framework for action. This transition enabled women to grow on a personal, cultural and social level through their participation in productive, educational activities.

Notes & References

1. Varnava-Skoura, G. and D. Vergidis. *Étude préparatoire à une action intégrée dans le département de Kozani* (preliminary study, integrated action in the department of Kozani), Athens, 1984.

2. *Idem*, p. 277.

3. Although funding for the project recommended in the participative study was approved by the FSE, the moneys were not used owing to the lack of experience in this field on the part of local administrative officials.

4. Local monthly publication *To Velvendo*, February 1993.

5. Report by the parliamentary commission on demographic issues, Athens, 1993.

6. Cf. D. Vergidis. "L'éducation permanente en Grèce dans le cadre de l'institution de l'éducation populaire", 1985 in M. Debesse, G. Mialaret, *Traité des sciences pédagogiques*, appended to the Greek edition, Éd. Diptyho-Athènes, Vol. 8, p. 610.

8. Publication *To Velvendo*, March 1985.

9. Cf. S. Tsioukardani. *The Velvendos agricultural and craft co-operative and its contribution to local development*.

Chapter 10
"TURKISH FACES & LANDSCAPES" AN EXPERIMENT IN CREATIVE WORKSHOP LEADERSHIP

Daniel Seret, Christine Mahy
Maison de la culture
Marche-en-Famenne, Belgium

LITERACY THROUGH IMAGERY

In 1981, volunteers instituted a literacy project in the rural area of Marche-en-Famenne. Belgians and Turkish immigrants who attended French-language training courses given by volunteers were contacted regularly over a period of a few years. This project was part of a comprehensive community development project underway in the "La Fourche" social housing project, in a complex called "La Chenille" [the caterpillar].

Very soon many simple questions arose, although answers did not come as quickly: Why was there such a high rate of absenteeism? How could young Muslim women be encouraged to attend the courses? How could newly acquired French skills be practised? Was a mastery of French really an asset in finding a job in this area? Why did the poor not attend the classes? Why did those in the Fatma family get along so well in our system? Why did this family speak French so well?

Did what we were teaching have a liberating or integrating effect? Where was the dividing line between adapting by learning a system of administrative, socio-cultural, and organizational codes (through spoken language, reading and writing), and diminishing, removing or subordinating the word?

Should we have helped our participants assimilate into the mass of ordinary people, without differentiating themselves from them, or should we have given them the means to decide for themselves the type of contact they would have with the mass culture? Should we hope that these minority groups, having as they do so little voice, join in the mass culture without a critical or discerning eye? Shouldn't the minority groups be demanding recognition of their distinctiveness?

Are academics the only ones asking these questions, or are they also being posed by those who became members of a minority group because of the kind of social decisions they made? Aspiring as we did to inculcate a critical outlook in our participants and to stimulate meaningful social change, we were dissatisfied with our work. Abandoning our literacy project remained as one of few options, but we never took that final step.

Unquestionably, there are always people who wish to learn to speak, read and write French. There are still groups that will teach these people what they want to know. Individual and group methodologies exist and volunteer teachers tend to give most attention to developing their students' free expression and powers of analysis. The vast majority of people attending these groups are political refugees; there are also Turkish immigrants and a few Belgians. They are all adults.

We turned for assistance to other languages and another methodology. At that time (nothing happens by chance), the team met an artist who wanted to give his art a social dimension. He had conducted experiments in some villages which showed him that artistic creation combined with work in a social context provided a means to portray the identity of a group or community. Becoming aware of one's identity and making an image of it would generate opportunities for change.

We decided to set up an initial project experiment in which **art** and **community** were closely linked, with a group of Turkish immigrants in Marche-en-Famenne.

Our action now is with **second-level literacy**, that is:

- a reappropriation of the group's cultural identity through its use of art as language,

- a codification of the group's use of art as language to compare its cultural identity with the cultural identities of groups that have been assimilated into the mass culture.

Both the language and the image required investigation.

CULTURAL MEDIATION

Social & Environmental Context

The town of Marche-en-Famenne, in the province of Luxembourg, has a population of 5,000, and is surrounded by nine small villages with a total of 10,000 inhabitants. The major town is in an area that has the typically rural characteristics of a widely dispersed population, an exodus from the country to the cities, no education beyond secondary school, small farm operations, the quasi-necessity of owning a car, tourism of extreme importance ("Durbuy, the world's smallest town"), Marche is the centre of activities for the area, service industries are highly developed, and there are many professionals.

Until you look more closely, Marche appears to be a "marvellous place for a holiday," a reflection of the province of Luxembourg. However, social housing is a major feature of the area (more than 2,000 people live in low-cost housing), jobs are scarce, unemployment is high, more and more families coming from the city find shelter in hazardous dwellings such as the trailers and cottages usually set aside for tourists. These families thought that they would be able to find what they are seeking in an area that affords very few opportunities.

Our project was conducted in the low-cost La Fourche housing development. La Fourche has 600 inhabitants in 150 dwellings, of whom 200 are of Turkish origin.

The first few Turkish families arrived in Marche in the 1970s, attracted by the then thriving forestry industry. Today, a large proportion of this immigrant community is unemployed. A small immigrant community in a rural area, it all looks so uncomplicated. And yet, the problem of cultural identity is evident both within the community itself and in its relationships with others. Traditions and customs remain very strong in this Muslim community. The fear of losing any part of its Turkish identity forces the community to turn inward and to perpetuate the rules of conduct that were the norm in Turkey 20 years ago.

The **Turkish Faces and Landscapes** project was carried out in this community.

At the outset, neither La Chenille social association nor Le Crean artistic association (set up by the artist) was financially able to conduct a project of this type, so they did it as volunteers, receiving special technical assistance from the Maison de la culture [cultural centre], which was becoming involved in continuing education and community development.

The social worker received a half-time salary from the Maison de la culture, and the artist was unemployed, taken on under an unemployment reduction program. Most of the other counsellors were volunteers.

Objectives

Our goal was to uncover the forms of expression used by a particular community in order to assist the community in defining and portraying its own identity. It is only when a community can recognize itself and be recognized by others that it can look to the future. Its self-awareness engenders a dynamic and creative attitude that leads to changes being desired and chosen. Our primary goal was to develop the community's skills and independence in terms of its lifestyle, its life environment and its degree of integration into the rest of society.

Tools

In order to make our project more easily understood, definitions of three concepts — cultural identity, art as language, and mediator — are required.

Cultural identity

In an environment that is atrophying and in decline, a generalized defeatist attitude prevents individuals and groups from planning or even imagining development projects. The mass culture obliterates individual characteristics, as well as the dynamic and creative attitudes that lead to a variety of desired and chosen changes. The mass culture generates a fear of what is different.

It is impossible to foresee changes if at the outset one does not have a liberating, positive image of one's identity that can influence the vitality of the individual and the group. We therefore placed our emphasis on the discovery or rediscovery of the group's cultural identity, their acceptance of it, and its ability to communicate that identity to others.

Art as language

Words are charged with the emotions and meanings that were incorporated into the dominant language. Those with whom we worked did not know how to use intellectual language, and it was therefore inaccessible to them. If we were obliged to use it, an obstacle was created and change became impossible. On the other hand, art is a means of expression with which we can tell stories without having to speak. A picture can paint a thousand words. The community's identity can be expressed through the images, and it can see itself.

Mediators

All of the activities were carried out by a two-member team of social workers and artists (the "workshop leaders"), who acted as mediators. Their goals were to decode the community's use of art as language, in relation to form and substance, as well as to issues of conflict and consensus within the community. As well, they hoped to codify or recodify the community's expressed views, in order to begin the appropriation or reappropriation of its identity; and further, to create artistic products that are the shape and colour of the community's repressed social sentiments. Once developed and perfected, these artistic products would provide the community with a way to describe itself to others, in other words, developing identity. And finally, to create conditions conducive to the receipt of the community's message, as expressed in art, by others, and to ensure that they cannot avoid coming into contact with the community's expression of its identity.

ARTISTIC EXPRESSION OF THE SUBCULTURE

Developing the Symbolic Language

Rather than inviting you to visit the **Turkish Faces and Landscapes** show, we shall try to have you experience how it came to be. First of all, let us consider the show as a painting. Painting is made up of **forms, colours**, and **lines**. Without these three elements, there is no image, as without letters or words, there are no sentences.

Clearly, if spectators are to see themselves in an image, they must look at it; and so the image must invite spectators to look at it. In the image, spectators must find themselves: not only a representation of themselves, but also forms, colours, and lines that are their own, thus reflecting a particular life environment and social group; what could be called the artistic expression of a subculture. However, while there certainly is community artistic activity, there is no independent community artistic production (the residents do not decide on the architectural form of the social housing development). The artistic expression of the subculture is hidden or implicit in the day-to-day environment.

In the workshops and during the preparation for the show, similar forms, colours and lines appear in the art produced by various participants (which includes art from children's workshops, interior carpets, paintings, photos of artists, and traditional lace). We have called these **formal similarities**. Using them, we can construct a system of signs of this particular environment: a symbolic language of the subculture. In the community's artistic environment, this language of the subculture, unfamiliar or repressed, is not known and very much in a minority situation. Our purpose will be to bring it into the mainstream. How?

Any artistic construct is based on a sign that co-ordinates the visual balance of the work, made up of the system of colours, forms and lines used in the image. Visual balance achieved using this sign makes possible coherent expression and effective communication, two elements that are essential if spectators are to look at an image and understand it or project themselves into it. And, if spectators are to recognize themselves in an image, the sign underlying the composition of the image must be part of the artistic language of the spectators' subculture. We must structure the show on the basis of this sign of the subculture, and surround spectators with it, so they will be caught up in an interaction between the overall structure and the exhibits. These exhibits carry within them the sign of the subculture, or a part of that sign: the repetition of forms, colours and lines has made it possible to discover and construct this sign.

Thus surrounded, spectators are at home or, rather, inside what is in themselves, inside something that is their own; they are inside something unfamiliar that is nonetheless themselves. In short, spectators are pleasantly surprised to find themselves there. We must take advantage of that fact.

Confronting Diversity & Conflict

The other important element of our approach is to confront diversity and the revealing nature of conflict smoothly. The formal similarities extend beyond the exhibits and beyond images representing negative or painful tensions. Images are thus perceived through an internal language, produced by oneself and thus acceptable and recognizable. People recognize their conflicting tensions and the sign of the subculture — a sort of common sign — that organizes these tensions esthetically. If this sign is common, it can be shared. The "dark side", the other, conflicting, side of oneself, becomes no longer frightening.

We shall outline here what has made it possible to identify the artistic expression of the subculture of the Turkish community in Marche-en-Famenne, starting with an initial show and celebration organized by the community itself, and based on our creative expression workshops for the Turkish children. We shall then give an outline of the **Turkish Faces and Landscapes show** in order to demonstrate how various and even opposing groups are brought into relationship during the workshop process, how the art produced as a result of this coming together appears, and how the sign of the subculture appears in that art.

REPRESSION & SIGN OF IDENTITY

As part of a celebration organized by the Turkish community at the Maison de la culture in Marche-en-Famenne, the Turkish community shows exhibits and reconstructs a living space combining tradition and modernity. In this midst of all this is a painting by a Turkish child. At the show, we can discover curious similarities between place mats and embroidery: the composition of both types of work is very geometric, and the small, lively touches of colour have the effect of beadwork. The subject matter and vibrant colour of the symbolic carpets are the same as those of the embroidery and paintings. Among many books of the Koran, a single one has been selected for the show. It, too, has the same vibrancy and fine mosaic motif.

Artistic Expression of Children

At the creative expression workshops for the neighbourhood children, we had already noted that, whether in the form of flecks, dots, blemishes on a face in a painting, or fragments of images, the fine mosaic motif is omnipresent. Other parameters are present. The carpet is traditional among the Turks; in our culture, the window is the picture frame. They make squares filled with colour: objects of beauty, unencumbered by narration.

Boys paint very differently than girls. They throw colour onto the paper in bold stokes. Initially they use lively colours; then they mix everything together, erasing their mosaics, and everything is turned to brown. We are reminded of modern, abstract art — Tapiès, Dubuffet, Pollock —, and we could exhibit these paintings as works of art. But, in so doing, we would seek to justify our own artistic expression, not that of the children: unlike artists, children are unaware of the art they are producing.

The interior decoration of the workshop and the houses in which the Turkish young people live has a much greater influence on the art they produce than does artistic culture. The colour of the walls, the calligraphy of texts of Turkish chants, and the relationship between the subject matter and light on tourist posters reappear in the way the young people handle brushes and use colour. When imagination is lacking, however, they all start to paint Turkish flags. For them, unlike us, the flag is a real symbol, which people still hang in their homes. Eventually, in order to staunch this apparent hemorrhage, we even had to advise that red not be used.

Although these sociocultural elements are determining factors in the art the children produce, the essence of the creative expression workshop is to have each child discover and accept their own forms, so that their creations are increasingly individual. The exercise is a simple one. It consists in having participants compose a collage of photos cut from a magazine, and then comparing the collage to a painting. After this comparative decoding, it will be noted that individuals each have their own forms. Often, these forms are hidden in one way or another. Individuals repress or are unaware of their own artistic potential, their own symbolic register.

Artistic Expression of groups

Despite two changes to the interior decoration of the neighbourhood house, the wallpaper of the room reserved for the children has not disappeared. The children have always objected to having it removed; but it is not Turkish at all: the mother of a social worker had donated it in order to decorate the house.

At the show, we had not wanted to show the children's favourite painting: dark green with yellow and blue spots. We feared that it would give the Turkish community a negative connotation in the eyes of the Belgians. The children wanted it to be shown. We said no. The young people asked for the same thing, and were also refused. Then the adults went to get the painting and hung it on the wall themselves.

When a community wants a work and decides to show it alongside familiar objects, it does so because, in that image, the community sees itself. Although the meaning of this artistic expression cannot be explained, we think it is a sign of identity, or the sign of an identity. The wallpaper had blue and yellow foliage with green stems, on a white background. The similarities between the painting and the wallpaper are clear: one is the negative of the other. Like individuals, then, groups each have their own artistic expression.

Artistic Expression of the Subculture

We seem to have here an artistic expression that belongs to the environment, the community and the neighbourhood and could be called an **artistic expression of the subculture**. These artistic similarities appeared regularly during creative workshops organized in various regions of the country. Artistic expression of the subculture, then, does seem to exist. We shall give here an example of artistic expression of the subculture that was apparently discovered by accident. It was on the basis of this discovery that we designed the **Turkish Faces and Landscapes** show.

REVEALING CONFRONTATION

In a village called La Forge, we had asked contemporary and traditional artists, both amateur and professional, to paint pictures on the subject of the forge. In so doing, we highlighted both the village's name and its lost economic activity. At the same time, we met the residents, by age group, and asked them about their past history and present experiences.

The young people told us that, whatever they did, there was no point: why bother? If they worked in the city, they would no longer live in the village: why bother? If they worked in the village, they would have to build a house; for reasons of costs, the house would have to be modern; a modern house would make the village uglier: why bother? If a house were to be kept as it is, it would have to be sold to other people, with money, who would restore it: why bother! For the old people, things have been finished for a long time. The last forge closed in the 1960s. For them, as for the young people, there is neither hope nor identity.

In the show, at our request, the village residents each indicated their favourite work. Among the old people, the favourite was a painting of a blacksmith at work, depicted naturally and done by an amateur. The young people chose an ecoline-enhanced photograph of the village landscape described as a nuclear explosion. For the old people, "It's gone," and for the young people, "Everything's gone."

In this void, what esthetic similarities exist? The two works, in differing styles, are based on the use of the same colours: red, blue, and green. Visitors — tourists or village residents from the surrounding area — chose a very different painting, in blue-gray tones. Red, blue and green are the colours of the village residents, the colours of their absence of prospects, their socio-economic repression, their sociocultural impasse.

Showing the facts as they are can only be an affront to the village residents, making them turn inward, and thus preventing any message from having an effect. Indeed, the young people denied what they had said at the time of the survey. If we show this reality by means of symbolism — which, as is shown by the choice of favourite works, reflects life experiences, results from those experiences and is recognized as doing so — people could see the reality of the facts. On the basis of this theory, we decided on the design of the **Turkish Faces and Landscapes show**.

The theory put forward here is also based on observations made in the pictorial expression workshops where the process is the same: bringing together the artistic expression of the individual and that of the subculture of that person's life environment. When these two expressions meet, the confrontation is revealing. In it, the individual seems to say, "I do exist, as I am, in a social group that recognizes me. I no longer have to be afraid of the outside world or defend myself from it. The criticism and self-criticism that victimize me and that I have imposed upon myself are falling away. I can open up." When this esthetic confrontation takes place, artistic progress follows.

What is experienced in the creative expression workshops must also be produced on visitors by the show. Visitors, however, do not paint. They must therefore be placed in a similar situation. The various components and coincidences of this confrontation must be reconstituted.

A TURKISH CHILD

We shall try to follow this evolution through the paintings of a Turkish child. We remind readers of the frequent appearance of the fine mosaic motif. Initially, we liked it very much: an abstract painting that professionals would envy. But the child is not pleased; he has to add those small mosaic touches, and the colour is made less lively. Still he is not satisfied, so he folds the sheet of paper in half, bringing the two sides together. We are disappointed; he is delighted.

Two interpretations are possible: either the child has ruined his painting and does not want to admit that to himself, or he really has done what he wanted. How can we tell? We had photographed three stages of this painting. We then showed these three paintings to all the groups of Turkish people who regularly visited the neighbourhood house: women, girls, children, men, and Belgians as well. The Belgians preferred the first painting; the Turks, the third one. These preferences must be significant.

We then suggest to the child that he paint using only small touches of colour, and instruct him only not to mix the colours, an instruction that both respects and contradicts the artistic expression of the child's subculture. When the child has finished the mosaic of the painting, he cannot help folding the sheet of paper in half. In doing so, he is not trying to make a butterfly; he wants to recreate the vibrant colour in the favourite painting that was brought to the show: the painting that resembles its positive image, the wallpaper in the children's room.

One evening, a film is shown on television; the following day, a painting is made to tell about it. The story was about a sheep; the child paints a landscape. The technique is that of a child, but the shape of the trees and clouds and the colours are the same as the involuntary arabesques of the third abstract painting whose evolution is described above. The following day, the child makes two paintings: two faces, which is surprising for a Muslim, and a landscape. The trees in the landscape are large in the foreground and small in the background; a black line in the foreground is lighter in the background: the painting shows perspective.

While the confrontation between the artistic expression of the individual and that of the subculture leads to artistic progress, it is also accompanied by progress in an individual's social and emotional relationships, that is, in that person's social side.

Today, this child is an adult. He has left Marche with his parents for a large city, found work there and, like every good Turkish child, brings all the money to his father, to the family. At the age of 18, in order to feel free, he needs a bit of money. So he has to steal it... and he gets caught. At a time like this, what does he think about, whom does he think about? He thinks about the painting he wanted to learn; he has come back to see us; and he would even like to come back to live and work in Marche.

VISITING THE SHOW

The colours of the posters announcing the show are white, pink and light blue. We noticed that this colour combination often appeared, as if these were lost colours, colours from home, from Turkey. As well, these colours often appear in the children's paintings, which, for the occasion, we moulded in polyester to make a carpet. Take off your shoes when you come in: we are in a part of the Turkish community. But that does not mean that people may not look each other fully in the face.

Looking Inside, Looking Outside

The women participants in the painting workshop made the Turkish men open up. For the show, the Turkish men chose portraits, regardless of style or quality, that best represented each of the women portrait painters. The women painters tried to get the Turkish women to open up, to be painted at home, and were categorically refused.

And the Belgian women, acting out of their own culture and habit, had to go home and make supper for their husbands and children, while the men, acting out of their own perceived position, followed the women in their cars and ogled them a little on the way home.

Formal Similarities & Social Analogies

Pieces of Ardennes lace, the creations of our grandmothers in the 1950s and Marche's heritage — still alive in the Walloon regions (as it is in Bruges and Brussels) — are shown alongside creations by the Turkish women of the neighbourhood. Once an activity of the poorest people, today lace-making is a fine craft. Is it a folk, ethnic, cultural or artistic activity? It is impossible to tell.

What we had already observed in the first show, the similarity between the fine mosaic motif, the subject matter and the vibrant colour, reappears in the stitches of lace. We shall compare here the work of a farm woman and a Venetian man, in both of which we shall see the fine mosaic motif reappear, and we shall use those works to enhance our perception of another piece of lacework.

Simone, the farm woman, offers a Nativity scene that she has painted herself, in order to put an end to racism. "After all," she says, "the three wise men had skins of different colours." The Turks tell us that the Virgin Mary is buried in their country, to our great surprise: we Christians believed she had ascended to heaven!

Italo makes masks using the faces painted by the children. Although in Islamic culture there are no masks, the masks are inspired by the children's drawings. They are covered with small touches of colour.

FROM CULTURAL MELTING POT TO MUTUAL MARGINALIZATION

A lampshade in lace, but in a contemporary style and, as it happens, in the Turks' favourite colours, pink and blue: formal similarity again — and, as well, a similarity of marginalization. How so?

This work by a local craftswoman was refused by the lace makers in Marche, who claimed, "You don't make coloured lace. Real lace is white!"

The immigrants' artistic activity and the local contemporary artistic activity, then, are both mutually exclusive and mutually similar.

Breaking Away

In order to bring the show smoothly to its conclusion, the decoration created used the forms and colours of the environment: small touches of pink and blue. As well, the floor was covered with a carpet made of children's paintings, moulded in polyester. This carpet, instead of limiting spectators' view with a vertical hanging of the paintings, was warm and solid underfoot: something on which to stand, something solid on which to rely for the future. Each element of the space a show occupies must have meaning. In the last exhibit, the Turkish women recreated a Turkish interior, a marriage bedchamber. The women came often during the show, the old women alone, the young women brought by their husbands. It was certainly an important exhibit.

Young adolescent women met in this room and danced for us, in front of Belgian men, something that was strictly forbidden. The Turkish men promptly came to put a stop to such dancing in public. But a breaking away had already formed part of the community's memory, to surface again as circumstances dictated. Six years later, Turkish women in traditional dress came to a neighbourhood dance without their husbands.

Before leaving, we stop at the painting commissioned by the municipality and done by an artist with the group of Turkish young people who regularly visited the neighbourhood house. Many discussion sessions were necessary for them to be able to tell their story, that is, to determine their own perspective, composition and colours. One may speak of women and mosques in the same breath, but not depict them side by side. How can this apparent contradiction, this criticism, be shown and made acceptable?

Familiar places, the hope of returning, homesickness: ochre, blue, pink. The comparison between this commissioned painting and the art produced at the children's creative expression workshops, and with the analysis of the forms and colours that dominate the interiors and favourite objects, sets the tone for the design of the show. Various activities have helped uncover this particular artistic expression. When the members of the Turkish community saw all this, they were silent, they spoke out, and they became angry.

The girls understood everything about the painting, but do not think that this type of pictorial experiment is appropriate for them right now. They go to a Catholic secondary school, whose administrators would certainly have some difficulty accepting the artist who did the commissioned painting.

Different cultures have different impasses.

When people open the invitation, they see that the accompanying map of the neighbourhood resembles a caterpillar. We did not design it that way on purpose; the neighbourhood was designed by the architect. And it was the children who live in this neighbourhood who named the neighbourhood house La Chenille. The spatial design of architecture influences the spontaneity of residents and their process of creating symbols. This unconscious relationship between art, society and expression, then, is analyzed and verified.

REFLECTIONS

What is the purpose of all these theories, observations and analyses?

If an individual or group is to indicate its social needs, it must be able to express itself. Expression assumes a language. Every language is the result of a history. How can a language be invented if this history is not recognized? For a language to have meaning for itself and for others, it must have signs that have meaning, for the language and for others; otherwise there is no communication. To recognize one's history and one's signs is to **create symbols**, something that is **necessary** for any form of expression and communication. In order to change, however, one must have accepted a self-image that is realistic and free of negativity and guilt about the societal causes of one's situation.

This is the purpose of creative workshop leadership: **to initiate a way out of sociocultural impasses**; without such a way out, any discourse on independence must be illusory. Prominent exploits are always possible, but they lead nowhere.

Genuine change at the local level cannot be expected without the means to implement this kind of activity at the regional level.

Chapter 11

OPENING UP LEARNING — RESPONDING TO THE LITERACY NEEDS OF THE RURAL COMMUNITIES

Sue Buss, Julia Clarke, Sue Craggs,
Sue Grief, Mary Hamilton,
Catherine Sauzier
United Kingdom

RURAL STUDENTS & OPEN LEARNING

The five case histories described here represent different practices of delivery, and were chosen because they depended upon action research to some extent, and involved ideas of open learning. The term "open learning" has several possible meanings,[1] which are relevant to rural education. In its wider sense, this indicates provision which is not limited by place, time, or the need for previous qualifications, so that any student may make use of it in a way appropriate to his or her needs. It may include attendance at a learning centre either regularly or occasionally, the use of telephone tutorials, written assignments, or individual study projects.

The second definition of Open Learning is a more precise one, connected with the use of individual study in a centre where there is access to computers and other information technology, audio and video tapes, and possibly local closed-circuit television. Tutors are available, but do not generally work one- to-one with students, and are seen as a shared resource, along with the printed and electronic materials.[2] Both meanings are referred to in the case studies, as both are useful to many rural students in particular contexts.[3]

RURAL AREAS & ADULT LITERACY IN THE UNITED KINGDOM

World-wide, there is a movement of population and economic power from the rural areas to the towns. In Britain, this process has been evident for at least 200 years, since the Industrial Revolution, and now means that most people live in towns.

The experience of some other European countries, of villages with aging populations almost deserted by young people, is less evident in Britain. Where depopulation is serious, it has often resulted from outsiders buying houses as second homes, at a price local people cannot afford. This has created half- empty villages in some popular holiday areas of Wales, Cumbria and East Anglia. In the past, the effect was countered by the availability of new, cheap housing owned by the local council and offered at subsidized rents; these allowed families to stay in their home area. Since the 1980s, local councils have been discouraged from building subsidized housing.

Town dwellers, including retired people, may move out to the countryside to find quieter surroundings. With the growth of computer-based businesses, some newcomers set up work at home, but make minimal contact with the local working community. Many of these affluent migrants have ignored the traditional social life of the district, with its complex network of related families, and its beliefs and customs. Younger members of local families may welcome the freedom and choice of action which has resulted, and the opportunity for school and college education, and urban-style entertainments. There has, however, been almost no effect in creating a strong base of local employment where the same young people can find work, or aim for promotion to managerial level, except for some services, such as school teaching and catering.

Because of mechanization, farming now occupies a fraction of its original workforce, and often less than a fifth of the present population. Employment is often seasonal, as in the holiday industry, and in farming at harvest time or lambing. Local contractors may take over the farm-based work of ploughing and combine harvesting. Traditional rural crafts, such as making fences and furniture have declined, because the labour cost makes them uncompetitive with factory-produced, imported products.

Community issues in rural areas have been researched, although rarely with a literacy component. Some organizations such as the Rural Development Council, REPLAN (a government funded body, now disbanded, concerned with unemployed people's education), and the Workers' Educational Association (a voluntary body) have funded short projects to research the needs for rural employment, businesses, transport and adult education.

There is at present (1993) a radical change taking place in the provision of adult literacy in England and Wales, as a direct result of Government policy.

While the necessity for literacy teaching and learning has now been accepted, its funding has been largely centralized and taken out of the control of local government. Until this year the main source of funding and staffing of regular literacy provision were the councils of the separate counties or metropolitan boroughs, along with Government-funded private commercial suppliers of training, and some voluntary schemes.

A variety of styles evolved over the last 15 years, partly because of the initial piecemeal growth of the literacy movement, and partly because of the general philosophy that the style of learning must be determined by local preferences and needs, albeit aimed at individual outcomes. This view accorded well with the traditional British expression of respect for individuality, and amateur (as opposed to professional) organization.

At the same time, action-research projects were organized, many through the Adult Literacy and Basic Skills Unit (ALBSU), a national organization established to promote particular forms of functional literacy. Their support for a philosophy of personal development and achievement became a hallmark of ABE services, with the aims of empowering the individual student to control his or her own learning and destiny. Much of the community-based provision made use of ALBSU's nation-wide network of training and information, by means of newsletters and regional meetings. Adult literacy became known as Adult Basic Education or ABE, and often included tuition in everyday mathematics, and English for Speakers of Other Languages (ESOL).

Since the 1980's, another strand of provision has been the Government funding of private or local authority schemes for training unemployed people for future work. Funding for literacy services is now to be channelled from the central Government through the Colleges of Further Education. Formerly part of the local education provisions, colleges were a source of vocational and certified courses for the 16- to 19-year old age group, and increasingly for older adults returning to formal study. Some colleges already played a part in local literacy work, by setting up classes and short courses with a literacy element, such as Return-to-Learn courses, including writing skills. The colleges have now been made independent and self-managing, no longer controlled by local education authorities. Along with the regional Training and Enterprise Councils, TECs, which receive central funding for vocational training, colleges now have responsibility for the largest share of literacy work.

The effect of the changes in adult education remains to be seen. There is an opportunity to make literacy provision truly open in the more general sense, by giving a choice of styles, and locations of meetings within reach of home.

It is almost certain, however, that any content of community development, present in some former ABE schemes, will be entirely replaced by aims involving the learners' own individual outcomes. There is a danger that these will be defined solely in terms of gaining work, achieving promotion, or progressing to certificated or vocational courses. Community development, such as the wider awareness of the learners' own roles in local society, and of the ways of determining the future prosperity or happiness of that society, will be largely left to chance. There may be a few literacy schemes with such aims, funded under other arrangements, such as local charitable organizations, national business-led trusts, or the European Social Fund.

FIVE CASE STUDIES

An Adult Basic Education GRoup in West Dorset

As in other areas of Britain, the offer of home-based individual tuition using volunteer tutors had formerly been seen as a remedy for the stigma of adult illiteracy. This was coupled with the view that individual tuition would be more effective for people who had failed in large classes at school.

Superficially, provision matched the definition of open learning which emphasises learners' choice in venue, timing, pace, materials and content. Tutors were supplied with resources, training and the support of a local organizer. In Dorset, one-to-one tuition was regarded as particularly appropriate for rural areas.

Attempts by educators or community workers to help others to identify or to articulate their needs are always problematic. This is particularly true with adults whose previous educational encounters may have been associated with failure or humiliation. Such learners will often communicate ambivalent or contradictory messages about their learning "needs". They may assert the wish to achieve success by "going back to basics" in the same oppressive and limited curriculum which led to failure in the past. This learner may alternatively be willing to explore wider approaches to literacy and education, which value his or her experience, and build on achievements in other areas of adult life. In the one-to-one relationship, whether in the home or in an Open Learning Centre, a tutor may support either course of action with the claim that the chosen program is meeting the learner's "needs".

When a group of adult learners with similar experiences is able to meet together, the tutor's control over the construction or interpretation of needs is diminished, while the learners are able to explore a range of possible shared or individual needs in discussion with each other.

In March 1991, a tape recorded discussion was held with such a group of adult learners. They met in Bridport with a paid tutor, jacky and two volunteer helpers. The adult students had a wide range of basic educational needs (literacy, numeracy, ESOL) and were at various stages of achievement and from differing social backgrounds. The group provided a supportive environment and learners followed individual programs.

One student, G., commented on the tutor's contribution:

"She just finds what I need to go on, you see..."

and on the sense of common purpose in the group:

"Well, I find it's good to be together, and everybody has needs: they're all not the same and one can help another... It's a social group. It's not only to read and write but you find each other, and if somebody is not there you are missing them... and you share problems as well."

Vicki explained how her own "curriculum" was extended through the interests of others in the group:

"Well, we learn other people's things like (Liz) and her buses and holidays, and booking up; and we learn off of (Liz) about booking and how she goes about booking; where she gets her pamphlets from."

Chris related this to broader aspects of communication skills:

"Yes, it's all useful. Yes it is... I think I've got more confidence in myself. I talk to people a lot better than I ever used to. I don't mind going back to shops if things go wrong. A while ago I wouldn't do that."

Three of the leaders in this group had previous experience of working with a one-to-one voluntary tutor, but all felt that the group supported a more independent approach to learning. Liz spoke of the volunteer tutors:

"Well, they're with you all the time: they're over your shoulder, but in a group they go round and you can do lots of things on your own."

When it was suggested to Sandra that she might now have the confidence to work without a tutor, she replied:

"I think you need to come as a group. Now I think if I had to do it at home... Well, Jacky wanted me to do "Women: the Way Ahead" (an open learning pack) at home, because I wouldn't be able to get to Waymouth, but I know I wouln't do it. I'm just not motivated enough... It's laziness, isn't it really?"

Any discussion of new models of literacy provision in rural areas must include an emphasis on the importance of social interaction to the learning process. If people are isolated in rural areas by the loss of village communities and the lack of public transport, there is a danger that distance learning approaches will only perpetuate such isolation. People may blame their lack of motivation on their own "laziness", rather than valuing the observation: "You need to come as a group."

The inter-dependance of members requires a commitment to regular attendance at specified times. The funders stipulate a minimum of six regular students to each paid tutor. In small rural communities, subject to the seasonal and casual employment patterns of agriculture and tourism, these numbers are difficult to sustain, this removes some of the flexibility possible with one-to-one placements. Using unsupervised volunteers in smaller groups is rarely an answer; the training and commitment required of a group tutor cannot be expected of a volunteer.

Thus, while a group can offer adult learners the most "open" approach to defining their own needs and curriculum, this is often possible only by imposing "closed" restrictions on timing, attendance and venue.

A Community Education Project in Peer Tutoring With Young Adults

In Suffolk, a grant was obtained for a two-year project from the Rural Development Commission. The aims of the project were to identify the reasons for the low referral rate to ABE, and to establish flexible opportunities in the area to cater for local needs of young people. Suffolk Association of Youth already ran a scheme in Ipswich, the largest town in the county, using young people of 16 to 25 years of age to teach other young people who wanted to learn to read. They wanted to discover whether the scheme could be extended to rural areas.

Two ABE project workers were appointed, for 5 hours each per week, one specifically to work with adults under 25 years of age. A considerable investment was made in publicity, both in printed leaflets and in staff time. Volunteer tutors were recruited and trained, and matched with new students. Some tuition took place in the homes, but church halls, community rooms and youth clubs were used when appropriate.

The use of one-to-one tutors, as previously discussed, had advantages in the flexible timing of sessions, but serious disadvantages in the lack of interaction between students. The careful process of matching students with suitable volunteers involved a complex set of factors, including personality, age, sex, and places where the participants lived and could meet. Many young people did not have their own transport, and there were considerations of confidentiality. All these factors led to frequent delays in matching.

As a solution to the needs of rural learning, one-to-one cannot deliver truly "open" learning, and the cost of supporting tutors makes it an expensive method. The cost of a truly "open" provision in a rural area will always be greater than in a town.

An alternative way to make provision more "open" in terms of place and time would have been the use of resources for independent learning. This was not possible, as the available learning packs offered a "closed" content, not suited to individual students' needs, particularly at a more basic level. A decision had to be made whether to spend the modest funding on training and support of staff, or on staff time to develop packs of learning material responsive to individuals' needs. One of the deciding factors to use the funding for tutors, was the practice of the Suffolk Association of Youth as co-leaders. They saw a greater value in developing the relationship of the young people concerned. Therefore independent learning was seen as less appropriate.

In the two years, about thirty people took up literacy and numeracy tuition in the area. Half were in the 16 to 25 age range. Awareness of the local service was increased, and referrals to regular provision continued after the project ended.

A Workshop in A Tertiary College

North Devon Tertiary College is the largest single provider of further education and training for adults and young people over sixteen years. The college aims to serve the needs of a large rural area with a population of 120,000 and receives funding for the development of Adult Basic Education. A recent growth in the college population increased students with lower levels of attainment in basic skills which presents the challenge of providing effective help to enable them to meet individual goals in education. A local development project was launched to develop core skills, across the college curriculum and to create 'open learning' provision for adults in the North Devon community.

The college chose the title of *Core Skills* in preference to Basic Skills because it focuses on the essential skills which are at the core of most education and training. Core skills encompass Basic Skills: reading, writing, listening, speaking, numeracy and English for speakers of other languages. In addition they include the learning skills increasingly required for recent developments in Tertiary Education placing a greater emphasis on project work, resource based learning, independent study, and the use of information technology.

The major task of the project has been to establish a new Core Skills Workshop in a redesigned centre for independent and supported study. Resources have been acquired which have a particular emphasis on independent learning and linked vocational skills which enable students to extend their study at home.

Part of our induction procedure includes an exploration of the best places to study. This is an issue for many students but particularly for parents who may not have established a set time or a private place for independent study. Such decisions may affect other members of the family and therefore it is necessary to incorporate: time management, negotiation, assertiveness, study skills, together with the specific skills of literacy in order to be able to study at home. The success or failure of individual efforts to return to study will often depend on the degree of support from other family members.

The workshop has proved to be attractive to adults for several reasons. Students may attend the workshop whenever they wish — they are not committed to set times. For many adults the workshop is their first contact with the college. The opportunity to improve basic skills provides an opening to further education and training and many adults progress to further courses with greater confidence. An increasing number of mature students are referred to the workshop at the time of interview, to develop specific core skills for a vocational area. Existing adult students refer themselves to the workshop to develop skills to support their main studies.

Open Learning provision has been supplemented by short courses such as 'Return to Study' which combines study skills with information and guidance. Many adults are apprehensive about returning to study. The workshop provides a supportive environment and a positive approach to meet individual needs.

The focus on mature students within the project should not detract from a consideration of the needs of young adult students within tertiary education who generally do not seek help with basic skills. The establishment of the Core Skills Workshop in the heart of a tertiary college has made it easier for younger students to acquire this. Forty-eight percent of the self-referred workshop students were young people aged between 16 and 18 years. Younger students have responded positively to the adult environment of the workshop where they have been encouraged to take responsibility for their own learning.

Working With Ethnic Minority Adults in A Rural Area

The Huntingdon area of Cambridgeshire is rural, but experienced a period of rapid economic and demographic expansion in the 1980's, mainly in three towns, Huntingdon, St Neots and St Ives. The level of unemployment was relatively low and newcomers were generally attracted by cheap housing and job opportunities in expanding local industries. For many years two air force bases also supported the local economy.

Nevertheless, some people have been experiencing the phenomenon of "rural disadvantage". These include some of the members of ethnic minority groups living in the Huntingdon area, recently estimated to number about 2,500 (2% of the local population). Through local research it was possible to recognize a range of educational and vocational backgrounds, reasons for coming to Britain, family and economic circumstances, and length of residence (up to 50 years in some cases) with an increasing number of young people born and educated in the area.

This part of Cambridgeshire has been slow to recognize and respond to the multicultural dimension of its population. Many people in areas such as this still view Britain as a homogeneous society with unchanged, unchangeable traditions; any newcomer is seen at best as an unfortunate problem and at worst as a downright threat to stability. Such attitudes have not always been helped by the criteria attached to central government funding for identifying and meeting their needs.

Since 1966, when the additional needs of ethnic minorities were recognized, the Home Office (the government department responsible for immigration issues) has given substantial funding to county councils. When the provision of separate external funding is too closely identified with English language deficiency, institutions may ignore the wider social and educational needs of speakers of other languages. It also places the onus on individuals to "learn more English" before attempting progression into education and vocational training, access to public services or full participation in society.

In Cambridgeshire most such funding was allocated to teaching posts in schools. Occasionally, as in the Huntingdon area, projects were also funded which had a community development dimension as well as a teaching role. In this case, over the 947 square kilometres, English language provision for adults amounted to ten hours per week for thirty weeks in the year, providing five groups in three towns. There was also some home-based one-to-one tuition.

The full-time organizer of English language support, which included literacy and numeracy, was also required to ensure the development of appropriate community support, both in accordance with the County Council's policy and in response to identified needs.

Increasingly the fieldworkers recognized that effective communication is a two-way process, and they realized that traditional styles of language learning were likely to be useless where transport problems isolated the learners. Further, the majority population was monolingual and generally had little language awareness.

The organizer's role therefore shifted from self-sufficient language teacher, trainer and organizer to a more outward-looking approach combining management, marketing and entrepreneurial skills. Much of the organizer's time was spent on establishing links with other education providers, networking to raise awareness of discriminating practices, promoting a small team of community interpreters to improve communication, and raising awareness of learners' needs and the use of the community as a resource for that learning.

For most adults, learning a new language is an exceedingly slow process which can suddenly disintegrate in precisely those moments of crisis when they most need to communicate effectively. The learning is hardly helped in areas where the rest of the community prides itself on being both "colour-blind" and "culture-blind".

Other people's perceptions of minority cultures can be extraordinarily limiting. Firstly by ignoring the rich heritage that ethnic minority individuals and groups have brought with them; secondly by denying them opportunities to maintain this culture through public services; and thirdly by failing to appreciate the dynamic nature of all cultures which not only change as a result of being transposed to a new environment, but also from generation to generation and even from one individual to the next.

Working With Unemployment in West Cumbria

West Cumbria Trades Hall Centre was established in Workington in 1981, to offer help to redundant workers after the closure of the foundry and iron works.

Other branches of national firms lost workers or closed down after this. By 1992 the unemployment rate was 18%. A project was needed to retrain people for new work, to set up local networks, and to lobby the authorities for better facilities such as housing and transport. At present, contributions come from three levels of local government and the work was administered by Cumbria Open Learning Trust.

The Centre provided educational guidance, computer classes, and referral to mainstream Adult Basic Education groups when desired. The coordinator was supported by a fixed term post of Project Worker, who also ran the Job Club, and a part time administrative officer. Volunteers were trained, largely for advice work, and some were recruited from the original clients.

A survey of nearly 200 local unwaged people's interests in education[4] found that most had left school with no formal qualifications, or had not studied beyond the then school-leaving certificate (CSE). The need for basic skills provision was confirmed by requests for English and simple maths, as well as a wide range of craft and hobbies courses.

The Trades Hall Centre undertook to publicize local educational opportunities, and to improve cooperation between agencies such as the health and social services, training organizations, churches and employers. In February 1992, a conference was organized to raise awareness in local and central government agencies of unemployed people's concerns. The proposed agenda for action included increasing the pressure for: partnerships between agencies, more development funds and housing, improvements in local facilities such as roads, training and equal opportunities for local people, provision of more jobs and improved working conditions and finally, support from local and national government.

Adult Learners' Week in 1992, a national event promoted by the National Institute for Adult and Continuing Education (NIACE) was an opportunity for publicity including a travelling exhibition in local libraries, and a market stall.

Outcomes have included personal gains in education, awareness of local issues, and ways to achieve self-help in looking for work. The computer courses were popular, and the provision of newspapers and Job Club notices were useful. It is difficult to see effects in the community as a whole, especially since much of the funding has now disappeared. The functional literacy element, however, has been noted, and the development of volunteers' skills through training. One Member of Parliament was quoted as estimating that each unemployed person costs the national economy £10,000 per year. Some of this could be recovered, and the people's dignity restored, if funds were put into creating local work projects.

GENERAL ISSUES

The need for partnerships

Literacy work needs to be linked with other activities, and may involve several agencies. Each case study illustrates different partnerships, showing some of the diversity which is possible in effective ABE work. Dorset emphasizes partnerships between the learners themselves. North Devon Core Skills Workshop argues the importance of linking literacy with vocational studies, and by involving other subject lecturers. The other three cases include partnerships between local agencies such as the Youth Service, funding bodies, and county councils. Cumbria has developed close links of ABE with practical issues, mainly employment.

Organizing resources

Resources include people, facilities, and learning materials. Practical access to transport and premises is of major concern to overcome rural isolation.

The types of resources and the teaching and learning styles which they best support have been discussed, and the variety of ways these may be organized in rural areas. The potential value of distance learning and individual study is set beside the need for more personal support where appropriate. The human resources of fellow learners, and of adequately prepared tutors are vital in maintaining the students' motivation, and counteracting personal isolation.

Open Learning Centres can offer distance learning resources such as packs, and audio and video tapes. Loan of printed materials may have to be organized by postal deliveries. Telephone and taped tutorials have been used in Leicestershire, with occasional meetings of small groups with a professional tutor.[5] All have cost implications.

Training and support of staff

Professional quality training enables local people to become effective tutors in their own home areas. In order to encourage a student-centred philosophy of ABE, the training needs to include counselling skills as well as teaching methods and the ability to use these flexibly in response to students' interests.

The importance in rural areas of adequately trained and supervised volunteers is reflected in one of the case studies. Some new students may need intensive support at first, preferring alternative styles of learning later on. There is a need to think again about the problems and potentials of involving volunteers in literacy provision. It is not a cheap option.

Training of ABE workers in community development methods is occasionally attempted. A suitable package, including marketing methods, was produced by REPLAN.[6]

Relationships between students and tutors

The ultimate aim of tutors should be to encourage self-directed learning. The five case studies offer a range of examples from intense to fairly impersonal involvement with tutors. The risks of employing under-qualified volunteers or paid staff has been discussed, when a possessive and limiting relationship can prevent the widening of horizons. Clearly, a relationship which depends on domination by the tutor or the curriculum is very unlikely to introduce wider issues, or to allow the student to develop his or her sense of autonomy and social effectiveness.

Respecting and responding to different cultures

In rural areas, there is a variety of lifestyles and cultural groups. New immigrant populations present a challenge to the traditional culture of the area. Whether these incomers are sophisticated and affluent people, or are more disadvantaged economic migrants seeking work, their relationship with the local mainstream culture cannot be left to chance. As the recent experience of other European countries has demonstrated, lack of respect for the differences between cultures, and narrow perceptions of other people's lifestyles can have devastating effects.

This indicates a need for the careful initial assessment of learning requirements, not only of individuals, but of whole local populations. The Cumbrian project, by surveying local opinion, came nearest to an objective appraisal of local patterns, even though these were related mainly to work. Equal Opportunities issues, i.e. the respecting of other people's different needs and opinions, must be brought openly into discussions, as in the Cambridgeshire project. This attempted to educate the local community, and not merely to teach life skills to minority groups.

Funding

In some ways, funding has been the major factor affecting the style and effectiveness of literacy teaching in Britain, as shown in these examples, and in the experience of many ABE workers. The quantity of funding, and the conditions attached to a grant, (target clients, required aims and outcomes, time scale, etc.) have had profound influence on the philosophy of projects, and their survival.

The effects of an initiative may take years to become apparent. Adult education is not a cheap service, because of the cost of professional tutors' pay, resources, travel expenses, and items such as creches, all of which are necessary in scattered rural populations. Tutor training and support are necessary to the quality of teaching and the relationship with students. Publicity is indispensable, for attracting new students, and as a tool for raising awareness in other people.

Resources may be expendable, or need to be distributed by post. Telephone contact is important for referrals and on-going support. There is a high student/ teacher ratio, and some students make progress very slowly. Therefore Adult Basic Education will always be labour and resource intensive, even in Open Learning settings, and costly to support.

REFLECTIONS ON LITERACY PROVISION

Much of the information available on the effects of literacy provision is anecdotal, whether it refers to former learners, or to their communities.

Research into the effects of local history classes on the views of their participants[7] suggested that outcomes were largely decided by the overt aims and teaching content of a course. Reflection on social issues, and the relevance of history studies to present day conditions, was not considered by students unless it was written into the curriculum, and discussed purposefully. It may be that larger local issues in literacy should be included in interactions with students, so that they can identify not only their own needs, but the underlying causes of local problems, and ways to address these.

In the present political climate of Britain, such awareness of social needs is not officially encouraged. Government control of literacy funding through the Further Education Funding Council has recently made some of its allocation conditional upon outcomes such as the numbers of learners achieving jobs or entry to further courses. This limitation of possible outcomes fits another aspect of traditional philosophy of adult education in Britain, which considers the teacher to be more capable than the students. Even recent emphasis on student-centred approaches still encourages tutors to respond to students rather than to hand over complete control.

There is, however, a strong base of practical experience among ABE tutors in Britain. They tend to plan and carry out the work with a pragmatic approach, and then to reflect on theoretical considerations afterwards. There is a tendency to describe the methods employed, and above all the intentions rather than the results. The stress placed on having clear aims (required by applications for funding and management of projects) obscures the need for appraisal of the actual results while the project continues.

Therefore reflective evaluation of the work is often minimal, and there is little information on the factors in ABE provision which have had the most successful impact on community development. ABE and adult education in Britain are not generally seen as tools for large-scale social change, either in towns or in the countryside. If providers of ABE wish to see functional literacy used for the good of local affairs in this way, (and such use would be seen to justify some of the expense, by helping to ensure a stable local economy), they would need to look not at the factors already inherent in ABE teaching in Britain, but at a very different issue: the aims and objectives of the funding agencies. The largest of these is now the national government. To ensure the use of ABE programs for more general social benefit, there must be changes in the targets set by all authorities in charge of funding, so that they foster a community development approach.

Notes & References

1. Bergin, S. et al., Open Learning in Adult Basic Education, *Research and Practice in Adult Literacy Bulletin*, 18, 1991, Bradford.

2. Sanders J., Open to Question: Opportunities in Adult Basic Education, *Research and Practice in Education (RAPAL) Bulletin*, 1990, Bradford.

3. Lee J., The Practicalities of Open Learning in Teesdale, *ALBSU Newsletter*, 48, 1993, London.

4. Lucy J., *Why Ask Me? Report on Preliminary Investigation into the Educational Needs of Unwaged Adults in West Cumbria*, West Cumbria Open Learning Trust, March 1987, Carlisle.

5. Herrington M., *Open and Distance Learning in Leicestershire; Final Report*, (unpublished report), ALBSU, 1986.

6. REPLAN, *Country Learning: A Development Workers' Guide to Supporting Unwaged Rural Learners*, National Institute for Adult and Continuing Education, 1989, Coventry.

7. Craggs S., *The Outcomes of Local History Classes and Projects*, (unpublished dissertation for Diploma in Adult Education), University of Liverpool, 1986.

Chapter 12
A NEW HISTORY FOR THE HUNGARIAN VILLAGE OF GYULAJ

Ferenc Balipap
Association for Community Development
Hungary

"BIRD-SONG WAS ALL WE GOT OUT OF THE FOREST..."

The village of Gyulaj is a small closed world that sits almost exactly in the middle of southern Transdanubia, bounded on the north by Lake Balaton, on the east by the Danube, the Austrian border on the west and the Drava River along its southern edge. Roads, traffic, commerce, culture, the rumble of civilization, have long ago passed these parts by. The hills and dales bordering the village on the north-northwest are covered by a pleasant forest which defined life here in the past and does so now, more powerfully — and paradoxically — more than anything else.

Historically, although most of this 7500 hectare forest always fell inside the boundaries of Gyulaj, never did it come to pass that the inhabitants of the village were able to exercise the rights of possession over it. They were completely at its mercy and subordinated to it! Such a prolonged condition of subordination and inequality affecting the community elicits collective notions, attitudes and responses in the community's confrontation with this situation and its will to resolve it. This makes the local conditions interpretable only by means of the theory of culture, the so-called basic acculturation. The unresolved situation results in a constant concern with the problem as well as a set of relationships among the people appropriate to this concern, that is of a cultural nature. This occurs when the debates, expressions of opinions and evaluations of them occur not in the various competent and official forums but become chronic in the sphere of everyday contacts. Public matters are transposed into the private sphere because, given the absence of true democracy, they cannot start functioning. In this way they start to take over the civic and private "domain," enriching it with information, skills and lines of communication. These are not verbalized because this would require taking an open stand, when one of the principal characteristics of this situation is that openness cannot always be undertaken.

But the less people talk about the tensions, the more likely it is that they are suppressed, thereby creating a culture "underneath". This is stifled by contact with officialdom and with the broader outside world but, in the final analysis, it vigorously gathers strength. In the case of Gyulaj, this kind of coexistence with the circumstances forced upon them from outside and the continuous implicit shaping of this culture forming their life-strategies, has been a factual way of life over many decades. Paradoxically, it is this "underneath" culture that is the most conspicuous aspect of local history and culture.

CHANGES IN THE LIVES OF THE VILLAGERS

It is not the victory of Communist principles that is impossible but only that these principles be realized in any other way but through absolutism. And therefore the victory of Communism will always be the victory of despotism.
Baron József Eötvös, 1854[1]

The historical settlement of Gyulaj was still an average Hungarian bourgeois (European, if you like) village until World War II when the number of inhabitants fluctuated markedly in the course of the difficult history of the Hungarians, though less so in the last 200 years. The decline in population only became more serious during the past 30-40 years.

In 1890, the population of this ancient settlement was almost three times what it is today: only 1162 inhabitants now, 3063 inhabitants then. There were good reasons for decline and outmigration on two occasions. The first occurred at the end of the last century when the local smallholders refused to allow train tracks to be laid across their fields. The second occurred after 1949 when the opportunity to farm privately was taken away by a stronger, more violent alien force than industrialization. On both occasions, those who wanted to live had to flee: in 1890, those who wanted to live differently, in 1949, those who wanted to continue living as before.

There is no doubt that, on one occasion, the village itself made the wrong decision about its future, when it resisted the building of the railway; but thereafter, practically nothing but wrong decisions, detrimental to the village, were made... by others.

Socialist anti-village and anti-peasant policies fiercely exploited Gulyaj by the early 1950's and between 1957-59, a new violent co-op organizing wave occurred. The village and the cooperative were "allocated" new outside leaders who knew nothing about either farming or villages, resulting in the complete depopulation (between 600-700 people) of the Szölöhegy part of the village where 600 to 700 people had been living in the valley near the woods. (Szölöhegy is a hill planted with grapevines. Here it also appears as the name of part of the village.) After 1960, those who could, fled into nearby towns, while those less able retreated into the village.

As a consequence of the generalized centralizing policy extending into every facet of life in Hungary at the beginning of the 1970s, Gyulaj lost its independent authority first over a part of its territory, then over its council and, for a time, over its institutions (the latter was soon restored) and finally even the co-op was turned into a "colony," with headquarters two villages away, at Döbrököz.

Traditionally, it was only in issues concerning its forest that the village had had no say. It is a consequence, however, of the past half-century — that is, exactly in the course of this socialism advertised as being for the community — that almost nothing was left of anything that had to do with their lives or destiny in which the citizens of Gyulaj could participate. It is even possible to say that, since the end of the last century, the majority of the population — close to 2000 people — did, in fact, "clamber aboard" that train which the burgers of that time had refused to allow across their fields.

GYULAJ & THE GYULAJ FOREST

Gyulaj owes its infamy as it does its world renown to the forest and the fallow deer living in it. The gifts of nature and the environment which lead to the flourishing of nearby settlements practically as a rule the world over, became in the case of Gyulaj, the basis for decline, neglect and abandonment, thus exemplifying the peculiar paths of Hungarian history and the nature of the powers that be.

At the beginning of the 18th century, most of this southern part of Transdanubia was covered by forests teeming with wildlife. The Gyulaj lands and forests were owned at that time by the family of one of the most prestigious members of the Upper House in Hungary, the Prince Eszterházys. There were glittering hunting parties from the beginning of the 19th century on, fashionable and ritual-like entertainments for aristocrats, renowned not only in the neighbouring countries but world-wide. The distinctive big game in the forest — since the time of the Turkish conquest in the 16th century, according to tradition — was the fallow deer.

The forest, however, yields no benefits whatsoever from its true worth and bounty to the people of the village. After 1945, possession of the choicest parts of scenery and nature continued to be the privilege of the country's (new) lordships. Communist comrade-lordships replaced the aristocratic lordships. This was the only change perceptible to the villagers. Not only were the people of Gyulaj gradually prohibited from entering the forest but their highway through the forest (to Tamási towards the Balaton) was also closed to them.

Citing the wildlife reserve and the necessity of protecting it, the village of Gyulaj was turned ever more into a "reservation," sealed off from the world. Nor was there need any longer for the village work-force either, since large-scale mechanization had been instituted in the management of the forest and the wildlife starting in the mid-70s. The fence around the reserve to protect the forest, the wildlife and the comrades was completed at the beginning of the 70s and the roads into the forest were closed off with barriers. Entry and exit have been controlled, rules strictly enforced, restricting entry into the "realm" exclusively to those with permission from the management of the Tamasi Farm.

As there is no need for the people to work in the forest, there is no need for people either. In these circumstances, the village and people of Gyulaj have no opportunity to develop natural inter-village and neighbourly contacts or relationships based on vehicular traffic, commerce, administration, and culture or to associate with their neighbours but must instead execute precepts, ukases and orders. As a result of measures by the higher-ups, Gyulaj has no neighbours. "One can only stray into this village, but that means the end of the rover's life," says a local old fellow who, nevertheless, adds that there is nowhere in the world where he would be as happy as here, in his village, at home.

A single hard-surfaced road serves Gyulaj, leading south to the village of Kurd, seven km away. Thus the forest and wildlife reserve, which are the only elements that could bring about the revival of the village are, instead, the cause of its isolation and a restriction on its development.

"It is not right that bird-song is all we got till now out of the forest," say the villagers ever more often these days since they see — as many of them already saw, even then — that the whole village community could indeed end up as outcasts just like the Gyulaj Gypsies, tossed by the vicissitudes of fate.

THE GYPSIES OF GYULAJ

Statistical data on the Gypsy population of Hungary is unreliable. The previous regime "handled" this matter as a political issue so that self-serving voluntary reporting and socialist propaganda were mixed in with the facts. For instance, contemporary figures report that 320,000 Gypsies were in Hungary in 1970 and 350,000 in 1980, estimates now show a figure somewhere between 500,000 to 800,000. Local Gypsies first appeared in a Gyulaj statistical report in 1768. (There is still an almost folkloric notion in this southern part of Transdanubia which says that the average village — about 800 to 1500 souls — "should be able to support 5-10 Gypsy families of its own".) At the end of the 19th century, however, about 80-100 Gypsies were brought in from neighbouring counties and settled on Gyulaj at the edge of the manorial forests bordering the village farms, according to the sources, to "log and clear the forest and to work as game-beaters," and to live a nomadic existence in squalid, dug-out hovels.

In 1958, obviously as a result of political pressure from above, and in agreement with the forest-management, village leaders decided to "do away with the medieval hovel conditions", compelling the Gypsies to settle down near Szölöhegy, already in the process of being abandoned anyway, but still outside the forest. They did not, however, provide them with any kind of housing but did "allow them" to build new hovels. A so-called Gypsy school was then built here in 1961, functioning more like a community centre. The children, and often their parents too, were given meals here and were taught first to speak, then to write Hungarian. Until 1970, only grades 1 and 2 operated with a single teacher in this school, which educators to this day describe as one covering a "broad age range." Those — few — who got to grade 3 went to the Szölöhegy Hungarian school where there still were two groups of students. But in 1967, at the culmination of the newest wave of flight by the Hungarian population, this time from the Gypsies, the village council closed the separate Hungarian school at Szölöhegy.

The Gypsies started to take over houses on Szölöhegy in 1962 and those in the village shortly thereafter, at first only houses belonging to people fleeing from the co-op conversion and mostly those which had no real value because of their decrepit state. (The "mixing" of Gypsies in among the Hungarians of course also speeded up the departure of the villagers).

Later, the village leaders and party members, resulting from direction and political pressure from above, undertook the sale of vacant village houses to the Gypsies, now made advantageous with official credit terms. Life for the Gypsies now forced to live among the villagers became wretched. Hostilities were fought out among themselves. The villagers were not willing to play the "domesticator" role forced upon them nor did they wish to carry out direct and personal assimilation.

"Systematic rural development" and the "solution to the Gypsy question" in its framework continued with unbroken momentum. It was not easy to divert the national and local politicians who were "implementing" socialism from their triumphant forward (!) march.

In 1967, an old house and its stable in the centre of town which had been converted a good 15 years earlier into a cultural centre was turned — in a few weeks — into a week-day student hostel for Gypsy children. This was the first institution of this kind in the country and its main peculiarity was that Gypsy children were separated from their own parents living in the same village. Starting in 1971, all Gypsy children went to the village school and 40 of them lived in the student hostel. Szölöhegy was abandoned by 1975 and the hovels still standing were knocked down and ploughed under by tractors from the co-op.

The earlier segregationist policy regarding the Gypsies was replaced by assimilation in the 60s. Here again, decisions were made without consulting those involved. They wanted to provide the adults with models and jobs and to use the school to the socialize the children into little Hungarians.

In 1962, the Hungarian Socialist Worker's Party announcement that "the laying of the foundations of socialism in our country is complete" meant for Gyulaj that decisions in every issue, affair or matter pertaining to it would now and henceforth be made outside and independently of it. Commerce, transportation, even culture would be organized and directed from "headquarters". Ideas , at least those that came to fruition, came ready-made from above.

The regime's designation for all of these centrally-run activities was that the village was being provided with services and "development", as a consequence of which there was decline, destruction and retro-gression on a scale never before seen in the settlement. The independence of its local council was taken away (it was annexed to Kurd), the co-op was placed under Döbrököz, the forest and wildlife reserve were run from Tamási, and the people managing by remote control did with the village as they pleased. And what was it that they pleased? The chairman of the district council stated publicly in the mid-70s that "Gyulaj is a settlement without a role. It is not worth developing and it must be abandoned, to disappear from the map."

BUT GYULAJ LIVES - & WANTS TO LIVE!

Because you can only be yourself if you undertake something for others, and you can only win at life if you renew the battle with death.
                              István Vas, from his poem titled "József Attila"

What is the situation in Gyulaj now? How did people react to the despotism of the regime ruling over them and how did they seek and find their own system of values and the opportunities to pursue their apirations? What kind of culture did they create and operate to survive?

There are 1162 people living in 397 dwellings in Gyulaj. A third of the population consists of elderly people on low incomes, mostly living alone and able to look after themselves only with difficulty. Another third, almost all of them now unemployed, are Gypsies. There is running water in half of the houses, given as a "gift" by the co-op, but there is no sanitary sewer system.

The kindergarten has 60 places and 13 teachers for the 121 elementary school students. A doctor, veterinarian, nurse and a so-called welfare system (which includes home-care workers and an old-people's home with a residence for indigents) have recently started operating in Gyulaj. The settlement council has been autonomous since 1990. Employment opportunities are extremely circumscribed even as far as casual jobs are concerned. The co-op headquarters are still in Döbrököz and its structure and profile are now in the process of being reorganized. More than 100 people, 70% of them Gypsies, were unemployed in Gyulaj at the end of 1992. (More than 80% of the Gypsies who were formerly employed have now lost their jobs).

And what kinds of desires, civic projects, community aspirations, confrontations with the situation and initiatives seeking opportunities for development can be found in Gyulaj today? Will the proletarian peasant who was subjugated, forced to make accommodations and constrained for decades be able to turn into a free citizen once again? Are the people of Gyulaj now able make a go of freedom and democracy?

Independence & Passive Resistance

First of all, we can put on record that Gyulaj, during the past half-century, like most Hungarian villages, was able to emancipate itself from the central authorities in many important areas and without particular problems. The socialist policy-makers left the daily life of village society alone (!) from the mid-60s on presumably because they believed that it was inevitable for the "legitimacy of Marxism to become operational" once the people were herded into the co-ops. That is, economic circumstances almost automatically determine everything else and that every further historical development could only bring the consummation of socialism closer. The village — defined by the policy — was harnessed to the cart of (Marxist) history from which — stripped of its possessions and freedom — it could not be torn.

In Gyulaj, however, as in most other settlements, the people soon found "small-scale freedoms". Those who had stayed behind, quickly discovered not only the opportunities for the "underneath" culture or so-called second economy (home-based, legal or illegal small enterprises) and the appropriate forums for expressing them. The dense network of family, friends, relatives and neighbourhoods rallying together, meant some sort of security and protection against the unilateral actions of the (service-providing) state/policies/authorities, distortions and scarcities. They created a sense of self and of community in time of trouble. The people exchanged and lent produce, small machinery and tools, knowledge and information on a broad scale. This is how individual and collective strategies for survival in local relationships operated as a sort of second public level and turned all this into local resistance in spite of the outside and higher authorities.

Having been compelled to do so, people gave up playing a role in social, public and community life (and even gave up the role too!) to get closer to the opportunities for economic survival. They gave up what they had lost anyway. They surrendered what [the authorities] wanted in any case to take away from them, so that they could live. They had their own opinion of the world enclosing, constricting and restricting them but they did not take on confrontation and engagement which had no hope of success but — yielding to ancient village and peasant instincts — they chose the common people's wise tactic of survival by outwitting authority. They strove to compensate for diminished freedom by working harder and with greater solidarity within their own world.

By the second half of the 70s, this relative independence, chiefly in the area of farming and business, slowly allowed some to achieve a relatively better standard of living, almost to the point of wealth. That which state services (redistribution) and collective farming did not guarantee to families, they created for themselves, chiefly by excessive work and exploiting themselves. (We report this noting that we also cite the validity of the typology created by the socialists Iván Szelényi and Róbert Manchin which says that some of the peasants forced into the co-op did become bourgeois in Gyulaj too; some took on a specific character by becoming a new "working class", the peasant worker, while it was formerly the better off and more bourgeois, interrupted in their progress toward middle-class status, who tried to achieve compensation in the private sector most vigorously.)

An autonomy preserved (or recreated) on the economic basis developed. It was expressed most typically in household plots which exist almost everywhere in Gyulaj, with animals, cultivation of small garden plots, raising vegetables and keeping orchards near the house, or small vineyards. We could almost say that families have remained self-sufficient in this respect. A few of them raised garden produce for sale or exchange in town. Gyulaj farmers still raise pigs and keep beef cattle too, and poultry-raising is also common and has now even appeared here and there among the Gypsies too. It is considered "shameful" not to be self-sufficient in these kinds of products or goods, that is, to have to buy them.

Conditions Related
to Private Production & Farming

We can highlight two of the more significant characteristics of the efforts of the former period in connection with grape-growing as a hobby which also typify the changes manifested through and in the culture.

All the areas at the edge of the village which are not bordered by the forest, except for the south, are surrounded by small vineyards. This means that almost everyone living in Gyulaj has some sort of private vineyard. Until the mid or late 60s, the grapes were of the direct-bearing indigenous variety. These were cut out, because of information and cultural influences from outside and replaced with choicer varieties. The Gyulaj villagers also switched from traditional growing practices to growing the grapes on raised wires, thus gaining additional space for vegetables and plants below the rows of grapes.

Also naturally contributing to the change in viticulture was the fact that the scarcity of land forced people to convert to more intensive farming methods giving better yields on smaller plots. Even those people who had moved just a few villages over still kept their vineyards and brought the culture of the new production method back to their "weekend property" from their homes away.

Another cultural characteristic related to grape-growing in Gyulaj is wine-cellar parties, held mostly by men. The ancestors or the previous generation built such press-sheds in their vineyards, often 2-3 km from home in which it was possible for the whole family to spend the night. Nowadays, very many of these press-sheds have been remodelled, especially by returnees, to serve expressly as sort of weekend cottages whereby personal and social contacts can

be carried on to a significant degree in these unofficial "green living-rooms." (In the old days, these press-sheds away from the village were the site where brandy was distilled illegally and game trapped on the sly was butchered; this, of course, still happens from time to time...)

Among the young people too, we came across many cases where, protesting against the activities run by the council cultural centre built in 1968, (which were disorganized and ignored their needs) they started group gatherings like their elders, spiced with songs and talk, held in the press-sheds. Press-shed owners who have moved to Dombóvár or elsewhere also come back here in summer to "camp out," thus increasing the significance of the role of vineyards as private community forums.

Although the organization of private and family-based village labour and community had ceased to exist in the old way because of the violent establish-ment of the cooperative and the despotic expropriation of community life, nevertheless the traditional family and village economic autonomy as well as the broader form of community cooperation based on it still survived in the culture of so-called home-based activities — and especially in grape-growing and in the relationships, social and recreational activities connected with it. Thus, alongside the constancy of the household plot that was restricted within the second economy, the elements and structures of civic society also existed and operated on a second (sub-official) level.

The situation described above, as well as the historical and political circum-stances did influence or, more accurately, prevent the new social links and relationships among citizens from becoming completely and openly formalized. That is why the culture created and operated by them together, the basic culture, was and could be the strongest factor for integration and identity-formation in the life of village society. The fact that the village did not disintegrate and that they did not obey the will of the higher-ups, that is, that the village was not abandoned, is due to this force of resistance and the self-preserving strength of the local culture and society meshing with the activities around the household plots and vineyards. And it is likely that every further act of resistance and vitality is the consequence of the shared capabilities and achievements which emerged and grew strong in this little place. In the midst of unrealities and absurdities on an enormous scale, it was enough for survival for the villagers of Gyulaj to have a piece of reality, a solid piece of land (figuratively and literally) where they could plant their feet.

Thank God that they did!

Evolution of the Relations
Between the Villagers & Gypsies

The villagers left behind did, basically, accept the Gypsies, at least formally. What is now a quarter-century of being confined together has tamed the former keen hostilities, placing them among the bearable burdens of daily life. One could say that the village accepted the Gypsies better than they themselves have fitted in. The two closed "systems" have congealed side-by-side. Perhaps the Hungarians have had to exercise the greater tolerance whereas the Gypsies have had to make the more difficult effort. The formerly happy-go-lucky fellow living on the forest edge did not exactly turn into a farmer, co-op member or tiller of the soil. There may be five or six Gypsy families at the most who are trying to follow the villagers' life-style and habits. Not much has come of integration in this respect, to this point. Employment has, however, become more common among the Gypsies, especially among adult men. Up until unemployment "exploded" in Hungary, most employable Gypsies were working on the neighbouring state farms in some sort of skilled or semi-skilled, chiefly seasonal, agricultural jobs. It was typical of many to work in these places for only as long as needed to entitle them to the family allowance and other social assistance. (This was previously possible after working for 15-16 days). A day or two after payday the little they had earned was blown on amusement or women.

A few of them also got jobs at the co-op in recent years but practically no one did in the forest reserve. The last report, issued in 1988, that is, before the emergence of unemployment, showed that 294 Gypsies lived in Gyulaj, including 157 employable persons (73 men, 84 women); 68 had permanent jobs (49 men, 13 women [sic]); 43 persons had seasonal jobs (15 men, 28 women); 14 persons (five men, nine women) subsisted on casual work; 32 persons (four men, 28 women) were not gainfully employed. (There were 14 Gypsies from the village, 11 men and three women, in jail at this time).

The village has kept its two-sided attitude toward the Gypsies: there is a an officially "handled" Gypsy issue and then there are the real, live, every-day human contacts. The official "provision of services" has been going on since they were settled on the village and concentrated there though it has become tamer in recent times. (At the beginning, the KöJÁL [Public Health and Contagious Disease Station] "swooped down" on the Gypsies every month or two and mounted enormous — and forced, if necessary — campaigns of disinfecting baths...).

Social assistance to the Gypsies is a moral and economic concern equally to the village to this day. Their health-related handicaps are obvious from the moment of birth and follow them for life (they marry among themselves — there has not been one marriage to a non-Gypsy yet; low birth-weight babies; inadequate nutrition, bad housing, etc.).

Official "efforts" at assessing the Gypsies have placed great emphasis on cultural factors. However, the Gypsies have not reached equal footing with the villagers to this day either in their behaviour or their ability to speak Hungarian. Their distinct culture is still a cause for clashes with the indigenous Hungarians. Not even half of the school-age Gypsies complete the eight elementary grades. The student hostel provided a great deal of study help but the segregated, isolated environment was unrealistic and could not bring about lasting results. In spite of every attempt, Gypsy children are set apart in school, struggle with disadvantages and do not assimilate. Regular school attendance has not been solved either. A 1986 report shows that one Gypsy child went on to a vocational school in 1980, two in 1981, six in 1982, two in 1983, four in 1984 and four in 1985. One Gypsy student from Gyulaj achieved admission to a vocational high school in 1985. One Gypsy girl from Gyulaj was able to complete kindergarten teacher training successfully.

A "Gypsy club" was set up in the village in 1983 as part of the official "provision of services". They wanted, primarily, to lure back those young people who had been in the student hostel or had grown up, in order to extend their educational influence over them. Another obvious motivation for this initiative was that the young people who had finished school very quickly fell back into their traditional want of ambition in almost every facet of their lives.

Basically, the Gypsy club attempted to organize technical and academic extension courses, on the basis of theories of child rather than adult education, and tried to develop self-run activities (raising small animals, cooking, photography, learning music, dancing and other amateur artistic activities were on the club program — and externally directed). After some early successes — participation in a few county club meetings — the club has now disintegrated almost completely.

It had no internal cohesion and organization from the outside created precious little motivation. The get-togethers started to degenerate into drinking bouts. A few villagers 'adopted' an individual Gypsy or a Gypsy family but no significant results came from these endeavours. It appears that the "parties" are characterized by a resigned coexistence: the village tries to avoid conflict with the Gypsies and expects the authorities to look after the Gypsies in their midst as a result of initiatives from above. The Gypsies, basically, expect the same thing. (The villagers say that their knowledge of their rights is much better developed than their knowledge of their responsibilities). There is, today, no earth-shaking difference between the opportunities available to or conditions of the significant majority of villagers and the Gypsies. This is because charitable and social assistance is extended to the Gypsies quite frequently though there is no doubt that many in the village look askance at their idle, unthrifty, imprudent and reckless life-style.

The conflicts between the Gyulaj villagers and the Gypsies have not been resolved but they are no longer acute. Resignation and helplessness have toughened this village in other respects and the majority of people are of the opinion that it is perhaps not the Gypsies who are the greatest cause of their handicaps. And almost no one disputes that it is only possible to clamber out of the current "historical quagmire" into which the masters of the country had toppled Gyulaj, together with the Gypsies, if at all. The people of the village have worked out a culture of coexistence with the Gypsies mutually acceptable and adhered to for some time now. This is as much as the community could manage and to expect more would be unrealistic. (Just as this is as much as the Gypsies could manage in the interests of their own "advancement"). The Gypsies were just as much "dumped" onto the backs of the villagers from above and outside as all the other burdens (the Gypsies did not volunteer to come to Gyulaj and came not of their own free will at all but most reluctantly). It is a shared, collective and honourable accomplishment on the part of both the villagers and the Gypsies that, in spite of it all, they learned to tolerate each other and have, even worked out some norms of coexistence. The so-called Gypsy problem is, however, not satisfactorily resolved in Gyulaj either for the Gypsies or for the Hungarians, just as the whole of Gyulaj as a complex of problems, is not yet resolved. The powers of this settlement were weakened and taken away over the decades to such an extent that one cannot expect it to revive and flourish without outside help. One of the most obvious areas where Gyulaj requires help is in the situation of the Gypsies as it has evolved here to the present.

Since 1990

As a result of the 1990 municipal elections, new opportunities opened up for the development of Gyulaj. In these new circumstances, it may be possible to openly pursue local, individual and community objectives which formerly had to be concealed. And though a lack of confidence is quite generalized, the village community has, nevertheless, started off on its chosen path of measures they want to implement.

Despite a very intensive, long-term and systematized series of setbacks extending over practically every facet of its life, Gyulaj is appearing capable of making a go on its own. A few of these promising manifestations are:

- The village retook legitimate authority to control official matters and its administrative institutions for itself in the course of the local elections. They elected a respected local 73-year old fellow-citizen as their mayor. His life is exemplary, he is a local man linked to this place through all his trials and efforts over the last decades; moreover, he has forged his own life to the struggle of the village to survive. These two elements — loyalty and commitment to the community by accepting the same fate — are not only compelling human values in Gyulaj today but are also the most important of the values. The person of the mayor is, furthermore, the guarantee for the rehabilitation of religion. In addition, the elected representatives are local members of the younger generation bound to the community with their lives and aspirations. (An interesting feature of the elections was that not only were members of the former political, administrative and co-op cadres not elected, but even educators were left out; on the other hand, the majority of village voters supported the election of a young Gypsy man). The people of Gyulaj elected a village council in 1990 which they dare to trust will serve and represent their affairs and interests — which they were formerly forced to conceal — or at least most of them.

- With its first two measures the local council did merit this trust. They made local interests the determining factor in the handling of rather serious social issues and in the selection of the new principal for the elementary school. They closed the week-day student hostel which had been stagnating and already abandoned for years. It was the Gypsies themselves who, in the final analysis, initiated the closure of this 'segregationist" institution. The council made its decision with considerable determination and demonstrated responsibility towards local concerns when it closed the Gypsy hostel which had, in its time, been considered a great triumph of socialism in Gyulaj. In its place, it created a seniors' home with room to look after 15 local old people who were unable to care for themselves.

  At the same time, they relieved the school principal of his duties and selected, instead, a Gyulaj-born teacher whose teacher-wife also came from here. This couple had, over many years away from their place of birth, proved their qualifications as educators and, in their application for the position in Gyulaj, their commitment to and love for the village. (Gyulaj now has, for the first time, a locally-born school principal).

  With these decisions, the council has left no doubt that it is striving with great determination to assert the interests of local citizens in the organization and operation of its institutions too and is thus taking control of the village and its affairs.

- The co-op is reorganizing and seeking new prospects. They are interested in developing manufacturing and sales activities to add to that of production. Meanwhile, some of the villagers are hoping to leave the co-op and get into private farming, since opportunities have opened up in this area too. Methods to resolve (or indeed, forestall) conflicts arising from this have not yet been worked out. It is likely that this is the area in which local citizens will have to make their most personal decisions since the council and co-op cannot be expected to represent or to endorse on a broad scale the interests or ideas of those wishing to become private farmers. A few determined youthful and more mature local families have already started on the difficult path toward private farming. The village is watching them with sympathy and cheering them on but most people are cautious and biding their time.

- The most spectacular development in the reorganization of the co-op was that a brewery was set up in Döbrököz and so a beer-garden is being opened in Gyulaj, too, where the local adults want to operate a club on Thursday evenings. (There has been a long-standing need in the village for a public meeting place of this kind that is not just for young people).

- The village had already handed its cultural centre over to the young people. The latter have now formed a free cultural centre circle as a club and, in this setting, organize their own entertainment and group programs. This self-run cultural centre is open Fridays, Saturdays and Sundays.

- Village leaders and citizens have brought up the idea of organizing a reunion for those who have left the village and emigrated. On this occasion, they would set up a foundation for the development of Gyulaj andmake plans for the required steps for development to take advantage of the intellectual capital of the "emigres". (At the initiative of the present mayor, former residents of Gyulaj contributed a significant amount to renovations to the church damaged by an earthquake a few years ago).

- The village is trying to arrive at a solution to their long-standing problem of isolation and seclusion. Public opinion holds that the most serious concern of the village from the point of view of its prospects and its revitalization is the prohibition on traffic through the forest, that is towards the north or east. The citizens demonstrated this concern in a petition campaign started during the spring of 1992. In effect, there was one person in every family dwelling who demanded that the feasibility of travel through the forest be restored. (It is obvious to many of the villagers that foreign tourism and visitors would be the best asset for development by the village. This is rendered impossible by the lack of roads and the obstacles to traffic, that is, its seclusion).

The village would even resign itself to not getting back its road to Tamási if a connecting road would be built to Szakály to meet the Siófok-Szekszárd road. (This would require the construction of an approximately four to five km paved road). The village itself has started building its municipal roads. Preparations for receiving tourists are proceeding systematically.

• The village council is no longer alone or lacking expertise. Help is being provided by the Hungarian Association of Community Developers and the Hungarian Institute of Culture (which hired the author as a regional development officer on November 1, 1992 to work in rural development at Gyulaj, among other places. - Incidentally, the author is himself a native of Gyulaj and has, during the past 15 years, endeavoured to provide assistance in the struggles of the citizens and institutions of his place of birth as director of the cultural centre in the former district capital.)

• The village has hired a new doctor and new veterinarian and is preparing to tackle the other problems of the elderly, the unemployed and of young people. It is now expressing its wishes and now garnering those experiences in satisfying its needs and achieving its aspirations.

EPILOGUE

"...increased attention must be paid to the misery of marginalized groups of people; these are the racial minorities, the abandoned, and the regions swept to the side-lines in the process of mass-production. It is the responsibility of society as a whole to ensure that they are drawn into the enjoyment of the fruits of society and share in them successfully. This is not easy because sometimes there are cultural differences which exacerbate the situation and make the task difficult but the responsibility of society as a whole is all the greater then. Once again it is the shared sin of both capitalism and communism that they neglect these people and favour mainly those who participate in the process of production in a decisive fashion while attempting to minimize the importance of these groups, which are gradually increasing in significance and in the danger they pose in the modern world, at least within their own circles. Bringing them into participation in the whole of society or making it possible for them to live their own particular way of life must become the responsibility of society as a whole."

(István Bibó, tape-recorded in 1971-72)[3]

The decades-long project to "improve" the Gypsies living in Gyulaj has become totally bankrupt since the Gypsies, who were meant to "get ac-customed" to working, have almost all become unemployed in recent months. The "Gypsy question" is once again being raised ever more vociferously in the village, in particular the social aspect, especially the problem of assistance, since the Gypsies have neither income nor skills with which to compensate for their lack of possessions or employment.

A Gypsy self-government body should be set up on an experimental basis. Cooperation of this body with the village council must be established by contract and it should be granted as much autonomy and responsibility as possible in the most important issues affecting the Gypsy people — public assistance, employment, business, education and development — and the decisions, expressions of opinion and recommendations on which they are based. The system of coexistence and cooperation between the Gypsies and villagers should first be structured in such a way that its workings would be determined and operated together by the Gypsy community (and their representatives) and the non-Gypsy village community (and their representatives). This system, based on cooperation at the beginning, would aim to achieve Gypsy autonomy mutually agreed upon by the village and the Gypsies. It is necessary to guarantee development assistance, which will, at first, be on a relative scale but will gradually become more complete. Opportunities must be provided for continuing education of the Gypsy community on many levels, directions and forms.

Based on the mood and public opinion in the village, we can assume that the time is perhaps not too distant when the civic organizations and the smaller and larger groups which see themselves as a community sharing a common situation, values and aspirations will make their appearance in Gyulaj.

Further tasks — of setting democracy, farming, culture and society to rights, to making life livable and bearable — lie ahead in this small Transdanubian village with a long, difficult history but now seeking itself again and striving to make its own way.

POST SCRIPTUM
(Laszlo Harangi, Association for Community Development)

The gypsy question has been an overall European minority issue, the roma population being one of the largest minorities in Europe. Most gypsies live in central and eastern Europe. Every country, from Finland to Spain, has its own gypsy minority. Hungary's gypsy population is estimated at 700 000.

The main characteristic of the "gypsy issue" is that it is a very complex phenomenon. However, the major obstacles in this issue have been intolerance, suspicion, misunderstanding, oversensitiveness, lack of self-moderation, the exaggerating of faults and hits on both sides, in one word a lack of social conscience based on education and literacy.

It may also be relevant to develop the social, economic and cultural aspects of gypsy minorities, considering that any sophisticated intervention should be based on the self-activation and inner dynamism of gypsy communities. The gypsies' values, traditions and their special ability should be recognized, as should their right to their own way of life, which is based on their rich and unique cultural heritage. It is only in this spirit that this nation and its representatives can be considered as responsible and equal partners, and not just as the objects of a minority policy, no matter what amount of goodwill it reflects.

The relationship between the roma and non-roma societies should be based on principles of tolerance and permanent consultation, communication and coordination of both groups' interests. Open lines of communication should be established between the two societies at the family, local, intermediary and national levels.

The majority should help the minority, in this case the gypsies. In such a balanced relationship, the dignity of the minority and the interdependence of all groups withina country should always be respected.

Assistance to gypsies as a minority is necessary but should not be in the form of assimilation. It should be a technical, neutral, non-political, non-clerical aid, as opposed to a paternalistic approach such as the so-called "socialist policy" that existed in the late communist countries. In other words, gypsies should be given tools that will enable them to act as independent and autonomous groups. "You give a man a fish, you feed him for a day; you teach a man to fish, you feed him for a lifetime."

Notes & References

1.   Baron József Eötvös, *A XIX század uralkodó eszméinek befojása az államra* [The influence of the reigning ideas of the 19th century on the state]. In Hungarian. 3rd ed. Budapest, 1885, Vol. II, p.48.

2.   Gyula Szeghalmi, Dunántuli vármegyék, [Countries of Transdanubia]. In Hungarian. Budapest, 1940.

3.   István Bibó. *Az europai társadalomfejlesztés értelme* [The significance of community development in Europe]. In Hungarian. In *Válogatott tanulmányok* ["Selected studies"]. In Hungarian. Vol.III.

Chapter 13
FUNCTIONAL LITERACY IN ROMANIA — BETWEEN MYTH & REALITY

Florentina Anghel
Education Sciences Institute
Bucharest, Romania

THE MEANING OF LANGUAGE

The text that follows is intended as an essay on the contradictory history of literacy training in Romania (during the period preceding and the period following 1989) and some of the objectives, problems and desired results of literacy training projects for development in rural areas.

The study's presentation in three parts, pre-totalitarian period, totalitarian period and post-totalitarian period, is justified, on one hand, by the need to emphasize the relationship that should exist between traditions and current projects. On the other hand, we have tried to point out current literacy problems in rural areas based on the idea that, during the totalitarian period, literacy really a "logocracy", a sub-system of the Ruling Power through which it imposed the codes, symbols and structures of "communist literacy".

We have tried to suggest new answers to questions raised about literacy research and action programs, such as: "What could be more normal than literacy training that intends, according to its objectives, to be something other than evangelism through language or a false social catalyst that is much too diluted to trigger the radical transformations it proposes?" The answers come only through understanding what language has meant in countries that have experienced totalitarianism: not so much a way of communicating, understanding, arguing and philosophizing but rather, a subtle, external form of manipulation designed to contaminate all messages by reducing them to a single code: that intended by the Ruling Power.

We have adopted the recognized meaning of "consciousness-raising",

177

because it fits the objectives proposed and our way of thinking. In Romania's case, literacy has to fulfill a training rather than an information function, because it is more than a sum of basic skills (reading, writing, arithmetic). It is a way of raising consciousness of a social and cultural heritage that must be mobilized and revitalized. Enlightened (participative, involved) literacy training must become a basic framework for cultural development in rural areas, as much an expression of the quality of new relationships between the individual and the community as the starting point for the individual autonomy that is necessary for Romania to consciously find a place in the outside world, to communicate with self or others, to participate more fully in social life. The overall purpose, in a word, is liberation, in its most generous sense.

GENERAL CONSIDERATIONS

Today, rural areas are obsessed with their own stagnation. Although they want to return (perhaps too quickly) to tranquillity, they do not have the means. In this social milieu, transition is difficult and painful. Peasants are thrust into a new role, that of farmer or owner, forced to deal with the new mechanisms of the market economy and expected to translate all their problems into prosperity or, at least, economic growth.

Economic growth, however, has to be questioned if rural areas are to represent anything more than just a preservation of the status quo, maintaining privileges and submitting peasants to new slogans imposed for political reasons that have not been explained to them. Real development includes becoming aware and experiencing what individuals can achieve in the general historical and community setting, when they have the opportunity to express themselves creatively according to their aptitudes, beliefs and personal preferences, and when society accepts their individual uniqueness, following models that enable personal and communal transformation. Development also means the opportunity to participate in every aspect of public and private life, allowing each individual the right to experience a conscious relationship with self and with the environment.

Rural areas, moreover, should not be considered a blank page that can be filled with new codes and rousing messages. No political authority (party or organization) can assume the role of writing and rewriting the history of literacy in the same terms as in the past. The peasants have negative experiences from the past and are very sceptical about new revolutionary action taken at their expense.

What, then, are the risks of too rapid a transition? First, there is moral crisis, lack of confidence in the new activism imposed, passivity, and/or a refusal to participate in community life — then isolation, a safe strategy in difficult times. The peasants have already learned the mechanisms of social protection by isolating themselves within the confines of their village or even their own home.

The village can easily fall prey to cultural pollution by mass media in unfair competition with authentic rural values, yielding disastrous effects.

Raising consciousness about change can compensate for the speed of negative change. What models are acceptable? What are the critical evaluation criteria for integrating contemporary urban models? What methods are there for renewing rural areas, and who are the social players (individuals, groups, organizations) ready to mobilize their resources? If an infrastructure or information structure exists, how can it assist the goals of literacy training?

It would be easy to believe that such an exalted purpose could only be unanimously accepted and recognized as an unquestionable national priority. Yet, the literacy training problem is still evaded, in post-totalitarian Romania, either by silence or by reducing it to a sum of insignificant, anachronistic problems.

Politicians do not consider illiteracy a real problem in rural areas, although there are concerns about other problems there (privatization, repossession by former landowners, production associations and so on). When, in spite of everything, literacy training is not forgotten, it is presented as an issue from the past or one that exists only for the aged.

Without question, however, 1989 was a year of profound change. The availability of information sparked an information explosion in reaction to the suppression of information by the past regime. For the moment, it finds expression in rural areas simply as an interest in information. But the time will come when peasants will express their need for access to information, and we must be prepared for that day.

The Option of Literacy Training

There are many "enthusiasts" who consider cultural development an invention of cultural facilitators/"agitators". Such enthusiasts cite statistics to show that it is impossible to raise the problem of illiteracy in rural areas. Here are some of the data:

- There are 11,307 schools in rural areas as opposed to only 2,540 in urban areas.

- There are 12,786 classrooms in rural areas and only 3,298 in urban areas.

- In every village or commune, there is a cultural centre, library and movie theatre.

- Out of a total of 157,838 students, 35,189 came from rural areas (in 1992).

To moderate the enthusiasm, we could cite other data. The number of schools in rural areas is approximately equal to the number of classrooms, because the schools are so small and old; 592 classrooms do not have indoor plumbing. More than 1,700 teaching positions in village and commune schools are held by individuals without specialized education, secondary school graduates. Most cultural centres have been transformed into restaurants, and many libraries are unusable, abandoned or lack readers. A survey conducted in three categories of populations at risk showed 15% were functional illiterates; 60% of them were from rural areas.

These figures reveal facts that we consider serious; inequalities between urban and rural areas are becoming more marked. Only the more cultured and better informed take advantage of expanded cultural dissemination: youth and city dwellers. Underprivileged social groups remain marginal with respect to culture.

In response to a radio survey in 1992, which was called "Your opinion about your village", we received hundreds of letters from young people in rural areas; the results reinforced the observations already made. In rural areas, there is significant interest in cultural activities (including traditional ones). The statement of a young girl, 23 years old, who lives in an isolated village in the Arad district is a moving example:

> I do not know why there is such indifference toward cultural life in my village, an indifference that seems to include everyone, toward the pollution of popular music and the lack of theatrical performances. Only newspapers with political content, no cultural magazines reach here... Although I work in a village school, I cannot say that there is anyone to talk to about books. All the discussions are... political! Sometimes I feel like an intruder in my own village. Our grandmother left us grandchildren all kinds of things she made with her own hands, but I could not say that I have tried to learn anything about what could be called "folklore".

Due to indifference, we are witnessing the slow death of popular culture, the death of a system of references, customs and beliefs marked by religion, folklore. Through songs, images, lay or religious holidays that gave meaning to life events, the system played the protective role of a basic matrix necessary for osmosis between individual and milieu. Popular culture has now left a vacuum that could well be filled by conflict and aggressiveness.

On that basis, we could formulate the fundamental objectives for enlightened literacy training based on an idea expressed in a study of education system reform in Romania:

> Transition from a totalitarian to a democratic society is not possible solely by a change of government, but rather by changes in skills, mentality, attitudes, social relationships and daily behaviour. As a result, although political and economic decisions are often in the foreground, transition is actually essentially social, psychological and moral in nature... It is obvious that transition is an educational process of national scope.[1]

The general objectives of functional literacy training in rural areas could therefore be specified as follows:

- restoring traditional institutions in Romanian villages (school, church, library, cultural centre, movie theatre, museum) and other activities that are cyclical or devoted to local events (social gatherings, agricultural holidays, activities for single youth and so on) for the purposes of literacy training;

- training specialized literacy facilitators for rural areas and preparing (mobilizing) individuals targeted so that they participate in their own literacy training; learning new linguistic codes and using critically communication channels;

- motivating each individual to participate in community life as a social player; mobilizing local groups (intellectuals, for example) and other individuals who are still tied to rural areas; discovering specific methods of inter-regional organization based on the theme of local solidarity among villages that have common problems.

It is, therefore, a matter of an overall view of literacy training and, implicitly, an overall view of the individual attaining literacy: "A literate person must not only be able to read, write and count, but must, above all, be an informed and civilized citizen... Literacy represents more than reading, writing and arithmetic skills. It is not a simple skill but a basic human right.[2]"

In spite of past destructive policies of natural, social, cultural and sacred space, rural areas have remained opposed to the compulsory codes of the Ruling Power, thanks to humour and hardy traditions. There is still acceptance in rural areas of the idea of social solidarity through culture and literacy training.

Initial Action

Here are some forms of action that we consider necessary for literacy training programs:

a) Preparing the matrix for participative literacy training, through cultural development in rural areas, based on the principle that the rural population is willing to participate in community life, but prevented from doing so by material or social conditions. The means must be found to distance the idea of cultural development from the conditioned reflexes that link it to socialism: to overcome centralizing tendencies and encourage local initiative in selecting and training facilitators. We intend to launch a consciousness-raising campaign for representatives of local authority, individuals who represent rural institutions and intellectuals, in order to recruit literacy program facilitators.

b) Encouraging change in cultural institutions through innovation or simply by adapting their objectives to consciousness-raising objectives. This involves restoring traditional cultural institutions that are still functioning (museums, libraries, cultural centres) by giving them new meaning corresponding to current needs.

Cultural centres, experiencing decline, should not make us forget that they were created as institutions for popular education. Material and human resources will be required to recreate this.

We will evaluate the real situation, with the co-operation of representatives of local administration, mayors and prefects. Within the context of the general program of education reform, our institute aims to create pilot centres to apply education reform programs (including rural areas) and to involve local resources in research and development programs.

c) Evaluating new partners. The State cannot bear the financial burden of supporting reform programs without participation by other agencies and associations. Once the idea of literacy training is recognized as a priority for contemporary Romanian society, we will be able to count on the support of several non-governmental institutions and even the private sector.

This approach to enlightened literacy training could be compared to a new flourishing of the cultural revolution, in contrast to what is called traditional literacy training. Let us clarify that active literacy training does not, in itself, aim to transform the village social and economic system, but rather to provide peasants with the means for civilization (and not politicization) enabling them to become increasingly capable of assuming responsibilities toward their community.

LITERACY TRAINING: FROM ITS REAL TRADITIONS TO MANIPULATING CODES

The Pre-totalitarian Period (1890-1945)

Before 1945, Romania had toward adult education the same concerns as other European countries. To cite only a few examples:

a)   Between 1893 and 1945, education legislation recognized literacy as the responsibility of the schools and literacy training in rural areas as a duty of the rural community. There were school-based programs for adults, just as there were in the same period, in the first basic education programs, for example in the United States, Canada and Portugal.[3] Such programs were aimed at the undereducated and their reintegration into occupational and social life.

The trend in Romania was progressive for the times: a concern for special programs, organized directly in the villages within specific institutional structures (the army, convents, prisons) and relying on local resources for educators and funding.

b)   Detailed statistical data gathered either by census or by special surveys also show that there was interest in literacy training between 1899 and 1932. Such data are missing in statistics after 1945, which we perceive either as a lack of interest in the problem or as an evasion of a reality that reflected poorly on the "success of socialism". We were supposed to conclude that the illiteracy rates of 67.4% (1912) and 35.1% (1932) in rural areas had disappeared thanks to the two-year socialist literacy campaign (1948 to 1950). After 1950, illiteracy indicators are lacking; it was to be taken as a given that socialist society had succeeded, in only two years, in eradicating a problem that arose from a system of social inequalities (capitalism), and thus affirming its superiority.

c)   Sociological studies of rural areas were numerous in that period; specialists in the field (I. Ivanescu, G.G. Antonescu, Simion Mehedinti, Stanciu Stoian, P.P. Negulescu, Dimitrie Gusti, Traian Herseni) devoted their studies to rural areas and to the problem of eliminating illiteracy. Dimitrie Gusti's scientific activity is remarkable; he undertook a literacy campaign in 54 Romanian villages, with only the help of his students, applying his sociological monograph method, which could be called action research before its time. His effort to create a museum of the Romanian village, in Bucharest, is also remarkable. Dimitrie Gusti conducted an extremely relevant analysis of categories of illiteracy and became one of the promoters of the rural university. In 1928, he described the goals of the rural university in these terms:

> "We must create a new ethos, raise a new level of consciousness and conviction: the peasants' belief in their peasant mission and the consciousness of their responsibility to their village and to the State to which they belong, their attachment to their village and to their land — those are the objectives of a post-secondary school in the rural milieu!"[4]

The concern for rural areas can be considered remarkable. The various forms of literacy training adapted for different environments and genders and instituted in adult education programs reveals the diverse needs of rural areas and the interest the State and intellectuals had in resolving a problem they considered crucial. Just as remarkable, the rural university projects sought to improve the peasants' awareness and to renew traditions of popular medicine, agriculture and folklore. Many of these projects would be worth fulfilling.

The Totalitarian Period (1945-1989)

The Facts

After 1948 (the year of the first socialist education reform act), the illiteracy problem was declared the fault of the former regime and even used to explain its failures. The authorities declared a campaign of forced literacy training (in the same way they had undertaken other campaigns for co-operatization in agriculture, industrialization, expropriation) for a period of two years. Subsequently, illiteracy was completely ignored. But the literacy training campaign proved to be a resounding success for other, more veiled, reasons and produced the first functional illiterates:

> After two years of studies in an educational centre, two years of secondary school and three or more years of higher education (in worker universities), a total illiterate could become a "specialist" in problems of the economy, society or culture.[5]

This marked the appearance of new specialists in a new profession, that of revolutionary. Thus began the destruction of intellectuals and the Romanian elite. A subtle and diabolical process of separating facts from the mystification of facts also began.

During the "golden age of communism", rural areas underwent heavy losses. First, they lost the intellectuals who were considered dangerous, well-to-do bourgeois. They became prisoners in political prisons and forced labour camps built for utopic industrial purposes. The destruction of peasant property began, in the hopes of actually destroying the natural relationship with the land through agriculture co-operatization campaigns that followed several so-called "agrarian revolutions". Soon Romanian villages had to endure another triumphal campaign — industrialization! The youth began to leave the villages to work in industrial mammoths that swallowed underqualified workers.

The Consequences

An ageing rural population, homes and families abandoned along with popular costumes, traditions, community models, languages and symbols of the rural world... Where were the advantages? Impersonal apartments, frustrating for peasants who were accustomed to a certain kind of communication: direct, oral, face to face, which played a specific role in social control; underemployment, alienation in the workplace, new models for social and cultural relationship that would lead, in short, to social anomie.

Those who could not completely adapt to urban life chose another solution: commuting between the city (or place of work) and the village (no longer serving any function other than dormitory). But they made the worst choice; rootlessness, instability, minimal time for reflection and development of critical opinions. Those who could not adjust became victims of literacy training imposed by the Ruling Power much more rapidly than those who chose total urbanization.

Other effects of revolutionary policies struck straight at the villages: indirectly, through the introduction of some polluting but grandiose industrial schemes on village land and, directly, as a result of a policy of "land systematization" that sought to transform villages into some kind of mutant hybrid known as "agro-industrial centres". The consequences are still visible: pollution, villages completely demolished or moved and the attendant results of that destruction. The villages around the city of Copsa Mica are a good example; a factory for the production of chemical substances was built there, and the vegetation and forests were practically totally destroyed. Another example is the small village of Ada-Kalech where Romanians and Turkish minorities used to peacefully co-exist; it was completely razed to make room for a hydro-electric station. Now, only a small museum remains, with picturesque images of the past, and a few ageing people, who speak about their former home with tears in their eyes.

An evaluation of rural literacy training shows that, during the most difficult stage of totalitarianism (1980 to 1989), results were spectacular. There was a school in every village, no illiteracy, free education for all, access to cultural activities and written information, original cultural productions, mass cultural demonstrations and so on. But over those great benefits and achievements hovered an amusing question that transformed all that prosperity into a paradox: How do we explain that, under capitalism, where it is worse, it is better, and, under socialism, where it is better, it is actually worse?

Communism's Mystifications

In order to assess the extent of the problem, we propose to highlight not only the linguistic and cultural aspects of literacy training, but, in particular, the socio-political and psychological implications of a policy based on overturning the rural traditions of marginalized peasants whose survival depended on an oral culture that they constantly had to defend against mystifications.

School for all and literacy training in school

One of the strongest indoctrination resources was the school, which soon became the only source of literacy training. Schools in rural areas were transformed into agro-industrial schools where basic education was largely neglected. There was a profound incompatibility between the very advanced level of the curriculum and the practical need to simplify knowledge for the purpose of making it operational. As a result, students were not given a good understanding of facts and were given even less instruction in basic skills (writing, reading, arithmetic).

Compulsory schooling up to 16 years of age, which should have thrust Romania into the ranks of the world's developed countries, had unexpected pernicious results: lack of objective selection and promotion criteria, many failures and dropouts, an increase in juvenile delinquency.

A teacher of Romanian who now works in a small country school made this edifying statement:

> I was obliged to announce incorrect percentages for the promotion of students to higher levels because, if I had students who had to redo the material I was teaching, I was considered a bad teacher, or, worse, an enemy of Party policy. In addition, my students were obliged to study politicized, so-called literary texts during class time and to read real literary works that I recommended outside school, almost with the feeling of committing a crime. I realize that I was one of the first to teach them the techniques of duplicity, but it was the only way to survive.

The purpose of literacy training based in the school was, in fact, the materialization of a myth. The myth of the "new human being" was, however, the prototype of the ordinary person, normal to the point of losing his or her own individuality. This myth cast a utopian light on all educational, cultural and political activity, becoming the most dogmatic and populist slogan of the time. The "person with multilateral training in all fields of activity" was, in reality, the materialization of the "superman" myth as opposed to the Promethean "man in revolt".

This "evil rewriting of man" wanted all spiritual concerns to be repressed in favour of a dogmatic and ultra-pragmatic approach, intending to create a prototype of an animal-like person, with a dormant conscience and primal concerns.

In spite of this situation, the peasants continued to live, love, learn, create. The Ruling Power proved incapable of evaluating their ability to survive, to endure suffering, injustice, the absurd. But peasants began abandoning their potential for authentic creation.

The ongoing revolution and its sacrifices

One of the most prevalent phrases in the past regime was "ongoing revolution", which contaminated many other concepts. Consciousness became "revolutionary", as did thought, history, activity, work. Paradoxically, despite the enthusiasm that was also supposed to accompany the underlying realities, individuals became increasingly passive toward change, because they were told that all their sacrifice was to further the "revolutionary values" they were meant to endorse.

As for the peasants, they were able to resist the pressures thanks to their deeply embedded roots in tradition. Perhaps it was what Fernand Braudel referred to as "the long term" or just the peasants' natural, common-sense loyalty to their own values. In any case, they resisted the pressure but became less communicative and less interested in participating in social life. In the villages today, the traces of post-revolutionary sadness are still evident on the faces of many of the elderly inhabitants.

Control and falsification

The Ruling Power of the former regime soon understood the importance of communication in society. It therefore decided to control the content of written and visual communication, finding oral communication harder to control and preferring to let it function as a release valve in case of potential conflicts. The Ruling Power thus meticulously considered and applied a program for a new kind of literacy training whose objective was to create the ability to understand and to communicate only the falsified codes imposed by the Ruling Power, by inventing a specific mechanism that could be called "control by falsification".

In rural areas, literacy training was conducted specifically through new or socialist folklore, an expression of the joy of socialist living, used to communicate the total harmony that exists between traditional and socialist values (such as collectivizing land, for example, or hatred of the rich and the exploiters) and to give due thanks to the Party and its leader. We had to endure "folkloric" creations transformed into songs or deformed poems of the genre: "Maple leaf and cabbage leaf / Come see me, my fine young wolf / If you take me as your wife / my co-op'rative's your life."[6]

Now it is impossible to imagine the peasants who created folklore that was either sober or full of humour, but always remarkably connected to their essential themes (the relationship between their feelings and nature, the sacrifice required for any real achievement, love) humming a song about collectivization or love for the Party. There were some individuals willing to present that kind of "creation" (that nobody listened to) on radio or television, given that the purpose of the Ruling Power was clearly to falsify a means of communication by very strict control of it.

The most useful tool for information control was systematic and strenuous censorship. Nothing that might threaten the dictatorship could be broadcast. Words that expressed fear, criticism of the prosperous socialist regime or simply meanings that the dictators did not understand (being themselves suspected of illiteracy) were cut out and locked up in the "prison for words".[7] Partial banning, requiring the author to substitute and compromise, was more subtle. Creative writers adopted various attitudes and strategies to survive the slow, insidious war of attrition. They adopted a form of literacy that could be called "survival literacy". They used any and all means to thwart Party vigilance: sacrificing part of their creation, adopting a bookish style, of a different time, glorifying nationalism (a subject greatly prized by the authorities).

In our projects for rural areas, we must first recognize the existence of certain cognitive structures (for understanding written text) that could not be wiped out by the political changes of 1989, after 50 years of totalitarianism. While the peasants soon learned social complicity, all their tools for duplicity changed over time into behaviour: reserve, passivity and little interest in what happens beyond their immediate concerns or their community's. The premise that they could simply and rapidly learn all that society asked them to learn is not very plausible without sustained and organized literacy training.

The mirage of gobbledygook

Communist speeches habituated us to a certain language that has been called "gobbledygook". Communist Party reports, lectures, and debates were full of technical details, figures, percentages, forecasts and indicators that bore no relationship to reality. The more technical and filled with stirring slogans the speeches were, the less credible and more ridiculous they were. The purpose of the speeches, however, was not so much to falsify data as to falsify communication and thought.

Gobbledygook was a tool for regulating interaction between individual and Party and between individuals, a real mental battle where: "Only the Party is right and can tell the whole truth. What it cannot express does not exist." Such axioms, which governed the literacy training strategies imposed by the Ruling Power, gradually caused a contagious disease of thought that attacked any attempt at opposition.

Gobbledygook was also another tool for imposing the codes of the Ruling Power: for building a standardized structure and criteria based on populist attitudes using certain conditioned linguistic reflexes. All institutions were mobilized in the fight against the mind: the press, school, radio and television, movies, theatre. They were all to become sources of collective suggestion that were then to create individual beliefs, followed by collective beliefs.

As an example of the contagious disease of suggestibility inflicted by gobbledygook, here is a typical text entitled "To achieve the precious ideals of our nation", signed by the chairperson of a village agricultural co-operative:

> We agricultural workers are convinced that after the last few years of building socialism, and, in particular, after the IX Congress, which began a period of great change in the history of Romanian agriculture, we workers of the land have been through an intense process of great transformation and revolutionary change. First of all, there is the significant fact of ever-increasing growth in agricultural production made possible by learning the "art of working the land" and the great investment made in agriculture.... The peasants' quality of life has improved in keeping with the benefits of hard work, increasingly modern and effective, based on the solid foundation of the "new quality" principle.... I want to thank our Secretary General of the Communist Party for the efforts made... for the emancipation and civilization of the villages of Romania, for the life the peasants lead, for their conditions of work, for the future of humanity."[8]

We believe that it will not be possible to implement a program of democratization without reconstructing the language in real conditions of contemporary rural life.

Humour as a source of survival for oral literacy

In contrast to this sombre picture, the dictatorship period is full of humorous creations (anecdotes, songs, poems and so on). This proliferation of oral expression could be explained as an antidote to official imposed literacy. In fact, the anecdote has its roots in popular tales that are very short, joyous and conclude with a moral. In our case, the moral purpose of these tales has been exchanged for finding release and responding to official propoganda.

The most representative illustration of the role of humour in rural culture and social psychology is found in the cemetery of laughter. In the little village of Sapinta in the Maramures region, there is a crazy, provocative cemetery, full of grotesque images, with epitaphs written as humorous, rhyming chronicles of the personality and life of the deceased, an iconoclastic cemetery.

Humour has reinforced the codes of the sub-text, representing another way to survive by laughing at our unhappiness (grin and bear it). The purposes of propaganda were subtle enough to allow the oral channels to function, while allowing the Ruling Power to take advantage of a mutually accepted deceitful atmosphere. How could it have lied so blatantly, if there had not been a natural setting for lies? In the atmosphere of constant lies, it wisely accepted humour as a generously offered illusion, the illusion that we could laugh at the Ruling Power. We thus participated not only in the devaluation of the truth, but also in the depreciation of the aspiration to know the truth.

THE POST - TOTALITARIAN PERIOD (AFTER 1989)

The Romanian Rural Environment

In Romania, the rural area represents more than a group of villages and communes. It is a world that includes about 2,688 administrative units and over 10,839,761 inhabitants (46.8% of the Romanian population), where the main occupations are agriculture (and related fields), light industry, business and services.

Today, there are no "empty" rural regions because the Real Property Act (no. 18 /1991) re-established the relationship between the peasants and their land, thus allowing the urban population to repossess and work the land again. Furthermore, the rate of unemployment (8.4% nationally) has brought about an increase in migration from urban to rural areas.

We cannot speak of homogeneity in the rural area; it extends, very evenly divided, between regions of plains, hills and mountains. Differences in geographic location have brought differences in economic and cultural development. There are also definite differences between the regions that were co-operatized and those that were not in terms of mentality, attitudes and community spirit. (In the hill and mountain regions, the land remained the property of the peasant.) In the regions that were not co- operatized, cultural development and private initiative was much greater, and cultural pollution was minimal. (The Maramures and Bucovina regions are good examples.)

There are regions inhabited by minority communities (Hungarian, German, Serb, Turk, Romany and so on) that form relatively compact cultural zones where they speak their mother tongue and want to preserve their particular cultural and occupational traditions and to develop their own language with the help of educational and para-educational institutions.

The New "Conditional Dictatorship"

In the three years following the removal of the dictatorship, Romanian society has accepted a widely used, but still misunderstood, concept: transition. For the peasants, the meaning of that concept is not clear: does it mean crisis, development, restructuring? Without some clarification (information about the problems as well as the real possibilities for coming out of the crisis), there is no way to convince the peasants that they can make plans for the future, for a new life. Projects for development and plans to motivate people to get involved in community life cannot be entertained without creating a stable foundation. How could we consider building projects based on the fragile structures of the new conditional dictatorship?

What methods are there for informing rural areas? First of all, radio and television are oral literacy resources that are often criticized for their partisanship. (They are national networks.) Then, there are newspapers, periodicals, books and magazines; although in 1991, there were 3,869 new books, 435 magazines and over 200 newspapers and periodicals published, only 10% of them reached rural areas. So written information is lacking as a resource to raise consciousness about change.

The cultural infrastructure itself is poorly utilized. In 1991, there were 2,585 cultural centres with 4,862 rural branches, but they are still underused and undervalued as information tools today.

The Problems of Informal Education

Because rural areas were bombarded by the new popular culture, and because popular creators were obliged to endure social activism and the pres-́ sure, at any cost, to be creators (of new agriculture, new relationships or new folklore), the peasants are now very wary of any cultural development initiative outside traditional institutions. As a result, it will be very difficult to choose informal methods (generally used in literacy training programs) and to avoid using voluntary facilitators (who had been facilitators under the old regime) who might rediscover their taste for outmoded activism.

We plan to involve the Church in our projects, because it once represented a means of escape into a sacred space. Sacred rituals were special occasions for participation in community life, and the only form of civic instruction tacitly opposed to totalitarian rule was found in religious education.

Today, religious education could constitute a form of literacy training suited to rural areas that would not give the peasants the impression of coming from the outside, because it is familiar to them. However, here again it could be said that there is a crisis of confidence as some members of the Church compromised with the Ruling Power in the past (and have retained important positions in society), and also because there is a profusion of religious rituals on television. Many of them seem to have political rather than religious purposes. As a result, there are criticisms and controversies about the role of the Church in society and, in particular, about its educational mission. If we want to associate the Church in literacy training (a role it played before 1945), we have to start with some projects and measures aimed at the Church itself.

The New Gobbledygook

Immediately after the events of December 1989, we thought it would be enough to burn all the communist books and speeches for gobbledygook to be forgotten. But totalitarian reflexes had been solidly entrenched and led to a new gobbledygook that uses new terms but with the same purpose: **communication without content**, particularly when it comes to official explanations of a crisis. Some members of Parliament adopted a "gobbledygook style", as it were, a baroque style consisting of long jingoistic speeches and journalistic language closely resembling the language used in the past by those who humbly served the Ruling Power.

For example, the following is an excerpt from an article on the problem of introducing religious instruction into primary schools, entitled "An opinion on anticonstitutional, anachronistic procedures":

> How could the more gifted students, the intellectuals, with their atheistic, materialistic and scientific convictions, be forced to assimilate religious beliefs that clearly contradict scientific data on nature and society and generally contradict the most elementary logic, and to accept the basic commandment of any religion, which is to believe without questioning.[9]

This resembles a paragraph from a manual on scientific socialism. It is not difficult to recognize the gobbledygook style, which serves here to express the indignation of a teacher still steeped in Marxist scientific ideas, writing in a popular rural newspaper.

RURAL LITERACY TRAINING PROJECTS

Operational Objectives for 1993-1995

- Abandoning the idea that only rural schools can provide literacy training; they have neither the material resources nor the teachers for formal adult education. The schools' objectives are to prevent functional illiteracy and to take on their still important role in the development of rural communities. They must also recognize their failures and the serious impact of functional illiteracy on the culture and way of life of these communities;

- discovering community-based methods and non-governmental agencies to launch some literacy projects; promoting the idea of local partnership and decentralization, encouraging development initiatives and organizing inter-regional networks;

- producing tools to raise awareness of functional illiteracy in Romania (the evaluation of this phenomenon is still being investigated), with a positive, completely non-aggressive presentation; we intend to use mainly local media to disseminate popular data;

- making use of projects and programs established by other agencies for the education of women, youth, training and requalifying the unemployed in order to combine the objectives of those programs with literacy training programs;

- enlarging the field of literacy training to include cultural minorities (Hungarian, German, Romany and so on), by taking advantage of their concern for the development of modern languages as well as of their own culture, although, at the moment, this is a rather delicate issue.

Expected Results

- Changing the peasants themselves (whom we consider the main players in efforts toward village cultural development) by changing their mentality, role and attitudes toward community problems;

- changing the attitude of local decision-makers toward development solutions; their direct participation in the development;

- mobilizing material and human resources, educational institutions and, in particular, cultural institutions for the development of their communities; restoration of cultural centres and rural libraries; creation of a rural university;

- introducing rural inhabitants to the new roles they will have to play on their community scene.

Some Methodological Points

We are trying to involve the whole group of individuals, institutions and rural communities in our projects, even though our programs are based on individual attitude and behaviour; therefore:

- achievement of change in the new role they will have to play will be through learning or re-learning how to participate and be creative, tools they can use in their personal life, in their work life and in their community;

- occupational, social, political and cultural preparation will be through various activities:

  - occupational (knitting, sewing, crafts, ceramics);

  - social and political (meetings on the theme of civic education, developing associations for helping large families and so on);

  - cultural (folk dance, naïve art, popular costume exhibits, traditional folklore, lay or religious demonstrations).

The research units (for the proposed purposes) will be the historical regions of the country (Moldavia, Muntenia, Dobruja, Oltenia, Banat, Transylvania, Maramures and Bucovina) within which we will choose the administrative regions, communes and villages that are most culturally disadvantaged.

The methods selected will be more qualitative than statistical, but we plan to use data from the 1992 census and public opinion surveys, mainly through interviews, because we consider direct contact with the rural inhabitants very important.

Foreseeable Problems

- Functional illiteracy is not officially recognized in Romania as its most serious cultural problem with widespread implications.

- There is still a false view of development, facilitators and mass culture.

- Negative phenomena from the totalitarian society are still present in the form of blocks, mainly psychological where rural inhabitants are concerned.

- Material (financial) resources are lacking.

- Political and educational decisions about adult education (mainly those concerning basic education and continuing education) remain to be made.

- The idea of literacy training based in the school is still held; local initiative to develop cultural infrastructures and communication methods is lacking.

Projects in Progress

Found a Rural University

The project for developing a rural university is underway, initiated by the Bucharest Education Sciences Institute. Its goals:

- highlighting Romanian traditions with regard to rural universities and other similar undertakings elsewhere in the world;

- renewing traditional peasant involvement in popular medicine, agriculture, winegrowing and other fields;

- utilizing human resources in rural areas to prepare courses and inviting rural environment specialists to give courses on current topics;

- increasing awareness and appreciation for original folklore creations and specific techniques (for weaving carpets, pottery, naïve painting and so on) in order to restore specific peasant occupations and traditions.

Functional literacy training is implicit (an introductory module exists entitled "general culture"), but we have at least made contact with the project coordinator.

Romanian and foreign non-governmental agencies have been involved in obtaining material resources for the project with the goal of the university being self-financing.

(Details about the project and further information may be obtained from Alexandru Darie, Education Sciences Institute, 37 str. Stirbei Voda, Bucharest, Facsimile: (40) (1) 312-1447.)

Evaluate Material Resources
& Produce Material for Literacy Awareness

We plan to launch a program to evaluate the human and material resources in rural areas, involving local decision-makers who will themselves participate in raising awareness of the rural crisis. We also plan to develop some tools for creating awareness, which will be prepared based on the results of the survey and direct discussions with potential partners in literacy training programs. Copies will be produced in volume and distributed in all regions of the country. The material will be circulated for critical review to those who participated in conducting the survey.

We wish to establish a national network of facilitators for rural areas and documents for their work. We expect to have to start from a real (informal) base to set up future literacy training programs, and we will need local support for the process in terms of its partners, the kind of documents, interests, needs, the real situation in cultural institutions and so on.

(Further information may be obtained from Florentina Anghel, Education Sciences Institute, same address as above.)

An Education Reform
to Include Rural Areas

This is part of the education reform project in Romania which aims to introduce, through pilot centres for reform implementation, the main consultation programs for restructuring the education system. The pilot centres are not represented only by rural schools, but also by any institution that commits to joint projects with our Institute for direct participation in experimental research done on reform.

The objective of these centres is to involve the players themselves in preparing public opinion for the implementation of the proposed restructuring; thus the centres serve to multiply the objectives rather than simply apply results of research on the planned curriculum, administration and evaluation systems in an experimental fashion.

(Further information may be obtained from Cesar Birzea, Director, Education Sciences Institute, same address as above.)

Notes & References

1. Birzea, Cesar, Ana-Maria Sandi, Gabriel Ivan & Romulus Brancoveanu. (1993). [*Education reform in Romania: Conditions and prospects*]. Bucharest: Department of Education, Education Sciences Institute.
2. Birzea, Cesar. (1991). Literacy and development in eastern European countries: The case of Romania. International conference on *Attaining functional literacy* held October 10-12, 1991. The Netherlands: University of Tilburg.
3. Hautecoeur, Jean-Paul. (1992). (Ed.) *ALPHA 92* [*Literacy research*]. Québec: Department of Education / Hamburg: UNESCO Institute for Education.
4. Gusti, Dimitrie. (1973). [Politics and cultural status. *Pedagogical works*]. Conference in Bucharest on January 10, 1928. Bucharest: [Instructional and Pedagogical Editions].
5. Birzea, Cesar. [Literacy and development in eastern European countries]. op.cit.

6. [*The new folklore*]. (1965). Bucharest: [Central Popular Creation Enterprises].

7. Vlad, Iuliana. (1992). [Censorship as a way of using. *Literary Romania*]. No. 39.

8. Birzea, Cesar. [Literacy and development in eastern European countries]. op.cit.

9. (1992). [*Europa Review*]. No. 103.

Chapter 14
TELEVISION & LITERACY DEVELOPMENT IN THE CZECH REPUBLIC

Stanislav Hubik
Palacky University
Olomouc, Czech Republic

THEORETICAL TENETS

There are several dimensions to the development of cultural literacy (Key Term: kulturni gramotnost = (cultural) literacy = alphabetisation) in rural areas of the industrial countries of Europe and North America, and several possible approaches for achieving it. Essentially the approach will depend on the concrete socio-cultural situation not only in the country as a whole but also in the region. The current situation in the Czech Republic is specific because Czech society is undergoing a major transformation as a result of the revolutionary events of 1989 and the years following. This is why the problems dealt with by our literacy development project have been increasing and why, in addition to the usual problems produced by industrialization, we find problems generated by privatization (and the restitution of formerly private property).

In light of the many dimensions of the project, and the possibility of several approaches, it is important to explain certain theoretical and methodological tenets underlying the observations that follow.

By (cultural) literacy, I mean the ability of a regionally and structurally delimited community to create relationships, processes and institutions aimed at a multi-faceted social, spiritual and mental cultivation of that community, based on its own indigenous resources (natural, human, social and cultural), possibly with help from outside.

The nature of literacy and the type of action taken to improve it will differ in different historical types of society. If we accept the methodological and heuristic approaches based on the classification of socio-cultural entities into

197

premodern, modern and postmodern[1], we can observe that:

In the **premodern** socio-cultural type, the ability to generate and reproduce cultivation processes through literacy efforts in a rural area is natural but not very dynamic or innovative. It is mainly limited to reproducing traditional meaning structures. Outside intervention is restricted and untypical, increasing only with industrialization, ubanization and democratization.

In the **modern** socio-cultural type, the ability to generate cultivation processes is increasingly disconnected from traditional meaning structures and ever more closely tied to processes of rationalization and universalization.[2] A never-ending flow of innovations deepens the gap between the modern culture and the traditional cultural bases of rural communities. This diminishes the ability to generate cultivation processes from inside the community. Internal generation is increasingly replaced by external intervention through the now dominant processes of industrialization, urbanization, democratization, Europeanization, etc.

In the **postmodern** socio-cultural type, the ability to generate cultivation processes through literacy efforts is reassessed. The assessment shows up the defects and limitations created by modern culture and at the same time it seeks out and finds possibilities for re-introducing resources for the general cultivation of a rural community, that is, resources of a premodern type. The toleration for the incommensurable which is typical of postmodern knowledge and sensibility[3] is reflected in efforts directed not at a search for a general, universal model of literacy development in rural areas, but rather at bringing together practical development projects and drawing inspiration from their heterogeneity.

Literacy development, understood as an intentional intervention in the life of a rural community, has three equally important dimensions: the **social**, the **educational** and the **cultural**. Since these terms are used differently in the various contexts of European thought, I should explain them briefly.

If the aim of a literacy development strategy is the general cultivation of a community and its individual members, then an integrated approach is needed. Development cannot be limited to activities for cultivating spiritual life, such as adult education, because it is also necessary to eliminate social tensions in the community - deviant or even pathological tendencies. These are not problems dealt with by adult education but by social work. Yet even that does not cover everything. Communities possess certain cultural skills and related meaning structures which take material shape in traditional culture and folklore. These must not only be protected[4] but developed, and that falls neither to adult education (except in special cases) nor social work but to cultural work.

So to the three dimensions of literacy (the social, the educational and the cultural), there correspond three modes of action: adult education, social work and cultural work. Literacy development strategy consequently includes all three.

The modern way of thinking, representing as it does the cultural logic of industrialism/capitalism, stresses the educational dimension of literacy. This links the cultivation of a community with systematic book-based instruction and the accumulation of rational knowledge and interchangeable skills. On this point, modern thought is the faithful inheritor of the Enlightenment ethos. As Habermas would put it, in a modern society, the social and cultural dimensions of literacy, along with the traditional base of the rural Lifeworld [Lebenswelt], are absorbed by the modern System.[5]

This absorption by the System can be described metaphorically using such terms as industrialization, urbanization and rationalization. But that is not important. What is important is that the creation of a socio-cultural gap between modern society and rural society (a gap to which the System/Lifeworld distinction can be applied, with some simplification) leads to a weakening of the community's natural ability to institute an internal dialogue leading to cultivation. The result is a vacuum, mainly in the social and cultural dimensions of the literacy problem (less in the educational dimension). Into this vacuum come modern interventions from the outside, particularly those of an educational nature.

The following table provides a simplified illustration of this way of understanding the problem:

Cultivation of a Rural Society by Literacy Development

Aspects of Literacy	Literacy Development Activities
education level of adult population	adult education in various institutional forms
social life and social relations	social work in various institutional forms
dialogue between modern and premodern culture (traditional culture and folklore)	cultural work in various institutional forms

The above table is not intended to describe a hierarchy and its terminology is flexible. Nothing prevents us from seeing adult education as a *sui generis* type of social work, or social work as a *sui generis* type of cultural work. The terms are not important; what is important is to examine the problem in all its aspects.

The value of this approach can be seen much more revealingly when a society is undergoing really revolutionary changes — certainly the case in the Czech

Republic and other postcommunist countries. What changes is not only the various aspects listed on the table but also the character of the institutions that look after literacy development. In some cases, the institutional base may even temporarily disappear (because of problems with the economy or privatization, or a legislative vacuum), and symptoms of anomie may then appear for a short time in certain well-defined spheres of social life. The result is a focus on revitalizing the community's own resources for cultivation as well as on more effective intervention from the outside — from the System (the state). Where the System is unable to act, either through institutions or through individuals, the only remaining possibility is to act through what might be called replacement institutions such as the mass media. The result is a seemingly paradoxical situation: in the absence of institutions, the most influential representative of modern industrial society — namely television, the "enemy" of the Lifeworld — becomes a beneficial method of intervention (in well-defined cases of course).

SOCIALISM & LITERACY

What then is the situation in the Czech Republic regarding the various aspects set out in the above table?

The development of Czech society after 1948 considerably disrupted the integrity of literacy. I do not mean a disruption in the sense of a basic disconnection of rural communities from their traditional bases, or a subsequent decay of the various aspects of literacy represented on our table. Rather there was a disruption and restructuring of sociocultural relations as a result of the ideological denial of various aspects of sociocultural reality. Ideological denial meant, for example, that social problems of capitalism such as unemployment, homelessness and poverty had supposedly been eliminated. The result was the disappearance of institutions and modes of action whose purpose was precisely to eliminate or regulate such "problems of capitalism".

Now that these problems are returning along with the restored social structures, the corresponding network of institutions and modes of action no longer exists (though it is in the process of developing). As a result, it is not possible for the time being to look after the sociocultural life of rural communities (and non-rural ones as well) in the same multi-faceted way and at the same level as in Western Europe, where social policy and social work have been developing without much disruption, and where at the same time social institutions and projects have been flourishing.

Massive industrialization and the collectivization of life in rural areas brought new forms of social behaviour as well as new meaning structures to traditional culture. The question thus arises whether, as a result, the old patterns of premodern rural culture were covered over, forgotten or erased outright. To answer this question, we must take into consideration the paradoxes of socialism. On the one hand there was massive industrialization and collectivization of the countryside; on the other hand the regime paid scrupulous — even exaggerated — attention to traditional culture. It must be borne in mind that the regime fetishized the "people" (though often in "folkloric" terms).

This fetishization served as a counterbalance to elitism and as a source of legitimacy for the regime (though unlike ideological indoctrination, it was of course never translated into practice). The "people" became a quasi-sacred entity, and this was reflected in programs in the fields of traditional culture (seen as "the motor force of history" and "the bearer of progress"), as well as in efforts to develop backward (mostly rural) regions. This paradoxical approach had some beneficial effects, such as an extensive institutional and organizational network within which adult education and social work were carried on. The work was deformed by ideology but there is no doubt that it protected traditional and more recently created values and enabled their further development.[6]

So unlike the case with social work, cultural and adult educational work still have an institutional basis (now undergoing considerable change) as well as a tradition. Both types of work tend to be structured in terms of Enlightenment ideals that do not take account of the need for a multi-faceted and integrated approach to the problem. For many reasons, the educational, cultural and social facets of literacy work are still seen as strictly separate and specialized activities.[7] This is going to make the complex task of developing literacy in the Czech Republic more difficult for some time yet.

A system for literacy development in rural areas was created after 1948 and it functioned over the next few decades, but it is now in crisis and in some respects dysfunctional. This has turned attention to the mass media — a completely different phenomenon from an institutional point of view. The mass media can be seen as a universalizing means of literacy development, and of a peculiarly modern type.

In a situation where — as is generally recognized — existing types of institution are undergoing basic change and are therefore weakened, it is only logical that other institutions, or in some cases individual personalities, will take up their functions. Naturally this includes the mass media institutions.

Literacy development is part of their mandate, and adapting to the characteristics of regions and communities is for them an economic necessity. I do not have in mind here specialty media such as professional journals or specialized television programs. I am thinking rather of the mainstream media that cover all sectors of activity, and in particular those programs which have the secondary or tertiary function of stimulating literacy development. In the situation of institutional crisis I have described, this secondary function comes to the fore.

THE BOOK OF PRESCRIPTIONS

In the Czech Republic and in Slovakia, the function of stimulating literacy falls to a television program called *Receptár*, which means "book of prescriptions" or "book of recipes". Analysis shows it to have considerable potential for all three aspects of literacy promotion.

This brings us to two important questions:

1) Can television — the messenger of modern industrialism — revitalize and mobilize the indigenous resources for literacy in a rural community?

2) Are these indigenous resources constituted by structures belonging to the premodern past alone, or by structures of the present alone?

With regard to question 1), the negative assessment of television and its role in the absorption by industrialism of the traditional cultures of rural communities is well known. Even postmodernists understand television mainly as a means of simulation that distances a society both from the past and from contemporary reality. The views of Jean Baudrillard[8] are very influential on this point. Yet it is precisely the simulation capacity of television — its ability to create a "second reality", a "hyper-reality" — that enables it to take up certain roles of institutions which are malfunctioning or nonfunctioning at all. Television can successfully simulate the roles of institutions involved in literacy development or in the creation of literacy strategies for rural areas. Thus a simplistic negative assessment of television cannot be accepted.

With regard to question 2), as we will see, this issue is related to the influence exercised on the public by television in rural areas. Traditional culture is not necessarily to be seen as made up solely of the indigenous heritage handed down from past generations, that which has come down untarnished by modernity, the "old". The definition of traditional culture and folklore in the UNESCO resolution mentioned above (cf. endnote 4) does not exclude a conception of the present as a source of the tradition of the near future. Thus the study and nurture of the non-systemic (in the Habermasian sense) cultural structures of the present are just as important as the reproduction and preservation of the cultural structures of the past. So there are two approaches of interest: a reproductive/preserving approach which draws on the past and its meaning structures, and a productive/living approach which draws on the present with a strong pragmatic and topical focus.

The problem of literacy development in the rural areas of industrialized countries, understood as a problem of the multi-faceted cultivation of these communities, has two aspects: a historical aspect and a contemporary aspect. A community's own indigenous resources for cultivation are created by the previously existing and reproduced tradition and also by the tradition of the rural Lifeworld which is currently in the making. This second tradition is a field of action which television can not only enter but also to a degree mediate, providing a model for it through programs such as *Receptár*. A brief analytical description of the program will show the functional potential of television for literacy development in rural areas.

The program explores, maps, collects, analyzes, selects and evaluates existing resources for literacy development in rural and other areas. Itself a tool of intervention, it has been part of the regular television schedule since 1987.[9] By late 1992, there had been 187 different episodes as well as re-runs. The audience is very large — 3-4 million (the Czech Republic and Slovakia together have 15 million plus inhabitants). About three-quarters of the regular audience live in rural areas. Thus *Receptár* addresses 2-3 million rural viewers in the two republics. Most of them are middle-aged or seniors.

The way the program works is simple. Information is collected from viewers (over 150 letters a week, dozens of telephone calls a day and other information of various types, especially following the launch of a new periodical or other publication). The information is analyzed, checked and evaluated; a selection (of ideas, opinions, projects, etc.) is then made and broadcast. During its seven years, *Receptár* has accumulated a large bank of data, only a small part of which has actually been broadcast.

After 1989, *Receptár* developed into a rather more complex cultural institution. A magazine was launched, which now has a quarter of a million readers. A *Receptár* Club was founded, which has some 80,000 members, and a Club Foundation (Nadace Klubu) was established. In addition, the group which prepares the program also publishes theme books and pamphlets and organizes *Receptár* Days (*Dny Receptáre*) outside the studio. Thus a fairly well structured cultural institution focused on mass communication has come into being.

The original mission of *Receptár* was to create a television program that would deal with viewers' hobbies. Its basic function was supposed to be broadcasting ideas, finds and projects to occupy viewers' free time in a sensible way. This notion of "sensible way" needs explaining, especially for those having no personal experience of life in one of the societies of "actual socialism".

One of the features of such a society was a lack of goods and services. Not a lack in the absolute sense (poverty) but in the sense of a structural shortage. On the socialist market, the structure of goods and services was separate from the structure of needs and demand. As a result, a "secondary economy" very soon appeared and was more or less tolerated and even encouraged by the authorities. This economy was based on the spirit of invention, imagination and mutual aid. It produced and exchanged what the "primary economy" could not. The program quickly became a database and "advisor" for the secondary economy. If we were to look in the magazines and other broadcasts of the period, we would no doubt find analogies, but *Receptár*, with its mass influence, went beyond any such similar cases.

Thus what started as a hobby program turned into something quite different.

But then this is not unusual: the intention behind an act is one thing; the result is another.

THE "BRICOLAGE" ECONOMY

The real effects and the real status of *Receptár* are remarkable, and I will try to explain them by referring to the work of that classic thinker of French structural anthropology, Claude Lévi-Strauss. The chapter of his book *La Pensée sauvage* [*The Savage Mind*] dealing with "The Science of the Concrete" reads like a description of the situation the viewers of *Receptár* were in before (and to some degree after) 1989. In the following passage, the key term is the French word *bricolage (domáci kutilství* in Czech), which refers to "do-it-yourself" activity:

> There still exists among ourselves an activity which on the technical plane gives us quite a good understanding of what a science we prefer to call 'prior' rather than 'primitive', could have been on the plane of speculation. This is what is commonly called bricolage in French.[10]

Receptár became the database and the "spokesman" for this bricolage. Lévi-Strauss continues:

> In our own time, the bricoleur is still someone who works with his hands and uses roundabout means compared to those of a professional... The bricoleur is adept at performing a large number of diverse tasks; but, unlike the engineer, he does not subordinate each of them to the availability of raw materials and tools conceived and procured for the purpose of the project. His universe of instruments is closed and the rules of his game are always to make do with 'whatever is at hand', that is to say with a set of tools and materials which is always finite and is also heterogeneous... [The set is defined by the fact that its] elements are collected or retained on the principle that 'they may always come in handy.'[11]

"Making do with whatever is at hand" was imposed by the primary economy of socialism on anyone who had come up against the barrier of structural shortages. The "means used by the professional" were those provided by the primary economy. Individuals then had to resort to *bricolage*, making do with what they had available, and this called for a remarkable spirit of invention, mixing together the logics and tools of premodern and modern culture. The world of socialism was a "closed universe of instruments" just like the world of *bricolage*. The end of the cited passage ("elements are collected or retained on the principle that 'they may always come in handy'") speaks directly to the reality of *Receptár*: it became, to use Foucault's terminology, a sort of official "archive" of the "discourse" of *bricolage*.

Of course the discourse of bricolage existed in parallel to the socialist economy, and there was a tacitly recognized *modus vivendi* between the two "orders of existence".

Western society does not know of such a situation, though there are analogies in the circumstances that existed during the last World War. Also, the West may not always correctly understand us on this point. Lévi-Strauss says that industrial societies "only tolerate [*bricolage*] as a hobby or pastime".[12] In this he was wrong: socialist society was undoubtedly industrial but it tolerated *bricolage* not only as a hobby or pastime but as an activity to fill in the gaps created by structural shortages. *Bricolage* as practised in Czechoslovakia before 1989 (and still practised now to some degree) was much more than what Lévi-Strauss described; it was a sociogenic and culturogenic phenomenon/process arising from the social reality of the time.

The program became de facto and de jure an institution/medium of *mass bricolage*. This term may seem to be an oxymoron, but then paradox is one of the features of postmodernity. The existence of *mass bricolage* proves that socialist society reached a highly specific stage in which it produced, by industrial means, elements of premodern society (namely the practice of *bricolage*). In this stage, society had aspects of postmodernism but not of postindustrialism.

Receptár came to play the role of a guide to *mass bricolage*, a sort of university where Lévi-Strauss's "science of the concrete" was pursued.

This is also the starting point for my analysis and evaluation of the role of *Receptár* after 1989. Did it retain its *mass bricolage* function? The total social transformation of Czechoslovak society began in 1990, and this meant the end of the "secondary economy" and structural shortages. *Mass bricolage* should thus have become history and reverted to hobby status. But the actual situation is quite different: *mass bricolage* has shifted from the economic sphere into other spheres of social life (on a temporary basis it would seem). These other spheres are precisely those of interest in the issues of literacy development strategy.

Thus while *Receptár* is no longer a guide to *mass bricolage* in the economic sense, it now serves as a guide to *mass bricolage* in the sphere of general community development in certain localities and regions, especially rural ones.

This is understandable. It is true that the parallel economy is dissipating as the market fills with goods and services and structural shortages disappear. However the transformation of society includes the disappearance of institutions, including those which developed and implemented literacy strategy. And this is precisely what is creating the temporary need for *bricolage* — this time to deal with problems in the three dimensions of literacy (the social, the educational and cultural).

Once again, *Receptár* is assuming the role of guide and database. Here are a few examples.[13] Recently the program publicized a project to manufacture wheelchairs. After two weeks, 54 private firms said they would be interested. The result was a signed contract between the *bricoleur* who designed the chair and a company. Production was started and new jobs were created in a region suffering unemployment. And of course there was a social aspect that went beyond creating jobs since there was a benefit to handicapped people.

In December 1992, the idea of manufacturing aids and accessories for pet owners produced a flood of 1500 letters and 800 personal visits to the author of the proposal and the original *bricoleur*-manufacturer. The manufacturing process was then professionalized and enlarged, creating jobs and so forth. The same thing happened after a project to make clothing suitable for waiters was publicized.

There are hundreds of similar examples, too many to describe them all or list them. Just as in the period prior to 1989, their common denominator is their source — the *bricoleur*. Their new feature is their clear contribution to community cultivation, the impulse they give to multi-faceted literacy development: social and cultural as well as economic development. We could track the various ideas and inventions and identify precisely the number of jobs and amounts of profit created, thus determining the project's concrete contribution to the cultivation of a region or locality. That of course would greatly exceed the scope of the present study.

A POSTMODERN LITERACY

After discussions with the authors of *Receptár*, I came to the conclusion that this program operates as a sort of author and director of community development work in all three spheres of literacy. It is a prototype for cultural action whose importance — as I suggest at the end of the article — could potentially be of even greater scope. It is simply a matter of strengthening the program's function as a model, in accordance with the real needs of regions and localities. Once the needs have to some extent been harmonized with the information and projects disseminated by the program, *Receptár* will serve a therapeutic function in the most general sense of the word.

What is remarkable here is that the source of the model (and the possible therapeutic function) lies not within the System but within the Lifeworld. It retains its nature as *bricolage* and in this sense it is identical to tradition. Would anyone deny that *bricolage* belongs to tradition? Certainly not Lévi-Strauss.

The UNESCO *Recommendation on the Safeguarding of Traditional Culture and Folklore* encourages giving "precedence to ways of presenting traditional and popular cultures that emphasize the living or past aspects of those cultures". I would emphasize the word "living" because *bricolage* — even when it uses television — certainly provides living testimony of what used to be or what is coming into being (what is becoming a source of future tradition).

Receptár carries out its educational/instructional roles in a conscious and planned way, not only with regard to the distribution of information about hobbies or economic issues, but also by overseeing a systematic exchange of information among, for example, pet-owners, gardeners, small landowners, beginner entrepreneurs and designers of public projects. It provides information to people interested in healthy foods traditional to a region. It helps with the organization of dozens of local and regional exhibits and related seminars. *Receptár* Club and *Receptár* Days activities are always important social and cultural events with intensive communication among participants. The democratic spirit at these events is not the least important of their features.

Let us now go back to our definition of literacy as "the ability of a regionally and structurally delimited community to create relationships, processes and institutions aimed at a multi-faceted social, spiritual and mental cultivation of that community, based on its own indigenous resources, possibly with help from outside". Looked at in the light of this definition, *Receptár* is an impulse from the outside, yet because it only interprets and provides a guide to what comes in from the *bricoleurs*, from tradition-in-the-making, it is also a resource (though given the nature of the mass media, a resource which is not connected to any particular local culture).

Receptár is an example of a program that takes up the functions of educational, social and cultural institutions when these have been weakened or even eliminated in the process of social transformation. These functions were not originally planned for the program; they are secondary functions, generated by the program itself. A necessary precondition to their development was the viewers' long experience of *bricolage* and *mass bricolage*, as already discussed. The program is only a prototype of televised community and literacy development in the rural areas of an industrialized country. However its existence, and our experience with it, suggest that its educational, social and cultural functions can be systematically strengthened and that they can then consciously replace, on a temporary basis (i.e. for several years), institutions which are lacking or ineffective. From a guide to *mass bricolage*, *Receptár* thus becomes a guide in the spheres of adult education, social work and cultural work.

At the beginning of this article, I indicated that there is a difference between the ability of a society to generate cultivation processes under modern conditions and under postmodern conditions. *Receptár* is a good illustration of how modern forms (System forms) can be linked to premodern content (content representing, for the most part, the Lifeworld). Such a combination is typical of the postmodern. Thus the postmodern re-examination of modern literacy development methods is a feature shared by contemporary postindustrial Western Europe and postcommunist Central Europe.

To conclude, then: under special social conditions where, as a result of the global transformation of society, certain institutions responsible for literacy development become dysfunctional or disappear, their function can be taken up by a television program which can serve, on a large scale, as a guide for processes originating in *bricolage* and analogous phenomena.

Such activity can be especially successful in societies which have lengthy experience in exchanging information from the world of *bricolage* through the mass media. The societies should also have little ethnic or socio-cultural differentiation.

Under such circumstances, the work of preparing literacy development strategies can be transferred to a public exchange through television. At the risk of exaggerating, we can say that this exchange remains in the hands of the *bricoleurs*, who serve as the mediators of a strange dialogue between the modern social System and the "secondary premodern culture" arising from *bricolage*.

The state authorities can play a role by offering moral and financial support.

Notes & References

1. I refer here to Giddens' characterization of the differences between premodern and modern societies/cultures, along with the characterization of postmodern conditions in the following works:

   Giddens, A., *The Consequences of Modernity*, Cambridge 1991, p. 102.
   Jameson, F., *Postmodernism or the Cultural Logic of Late Capitalism*, London/New York 1991.

   Nelson, B., *Ursprung der Moderne* [origins of modernity], Frankfurt-am-Main 1986.

2. Nelson, ibid., p. 23.

3. Lyotard, J.-F., *The Postmodern Condition: A report on Knowledge*, Manchester, 1986, pp. xxiv-xxv [translation of La Condition post-moderne: rapport sur le savoir, Paris, 1979].

4. See the *Recommendation on the Safeguarding of Traditional Culture and Folklore*, a resolution adopted at the 32nd Plenary Meeting of UNESCO on 15 November 1989 (parts D and E).

5. Habermas, J., *Theorie des kommunikativen Handelns, Bd. II* [*Theory of Communicative Action, Vol. 2*], Frankfurt-am-Main, 1981, p. 182 and elsewhere. Using an opposition between Lifeworld and System, Habermas moves from Husserlian phenomenology and phenomenologically inspired sociology (Schutz) to Mead's interactionism. The Lifeworld is the spere of what is near and known to everyone, the sphere of an intimate community arising from "presystemic" and "prescientific" forms of social life. The System, on the other hand, refers to the power of institutions not based on a reality known to all or close to the community, but based rather on the abstract systems of the modern era, systems that absorb the Lifeworld (tradition) and the "prescientific" community. This pair of concepts is quite well suited to grasping the problem of literacy development in rural communities (Lifeworld aspect) which exist in an industrial invironment (System aspect).

6. New agencies and institutions started to operate in 1990 under the terms of the UNESCO *Recommendation* (see note 4), for example the "Folklórní sdruzení" (folklore association) in the Czech Republic and the "Folklórní unie" (folklore union) in Slovakia.

7. This is reflected even in the structure of government institutions: the three aspects are looked after by the Ministry of Education, the Ministry of Culture and the Ministry of Labour and Social Affairs respectively. Very different ideas are to be found at academic institutions. For example, we at the Faculty of Philosophy of Palacky University in Olomouc (Chair of Sociology and Adult Education) follow a concept developed by Jochmann in the late 1960s and see literacy development as a multi-faceted, integrated process.

8. See for example his *Selected Writings*, Cambridge, 1988.

9. This and other information has been provided by the creator of *Receptár*, Dr. Premysl Podlaha and his colleague Kamil Knotek, an engineer. I would like to thank them both for all the assistance they gave me in November and December 1992.

10. Lévi-Strauss, Claude, *The Savage Mind*, Chicago, 1966, p. 16 [translation of *La Pensée sauvage*, Paris, 1962]. Lévi-Strauss's idea of *bricolage* will be essential to our further analysis of *Receptár*, especially the description of its functions. Lévi-Strauss conceived the notion as part of his study of pre-scientific and mythical thought. He said that *bricolage* is an activity in which we use non-specialized tools which are already available; the tool for any activity can be created out of whatever is already there at hand. This art of taking something existing and using it for any number of other purposes is developed by the *bricoleur*, an individual who always operates in the same closed world, where the new is arrived at by re-arranging the already available. What I am pointing to here is a logical and historical-cultural chain of thought that begins from the world of *bricoleur*, from Habermas' Lifeworld — both of which are connected to the rural world under

discussion here.

11.   Ibid., pp. 17-18, with two corrections to the English translation.

12.   Ibid., p. 33.

13.   cf. *Receptár* archives and interview with P. Podlaha.

Chapter 15
EMPOWERING PEOPLE & BUILDING COMPETENT COMMUNITIES

Priscilla George
Ontario Ministry of Education
Toronto, Canada

LITERACY INVOLVES THE WHOLE COMMUNITY

For the Aboriginal peoples of Ontario, literacy is a process involving not only the individuals, but also the whole community. Literacy leads to development and empowerment which will contribute to self-determination. Cox, et al[1] describes community development as "a process designed to create conditions of economic and social progress with the active participation of the whole community and the fullest possible reliance on the community's initiative". Tribal Sovereignty Associates, an Aboriginal consulting firm whose focus is community development, sees the community as performing five basic functions — economic, political, social, educational and cultural. "In order to meet the human needs within a community, programs and services must be structured within these areas. These areas do not operate in isolation of each other, rather, they are interdependent."[2]

For example, while community-based Aboriginal literacy programs are ostensibly **educational** in nature, the program participants are having their **social** needs met, and their social skills developed. In addition for the program to be effective, it must have **political** support (endorsed by Band Council or the Board of Directors). Of necessity, the programs are **cultural** in focus (we do not want to be a group of Aboriginal peoples perpetuating the non-Aboriginal approach which did not work for us in the first place). These programs also impact on the community **economically**. They provide paid employment for people indigenous to the neighbourhood[3] and either develop or enhance the employment skills of program participants.

Uppermost in peoples' minds is the question, "In what languages should Aboriginal peoples become literate?" Presently, in Ontario the official languages are English and French. However, the languages of the original inhabitants of Ontario fall into two major linguistic groups, Algonquian and Iroquoian. The Algonquian linguistic group includes Algonquin, Cree, Ojibway, Delaware, Odawa and Potowatomi. The Iroquoian linguistic group encompasses Mohawk, Cayuga, Oneida, Onondaga, Seneca and Tuscarora. Further, Ojibway, Cree and Mohawk each have dialects. Through intermarriage and migratory patterns, Aboriginal peoples from other language groups reside in Ontario. Current policy of the Ontario Ministry of Education states that if the parents or guardians of 15 or more qualified students request an Aboriginal language program, the school board must provide the program pending the availability of a qualified teacher. Where this policy does not take effect, instruction is provided in English and/or French. Aboriginal peoples contend, however, that it is our right to become literate in our language of origin as well as English and/or French.

Many people choose to focus on the grim statistics and social indicators of the plight of Aboriginal peoples. According to the Indian and Northern Affairs Canada customized data, based on the 1986 Census of Canada, the percentage of the Registered Indian population with less than Grade nine education is 37.1% as compared to 17.1% for the general population. Further, the percentage of the Registered Indian population with at least high school education is 27.5% as compared to 55.9% for the general population. Due to lower levels of educational attainment, Registered Indians are likely to continue to experience lower levels of employment success, a tendency to be employed in unskilled jobs of shorter duration and lower earning power.[4] Phil Fontaine, Grand Chief of the Manitoba Assembly of Chiefs says, "We are the poorest of the poor".

However, Aboriginal literacy practitioners choose to heed the words of Penner,[5] "massive improvements in the quality of education of Indian students are absolutely essential to the success of the current drive for Indian self-determination and self-government." For the past six years, we have been taking the community development approach in literacy to make those massive improvements in the quality of education for program participants.

Inherent in their lower levels of educational attainment is the disproportionately low number of Aboriginal peoples in positions of political power. For this reason, we feel that literacy is an important first step in self-government.

AN OVERVIEW OF ABORIGINAL SELF-GOVERNMENT

In 1492, Queen Isabella of Spain sent Christopher Columbus on a mission to the Indies. Unfortunately, his ships went off course and Columbus landed on the shores of North America. Because he thought he had reached India, Columbus mistakenly identified the Aboriginal peoples who greeted him as "Indians".

Since then, this misnomer has been applied to Aboriginal peoples.

Before Jacques Cartier set foot in 1534 on what is now known as Canada and for a couple of hundred years afterwards, Aboriginal nations existed with their own complex institutions of government. The common theme running through these various types of governments is that laws and customs were given to the Aboriginal peoples by the Creator and that no one could take them away. Aboriginal peoples chose their own leaders according to their own traditions. One of the best known, the Iroquois, also known as the Haudenosaunee Confederacy, governed through a formalized constitution and a code of laws for its people. Each clan was represented by a male and a female leader. Consensus was the form of decision making. This confederacy was the model American colonies used for their first union.[6]

The passage of *The Indian Act* by the Canadian Parliament in 1868 (and its revision in 1876) marked the removal of self-determination from peoples who had, up until that time, governed themselves. This Act defined who was legally recognized as "Indian" and who was not, thus the terms "status" or "registered" and "non-status". Under the provisions of this Act, certain tracts of land, known as "reserves" were set aside for Indians. Those who fit the definition of the Euro-Canadian authors of the Act now had to live on these reserves. These groups of people became known as "Indian Bands'. The federal government allocated funding for these bands. "Indian Agents" also lived on the reserves. These Indian Agents were non-Indian employees of the Department of Indian Affairs. It was their responsibility to administer the funding from Indian Affairs and to ensure that the Band members lived according to the provisions of *The Indian Act*.

In effect, Indians were wards of the federal government. The focus of the government was the systematic assimilation of Indians into the ways of the dominant society. Indians were not permitted to practice their own spiritual traditions. Ceremonies were outlawed. Indian students were sent to residential schools where they were not allowed to speak their language. Not only did *The Indian Act* strengthen the government's control over Indians and reserve lands, it imposed for the first time on Indians the concept of an elected band and council. Once a people free to roam across the continent, Indians found themselves confined to land that they were allowed to use, but could not own.[7]

Under the provisions of *The Indian Act*, those legally defined as Indians were entitled to certain rights:

- statutory, such as tax exemption under certain conditions;

- treaty, such as hunting and fishing on their reserves; and,

- discretionary, such as medical and educational coverage.

Those who did not fit the definition of Indian were not allowed to live on these tracts of land, nor did they have the above-outlined rights. Further, a non-Indian woman who married an Indian man could gain these rights, and an Indian woman who married a non-Indian man lost them. In 1985, *Bill C-31, An Act to Amend the Indian Act*, restored to women and their first generation children rights they had lost.

As a result of *The Indian Act*, the provincial governments regarded Indian peoples as the exclusive responsibility of the federal government. While programs and services were provided to Indian peoples by the federal government, they had virtually no say in how these programs and services would look. Indeed, it was not until 1960 that Indian peoples were given the right to vote in federal elections. However, in the mid-1980's, Aboriginal peoples began to receive provincial services in a non- discriminatory and culturally-sensitive manner.[8]

On June 25, 1969, the Minister of Indian Affairs, stood before the first session of the 28th Parliament to read, *The Statement of the Government of Canada on Indian Policy*. This "White Paper" of 1969 contained six basic points:

1. *The Indian Act* would be repealed leaving Indians with no different status than any other Canadian;

2. other federal departments and levels of government, particularly the provinces, would provide services for Indians in the same way they provided services for other Canadian residents;

3. the Department of Indian Affairs would be dismantled within five years;

4. Indians would be given control of Indian lands;

5. everyone in Canada would recognize the "unique contribution" that Indian people have made to the country — those furthest behind would be helped the most; and,

6. "lawful obligations" would be met.

The reasoning behind the government's proposed abolition of *The Indian Act* was that the special status conferred upon Indians by the Act and a separate government department to look after their needs was the key to discrimination. Government felt it was the major stumbling block to Indian progress.

Indian leaders reacted very strongly to this announcement citing that there had not been any consultation with the Indian community regarding the abolition of *The Indian Act*. Provincial governments who were being asked to accept responsibility for Indian peoples and the programs supporting them also denounced the White Paper. After several months of stormy debate, it was officially withdrawn in the spring of 1970.

One positive impact the White Paper of 1969 had was to unite Indian organizations and leaders in the superordinate goal of opposing government's unilateral attempt to make decisions on behalf of Indian peoples without their input. From the scattered Indian organizations with undefined and general goals in 1969, there are now groups with a clear vision of what self-government entails.

In the meantime, the terminology referring to the original inhabitants of

Canada evolved. "Native" reflected indigenous. "Aboriginal" was preferred by most political organizations as it encompasses Metis, Inuit, status and non-status.

On August 6, 1991, the Premier of Ontario, and the Minister Responsible for Native Affairs, signed the Statement of Political Relationship with the Chiefs-in-Assembly. The Chiefs-in-Assembly represent those Aboriginal peoples who have a land base, i.e., they originate from a reserve. ("First Nations" has been adopted to refer to these people. The term was chosen to correct the misconception that the English and the French, are the two founding nations of Canada.) The basic premises of this statement for the Aboriginal peoples of Ontario are:

- the recognition of the inherent right of First Nations people to self-government (establishes a basis for negotiations to take place which will facilitate the re-emergence of First Nations jurisdiction, through our laws based on our traditions);

- the establishment of a government-to-government relationship between First Nations and Ontario (examines how to remove the assumed provincial jurisdiction over our lands and peoples);

- the commitment of First Nations and the Government of Ontario to negotiate the exercise and the implementation of First Nations jurisdiction and their right to control their own lives.[9]

This Statement of Political Relationship does not include some independent First Nations and non-land- based Aboriginal peoples not represented by First Nations (including non-status and Metis).

As part of the movement towards self-government, Aboriginal communities and organizations are assuming more control over their own affairs. Education, including literacy, is key to such control.

LANGUAGE ISSUES

In recent years, Aboriginal issues have come to the forefront of the political agenda. Aboriginal literacy is no exception. The following comprehensive national initiatives examined literacy as it pertains to Aboriginal peoples.

- *Aboriginal Literacy Action Plan*, Saskatchewan Indian Institute of Technologies, 1990. Six working groups of practitioners involved in the delivery of educational services to Aboriginal peoples across Canada met to discuss Aboriginal literacy issues and to formulate a strategy;

- *You Took My Talk: Aboriginal Literacy and Empowerment*, the fourth report of the Standing Committee on Aboriginal Affairs, House of Commons, Ottawa, 1990. The Committee is a permanent structure which reports to Parliament. The Committee invited written and verbal submissions from Aboriginal literacy practitioners across Canada. Based on these submissions, the committee made recommendations on Aboriginal literacy to parliament.

- *Towards Linguistic Justice*, Assembly of First Nations, Ottawa, 1990. The Assembly is a national organization whose members constitute many First

Nations communities across Canada. All First Nations were invited to complete a questionnaire. This questionnaire identified number of speakers, and extent of use, of Aboriginal languages. The report made recommendations on assistance needed to address problems being encountered.

- *The Native Literacy Research Report,* Native Adult Education Resource Centre, Salmon Arm, B.C., 1990. The authors of this report devised a questionnaire identifying barriers to education for Aboriginal peoples. They also researched existing Aboriginal literacy programs. They made recommendations about Aboriginal literacy programs.

Consensus amongst these reports was that Aboriginal languages (and culture) are in need of revitalization. The dual forces of language and culture help communities sustain and maintain a strong identity.[10]

The dilemma for Aboriginal peoples in Ontario is that English and French are the official languages. Literacy in one's mother tongue strengthens acquisition of literacy in a second language. According to Betty Harnum of Yellowknife, "...literacy in a native language must not be viewed as a vehicle for developing English/French literacy. It must be viewed as a goal in itself, and as the only desired form of literacy for some individuals...We must be cautious that we do not insist on literacy as a vehicle of assimilation, but, rather, as a method for individuals to seek knowledge and make informed choices."[11] Aboriginal literacy components, therefore, must examine reasons for existence.

PLACING EDUCATION INTO CULTURE

For Aboriginal peoples, "learning must be associated with spiritual, physical, and emotional growth, as well as academic growth. Traditional First Nations methodology of teaching and learning must be considered. It is imperative that First Nations use the strategy of placing education into culture rather than continuing the practice of placing culture into education".[12]

How does an Aboriginal literacy practitioner place education into culture? First and foremost is the holistic approach. Life cannot be compartmentalized. Each and every thing in the universe is a part of the whole creation. In honouring the creation, we honour the Creator. In fact, we derive our teachings from the creation. These teachings permeate our everyday lives.

The most common teaching, the circle, can be used to explain the holistic approach. The Creator has given us ample evidence of the importance of the circle. The sun, moon and the earth are in the shape of a circle. Life is a series of cycles, which can be likened to circles. We experience the cycles of the days, months and seasons. Picture a series of four concentric circles, with the inner circle being "self", the second circle being "family", the third being "community", and the fourth being "universe". We have a responsibility to keep "self" physically, mentally, emotionally and spiritually healthy. "Self" interacts with the family which, in turn, impacts on the community and finally affects our relationship with the universe. The energy from these interactions flows in both directions — inwards and outwards.

The elements of self, community, family and the universe are to be considered in setting up the program. Further, literacy is a tool in personal empowerment and community development. It is, therefore, useful to keep in mind how these programs can enhance the spiritual, economic, political, and social aspects of community, in addition to the educational.

Self

The institutional educational system has, for the most part, not promoted the strengths, needs and aspirations of Aboriginal peoples. The curriculum, teaching styles and, in some cases, the entire structure, has disempowered Aboriginal peoples.

Many Aboriginal peoples were educated in a residential school system. For over the first half of the twentieth century, Aboriginal children were systematically removed from their families and communities and sent to a residential school. In these schools, the focus was on teaching the non- Aboriginal society's way of life to Aboriginal students. One of the tragic results of this approach was that the culture and languages of most Aboriginal peoples was weakened and almost lost.

Aboriginal communities are in various stages of "healing" from the aftermath of the residential school system. Community-based Aboriginal literacy programs are an integral part of this healing process. Healing means the revitalization of our language and culture. "Language is our unique relationship to the Creator, our attitudes, beliefs, values, and fundamental notions of what is truth. Our languages are the cornerstone of who we are as a People. Without our languages, our culture cannot survive".[13]

Nevertheless, it is important to remember that some Aboriginal peoples have adopted the ways of the non-Aboriginal society. We must respect their choice. There are others who are lost between the Aboriginal and non-Aboriginal cultures. A strong cross-cultural component to the literacy programs raises their awareness of what is happening to them and allows them to choose with which culture they will identify.

Geography is another important consideration in literacy programming. There are 138 First Nations Territories in Ontario. Some of these are near urban centres; others are remote. Some are in the north; others are in the south. Some are able to generate their own revenue; others are dependent on transfer payments from provincial and federal governments.

The quality of life in First Nations communities can vary from that of relative self-sufficiency to that of abject poverty. Approximately fifty percent of Aboriginal peoples in Ontario live in urban centres, either because they so choose or because they do not have a land base. "What they have found more often than not in these concrete jungles is a world where they are unwelcome, where their facial features, accents, hair-styles, history, and way of thinking keep them apart from other city dwellers, a world where they exist in a political vacuum, the responsibility of no one in particular and considered the burden of many".[14] Thus, the needs of Aboriginal peoples in each of these settings vary widely.

Family/Intergenerational

The residential school system has had a debilitating effect on family relationships as well. Government made unilateral decisions to remove Aboriginal children from their homes for long periods of time to be educated in the non-Aboriginal environment. In the absence of a supportive, home-like atmosphere during their formative years, many individuals found it difficult to develop healthy ways of relating to family. However, because of the current revitalization of culture, Aboriginal peoples are, once again, able to place a strong emphasis on family, including extended family.

The family is the primary medium of cultural continuity and an invaluable part of the social context in which literacy occurs.[15] Intergenerational literacy components are natural ways to teach mothers and/or fathers meaningful ways to interact with their children.

Further, Elders can be an integral part of literacy. Traditionally, Elders played a vital leadership role in passing on cultural teachings and knowledge. Living in closely knit extended families, they played a key role in passing on history, culture, language and skills to younger generations.[16] Through literacy programming, Elders can again transmit their wisdom to the community.

The Community

The Assembly of First Nations developed a policy paper, *Indian Control of Indian Education*, which firmly laid out the principles of local control and parental responsibility as the basis for First Nations jurisdiction over education. In 1973, the Government of Canada accepted the policy paper in principle as the national policy statement. The National Review of First Nations Education (1984) found that, in practice, First Nations have very limited jurisdiction over education programs. In fact, the first time that many Aboriginal communities and organizations had control over their own educational programming was in the development of community-based literacy programs.

"Community" has two meanings. For on-reserve programs, community refers to the actual geographical location. People living in this region have common experiences, concerns, and aspirations. They could be political, educational, spiritual, cultural or economic. For off-reserve programs, community encompasses the individuals who identify themselves as Aboriginal peoples. What they have in common with on-reserve programs is an Aboriginal identity.

Off-reserve Aboriginal peoples may want to preserve their language and culture. They may have had no exposure to it and now want to learn.

One of the greatest limits of the Aboriginal community is the demands placed on their time and energy. Those who have the skills and knowledge to be actively involved in community issues are asked to be on numerous boards and committees. While Rupert Ross was describing a reserve, the same could be said of Aboriginal communities off-reserve:

> The amount of administrative and other talent it takes to apply for, create and then maintain essential services in small reserve communities is, in a word, staggering. The same few councillors must be the school board, the police commission, the welfare office, the housing authority, the social services agencies and the provider of virtually all jobs. If our municipal politicians ever had their duties expanded to such a degree, there would be resignations everywhere. Yet, even in communities as small as three hundred people, that is the load borne by band councils.[17]

Universe

"With education comes the opportunity to exercise choice."[18] Traditional Aboriginal cultures have always viewed themselves as a part of the universe, not apart from the universe. *The Indian Act* set Aboriginal peoples apart by segregating them onto reserves and creating further divisions such as status and non-status. In the realities of a multicultural society, Aboriginal peoples must have the choice of where and how they wish to live. Aboriginal literacy programs need to find ways to assist Aboriginal peoples to exercise choice.

THE ONTARIO NATIVE LITERACY COALITION (ONLC)

The ONLC is comprised of the thirty-one literacy projects funded through the Ministry of Education. Sixteen of the projects are urban-centred, fourteen are on-reserve, and one is in a Metis community. The projects operate either through a band council, local friendship centre, or a training program. Thirty-nine literacy practitioners, thirty-one female and eight male, are working in these projects.

The mandate of the ONLC is to support Aboriginal literacy through:

- information and opportunities for effective networking;
- their video, *Native Literacy: A Healing Energy* and other means as required;
- training for Native literacy practitioners;
- culturally-sensitive program materials; and,
- advocacy on a community, regional, provincial and national level.

The Practitioners

The practitioners are people from the home community. This has important implications in that they have knowledge of the community (and its individuals). They have knowledge of the Aboriginal culture. In some cases, the practitioners are fluent in the Aboriginal language of the community.

Other qualifications include: a sincere belief in the student; experience with some of the issues the students are encountering; creative abilities (including artistic or musical talent); good organizational skills; and, a deep commitment to improving the quality of life for Aboriginal peoples.

Of all the practitioners whom I interviewed, only two offered their level of formal education as a qualification for their position. This makes a strong statement that Aboriginal as opposed to Western qualifications are much more beneficial to those working with Aboriginal peoples.

The Co-ordinator

Co-ordinating a community-based Aboriginal literacy program is a demanding position. As the programs offer one-to-one and/or small group tutoring, the co-ordinator must recruit students and, where possible, tutors. The co-ordinator usually does the tutoring. For those programs who are able to recruit tutors, the co-ordinator provides tutor training which encompasses literacy awareness, cross-cultural awareness (the holistic approach); and, techniques for teaching adults. Because of the student-centred approach, the co-ordinator must either develop curriculum or adapt existing materials to make them applicable to the students' situations.

Further, because the grants from the Ministry of Education cover only core operating costs, most programs do fundraising. The most successful programs find that it is best to involve the students. This way, the students feel ownership of the program and know that they are giving something in return.

The Programs

Because the literacy programs are community-based and student-centred, a variety of models have emerged. A number of communities have initiated Moms and Tots Reading Circles so that young mothers can learn to read to their children and to interact meaningfully with them. There are also homework nights for the youth to address that high drop-out rate that is such a concern to the Native community. Further, because literacy programs are seen as a way of revitalizing the culture and language, the program participants often host cultural events.

The most successful in terms of impact was the *Winds of Change Peace Assembly* by the Chippewas of Nawash program. The Assembly attracted hundreds of people from across the country for a weekend of teachings by Aboriginal Elders and traditional teachers.

The students identify what it is they want to learn. Most programs use the whole language approach. The students' own stories comprise the curriculum. Various comprehension, vocabulary and grammar exercises are devised from these stories. In many cases, the students will request life skills exercises — dealing with grief/loss, positive parenting — all from an Aboriginal perspective. Often, the students request educational and moral support with correspondence, community college and, in a few cases, university courses.

Finally, students have gained the confidence to request literacy in their Aboriginal language. There are fourteen projects throughout Ontario in which the program participants are doing innovative things such as devising crossword puzzle books in the Aboriginal language, and developing theme units complete with pictures in both English and the Aboriginal language of the community. Because the students are involved in the process, they are empowered and becoming more active in the community.

SPECIAL INITIATIVES

Students have been instrumental in a number of special literacy initiatives. Their requests and needs have resulted in innovative approaches to literacy.

In Kenora, numerous students requested assistance in getting their drivers' licences. They found studying the drivers' manual boring and difficult. The co-ordinator then devised a game similar to *Trivial Pursuit*, but based on the drivers' manual. The game is in plain English, making it easier than the driver's manual for the students to understand.

The Chippewas of Saugeen students wanted to go to art school, but were not eligible because of the Grade 12 admission criteria. The co-ordinator then decided to bring the art school to the students. She obtained a grant to pay honoraria and travel expenses for Aboriginal artists from all over the province to share their skills and to transmit their artistic knowledge. In addition to enhancing their artistic abilities, students honed their note-taking, critiquing and listening skills. Further, each student donated one piece of artwork to the program to be used for fundraising.

In the Metis community around Burleigh Falls, the students themselves produced the community newsletter, circulating 2,000 copies monthly. The newsletter provided an important community information service, and outreach tool for recruitment of students in the program and participants in other activities of the host organization. Students gain marketable skills such as word processing, desktop publishing, layout and design, as well as practice in writing. The newsletter also provides an opportunity for them to display their artwork.

In Sioux Lookout, students are involved in running a bookstore. This project began through book sales which were a tremendous success because of the introduction of an extensive selection of books for adults and children by Aboriginal authors, and the fact that the nearest good bookstore was a six hours' drive away in Winnipeg. Students are involved in writing bibliographies of the books, taking inventory, and making transactions with customers. The bookstore will be an important fundraising venture for the program. Although it is only in its initial stages, the project co-ordinator says the bookstore is well-received in the area. These are just a few examples of how students not only guide the direction of the program, but give back to it and the community.

TRAINING FOR THE PRACTITIONERS

In early 1990, the board of directors of the ONLC and I designed a training plan with Tribal Sovereignty Associates. Many practitioners reported a feeling of isolation (most Aboriginal literacy practitioners are a few hours' drive from each other). The practitioners could be brought together for a week at a time every three months for five sessions. The courses would lead to an Aboriginal Literacy and Communications Certificate through the First Nations Technical Institute. The practitioners had input every step of the way. They chose to meet in different parts of the province where there are successful programs operating. They then saw what the practitioner in that area has been able to accomplish, giving them the incentive to do likewise in their home community. In addition to the formal workshops, a lot of ideas were exchanged after hours.

I will now describe what the practitioners have identified as the two most important courses in helping them to enhance self-esteem in their students.

Healing Circles

By far the most effective technique is the Healing Circle, conducted by someone who has been trained in co-counselling which is based on the principle that we, as human beings, are naturally wholesome and good. We are also naturally moved to feeling caring and loving about ourselves and others, are intelligent and have the ability to operate logically and rationally. However, these abilities can be seriously impaired by stressful events which have not been resolved. We, therefore, need a way to "discharge" the emotions that inhibit enjoyment of life, or block new learning. The person requesting a healing invites people he or she can trust. These people and the co-counsellor sit in a circle facing each other.

The Healing Circle usually begins in the traditional Aboriginal manner. In Southern Ontario, we use sweetgrass which grows in marshy places and is regarded as Mother Earth's hair. It is braided into three to represent the mind, body and the soul. We light one end of the sweetgrass with a match. The smoke that ensues represents our thoughts going up to the Creator. We brush this smoke over our eyes so that we will have a good vision, over our ears so that we will hear good things, over our mouths so that we will choose our words wisely, and over our hearts so that our thoughts will be positive. Each person in the Circle "smudges" in this manner and someone in the Circle says a prayer to the Creator.

The Healing Circle follows the cycles of performance identified earlier. The person (co-counsellee) requesting the healing shares with those present the troubling issue so that they have an "awareness" of it. Trust is critical. The co-counsellee then goes deeper into the issue to identify the "struggle". The co-counsellor will direct the person to "feel" and not to rationalize. Often, the co-counsellee goes into a "discharge" reliving the painful experience. The co-counsellor guides the person through the process, all the while providing assurance that they are in control of what to do with that feeling and that the feeling is not controlling them. When the discharge is complete, the person is ready to move into the "building" stage. The co-counsellor brings the person back to a state of emotional well-being by pointing out the positive that has come out of that experience, and encouraging a positive statement about the experience. When the co-counsellee is able to repeat the statement with conviction, they usually are able to see the next step to ensure maintenance of the good feeling.

Others present will be experiencing empathy throughout the process. At this point, they will share how they handled a similar experience or will remind the co-counsellee of other examples in which they demonstrated the ability being pointed out. The bonding that takes place during these Healing Circles has been conducive to excellent networking when the practitioners are back in their home communities.

Prior Learning Assessment

The second most effective component of the Aboriginal Literacy and Communications Course is the Portfolio Development process, also referred to as Prior Learning Assessment (PLA). PLA assists people to identify college level learning which may have occurred outside of the formal classroom. The focus of this process is the student's prior learning experiences. These experiences may have been gained in the workplace, the business or service world, or through involvement in home and/or community activities. The student is shown how to:

* identify and record prior learning experiences;
* determine individual strengths, weaknesses, interests and needs; and,
* share information with other participants.

In preparing a portfolio, an individual analyzes significant events and/or people in their life. The object of this analysis of **self** is to determine knowledge, skills and attitudes learned in each instance. Then examines **family** relationships to identiy any helping philosophy that was learned. Following this is an exploration o how this helping philosophy was applied in interactions in the **community**, be they positive or negative. Finally, the individual explores their support systems in relations to the larger **society**. The portfolio is prepared with the tutelage of someone with expertise in the PLA process. It can take up to a year to complete for an individual who is also working full-time while taking the course.

Several important documents accompany the portfolio. They include an up-to-date resume; a list of resources contributing to the individual's growth; and several references. Upon completion of the portfolio, the individual then meets with faculty members for an oral discussion which will centre on claims in relation to course outcomes and competency guidelines.

PLA is a lengthy and involved process. However, in addition to receiving advanced standing in one or more of the courses in the Aboriginal Literacy and Communications Course, the practitioners are then able to apply the principle of validating life experiences of their students.

TO PRESERVE ORAL HISTORY
& TO ENHANCE THE PRESENT

> Paradoxically...oral cultures must interact with the printed word and the symbol, both for renewal and survival. Oral cultures are fast disappearing. Cultures can no longer be perpetuated through orality.[19]

In this renaissance of Aboriginal culture, people are turning to the wisdom of the past. In 1990, International Literacy Year, several programs undertook Oral History projects to document the teachings of the Elders. The students in one program even wrote their own project proposal. They identified what they wanted to learn, who would be able to teach them, and by what means this information could be preserved for posterity.

Students in the West Bay First Nation literacy program created an exhibit on the traditional clan system. In Aboriginal culture, clans are named after animals. Students researched the skills, attributes and responsibilities of the animals whose clans are represented in West Bay. By assembling a display, the students were able to pass on these teachings to community members.

In other communities, students interviewed Elders. The Elders either gave a bit of history of the community or they passed on a teaching. Students then transcribed the audiotapes. In some cases, the Elders loaned pictures that they had kept for years to the literacy program. In other cases, the students illustrated the words of the Elders. These pictures and transcriptions were compiled into booklets.

Aboriginal literacy practitioners recognize that the written word is not the only way to express oneself. Theatre is another medium. The Nokee Kwe program in London developed a play entitled *Grace and Lillian*. The script was based on a composite of students' stories. The play toured the Southwestern Ontario region. It served as a promotional tool for literacy and as a fundraiser for the sponsors.

The co-ordinator of the Fort Erie program is a student in the very program she co-ordinates. She had been labelled "dyslexic" in the institutional educational system. She was initially a volunteer and a student in the program. Funding became available for her to do a work placement with the program. When the co-ordinator left, she capably assumed his position, and continues with her tutoring sessions. An assistant transcribes letters and reports that the co-ordinator dictates into a tape recorder. This woman re-wrote an Aboriginal legend into play format, and then recruited students and volunteers in the program to act in the play. Program participants prepared and served a traditional feast after the play. This "dinner theatre" served as a promotional tool and fundraiser for the literacy programs. Practitioners have been ingenious in helping students to develop literacy skills while capitalizing on various media to transmit information.

REFLECTIONS

Of the 31 Aboriginal literacy projects, fourteen have a Literacy in an Aboriginal Language component. Practitioners have had to be very creative in how these components are funded. Some projects are funded from the federal government as pilot projects. Funding is for one-time only projects. In other cases, the co-ordinator is bilingual and is able to offer literacy in English and/or the Aboriginal language of the community. In still other cases, the local program may have a private arrangement with the instructor of the Aboriginal language literacy component. In one of the northern programs, the instructor teaches one evening class a week in return for a monthly bus pass.

One concern is that the instructor may or may not be teaching the dialect of the community. Geography is a factor that determines dialect. Aboriginal peoples tend to be migratory, perhaps in search of a job. In addition, intermarriage may mean that parents speak two different dialects and the children of that union are thus exposed to both. This raises the question, "What dialect should be taught in the program?" Quite often the determining factor is the available instructor. As with the literacy practitioners, Aboriginal language instructors spend hours preparing curriculum materials. Often these materials cannot be distributed widely as they are prepared in the dialect of the instructor.

Staff in the Literacy Branch of the Ministry of Education desired that the written form of the Aboriginal languages be standardized to facilitate distribution of materials. We believe that if the communities want standardization, it would have to be done in two streams. Stream A would be for those Aboriginal languages in which there already is a modern linguistic foundation. A linguistic conference could be used to settle the most basic questions of standardization, e.g., writing systems, word formation. Ideally, there should be a linguistic conference for each group of a specific language community, with conferences to be held over the next five years.

Stream B would be for those Aboriginal languages which require further linguistic work. The Ministry of Education, in co-operation with linguists, Elders, Aboriginal language specialists and teachers, as well as the Aboriginal community organizations, will co-sponsor the preparation and publication of dictionaries and grammars as the foundation for standard, literary languages. Once basic linguistic tools, such as dictionaries are available, linguistic conferences can be held to establish a literary language.

Stream A and Stream B are in the initial stages. We have identified co-sponsors from the Aboriginal community. The Ontario Government will provide only the funds for standardization. It is the Aboriginal communities themselves that will decide what direction the project will take.

Further, the ONLC is in the initial stages of setting up an Aboriginal Literacy Foundation. The tasks for the ONLC in setting up the proposed foundation include:

- to open dialogue with provincial and federal sources to facilitate funding for continued support of Aboriginal literacy programs and the expansion of literacy programming to all Aboriginal groups within Ontario;
- to secure funding from private sectors for development of language initiatives;
- to create a First Nations Languages Advisory Council; and,
- to create a regional advisory board to help give focus and direction to the Board of Directors of the foundation based on the interests of their various regions and supporting bodies.

The growth within the last five years has been encouraging. Within the next five years, Aboriginal literacy projects will be seen as a viable force within their communities. Indeed, several of the regional and provincial Aboriginal political organizations are now beginning to agree with the ONLC that literacy is an important first step in the self-determination process. All in all, the ONLC is instrumental in assisting practitioners to use literacy to empower individuals and to build more competent communities.

Notes & References

1. Cox, E. et al (Eds.) Strategies of Community Organization: A Book of Readings (2nd. Ed.) Itasca, Illinois: Peacock. 1974.
2. Antoine, R., Miller, D., and Myers, B. *The Power Within People*. Peace Tree Technologies, Deseronto, Ontario, 1986.
3. Ibid.
4. Hagey, N.J., Laroque, G. and McBride, C. *Highlights of Aboriginal Conditions, 1982 - 2001, Part III, Economic Conditions*.

5. Penner, K. Indian Self-Government in Canada, Report of the Special Committee. Ottawa: Government of Canada. 1983. Comeau, P., and Santin, A. *The First Canadians, A Profile of Canada's Native People Today*. James Lorimer and Company, Toronto, 1990.

7. Ibid.

8. *Self-Government and Land Claims Task Group Framework Statement*, Ontario Native Affairs Secretariat, 1992.

9. *Special Bulletin, Statement of Political Relationship*, Chiefs of Ontario, 1991.

10. *You Took My Talk: Aboriginal Literacy and Empowerment*. Fourth Report of the Standing Committee on Aboriginal Affairs, House of Commons, Ottawa, Ontario, 1990.

11. Ibid.

12. *Towards Linguistic Justice for First Nations*, Assembly of First Nations, Ottawa, Ontario, 1990.

13. Ibid.

14. Comeau, Pauline and Santino, Aldo. *The First Canadians*, op. cit.

15. *You Took My Talk*, op. cit.

16. Ibid.

17. Ross, Rupert. *Dancing with a Ghost, Exploring Indian Reality*, Octopus Publishing Group, Markham, Ontario, 1992.

19. Comeau, Pauline and Santin, Aldo. *The First Canadians*, op. cit.

Chapter 16
LITERACY: A CRITICAL ELEMENT IN THE SURVIVAL OF ABORIGINAL LANGUAGES

Lynn Fogwill
Adult Education
Northwest Territories
Yellowknife, Canada

> When I speak in my own language, I can go anywhere with it... I can express myself... my thinking... it means so much. In English, I have to flip through my file index of words... using the same words over and over again. My own language allows me to be like a mermaid in the sea; I can flip and twist and dive and breathe air and swim anywhere. (Fibbie Tatti. 1992)

> No matter how many speakers there are of a particular language, no matter how small the nation, these people have the right to their language and to have it survive and be carried on.[1] ("You Took My Talk", 1990. Page 69)

A CULTURE ROOTED IN ORAL TRADITION

In Canada's Northwest Territories 57,000 people speak eight major different languages. Six of these languages, with a rich variation of regional dialects, are the ancient languages of the aboriginal people who form the majority of the population. The culture and language of the people was rooted in an oral tradition. Wisdom, knowledge, mores, survival skills and care of the land and the animals were passed from the elders to the children and youth through storytelling and the telling of legends and truths from the ancestors.

English and, to a lesser extent, French are also spoken. These languages came to the Territories with the non-native people who came for whaling, trading, trapping, mining and to Christianize the population. English became the dominant language and culture of business and industry, of government, of the print and electronic media.

In 1990, the Legislative Assembly of the Northwest Territories passed legislation which made the eight languages official. For the first time in a Canadian province or territory, aboriginal languages were recognized and given equal status with the two dominant languages of the country. Passing the Official Languages Act gave the highest political recognition to the desire and desperate need of aboriginal people to reclaim and revitalize their languages and their culture.

Their will to survive as a people pits their culture and language against the overpowering presence of a Southern, non-native, industrialized, urban culture and language. The traditional, land-based language and culture of the people competes with a dominant language and culture, epitomized by American television programs brought from Detroit, USA by satellite to the most isolated communities of 500 or fewer people.

The legislation is important but legislation alone cannot ensure that the languages and the culture will survive into the next century. Intensive strategies are necessary to support the people in their efforts to reclaim their language and culture and literacy is a critical element of any survival strategy.

BACKGROUND

The Northwest Territories (N.W.T.) includes most of the Northern part of Canada. It has an area of 3,376,698 square kilometres, forms approximately one-third of the total land mass of Canada, is about the size of India and encompasses three time zones.

The N.W.T. is the only jurisdiction in Canada in which aboriginal people form the majority of the population. Fifty-eight percent of the population is of aboriginal ancestry; 35% are Inuit (sometimes referred to by others as Eskimos), 16% are Dene (sometimes referred to by others as Indians), 7% are Metis.

The Territories has the youngest population in Canada as well as the highest birthrate, nearly three times the national average. Approximately 45% of the population is under 20 years of age, while only 2% is over 65.

The population of 57,000 is small compared to the land mass. People mostly live in 62 communities scattered across the land; although many people still spend some time in camps each year, living out on the land and following their traditional pursuits of hunting, fishing and trapping. Most of the communities are very small with fewer than 1000 people. There is one large city of 15,000, the capital Yellowknife, which has a majority non-native population.

The smaller communities, which are populated by mostly aboriginal people, have the highest unemployment rates (27%), the lowest rate of participation in the labour force (84%), a very limited economic and transportation infrastructure and are dependent upon a domestic, traditional, subsistence economy. The few larger communities are much more developed, populated by mostly non-native people, experience very low rates of unemployment (7%) and have a dominant wage economy.

Only in the last 20 years has some measure of local control of government, politics and economic activity come to the Northwest Territories. Until the late 1960's the Territories were run by the central government from the Canadian capital of Ottawa. It was not until 1975 that there was an elected legislature that governed the Territories. Currently, the majority of the elected members of the Legislative Assembly are aboriginal people, as is the government (cabinet) which is elected by the members from amongst their own numbers.

The aboriginal people, through their political organizations, have fought for rights, for recognition and for compensation through the courts and a process of long, complicated land claims negotiations. Three land claims have been negotiated and settled by the Inuvialuit (the Inuit of the Western Arctic), the Inuit of the Eastern and Central Arctic and the Gwich'in — the Dene of the Mackenzie Delta in the Western Arctic. Two other claims, by two other Dene groups, are currently in negotiation. These land claims provide some measure of self government for the people within their settlement region, control over the use of the land and resources within their region, and cash settlements.

The Inuit land claim settlement provides for the division of the Northwest Territories into two regions. An Inuit homeland "Nunavut" will result, and the remainder of the existing Territories will become a new political entity. Major challenges in terms of constitutional development, methods of government and taking control of their political, social and economic destiny confront the aboriginal people in both of the proposed new territories.

The Inuit form a clear majority of the population in all their communities while the Dene are in fact an overall minority in the Mackenzie Valley region they occupy. The impact of Southern, non-native culture has had a more intense impact upon the Dene than upon the Inuit.

As a result of missionary activity, many of the traditional spiritual beliefs of both the Dene and the Inuit were lost. By the middle of the 19th century, the Dene had become dependent upon the fur trade for their livelihood. Whaling had an impact upon the Inuit but it did not create the same degree of economic dependence. In both cases traditional culture was changed, foreign diseases brought death, ancient family territories were disrupted, the traditional lifestyle was changed forever and entire aboriginal groups died out. In the last decade, the impact of the anti-fur movement in Europe has had a devastating impact upon the aboriginal people of the North, particularly the Inuit. For most communities and families, the fur trade was the only source of cash income and its disappearance has crippled their economies.

Similar to many indigenous people around the world, the results of a colonial period have left a legacy of many problems. Most communities in the N.W.T. are confronted with a complex of interrelated problems. The N.W.T. has one of the highest rates of suicide in Canada, incidents of family violence are extremely high and alcohol, drug and solvent abuse are major problems confronting every community. There is a serious lack of adequate housing in most communities. Lack of employment and welfare dependence have a deeply negative impact upon aboriginal people, especially the large population of young people in the smaller communities.

HISTORICAL CONTEXT OF LANGUAGE & EDUCATION

For tens of thousands of years the Dene and Inuit occupied the land and developed a complex and highly successful society. Culture, beliefs and values were passed from one generation to the next through oral tradition. The language was rich in its power to describe, express and analyze.

Elders, parents and other family members were responsible for the education of the children and for passing the cultural traditions from one generation to the next. Children's education began at a very early age because they were included in the daily activities of the camp. Girls were taught to prepare skins and sew clothing by their mothers, grandmothers and aunts while the boys were taught to make tools for hunting and taught to hunt well by their fathers, grandfathers and uncles. As children achieved levels of competence they received respect from the members of the camp and became adults.

Schooling in the N.W.T. can be described in three historical phases; the mission period from the mid-1800's to 1950, the federal government period from the mid-1940's to 1970 and the territorial government period which began in 1967.

Formal schooling came to the North first with the missionaries, in the Mackenzie Valley of the Western Arctic as early as the mid-1800's and in the early 1940's in the Eastern Arctic. For the most part, the schools that were established were residential. Children were taken from their families to residential schools operated by either the Anglican or Roman Catholic church, often for as much as two thirds of the year.

In the residential schools they were immersed in a foreign language and culture and given a "basic education'. In the summers they were returned to their families and to the traditional camp life and culture. Frequently, in the residential schools, children were forbidden to speak their own language and their own culture was denigrated in the face of the Southern, "civilized" culture of the teachers.

> The experience of the child in school was that of being judged within an imposed culture; for example, putting up your hand to answer a question — within the Dene culture, you never draw attention to yourself. So the child is worried about two things at the same time, not just the answer to the question, but how to say it; am I saying it right? The child is being judged within a culture that conflicts with her own.
> (Fibbie Tatti. 1992)

At the best, children suffered from the strain of the terrible dichotomy between these two worlds. At the worst, the time they spent with their families and with their people was too little and they lost their language and their culture. They returned home after completing their schooling, without the knowledge, skills and language that permitted them to participate in the life of their communities. The elders and the adults of the community had their traditional role of educator usurped and saw a schooling system, which alienated their children from them, take their place.

The federal government established public schools in the late 1940's and early 1950's and for the next several decades schooling was highly centralized, with an administration system far removed from the communities and the people it supposedly served. Although there continued to be residential schools, gradually schools were established in communities as a flurry of building ensued. This also resulted in a growing, non-native bureaucracy to administer the schools.

Families were encouraged to stay in the communities in order for their children to attend school. Eventually, most families chose to stay in a community, although it disrupted the traditional way of seasonal camp life. Even though children were now able to stay with their families and attend school, traditional lifestyle gave way to settlement life, the lessons taught were imported from the South and the language and the culture was no longer passed from elders to children.

Although control of education passed from the federal government to the government of the Territories in the mid-1960's, most of the teachers were still non-native people from Southern Canada. They often stayed only one or two years in a community and rarely developed a deep understanding of the culture and values of the children they taught and their families. Moreover, the curriculum and the teaching materials were from the non-native, urban culture of Southern Canada.

Very few children did well in the educational system and their parents were alienated from it. Many parents saw little in the schooling system to value and to support. If their children succeeded in the elementary school within their community, they then had to go far from home to a residential school for their secondary education. To a large extent, the schooling system resulted in a loss of language and a loss of culture for several generations of children, particularly among the Dene.

In 1982, the Legislative Assembly established a Special Committee on Education to inquire into problems and public concerns with the schooling system. The comments from parents and community leaders at public hearings with the Committee give eloquent testimony to the crisis in schooling that existed.

> The way 14-year-olds are treated in the traditional society and the way they are treated in the school is quite different. In the traditional society, they are treated as adults; in the school, they are not.

> (The) problem with kids dropping out is that they are caught in the middle. They cannot go out hunting, there are no jobs for them, they don't have an education.

Culturally, they are caught in the middle and can't support themselves either way.

But we recognize the world is changing, and the school, ideally, should give our children the skills to make their living in other ways. But it should not conflict with the traditional education parents and elders still want to give their children. It should not confuse children with values and a vision of the world that is foreign to their own. It should give them the tools to make a choice as to how they want to live.

We cannot afford to bury our language with our elders.

There is a need to have language retained. I can't even speak to my own children and be understood completely, and they cannot act as interpreters for me — and this disturbs me.

Learning: Tradition and Change in the Northwest Territories, 1982

The Special Committee recommended serious changes to the administration and delivery of schooling in the Territories. Most of the recommendations were intended to bring educational decision-making and control to the community level, to increase parental and local participation in education and to make the schooling system more responsive to the needs of individuals in the community.

In the last decade, a number of significant changes to the delivery of education programs have been made. Regional boards of education were established which took direction from community education councils. The fledgling teacher education training program was strengthened and de-centralized in order to support the recruitment of more aboriginal teachers for northern schools. Regional centres were established for each major language group to develop curriculum and materials in the aboriginal language and to support the teaching of the languages in the schools. However, major changes are slow to implement and the impact is difficult to measure.

THE CURRENT SITUATION

Although there has been some progress towards community control of education, culturally-relevant curriculum and an increase of aboriginal teachers, the current literacy situation is still grim.

In the dominant language of English, the Northwest Territories has the highest rate of "functional illiteracy" in Canada. Using the UNESCO standard of measurement, 44% of the overall population has less than a grade nine completion. However, of aboriginal people 72% of adults have less than grade nine.

The numbers of aboriginal children who make it through school to graduation or grade ten are still significantly low. Although aboriginal children make up 72% of school enrolment, only 5% will graduate from grade 12. Whereas in Canada 30% of school-aged children and youth leave school before graduating, the rate in the Northwest Territories is approximately 80%.

The low English literacy levels amongst aboriginal youth and young adults hinders their ability to access training and wage employment. Because youth are such a large component of the population, the picture in most communities shows many undereducated, unemployed youth. Often they use neither their mother tongue nor English well. In many communities they are called the "walk abouts" as they aimlessly pass their days. Although the English literacy situation amongst aboriginal people is a major concern, this paper is focused on the situation with the aboriginal languages.

The loss of language for aboriginal people is alarming. Overall, 16% of aboriginal adults over the age of 15 years speak their native language only, 60% speak their own language and English as well, while 24% speak English only.

Both Dene and Inuit elders, the traditional teachers, express deep concern that the children and youth are losing their language; that the language they speak is very poor and is mixed with English. The young people have lost the richness and complexity of their language and their ability to describe and communicate. Although 94% of Inuit 15 to 24 year olds speak their language, it is often a mixed Inuktitut and English with a great loss of words.

The Inuit have a more deeply entrenched history of writing their language; 77% can read their language and 74% can write it. Amongst the Dene only 16% can read their language and 11% can write it. The language of the Inuit can be classed as still vital and highly viable, with a remarkable degree of homogeneity of the language across the circumpolar world from Greenland to Alaska. There is a relatively wide array of publications available in Inuktitut as compared to the Dene languages.

Use of the Dene languages is declining. This is indicated by the fact that the percentage of 15 to 24 year olds (62%) who speak their language is substantially lower than the rate for older people (75%). Although some of the Dene languages still have relatively large number of speakers left, others are in difficulty. The number of speakers of Gwich'in, the language of the people in the Mackenzie Delta, remaining is dangerously small. Even those languages which are not so seriously endangered are in need of aggressive intervention to ensure their survival.

THE CHALLENGE

> ...language cannot be separated from the living culture from which it arises. The recognition of language is not just the recognition of a system of words, but of a unique perception of the world and of the peoples and societies which hold these perceptions. (The Report of the Task Force on Aboriginal Languages, 1986. Page 18.)

The overall challenge is to ensure that in the Northwest Territories aboriginal languages do not die out. The languages must survive in order to bridge the traditional and modern worlds that the people carry within themselves and confront in their daily lives.

According to the Canadian Assembly of First Nations, Inuktitut is a "flourishing" language in need of prevention strategies to ensure its health and survival and the Dene languages are "enduring" languages in need of expansion strategies to ensure their continued survival. (Towards Linguistic Justice For First Nations, 1990)

Within this overall challenge, there are three aspects that are particularly critical if the languages are to flourish. First, a new schooling system must provide an education that meets the cultural and linguistic needs of the children and their families in each community. The community school must become a part of the traditional passing of the culture and the language from one generation to the next.

Second, the damage and loss from the past must be undone. The adults, especially the young adults, must be provided with an opportunity and a reason to recover their language and culture. People need to see some value and to have the opportunity to integrate the traditions of the past with the life of the present and the future.

Third, the languages must not be relegated to languages of the past alone, because if they do they will die with the elders and their way of life. The languages must become the living languages of the present, as comfortable and as expressive with computer technology, medical terminology and legislative writing as they always have been with the knowledge and wisdom of the land.

EXPERIMENTS & ACTIONS TO MEET THE CHALLENGE

The aboriginal people of the north are reaching for and taking control of the political, economic and social forces in their society. This is most obvious in the changes of the last two decades. In the beginning of aboriginal dominance in the political apparatus of government, in the movement towards the settlement of land claims and the three successfully completed claims.

Within this context of political and socio-economic change, the people have demanded change in the schooling of their children. At times there has been a conscious recognition and other times an intuitive understanding that providing a more culturally relevant school program for children will not be enough. There must also be opportunities for adults to recover their language and their culture. There is also a deepening recognition that if the languages are not used in all aspects of everyday life, no amount of schooling or community programming will enable them survive.

Instinctively, there is an understanding that aboriginal languages and literacy must be an integral part of family life, school life, business life, political life, community life. Therefore, the use of aboriginal languages, oral and written, must be promoted, encouraged and ensured an ongoing, integral place in the life of the community.

Taking Back the Education of the Children

As the administration of the schooling system was decentralized, parents were able to develop some control over the education of their children. They believed that the school had a responsibility to teach the children the language and to incorporate the cultural strength of the community into the child's learning experiences.

Not all parents felt or feel this way. Many parents are so alienated from the school system that they do not care what is taught, how it is taught or whether their children attend. Many families are so troubled with violence and addictions, that education does not have a place in their daily lives. Some parents have learned their own school lessons all too well and believe that the best future for their children lies in them learning English well and becoming accomplished in all the skills required by modern Canadian society. They feel that learning the mother tongue and the traditional ways is not important and will hinder their children's chances of success.

In spite of these obstacles, parents have formed community education councils to run the schools and a growing number of Northern, aboriginal teachers have joined them in designing and implementing significant changes to how children are educated.

Initially, small interventions were tried. The elders were brought into the schools and the classrooms to teach the children traditional skills, to tell stories and make the mother tongue part of the school environment. Time was set aside in the school week for language lessons. The education councils designed land-based programs and the teachers took the children out to the bush or on to the tundra for a few days each year, so they could experience the lifestyle of their elders.

The Board of Education for the Baffin region began immersion Inuktitut programs for elementary aged children and also determined that they would devote some part of the budget to publishing Inuktitut books for young children.

In 1989 the Baffin Board of Education took a further step and developed an integrated curriculum that was more than a language or cultural program added on to the main purpose of school. They believed that thinking and learning needs to take place in the mother tongue of the Inuit before it can occur effectively in a second language. *Piniaqtavut*[5] develops learning experiences for children from an Inuit perspective. Materials are developed by Inuit in Inuktitut and the content begins with the experiences of the child within the family, the community and the culture. The philosophical base incorporates Inuit relationship with the sky, the sea, the land and the community. Learning experiences include land-based classes and returning to the elders their traditional role of teacher.

Similar developments are gradually taking place with the Dene. After some years, it was obvious that teaching the language as a small part of the curriculum or having elders visit the school was not having enough of an impact.

The philosophy behind *Dene Kede*, a Dene curriculum, begins with the Dene story of creation which

"tells us that as human beings, we are dependent on the land for survival and that continued survival requires not simply knowledge of, but respect for all things on earth. The purpose of this curriculum is to give this perspective back to our children. There is a need to root ourselves in tradition not for the sake of the past but for the sake of the future. Our children, with the gift of their culture, can work towards ensuring our future survival as well as the survival of humankind." (Dene Kede, 1992).

Dene Kede was developed under the guidance of a council of elders. This fact is absolutely critical to the curriculum's authenticity and to the respect and validity it will have in the Dene communities. It is currently being implemented in the schools of the Western Arctic. However, there are still obstacles to overcome. The majority of the teachers are still not aboriginal or from the North. Some have actively resisted the *Dene Kede* curriculum; questioning how will they test the students and questioning its value in the education of the children. Others cannot bring the cultural background necessary to teach the curriculum. Until the majority of teachers in the school system are from the North and are aboriginal it will not be possible for aboriginal people to fully have control of the education of their children.

There are further obstacles if the children do not have the language and culture reinforced in their families and community. There is a danger that their mother tongue will become just a subject taught in school unless it is a vital part of their everyday lives.

There are several generations of adults who are not fluent or literate in their own language. This is especially true amongst the Dene, but there is a noticeable loss of language amongst young Inuit adults as well. These adults and parents speak a mixed mother tongue and English language at home and in the community. It is not the rich, complex language of the elders. Moreover, the mother tongue is not used in places of business, of recreation, or in local government. More than recovering control of children's education is needed.

Undoing the Damage & the Loss

Community-based programs in aboriginal language and literacy development respond to the needs of adults to recover their language and rediscover the richness of their culture. Any project is developed and designed by people in a community to meet their particular needs, and then further developed and managed by a community-based organization, which is a political organization, an educational council, or sometimes a cultural organization.

Since 1989-90 there have been projects in nearly half the communities. Some have been very successfully in meeting the needs of the community, others have faltered. The following vignettes provide a glimpse of some of these projects with some analysis of what factors have made them succeed or falter.

Coral Harbour

Coral Harbour is a very small Inuit community of 600 people on the coast of Hudson Bay. For the most part, the community is still very traditional in lifestyle but over the past four years, people in the community have organized a number of successful Inuktitut literacy projects. Each of the projects have interwoven with and supported the others, so that there is a sense that something whole and important is happening in the community.

Probably the most critical component of language and literacy activity in the community over the years has been the Elder's Writing Project. Elders from the community have been involved in writing and publishing books on the history, traditions and culture of the Community and its people. The publishing of the books caused many of the younger adults in the community to place a new value on being fluent and literate in their own language. The books written by the elders provided Inuktitut language materials for the school children in their own dialect and about something that was of intense interest to them, their own community.

A second component of the project, introduced a little later, brought Inuktitut language instruction into the adult (English language) academic upgrading program at the community college learning centre. Young adults, who were preparing for entry into the wage economy, received instruction in their own language, validating it as a language important for their adult work life. As part of their Inuktitut language program, these young adults worked with elders to write booklets on subjects that were of interest to the community. Thus more written material was made available in the language for the community to use. They researched the histories of the families who had settled in the community and developed family trees that linked them as a community and to other communities of Inuit.

One component of the language and literacy work in the community that has had an immense impact has been the use of the community radio station which is controlled by the people in the community. Nearly everyone listens to it daily. The radio has been used to stimulate discussion on language issues; everything from how many different dialects are spoken in the homes of the community to what are the things people want to see written in the books and whether they should develop their community dictionary (they did). The radio was also used for fun things like telling stories and holding language quizzes and contests. Use of the radio had a major impact in promoting the importance and value of the language in modern society. Last year more than 100 people regularly participated in the radio language programs.

For a period of time in 1990 and 1991, the momentum slowed. There were no people who could or would get involved to coordinate the projects, so things stopped for a while. By late 1991, people came forward again and the projects re-started. In very small communities, this is not uncommon. There are a limited number of people who can provide leadership because of the harsh demands of the Northern traditional lifestyle and meeting the many needs of frequently troubled communities. In another community an entire literacy project came to a stop because nearly every woman in the community was engaged in making special craft items for the 1992 EXPO in Spain. They had an opportunity to earn some wages for a period of some months and all else became second priority.

In Coral Harbour, the strength of the ongoing projects has been the consis-tent support and involvement of the elders and the sheer perseverance of a handful of individuals who would not give up. The creativity of the projects in using community radio and publishing meaningful materials ensured that language, oral and written, was deeply rooted in the life of the community.

Hay River Reserve

In Hay River Reserve, which is a very small South Slavey community of 200 people near Great Slave Lake in the Western Arctic, there are a couple of exciting projects meeting with some success and some problems. From 1990 until the spring of 1992 there was a very innovative Slavey literacy project in the community. The project was initiated by the commitment of one woman, deeply concerned about the loss of the Slavey language. She did the community research, convinced the Band Council to support her, prepared the funding proposals and put the program together. There were three main components: first, introducing a Slavey language component into the College English up-grading program; secondly, student-created projects that re-introduced written Slavey into community life; and thirdly, a desk-top publishing venture to create and publish Slavey language printed materials.

The adult students involved in the project first worked with the instructor to improve their oral skills in their language and to learn to read and write it. Once they were confident of their language abilities, they consulted with people in the community, particularly the elders, in order to design projects for themselves that also would be meaningful for the community. Some of the students mapped the traditional hunting and fishing areas of the community with the traditional Slavey names, which had been replaced with English names. A large map was put up in the Band Council office and small maps that could be carried in the pocket were given to every member of the community. Reclaiming the names of places was very important to the community and especially the elders.

The students also produced regular newsletters in Slavey and distributed them to every resident. The newsletter became an important part of community life. Some of the students chose to produce some simple books in Slavey for their own children and for the school. Others interviewed every member of the community and produced a calendar in Slavey, in which every person's birthday was listed.

At the same time as this project was happening, the Band Council was close to achieving a dream of many years. An alcohol and drug treatment centre was under construction in the community. People who seek treatment must either go to the capital, Yellowknife, or to Southern Canada and the political leaders of the community fought for years to build a facility in the region that they would control. As the construction of the building began, the leadership began to plan how the centre would operate. They are determined that the centre will be managed and staffed by people from the community and have put training programs in place so that personnel will be ready when the building is ready.

They also believe that treatment programs are most effective if they provide the spiritual and cultural basis that leads to the healing of the whole person, and they decided that the treatment centre must operate in the Slavey language and initiated a project to develop Slavey terminology for the addictions treatment and counselling field. This work is now nearly completed and when the centre opens in the summer 1993, all counselling, all patient records, all documents will be in the Slavey language.

However, the other project has come to a halt. The woman who was the single driving force behind the project accepted a job teaching in the nearby high school. She is still teaching Slavey, but the project she started in the community has ceased without her. In part, this is because there are very few people sufficiently fluent and literate in the language who could take over her role in the project. It is also because, as in other small communities, when a committed leader turns to another project, there is often no one immediately available who will pick up the work. Hay River Reserve has a group of committed people working towards a sober, healthy community in control of its own destiny. Speaking, reading and writing their language is part of working towards that reality; but if the people in the community are going to continue in their language and cultural recovery work, more language resource people are needed.

Lutsel K'e

Lutsel K'e is a small Chipewyan Dene community of 250. Like Hay River Reserve, in recent years the political leaders, the Chief and Band Council, have also placed great emphasis, at least verbally, on developing a sober and healthy community as well as developing the Chipewyan language, particularly in its written form. The Band Council aggressively developed a project and sought government funding for a Chipewyan literacy program for the community.

Initially, a pilot project was developed to train two local women to be the teachers and to develop a learning program and materials that would meet the needs of the community. There were one or two long community meetings to discuss the project.

Many of the elders were very disturbed about the new orthography writing system and wanted a return to the old syllabic writing system that they knew and could use. This is an issue in many of the Dene communities; the elders still use the old writing system taught by the missionaries while the children are learning the new system developed by Dene educators and linguists. The new writing system is here to stay but it causes splits in communities and separates the elders from the children.

The project in Lutsel K'e faltered very early and never took hold in the community. The difficulties began in the pilot phase. The trainer came from outside the community and used a whole language, language experience approach to teaching literacy. The women who were being trained wanted to be taught and to teach in the very prescribed way that they remembered from their own schooling. From the beginning they made it very clear they would not use any of the methods they were being taught and they felt the pilot project was a failure and a waste of their time.

Once the project itself started, there was one teacher who organized the teaching program, but there were no students. Although the Chief and Band Councillors had committed themselves and the staff to participate in the program, to be role models for the community, they never did. Too many other demands occupied their time.

A few students came for a short time but they stopped attending. The teacher was experiencing personal problems at the time and lost her enthusiasm and commitment for the project. At the end, the only person who came for classes was the non-native adult education instructor who wanted to learn the language.

Rae-Edzo

Rae-Edzo is the largest Dogrib Dene community in the Western Arctic with a population of 1500 people. Many people in the community are fluent in their language but very few can read and write it. The community is the centre of Dogrib politics, economic activity, social and cultural life.

About a year ago a number of employers in Rae-Edzo came together to discuss the use of the Dogrib language in the workplace. They formed a committee to further explore the interest in Dogrib workplace language and literacy programs. The committee represents the band council, the community economic development agency, the hamlet council, the parish council, the friendship centre and the government offices.

They conducted a needs assessment to determine the interest, commitment and support of employers and employees for Dogrib language use in the workplace. Twenty-two of the 26 employers in the community were supportive and response from employees was enthusiastic. Since most of the residents of the community are Dogrib speakers, people believed it was important to provide services in the language of the community. They noted that most workers in the offices spoke to each other in Dogrib when they were talking about personal or social matters, but many would switch to English when the subject matter was work-related. The staff at the nursing station believed they should be keeping patient records in Dogrib. Meetings of the Band Council or the Hamlet Council should be available in Dogrib as well as English.

The needs assessment and subsequent report is a model currently being shared with other communities. The committee has now launched a Dogrib literacy program, establishing a model whereby employees have time off from work one afternoon a week to go to class and give one evening of their personal time for class.

The program has two goals. The first is to simply offer Dogrib language development and literacy classes for employees in the community. The second is to develop and standardize Dogrib terminology for modern office use and to share that standardized terminology with the other Dogrib communities. For example, the Dogrib (or any aboriginal) language does not have a word for fax machine or photocopier or computer. The language provides rich words and expressions for all the things of the traditional culture and lifestyle. Now, the people are developing and agreeing on the words to describe the modern work environment they also inhabit.

The project so far appears to be very successful. There are a number of critical factors in the success of the project. The Dogrib language and culture in Rae-Edzo is very strong and there are quite a few resource people to share the roles of teaching and developing terminology. Dogrib people are a significant part of most workplaces generating a high degree of agreement on the importance of providing services in their language and ensuring their language is used in the workplace. There is a strong tradition of political leadership within the Dene Nation as a whole that comes from the Dogrib communities. But most importantly, the project came about because those involved felt it was necessary and important and they were committed to participating.

Using the Languages in New Ways

Flourishing languages change constantly and adapt to new circumstances and new technologies. As oral tradition languages adapt to the changing circumstances of the modern North, they must become more than an expression of the past and of traditional culture. As aboriginal people take control of the political, economic, service and governmental sectors they will bring their languages into the workplace, whether the work is providing government services, expediting mining exploration, providing patient care or developing models of aboriginal self-government.

Because the aboriginal languages of the Northwest Territories have only recently developed as written languages, there is not a heritage of literature or written discourse. Creating a written literature is part of re-creating the languages within a new context for ancient cultures.

In the last decade there has been a great deal of effort put into recording the stories, legends, knowledge and truths of the elders who are the carriers of the history. These oral traditions projects have documented traditional medicine, traditional place names, traditional scientific knowledge and much more. Some of the stories have been illustrated and published for children for use in the schools. But there has not yet emerged a strong aboriginal language literature. There is a distinct danger that if the only written materials are stories and legends from the past, that the language and the culture will exist only in the past.

In the last year, the Literacy Office has initiated a series of workshops to develop writers as one action to encourage the development of a Northern, aboriginal languages literature.

In any workshop there must be three to four speakers of a language in order for them to work together, writing, reading their work to each other, brainstorming, editing and re-writing. Each workshop usually brings together three language groups at once. The language of interaction within the workshop is English — the common language between the participants as well as the language of the instructor. Each group of people participate in two workshops separated in time by several months to allow for reflection and ongoing writing. By the end of 1993 workshops in every language will be completed.

The first book of writings from these workshops will soon be published and several more will result. They will be an important addition to the small number of books in aboriginal languages.

Most of the participants are those who have written a lot in their language, transcribing stories from the elders, writing word and picture books for children and documenting traditional knowledge and skills. These have been language survival activities. Many of the participants have exclaimed that they have never thought of themselves as "writers" until they experienced the writing workshops. For the first time they are deciding to write, in their language, poems, stories, books that come from their own experience and their own imagination.

In addition to creating experiences that enable these people to begin writing freely, the workshops provides them with the models and experiences to deliver future workshops in their own regions for others. In the future, there will be support for more workshops delivered by the original participants to develop more writers.

One of the greatest obstacles will continue to be the difficulties in getting aboriginal languages materials published. The North American recession is creating enormous difficulties for Canadian publishers, but even in the best of times they were not interested in publishing aboriginal languages books. There is too small a population and market for such books and publishing them is not cost-effective. One Northern publisher has, in partnership with some of the regional boards of education, published books for children in the aboriginal languages.

Perhaps the single most important and difficult challenge facing the aboriginal people of the North is to create a viable publishing venture to publish books in their languages.

REFLECTIONS ON THE ROLE OF LITERACY

The message we received in school was that our language was not important. It was not taught. English was important and we were taught to speak and read and write English. So, to read and write a language makes it important. Reading and writing my language validates its importance and that is the point of literacy. (Fibbie Tatti. 1992)

The experiences of the people of the Northwest Territories indicate that there are three important roles for literacy in the survival and re-vitalization of the aboriginal languages of the North. The first is validating the contemporary value of the languages; the second is preserving the traditions of the past for future generations; the third is re-creating the languages within a changing society.

The act of using a written form of an aboriginal language begins to undo the damage of the past by validating its value as a language within the society, alongside the dominant language, English. Written material — books, stories, newspapers — in aboriginal languages counters the message from the past that only English is important and has value because it is written and people are taught to read and write it.

The elders tell us that writing the language, writing down the stories, the history, the knowledge, the wisdom, the traditions, is the preserving role of literacy. It is necessary to prevent the culture and the language from disappearing. Writing the language allows the people to reach back to the people of thousands of years ago and to also reach forward to the people of the future. They have said that the wisdom, the culture, the traditions of the past can no longer be passed to the next generation through oral means alone. As the elders pass from us, we lose the experiences of the last generation to live totally the traditional lifestyle. If we tell their lessons and their stories in writing, that experience is not lost for us or for our children and their children.

In addition to the validating and preserving role of literacy, there is the critical role of creating a changing language, an adapting language, a literature of a changing culture. In the face of an overwhelming English language culture, the aboriginal languages cannot afford to use the English words for fax machine or computer or pneumonia. Terminology must be developed that brings technology or foreign concepts and words within the language and culture of aboriginal people. In the face of newspapers, magazines and books in English, aboriginal languages literature and publishing is essential. There is little point in people learning to read and write their language unless there is material to read and a publisher for the writing. The languages will flourish when they are used, orally and in written form, in every facet of community life; to keep patient records at the community nursing station, keeping records of Band Council meetings, to mark buildings and streets with signs as well as in the personal communications between individuals and within families.

The aboriginal people of the North are involved in actions that address these three roles. The work in the schools, to take back the education of the children, is a major action to validate the language and the culture of the people, to preserve the traditional role of the elders and the adults as the teachers of the children and to create a school system that reflects the culture, both past and present. Until most of the teachers are from that culture and until the children experience their language and culture in the home and in the community as well as the school, the goal will not be reached.

Community-based literacy projects also serve to validate the language and the culture of the aboriginal people alongside the dominant English language and culture. At their best, these projects provide actions and products that not only preserve the past for the present and future generations; they also provide materials and information that are important and useful to the people and create new uses for the language in the daily life and work of the community. The projects work well when the whole community is involved, but the elders are especially important. Even then, the projects are often fragile and operate on shaky ground because there are no longer enough people fluent as well as literate in the language. If one person leaves the community, falls ill, has a baby or takes a salaried job an entire project can falter.

New ventures in writing and publishing books are the challenge of the future. If children can participate in an education that reflects their heritage and culture; if the language is a changing, living, adapting part of the daily life of the community, then creating aboriginal languages literature will complete the circle.

Notes & References

REPORTS

Learning, Tradition and Change in the Northwest Territories, The Final Report of the Special Committee on Education, Northwest Territories Legislative Assembly, Yellowknife, N.W.T., Canada, 1982.

The Report of the Task Force on Aboriginal Languages, Government of the Northwest Territories, Yellowknife, N.W.T., Canada, 1986. Page 18.

Towards Linguistic Justice For First Nations, Assembly of First Nations Education Secretariat, Ottawa, Canada, 1990.

"You Took My Talk": Aboriginal Literacy and Empowerment, Fourth Report of the Standing Committee on Aboriginal Affairs, House of Commons, Ottawa, Canada, 1990. p. 69.

Dene Kede, An Educational Perspective, Department Responsible for Education Culture and Employment Programs, Government of the Northwest Territories, 1992.

Piniaqtavut Integrated Program, Baffin Divisional Board of Education, Iqaluit, N.W.T., 1989.

ORIGINAL MATERIAL

Conversations with Fibbie Tatti, Slavey Language Project Coordinator, Department Responsible for Education, Culture and Employment Programs, 1992.

Chapter 17
CHALLENGES OF LITERACY & DEVELOPMENT IN RURAL QUEBEC

Hughes Dionne and Raynald Horth
Université du Québec à Rimouski
Québec, Canada

EVOLUTION OF VILLAGE DEVELOPMENT

When we first met with Alpha, the local literacy group, in the spring of 1992, we knew relatively little about the small village of Saint-Paul-de-la-Croix in the Lower Saint Lawrence region, which can be considered representative of the challenges facing rural development in Quebec. It is a typical Quebec lumber town founded barely a hundred years ago, now struggling hopefully to maintain its population by seeking new jobs and developing a new vocation. Certainly, we could have picked any one of a number of unique and dynamic village projects to demonstrate the originality and vitality of rural development, but we preferred to describe an ordinary, unremarkable situation in a "typical village" attempting to redefine its future.

Nearly half of Quebec's municipalities — 600 villages — have fewer than 800 inhabitants. Most must face new challenges of rural development, given prevailing conditions of economic, social and political insecurity. Rural decline, the exodus of young people to the cities, and an aging rural population are trends found in many industrialized countries. Keeping small localities (villages) alive and well is thus a central issue for rural Quebec.

To understand the evolution of village development, it is useful to trace major historical changes in rural Quebec, with particular attention to high population mobility across North America, and the efforts of rural populations to defend threatened communities. In the Lower Saint Lawrence region, the grassroots fight against rural marginalization has been waged primarily through an organization called *Coalition urgence rurale*. The first section of this article will provide an overview of these challenges for the development of rural areas and outlying regions.

The village of Saint-Paul-de-la-Croix will serve as an example for the examination not only of issues in local village development present and future, but also of cultural challenges to identities and to the bonds that tie people to their communities. The local Alpha group is involved in redefining the terms of educational practices and strategies that it is employing to help give citizens a voice, helping them symbolically take possession of their communities, giving them full command of their social, economic and cultural environment. The second section will deal with these literacy practices.

The reflections at the end of this article explain how the traditional literacy practices in rural areas risk being ineffective because they lack sensitivity to the local dynamic and to the regional resistence to decline and marginalization.

CHALLENGES OF DEVELOPMENT IN RURAL QUEBEC VILLAGES

Decline of Rural Regions

Canada is often thought of as a wide open, thinly-populated space, ice and snow as far as the eye can see, and vast tracts of virgin land. To be sure, these are stereotypes, but they are in fact based on the scattered distribution of Canada's population across one of the world's largest countries. Yet, these rural areas are now dotted with major urban concentrations sprawling ever wider. Less than a quarter of Canada's population of 27 million is rural. Fifty years ago, 30% of the population lived on farms; today, the figure has fallen to 10%. While this is a phenomenon common to many industrialized countries, in Canada this came about in a short period of time and is reflected in the distribution of Quebec's rural population. It is important to understand this phenomenon.

Quebec is Canada's largest province and 80% of its population speaks French. It has an area of 1,535,,843 square kilometres and a population of 6,895,963 inhabitants, of whom 1,544,752 are rural. Agricultural lands cover only about one-tenth of Quebec's area. Farming in Quebec must adapt to wide climatic variations and varies from region to region. The majority of rural inhabitants are scattered among 1,200 villages of under 2,500 people. Most city-dwellers live in 100 cities of over 10,000 inhabitants, two thirds of them within the immediate sphere of influence of Quebec City and Montreal.

The Monteal and Quebec City regions cover 4.8% of the province's territory and are home to 72.7% of its population. Five large regions with resource-based economies make up the bulk of Quebec's territory: the Gaspé Peninsula, the

Lower Saint Lawrence, Abitibi-Témiscamingue, the North Shore and Northern Quebec. These outlying regions cover 88% of Quebec's area but contain only 12% of its population.[1] This distribution of Quebec's population is a result then, of far-reaching and fast-paced changes in occupational structures.

Rural Quebec has been undergoing these profound changes since the mid-20th century. Traditionally defined by agriculture, Quebec has experienced major demographic and socioeconomic transformations since the 1950s, when intellectuals launched what has become known as the "Quiet Revolution," a movement essentially aimed at catching up to the modern world by building up urban centres and increasing provincial government support.[2] The structure of the traditional family farm was undermined. The modernization of agricultural concerns led to the disappearance of less productive farms, increased specialization, and integration into mass production systems and markets.

All of these changes in turn led to a massive exodus of rural populations to urban areas, where most jobs in the secondary and tertiary sectors were being created. The Quebec government sought to manage internal migration through regional planning strategies aimed at harmonizing the distribution of Quebec's population by strengthening some regions. Specific regional development policies were introduced and in 1966, the government divided Quebec into 10 administrative regions. (In 1987, a new regional division split the province into 16 administrative regions to augment these policies.)

But the farm population has been shrinking steadily. For example, during the 1981-86 period alone, the farm population declined by 26.5%. The profile of the Quebec village has been refashioned by rapid transformation of rural occupational structures, rural society has ceased to be synonymous with agriculture; bedroom suburbs coexist with traditional land uses.[3] The flight of urban populations to the urban periphery over the past 20 years has been eating into rural zones in the belt around the cities.[4]

In the 1981-86 period, the overall population of the exurbs of metropolitan areas grew by 21.5%. This movement to the periphery was accompanied by a demographic decline in 665 rural localities of under 3,000 inhabitants,[5] causing them to suffer demographic and socioeconomic decay. "The least urbanized, most thinly populated regions — i.e. outlying regions — are the most strongly affected."[6] The balance of migratory movements confirms a trend towards concentric settlement around the cities, the so-called "doughnut" effect: the city core is losing population, the suburbs are growing, and beyond the suburbs rural municipalities are shrinking. The process is similar throughout Quebec.

The apparently irreversible waning of socioeconomic vitality is making these areas increasingly fragile. Growing awareness of the threat to existing communities is generating new diagnoses and citizens are mobilizing against this specialization of settled areas. Given that 46% of the population lives in municipalities of under 2,500 inhabitants, we can easily see the repercussions of this demographic trend on small rural localities, which increasingly feel their development to be compromised. Analysis shows population losses of over 60% in some villages over the past 20 years, with the nearest town often struggling to maintain its current population.[7]

The shrinkage of the inhabited land area and rural decline prompted rural leaders to organize the *Etats généraux du monde rural* (Rural Summit) in February 1991, under the aegis of the Quebec farmers' union, the *Union des producteurs agricoles* (UPA). After identifying the structural causes of the current rural decline, particularly the harmful effects of the productivist model of development, the participants formulated a new approach to rural development emphasizing the upgrading of human resources in rural communities, economic conversion "from below," the development of sustainable, environmentally-friendly alternatives and increased local powers.[8] In fact, analysis reveals a split between centrally located, agriculturally productive rural regions, which are faced with technological and environmental choices in areas threatened by urban sprawl, and the outlying regions, which are attempting to develop organized economic activities to replace traditional local economies, which are under pressure from processes of social and cultural marginalization, economic dependence and demographic erosion.

The strategy launched in the 1960s has not succeeded in overcoming regional disparities in Quebec. The specialization of the areas surrounding Quebec's large and medium-sized cities is still compromising the development of outlying rural zones. For example, the population of four of the five outlying regions has declined as a percentage of the Quebec total: together, the Gaspé Peninsula, the Lower Saint Lawrence, Saguenay-Lac-Saint-Jean and Abitibi-Témiscamingue have lost 5% of their population over the past five years. During the same period, Quebec's total population grew by 5.6%. The two regions which registered the biggest drops were the Lower Saint Lawrence (-2.7%) and the Gaspé Peninsula (-5.8%). This situation jeopardizes the future of these marginalized regions.

THE LOWER SAINT LAWRENCE

The socioeconomic situation in the Lower Saint Lawrence illustrates the issues and challenges for rural development in Quebec's outlying regions. The main resources are timber, especially in the highlands, and agriculture, especially along the coast.[9] There have been structural changes in the region's economy but these have consistently fallen short of the demand for jobs, resulting in a steady average unemployment rate of 15% and nearly 20% among young people (aged 15-29).

Coalition urgence rurale

For more than 20 years, the population of the region's highlands has been fighting to safeguard and develop its rural areas. As early as 1970, rural leaders launched the grassroots *Opérations-dignité* movement to fight government plans to close some areas to habitation and transfer residents to mini urban service centres.[10] A number of co-ops and community-based businesses were set up to counteract the marginalization of rural areas. Alternatives based on global community development and integrated resource management were urged against the government's primary resource exploitation strategies.

Twenty years later, however, local development initiatives have not succeeded in stemming the sociodemographic erosion of these areas. Some villages have lost over half their population in 30 years.[11] Underemployment has led to an exodus of young workers and college graduates, an aging population and reduced public services (the closing of post offices, the closing of elementary schools). The gradual disintegration of social environments is making any economic development initiative more difficult and contributing to the degradation of both the natural and man-made environments. These trends add up to a process of rural devitalization which has been a matter of concern to rural leaders in the Lower Saint Lawrence for several decades. The awareness of rural decline has grown stronger in the early 1990s and the grassroots movement has been channelled into the new regional pressure group called *Coalition urgence rurale*, which is attempting to break what has been called "the vicious circle of rural maldevelopment".

Coalition urgence rurale is the logical continuation of the *Opérations-dignité* movement of the early 1970s. Disappointment with promised development initiatives and persistent unequal development have prompted rural leaders to fight the weakening of their communities. There is more talk of "empowerment" over local and village development; citizens are holding demonstrations to show they want to stay in their communities; manifestos are being published demanding the right to live in the villages; rural youths are returning from the cities, disenchanted or searching for a new relationship with nature; city workers are coming to live in more peaceful surroundings. At the same time, a new sense of community pride is emerging and regional and sociocultural identities are being reaffirmed.

Coalition urgence rurale is developing an original rural policy to support proposed local projects.[12] In winter 1991, a broad consultation was organized on this policy throughout the Lower Saint Lawrence (22 public assemblies with over 1,500 participants in all). The movement's actions are guided by two general goals: to stabilize rural populations in the Lower Saint Lawrence and support all initiatives likely to promote community empowerment. They confirm the desire of local populations to stay on the land and exploit all its resources which implies stabilizing employment, upgrading services and enhancing rural identity.[13]

A series of resistance actions was subsequently launched: mobilizations against the closing of post offices, elementary schools and public television stations (local CBC stations); public assemblies, round tables, training seminars, forestry development projects (tree farms); the creation of local chapters of *Coalition urgence rurale* in a number of Lower Saint Lawrence localities. The movement is working throughout communities to shatter the backward image of traditional rural society and develop a social agenda based on a contemporary redefinition of rurality.

Loss of literacy in rural regions

Since the spring of 1992, *Coalition urgence rurale* has been involved in a variety of educational initiatives to support local bids for control over community development. It has called upon other institutions to work in partnership and organized twice-yearly general assemblies to publicize local development initiatives and promote policies to strengthen decaying village communities. Using testimonials, theme workshops, theatre and visual tools (posters, buttons, mailings), *Coalition urgence rurale* is attempting to mobilize community resistance through local job creation.

This challenge is a matter of survival for rural communities. The old local economies were more self-sufficient, allowing more dispersed settlement and extensive use of space in a predominantly agricultural society. The village was a suitable population centre for these scattered communities, which did not consume the specialized goods and services of our day. The village-based community, the family unit and the guidance of the Church sustained a continuous and relatively independent process of rural development.

The collapse of these rural social and cultural structures occurred over a brief period of barely 40 years. The drive to "catch up" and modernize shattered the old cultural systems, ushering in values and behaviours adapted to advanced industrial society. Modern production and consumption networks led to more specialized land use and the exclusion of some less productive zones, which were too far removed from major centres of industrial production. The new organizational and technocratic system imposed its own rules, shaped the organization of space and demanded new values adapted to the imperatives of modern economic growth. It became increasingly difficult for people to stay in their communities. Villages emptied; the suburbs of large cities filled up. The functional logic of mobility defeated the territorial logic of continuity of place and village development. Territorial economies, both local and regional, came to be seen as impediments to development.

Modern society is unburdened by this nostalgia for the past, this "obsolete" attachment to a land, a village, a community. The development of many small communities was compromised. The national economy's overarching rationality has no use for these areas which do not produce for major markets.

As a consequence, villagers are gradually losing mastery of the tools and knowledge they need for local development. This state of alienation, loss of control over the instruments of development and cultural disfunction leads to a loss of literacy. Social actors become illiterate in the sense that they lose all guideposts to the system in which they live. They become slaves to the imperatives of the productive apparatus and lose access to the codes which define the productive system's preferred or requisite practices. The complexity of modern economic processes and the transfer of control to increasingly specialized managers served to widen the gulf between the specialists, who control information and knowledge, and the population, which is uninformed and most importantly, untrained in the new forms of knowledge.

Thus, rural communities are being weakened by a loss of control over economic norms and mechanisms, and alienation from their own social and cultural environment; they are growing increasingly dependent on modes of development defined in political or technocratic terms. The individual's loss of social and cultural references is the clearest expression of the loss of literacy in village populations. Loss of literacy is a collective process resulting from structural factors of a social, cultural, political and economic nature which affect the lives of individuals. In many marginalized rural populations, loss of local autonomy contributes to prolonging a state of dependence, isolation and indeed incomprehension of the collective mechanisms that control their way of life. The loss of respect for rural communities gradually seeps into the consciousness of residents and discourages them from fighting against their own marginalization.

The fight against loss of literacy

In Quebec, consciousness-raising for rural renewal has proceeded primarily through sociopolitical strategies: writing manifestos, mobilizing citizens around political events (roadblocks, sit-ins), organizing conferences, setting up task forces. Growing awareness has led to the creation of study groups and action groups to exert political pressure and develop local projects. These democratic practices are the legacy of professional community organizing and community development efforts in rural areas, approaches which have developed specific sociopolitical cultures of collective action. Consciousness-raising strategies include economic studies of the local situation, the formulation of projects (to obtain grants under government programs), the publication and distribution of local papers. These educational activities are aimed at bolstering developmental actions and strengthening often- marginalized local rural identities. They are part of a movement of local defence and identity affirmation aimed at maintaining local spaces and living environments.

Coalition urgence rurale is now (early 1990s) also setting up local chapters to educate village communities about demographic and socioeconomic disintegration and the need to promote rural renewal. In many villages, citizens are involved in a multitude of local committees, working to affirm their commitment to the community and promote projects to support village development.

The situation in the village of Saint-Paul-de-la-Croix in the Lower Saint Lawrence region is typical of this process. A local chapter of *Coalition urgence rurale* was set up in 1991. A number of local action committees and service groups had been created in the village over the years; they served to support a myriad of volunteer efforts dedicated to maintaining and developing the Saint-Paul community. The local Alpha group was among them.

Our involvement with the local Alpha group in Saint-Paul-de-la-Croix in 1992 was part of this process of local resistance, identity affirmation and repossession by individuals of their general environment. Alpha's openness and enthusiastic response to the project made our action-research effort possible. They joined with us in a process of identity affirmation based on speaking and writing the history of their village. We undertook to accompany them in the process and work with them on this reflexive research project on rural literacy education. The project proceeded gradually over the course of a year. In this paper, we describe our rewarding collaboration with the local Alpha group in Saint-Paul-de-la-Croix.

LITERACY EDUCATION IN SAINT-PAUL-DE-LA-CROIX

A Typical Village

A person arriving in Saint-Paul-de-la-Croix for the first time cannot fail to be charmed by the panoramic view from the road leading into village, as it passes over a hill overlooking the small rural community. The first thing a visitor notices is the large grey church and its steeple. Across from the church is the main street, built atop an elongated plateau, lined by two rows of houses which form the spine of the village. A few side streets cross the plateau in front of the church; other roads branch out near the church, leading to neighbouring villages located 15-20 kilometres away. The village is surrounded by sparsely populated, undulating lands covered by forests and fields suitable for grazing — primarily dairy cows — and grain growing. Behind the church rise three large buildings: a huge rectory, the parish hall and the elementary school. On the other side of the road, across from the school, are the post office and a small grocery store. A little further, on the main street, there is another, larger grocery store, reminiscent of the era of the "general store," which was the commercial hub of the village and the surrounding farms on rural roads.

The approximately 150 houses in the village are still fine, warm, roomy structures. Many were built over 50 years ago for families with eight or 10 children — sometimes more! They are inhabited to this day, although many have become too large given the sharp drop in the village's population over the past three decades; they have become the homes of much smaller, aging families.

There are also a few recently built houses, put up during the past twenty years for a few young families who came back to the village during the 1970s after working in the city during the prosperous years of the Quiet Revolution. A number of young people have since left the village in search of jobs. This process is not unique to Saint-Paul-de-la-Croix; it is representative of the situation in most small localities in the Lower Saint Lawrence, or at least the ones which are furthest from the region's urban centres.

Fundamental changes

The village of Saint-Paul-de-la-Croix is located in the Lower Saint Lawrence administrative region, in the Riviére-du-Loup regional county municipality (MRC). Village residents are in contact primarily with the three municipalities located north of the village on the St. Lawrence River. Forty kilometres to the northwest is Rivière-du-Loup, a town of 15,000 on the St. Lawrence. It is the region's main town. To the northeast, at about the same distance, is Trois-Pistoles, another small service town, population approximately 5,000. To the north is the village of Isle-Verte, population 1,500, a former administrative centre from which a number of families came to found Saint-Paul.

The municipality of Saint-Paul-de-la-Croix was founded only 120 years ago. It is therefore a recent settlement, as are all the villages located in the region's highlands, away from the river. The village prospered during the first half of the 20th century and reached its peak population in 1929 with 1,250 inhabitants. Farming and lumber provided a harsh and simple existence, under the guidance of rigorous family and religious standards. The self-sufficient barter economy allowed dealings with merchants in coastal villages and enabled the population to maintain itself. The chief occupation was crop farming. There were 112 crop farms at this time; the farmers lived from subsistence farming and their woodlots.

In the 1950s, the locality had a population of over 1,100. Rural life and agriculture were synonymous. Farming dominated the economy and all other economic activities in the community were bound up with it. The 163 families had an average of seven members. Over the last four decades, Saint-Paul-de- la-Croix has experienced profound economic, social, demographic and cultural changes. In the mid 1970s, the village lost half its population to the cities. The ensuing drop in births further contributed to the demographic decline.

Today, the municipality of Saint-Paul-de-la-Croix has a population of 442, but while the number of individuals has dropped, the number of families remained the same in 1991 as it was in 1951, at about 160 with each family unit now having

an average of three members. The farm workforce has also declined dramatically. In the 1950s there were 112 farms; today, there are only 14: 12 dairy
producers and two beef producers. To develop, agriculture has had to adopt
principles of industrial production.

Today, though production has increased due to more effective technologies
and farm specialization, industrial agriculture can no longer maintain a large
workforce without compromising its viability. The loss of jobs in the agricultural
and processing sectors, coupled with the attraction of city life, has transformed
the exodus from the farm into an exodus from rural areas as such.

Meanwhile, lumber is in a slump due to the international crisis in the sector.
The forest was exploited primarily for timber, which was then used in pulp and
paper production. The recent collapse of that industry has caused the loss of a
large number of jobs. As the increase in service sector jobs is primarily an urban
phenomenon, Saint-Paul-de-la-Croix has been unable to create a significant
number of new jobs and retain its population, particularly young people. A few
new businesses are trying to establish themselves by developing markets for
their goods and services beyond the boundaries of the village. The rapid
disappearance of traditional crafts and the recent economic slump have made
fast conversion to new jobs difficult. About forty people live in the village but
work in nearby towns. According to our survey, residents practice some fifty
different trades, which account for about 53% of employment in the locality.
Some of these trades are practised primarily in Saint-Paul and a number of
people have to practice more than one trade in order to stay in the village. For
example, many residents have woodlots to provide for basic needs; most have at
least one. The unemployment rate is around 20%; 53% of income derives from
employment and 37% from government payments. To a growing extent, the
village's population consists of senior citizens.

Local activism

The present challenge in Saint-Paul-de-la-Croix is to consolidate a living
environment and develop a community which is convinced of the advantages of
life in the countryside and of the need to become involved in the community and
participate in social and cultural activities to affirm their identity and their rural
existence. This dynamic of identity affirmation and local resistance is clear and
enjoys the active support of a segment of the population. Of the 442 people in
the village, over 90 are involved in a total of 26 committees working to develop,
upgrade and expand various services which are important for the quality of life
in Saint-Paul-de-la-Croix: public services (volunteer firefighters and emergency
preparedness), religious life (pastoral work in the school, in the parish, religious education, liturgy, choir, parish council), social and health committees
(ambulance drivers, blood pressure clinic, golden age, young people, volunteer
work), education (school committee, guidance committee, Alpha group work-

shops), sports and recreation (leisure activities, hockey, cultural events, golf), women's activities (*Cercle des fermières, Association féminine d'éducation et d'action sociale*), village planning committee (beautification campaigns), social and economic committees (*Alliance des gens d'affaires de Saint-Paul-de-la-Croix, Coalition urgence rurale*). These efforts are helping to unite the community against the threat of village closure.

This solidarity was expressed with particular force during an event which occurred during the past year. It happened on May 4, 1992 at a day-long study session organized by *Coalition urgence rurale*. One hundred and fifty people took part in this event and attended workshops to discuss current issues and challenges for village development. A number of conclusions emerged. The municipal government was called upon to improve the roads and promote residential and industrial construction. Other priorities were maintaining rural schools, organizing health services on a volunteer basis in order to improve the quality of life in the community, setting up a body to promote local businesses and jobs for young people.

On the agricultural front, participants called for the creation of a list of farms with no children to take over and a list of young farmers without farms, so as to prevent the abandonment of farms. With respect to the development of tree farms, they called for easier access to available forestry credit and the creation of a group to collectively purchase woodlots. In the field of culture, the priority was to put out a paper to serve all the local organizations and the local population. Tasks were distributed, notably to a follow-up committee, and in some fields to elected municipal officials.

It is always a challenge to translate the results of discussion sessions into concrete action. While a number of people undertook to act on the various recommendations, the village's economic and social recovery remains a long-term challenge demanding activism on a daily basis. The strengthening of solidarity in the village and indeed the region is also an ongoing challenge. Beyond the opinions and duties of each of the individuals seeking solutions, joint action at the local level is essential for the village's survival; it can be developed only in partnership with community and business leaders and elected officials (the municipal council). Some village leaders want to see the regional grassroots movement of the past twenty years take on a significant local dimension in Saint-Paul; they want *Coalition urgence rurale* to develop a base in the village. The hesitation of some leaders about the best strategy to adopt, the role of municipal officials and action priorities is prompting discussion, local negotiations and new forms of activism.

The debates and challenges for local development were framed in the following terms during the summer of 1992. To launch local and community development actions, solidarity would have to be strengthened and local identity renewed. At that time, the local Alpha group in Saint-Paul-de-la-Croix did not consider these discussions on the village's future to be its concern. As in years past, the group's activities were based on teaching functional literacy. But the group's facilitator, who was already actively involved in a number of local committees and in following up on the *Coalition urgence rurale* meeting, was interested in getting Alpha more involved.

ALPHA

There has been a local Alpha group in Saint-Paul-de-la-Croix since 1989. It is part of the *ABC des Portages* project, which was set up by the Rivière-du-Loup school board's regional adult education department in cooperation with the Des Portages central lending library (BCP). *ABC des Portages* is an independent popular education organization accredited and subsidized by the Quebec Department of Education.[14] The local Saint-Paul-de-la-Croix group's approach to literacy education is in line with the traditions of the popular literacy education movement in Quebec, which, since its beginnings about 15 years ago, has favoured consciousness-raising over formal education.[15]

In the fall of 1992, there were nine people enrolled in the local Alpha group. Our action-research project was developed in conjunction with this group. Our first contacts with the group facilitator revealed that she was interested in a literacy education approach which could be more directly relevant to the problems of socioeconomic development in the village. She felt the Alpha group could become an arena or instrument for promoting identity affirmation, fostering community development and thereby enabling individuals to become more involved in initiatives for social, cultural and economic empowerment. It was with this outlook that the project with the local Alpha group began in the spring of 1992.

In our first meeting with Alpha, we identified the group's main expectations and together defined an educational project. The goals which emerged were primarily of a sociopolitical nature. The need to have a say, to create arenas where citizens could speak, to share ideas and options, to develop a positive but critical attitude all reflect a desire on the part of participants to break out of their isolation and gain a hold on their environment. It became clear that group members felt powerless, felt they had lost control over their own development, that their village no longer belonged to them. We interpreted the need to forge bonds of solidarity, to build self-confidence and personal independence, as stemming from the group's desire to regain control over its environment. Alienation from the social and economic environment is often expressed as nostalgia for the past. These expressed feelings and perceptions would serve as the basis for our action-research initiative with the group facilitator.

The facilitator was sensitive to these basic demands on the part of the group and wanted to pursue an educational approach which would allow participants to express their knowledge of the local environment and foster greater self-knowledge. Their vast store of acquired empirical knowledge had to be harnessed. Participants had to be given a voice; they had to acquire symbolic codes of transmission to make that voice clear. The goal of self-knowledge implies an educational approach centred on each participant, sensitive to each participant's pace and learning style, capable of fostering the development of each individual's unique skills and abilities. To establish real communication and build a relationship of mutual trust, one must know the group's interests and main motivations. Knowing people means knowing their family, socioeconomic and cultural background, so the facilitator will be in a position to communicate with them on the basis of their real-life experiences and respect their values. The facilitator's deep local roots were a major asset in making the process relevant for the participants.

The local Alpha group's approach was built on these foundations, using the project method and life stories approach.

The project method
& the collective life stories approach

The project method is based on doing, on action as a way of learning. Learning by acting is an expression of a basic empirical process.[16] The educational process is organized around and guided by the project: developing it, carrying it out, evaluating it. This approach cuts the gap between action and reflection to a minimum. Knowledge is conveyed through the activity and the questions it raises. A "relevancy principle" inevitably bears upon the knowledge being presented and the way it is presented. The group's activity or project determines the body of knowledge which is conveyed. Defined and executed by the group, the project forces participants to become involved because it grows out of the group's desire to transform a specific reality in a concrete way, to achieve tangible, communicable results of practical utility. The project method is based on the individuals in the group, their social environment, and their own real-life experiences, which they understand and influence. The resource person uses the project method as a means for developing self-confidence, solidarity and mutual aid, and to help each individual assimilate knowledge, know-how and social skills.

The collective life stories approach examines social reality from within with a focus on the members' own interpretations of reality.[17] Behaviours are understood in relation to the meanings participants assign to things and to their own actions. This is the starting point for all subsequent learning. In this sense, individuals are not prodded to overcome ignorance and false beliefs. Their perceptions of reality are accepted as valid and serve as the point of departure for a critical analysis of their environment permitting them to reconstitute their social reality not through an objective analysis of structures but based on their lives.

The method attempts to uncover the role of structural factors as the root cause of individual problems and pursues the goal of individual empowerment.

The adults are in an egalitarian relationship with the resource person and they are encouraged to play an active role in the educational process and to change the power relationships within which they operate.

During the summer of 1992, more precise orientations were established for the literacy education program, using these methods as a point of departure. Focused on strengthening cultural identities, these were seen as the driving force behind local development. It was important for us to develop an approach which would integrate as far as possible public literacy education resources into the process of mobilization, education and action led by the grassroots *Coalition urgence rurale* movement which was already involved in promoting various customized training programs and pushing for "recognition that the village school is a socially and economically viable force for community development".[18]

Project implementation

During the fall of 1992, five men and four women regularly attended Alpha's activities two evenings a week. The approach was simple. We invited group members to talk about their perceptions in three stages: their memories of the past (going back to the 1950s), their diagnosis of the current situation, and their forecasts for the near future (up to the year 2000). Different subjects were discussed each week: farming, forestry, business, public services, transportation, politics at the school board, municipal, provincial and federal levels, participation in the life of the village, family, religion, education, information media, demographics, holidays, recreation, bees, values, ideas about life, etc. All these aspects of community life in the village were the subject of lively discussion at Alpha meetings. On Thursday evenings, participants took the floor in turn to express their views on the topic for the evening. Notes were taken on the discussion, faxed the next day, and corrected and approved by the group on the following Tuesday. This procedure allowed the group to add information and also served as a reading and writing exercise.

In this way, the group members had an opportunity to express their perceptions of the village's development in the group and share their hopes for the future. The meetings were lively, with each participant spontaneously analyzing the themes suggested by the facilitator. The group thus discussed development in the village in a systematic way. The presence of members of the research team once a week to ensure continuity did not create any problems. In the course of sometimes passionate, sometimes nostalgic discussions, participants in the Alpha group gradually described the changes which had occurred in the village and attempted to define a viable future.

Participants found their voice. In the course of the exercise, group members could develop an effective and genuine discourse. Through this discourse, they committed themselves, became involved and engaged. All participants were able to speak freely, to express their opinions, ideas, feelings, experiences, peeves, criticisms, questions, uncertainties, doubts. Discussing freely in a group, claiming the floor, listening to others are things which must be learned. Group members were somewhat surprised by the opportunity to do so in what was at first a more formal setting. The facilitator validated the comments of all participants and proposed rules of order to govern the discussion: going around the table and keeping track of the quantity, length and order of comments.

Group members thus addressed topics close to their reality and real-life experience: farming, forestry, politics, housework, etc. The village's profile gradually grew clearer, like a group portrait being dusted off so it can again be appreciated. As each person spoke, personal identity emerged and found expression. Each participant also learned to analyze reality, to more fully understand it, question it, transform it. Claiming a voice is a first step towards taking possession of the social environment and gaining control over living conditions.

Participants received encouragement and confirmation for talking about their lives and work. They were invited to relate their living and working habits, without being pressured. For example, the subject of agriculture was directly relevant to each participant: three owned farms and all of the others were living on a farm or had done so at one point in their lives. The question affected them and they wanted to share with others their reading of the current situation, their often nostalgic memories of the past, their understanding of the loss of control they have suffered over the years, their hopes for a viable rural future. Describing the changes in farming over the past 40 years gave them an understanding of the influence of structural factors on their individual situations.

For example, group members had to try to explain why there were 110 farms in Saint-Paul-de-la-Croix in 1950 and only 12 agricultural producers in 1992. From the discussion prompted by this fact, there emerged a number of explanatory factors for the profound changes in agriculture and rural regions. Industrial production has imposed on farming the imperatives of efficient sustained yield production for national and international markets. Participants also noted the mechanization and specialization of farms, the loss of jobs from the abandonment of farms and small traditional businesses, government development policies and strategies geared to urban centres, the drop in the birth rate, the exodus of young people and the rapid aging of the population.

The other topics aroused equal interest on the part of participants and prompted enriching group discussions. The discussions also served to teach oral and written expression. We noted progress in communication skills, vocabulary, syntax and spelling.

Producing a book

A few weeks after the beginning of the project, the idea of sharing the group's analyses and broadening the discussion to other groups in the village was raised. Alpha's activities acted as a catalyst and motivated group members to disseminate the results of their discussions. It was agreed that by the end of the fall program, there would be a document reflecting the group's discussions in its 20-odd meetings on the village's past, present and future. The title was to be *Saint-Paul-de-la-Croix d'hier a demain* (Saint-Paul-de-la-Croix from yesterday to tomorrow). The book would cover all the discussion topics and express the members' pride, identity and determination to stay in their communities. They dubbed themselves "the craftsmen of the future," expressing pride in work and mastery of all its facets. The reference to the future testifies to confidence in a viable future for the village and for rural regions and to hope for the generations to come. The group's name therefore combines attachment to past and future.

In early December 1992, Alpha celebrated the launching of the book. Everyone gathered around a large table in the tiny village library. The room was hung with Christmas decorations. Every face beamed with pride. They were eager to see their book. The copies were handed out in silence. Each person handled the precious document with care. Their discussions had been transformed into a physical object. They started to flip through it with a thrill of recognition, connecting sentences to group members. People commented on passages or reiterated their views and they returned nostalgically to discussing the situation in the village. Memories stirred: this was their story, they were the characters. They had become aware of their right to speak; they had claimed a voice.

Shortly after Christmas, we learned that all copies had sold out in a few days. It was the talk of the village! The distribution of the book fostered awareness of the fight and helped focus groups and organizations on common projects for the survival of the village. A few kilometres away, the inhabitants of the tiny village of Saint-Clément occupied the post office for two months to protest its closing. The same concerns were expressed at La Rédemption and elsewhere. *Coalition urgence rurale* worked to coordinate the protests and to initiate or support local development projects. People joined forces to express their determination to preserve their communities and protest the decline of their villages.

REFLECTIONS

Rural populations have become more aware of the disintegration of their communities and many groups are developing grassroots actions.[19] Rural movements are organizing. *Solidarité rurale,* the organization which grew out of the *Etats généraux du monde rural* (Rural Summit), is working to coordinate these various actions. We have chosen to report on the activities of one local Alpha group in order to highlight the potential of these literacy education groups in the current situation. Many leaders have become aware of the issue of manpower training in rural regions and are attempting to develop original strategies to counter rural decline but these strategies usually neglect rural literacy education structures. The Alpha groups are part of a formal process which often fails to take account of specific situations in local communities and of the socioeconomic environment of the adult participants. We considered it important to work with an Alpha group both to investigate the group's potential to support community development and to postulate other forms of intervention to nourish individual and local initiatives. Given the expenditure of public funds on these operations, home-grown approaches adapted to local conditions ought to be encouraged.

The Saint-Paul-de-la-Croix Alpha group's initiative is not an isolated one. It is part of the current movement of resistance to rural and regional decline. By a simple, unglamorous act, the group eloquently expressed its desire to stay on the land. The village was established recently, like many others in Quebec. A hundred years ago, settlers were encouraged to open up new territories, to clear new lands and live on them with pride. Today, their presence there is seen as an inconvenience.

One important conclusion which emerges from current local development practices in rural regions is that local identities must be strengthened and used as the basis for development initiatives. Cultural roots are a prerequisite for local development.[20] Sense of community must be recreated; positive identities must be redefined. For the process of community empowerment to begin, a lost and tarnished identity must first be recovered.

At first, the movement expresses itself through a negative identity which seeks to defend its own living conditions, progressing towards a more positive identity. Original initiatives are launched, special projects are developed, citizens reclaim the standards which regulate their lives and reformulatethem on the basis of the way of life.

The Saint-Paul-de-la-Croix Alpha group's approach was focused on expressing this cultural identity and sense of community. The process of identity affirmation embraced three facets of identity: the community's history and heritage, which is an object of pride and of nostalgia sustained by the major events of the village's history; a forward-looking identity which casts the community as a guardian against the destructive logic of a system gone haywire; and an identity rooted in experience and the relative advantages of the rural lifestyle as it exists today.[21] By publicizing its discussions, the group helped expand this growing sense of identity in the village, and this sense is gaining strength in Saint- Paul-de-la-Croix. Recent examples of community-based efforts and development initiatives include bees, the arrival of new families, economic promotion, holiday activities, economic and social activities. The high level of participation in the various committees indicates a vigorous local community life.

In the final analysis, this local literacy education group is calling upon us to redefine the state of literacy in industrialized countries, which are developing rigid and elaborate systems alien to human needs and aspirations. The loss of understanding and control over the system's workings may well be an expression of a basic loss of literacy among many social groups.

The cultural challenge of reinventing rural societies in Quebec on a day-by-day basis demands a process of literacy acquisition aimed at overcoming dependence on a socioeconomic system which imposes standards and lifestyles opposed to the village-based model of local development. The renewal of rural communities and of basic education is bound up with reinventing what it means to be human in relation to the land and society, with recovering a deeply rooted living space and a community support system. The process of dispossession and deterritorialization of individual living spaces reflects a state of dependence and a dramatic loss of sociocultural knowledge. Becoming illiterate means, first and foremost, losing control over one's environment. Trendy talk about empowerment camouflages this state of alienation from our living environments, our communities, our own identities. Many villages in rural Quebec are engaged in this movement of rural redefinition. Saint-Paul-de-la-Croix is one of them.

Notes & References

1. Dugas, Clermont, "Distribution spatiale de la population du Québec et vitalité des régions," *L'action nationale* Vol. LXXVIII, No. 6, June 1988, p. 434. (On this subject, see the recent discussion by C. Dugas and B. Vachon in "Le Québec rural des années 90: son territoire, sa population, sa structure institutionnelle" in Vachon B., *Le Québec rural dans tous ses états (Montréal: Boréal, 1991), pp. 19-38.*

2. Rocher, Guy, *Le Québec en mutation* (Montreal: Hurtubise HMH, 1973).

3. Jean, Bruno, "La ruralité québécoise contemporaine: principaux éléments de spécificité et de différenciation" in Vachon, B., *op. cit.*, p. 84.

4. Vachon, Bernard, "Le peuplement des régions rurales du Québec face aux phénomènes de dénatalité et de désurbanisation," in *Espace, population et société*, Vol. III, 1986, pp. 85-94. *See also Dugas, C. and Vachon, B., op. cit.*, p. 24

5. This topic has been widely discussed in Quebec in recent years. See Conseil des affaires sociales, *Deux Québec dans un* (Boucherville: Gaëtan Morin, Gouvernement du Québec, 1989); Côté, Charles, *Désintégration des régions* (chicoutimi: JCL, 1991).

6. Dugas, Clermont, "Distribution spatiale de la population du Québec et vitalité des régions," *op. cit.*, p. 438.

7. See *Les villages ruraux menacés*, Actes et instruments de recherche en développement régional, No. 7 (Rimouski: UQAR-GRIDEQ, 1989), 253 PP.

8. Vachon, Bernard, ed., *Le Québec rural dans tous ses états, op. cit..*

9. See for example Jean, Bruno, *Agriculture et développement de l'Est du Québec* (Saint-Foy: Presses de l'Universite du Québec, 1985).

10. Dionne, Hughes, ed., *Aménagement intégré des ressources et luttes en milieu rural*, Cahiers du GRIDEQ No. 11 (Rimouski: Université du Québec à Rimouski, 1983).

11. Larrivée, Jean, "Evolution de la population des municipalités régionales de comté (M.R.C.) du Bas-Saint-Laurent: le déclin rural 1951-1986" in *Revue d'histoire du Bas-Saint-Laurent*, Vol. XV, No. 2 (41), Rimouski, June 1992, pp. 22-25.

12. La Coalition urgence rurale du Bas-Saint-Laurent, *Notre politique de développement rural* (Rimouski: 1990).

13. Dionne, Hughes, "De la région-ressources à la région-milieu de vie: à la recherche de nouveaux partenaires," in Gagnon, C. and Klein, J.L., eds., *Les partenaires du développement face au défi du local*, GRIR (Université du Québec à Chicoutimi, 1992), pp. 371-401.

14. Under the Programme de soutien à l'alphabétisation autonome (Independent Literacy Education Support Program). The organization has a Board of Governors and about 15 part-time employees. It receives federal and provincial government subsidies and also teaches courses for the school board on a contract basis.

15. Hautecoeur, J.P., "Politique d'alphabétisation au Québec" *in Alpha 90* (Ministère de l'Éducation du Québec/Unesco Institute for Education, 1990), pp. 31-49.

16. There are a number of books on this aspect of adult education. The most recent discussions are influenced by the action research approach espoused by U.S. researchers Chris Argyris and Donald A. Schon, and in Quebec by Yves Saint-Arnaud, Connaître par l'action (Montréal: Presses de l'Université de Montréal, 1992).

17. Filman, F., "Groupe de recherche et d'action pédagogiques," *Revue Internationale d'action communautaire*, 2/42, 1979. For a recent summary of the life stories approach, see Mayer, R. and Ouellet, F., *Méthodologie de recherche pour les intervenants sociaux* (Boucherville: Gaëtan Morin, 1991). The method generally used a primarily individual and private approach, not a group approach.

18. La Coalition urgence rurale, *Notre politique de développement rural, op. cit.*, p. 13.

19. Conseil québécois des affaires sociales, *Un Québec solidaire, op. cit.*

20. Guindani, S. and Bassand, M., *Maldéveloppement regional et identité* (Lausanne: Presses polytechniques romandes, 1982).

21. Centlivres, P., *Identité régionale: Approche ethnologique, Suisse romande et Tessin*, Rapport de synthèse, mimeographed document, (Neuchâtel: Institut d'ethnologie, 1981), p. 52. Cited in Bassand, M., *Culture et régions d'Europe* (Lausanne: Presses polytechniques et universitaires romandes, 1990), p. 219.

Chapter 18
MIGRANT & SEASONAL FARMWORKERS: AN INVISIBLE POPULATION

Loida C. Velásquez
University of Tennessee
Knoxville, Tennessee, U.S.A.

IN SEARCH OF INFORMATION ON MIGRANTS

Migrant farmworkers have been labeled the most disadvantaged of all minority groups. By definition, they are people on the move with little time to establish community ties; they live in isolation even when they live in high density areas;[1] and when they stop to work in local farms, they are hardly noticed by most community members. For the most part, migrant farmworkers' needs, problems, dreams and aspirations are kept hidden and go unmet and unfulfilled.

Migrants are the most undereducated major sub-group in the United States. Their high school dropout rate is higher than any other group, 43 % according to the National Council of La Raza.[2] Mobility, language and cultural differences combined with health and nutrition problems do have a negative effect on school achievement. The constant interruption of the educational process, as well as the inability of schools to understand their culture and meet their needs, leads to confusion, frustration and a feeling of alienation among migrants. Hodgkinson[3] reports that over 70 % of all migrants have not completed high school and 75 % are functionally illiterate.

Migrant agricultural labourers who travel within the geographical boundaries of the continental United States and Canada move along identifiable streams: the Eastern stream, the Mid-Continent stream, and the West Coast stream.[4] The Eastern stream is made up of Puerto Ricans, Mexican-Americans, Anglos, Canadian Indians, and Blacks and flows up and down the region east of the Appalachian Mountains. The Mid-Continent stream, composed of Mexicans, Mexican-Americans, Blacks, and most recently Viet-namese and Cambodians, traces the Mississipi river basin. These migrants move in all directions to and from different regions in Texas. The West Coast stream is the largest movement, extending from California and Arizona to Oregon and Washington. This stream is comprised primarily of documented and undocumented Mexicans, Central Americans, Vietnamese, Filipinos, and other Western Pacific immigrants.

For decades the economic health of this nation has depended on a steady stream of migrant workers moving through our farmland, yet we know very little about who they are, what their lives are like, what their needs are. A search of the Adult Basic Education (ABE) literature, for instance, reveals very little about the educational needs of the migrant adult. Educators interested in planning programs to reach this particular segment of the population find scarce information giving insight into the culture of migrancy. Most of what we have learned about the educational needs of migrant adults comes from research and articles on the educational needs of migrant youth. The Prewitt-Diaz, Trotter, & Rivera[1] ethnographic study, although intended to provide the necessary information to improve the identification and recruitment of migrant children for state school systems, gives us some insight into the needs of migrant parents. Research articles on migrant student dropout rates and drop-out prevention provide information on potential ABE program partici-pants.[5,6,7,8,9]

Migrant seasonal agricultural workers who follow the crops and harvests across the United States and Canada have little time to establish community contracts and are hardly noticed by most community members. The need to harvest a crop creates the demand for farmworkers. When that crop is har-vested, the migrant worker packs up his wife, children and possessions and moves on to find new work. Lacking adequate education, and without advocates to protect their rights, migrant workers accept jobs that offer no benefits other than per hourly or by-bushel pay. Migrants are paid an average of $4.80 an hour or 40 cents for each bushel and do not receive retirement pension or have a hospitalization plan.

According to King-Stoops,[4] the first real migrant movement began after the Civil War when freed slaves fled north and were hired to do agricultural work. As the season changed, they would move with the crops, taking with them family and relatives. Migrancy became a way of life for them. All family members, children included, participated in the harvest. Children followed the migrant footsteps of their fathers, generation after generation.

The main reason migrants move from one area to another, from one state to another, is to find work. They may have a home-base to return to after the harvest or they may not. Prewitt-Diaz et al.[1] found that, contrary to the media stereotype, most migrant workers are U.S. citizens. Undocumented workers represent only 15% of all migrants.[10] Green card workers migrate annually from Mexico to California to participate in the citrus and grape harvest.

Prewitt-Diaz et al. have divided the migrant population into subcategories by ethnic background. The early migrant farm workers on the West Coast were Chinese, Japanese, Filipinos and Mexicans. A second group was composed of Blacks on the East Coast. The third group was Spanish-speaking migrants from Puerto Rico and Texas. This latter group moved into the midsection of the country.

In the first decade of this century, Blacks, primarily from Florida, moved to the Northeast. The predominant place of their resettlement was New York. Later, Blacks from other Southern states moved to industrial centers in the North. During the 1930s, the cultivation of winter vegetables attracted Black workers from other Southern states to Florida.[12] Migrant Blacks became a significant part of the farm labor force in the South. Years later this work force moved to the Northern states. The pattern continues today, although a marked decrease of Black migrant workers has been noted.

Mexican-American migrants are predominantly from Texas, Arizona, New Mexico, and California. The Mexican-Americans, the largest group of Hispanics in the United States, are approximately 13 million. There exists no reasonable estimate of the percentage of Mexican-Americans who are migrants; however, the Department of Education reports that about 60% of all migrant children accounted for by the education system are Mexican-American.

Puerto Ricans comprise the second largest Hispanic group in the United States. Their migration to the mainland began after World War II and constitutes the first airborne migration to the United States. They settled in the Northeastern states, as well as in Illinois and Michigan.

About 20 % of migrant farm workers are Anglo (of European extraction). They are located predominantly in the Northern states (Washington, Idaho, Montana, Illinois, Pennsylvania, and Maine). This population works primarily on dairy farms or on farms where crops are cultivated and harvested by picking.

MIGRANCY AS A CULTURE

Although migrant workers share a certain lifestyle and many behavioural patterns, migrant groups differ in social and educational backgrounds. While many Asian and Hispanic-American migrants have some knowledge of English, some recently arrived immigrants are not literate even in their own language. For some, illiteracy is a result of their social and economic status, for others, illiteracy stems from the disruption in education caused by recent moves or political turmoil.[1] Some migrants from Haiti, Khmer, and Hmong come from areas with no written language or where there is a strong oral tradition of language learning.

A culture is broadly defined as the distinctive modes or ways of behaving that are shared by a group. The ethnographic study by Prewitt-Diaz et al.[1] focused on migrant children but in the process opened a window into migrant families and their shared behaviour patterns. Some of the patterns mentioned in the study are:

Male & Female Roles

In most cases women are expected to work in the fields and do household chores. Men and children are usually exempt from household responsibilities. Marriage at a young age is common for female migrants and signals the end of schooling. In most migrant families there is enormous pressure for the males to support the family, and for females to have children. These complementary roles assist young migrant couples to survive but severely limit the chances for educational success and advancement.

Adult/Child Roles

Although all cultures differentiate between adult roles and children's behaviour, the age at which children begin to adopt adult roles varies for different cultures. In many migrant families, boys begin to be treated as adults when, at age 15 or 16, they can earn as much in the fields as their fathers. Girls start being treated as adults when they are capable of having children and managing a household. The difference between the role expectations of migrant families and those of the dominant society has serious consequences for educational programs. Most migrant children drop out of school when they are able to work in the fields and earn money. Migrant parents allow their children to make the decision between dropping out of, or staying in school.

Dealing with Social Institutions

Educational, health care and social service agencies are created to facilitate living in a complex society. One of the functions of culture is to teach how to best use the system of agencies. Migrants, especially those who come from a different linguistic and cultural background, are at a serious disadvantage because they do not understand the system. Some migrants strive to be independent and take pride in meeting their family needs; others suffer in silence because they do not know who could help them in time of trouble.

Powerlessness & the Migrant Cycle

The cycle of migrancy is very hard to break and many migrants feel trapped, with little hope for a better future for their children. This feeling of powerlessness is sometimes misinterpreted as apathy by educational agencies. Although migrant parents express support for education for their children, they also feel that migrancy is the fate for them regardless of anything they say or do.

Attitude toward Authority

Migrants have a generally positive attitude towards authority, especially toward the schools. However, this attitude is occasionally expressed in a way that is culturally confusing to school personnel. Migrants trust the schools to know what is right for their children and feel that their questions about the appropriateness of their children's educational program will be construed as a challenge to the teacher's authority and prestige. The institution with which migrants most often interact is the school; ironically, the migrant lifestyle is the greatest impediment for their children's educational success.

Freire[11] stated that the lack of education is a form of oppression. For him the role of the educator is to understand and become part of the learner's culture, to stimulate learning in order to "free" or empower the individual. To reach the adult migrant population and to provide programs that would empower them, it is imperative that adult educators learn more about their culture. The studies cited by this article provide a starting point to understanding the educational needs of migrant adults but further research, particularly ethnographic research, will be useful to ABE programs intending to serve this population.

MIGRANT EDUCATION: A MULTIPLE SATELLITE PROGRAM

Federal legislation in the United States concerning migrant and seasonal farmworkers has historically included regulatory measures designed to improve the substandard working, occupational health, housing, and educational conditions encountered by this segment of the population. As part of an overall strategy in educational issues, program priority has been given to migrant and seasonal farmworker children. Early on, primary attention was given to primary school education, but in the past 10 to 15 years the attention has turned to supporting migrant youth in completing secondary education.

The programs designed to help migrant youth who dropped from school to complete high school requirements, are increasingly serving migrant adults. The College of Education at the University of Tennessee has been involved in the design and implementation of dropout retrieval programs for migrant and seasonal farmworkers since 1982. Funded by a grant from the Office of Migrant Education of the U.S. Department of Education, the University ran a residential program for migrant and seasonal farmworker school dropouts from 1982 to 1986. The goal was to prepare students to take the high school equivalency test, expecting that the college atmosphere would serve as incentive and motivate these students to continue their education. The residential program was highly successful in assisting the recruited students to complete high school requirements but very few decided to enter higher education and there were very few changes in their quality of life. Very early in the recruiting process the University of Tennessee High School Equivalency (UT HEP) staff discovered another characteristic of these particular populations: although very few had a place to call home, they were very reluctant to leave family and friends to come to a strange place away from loved ones. Many were already involved in farmwork and their income was needed for the family sustenance.

The proposal presented by the University of Tennessee to the Department of Education for the 1987-1990 three-year cycle was for an ambitious multiple satellite program. The UT HEP targeted four states and proposed the establishment of four HEP sites. The intention was to bring the program to the student instead of bringing the student to the program. The four HEP sites were located near to areas with high concentration of migrant and seasonal farmworkers in North Carolina, South Carolina, Georgia, and Tennessee.

Most recent research on the barriers to adult education participation point toward lack of motivation and interest as the major participation deterrent. The University of Tennessee High School Equivalency Program tested the veracity of this research conclusion. After four years of administrating a satellite program they have concluded that if you control external variables (i.e. transportation, child care, fees or cost, the time of the day, and location), migrant students are normally motivated and interested in completing their secondary school education. The yearly target was to serve 170 students, and each year of the three year cycle the program has surpassed the enrollment target.

PROGRAM EVALUATION

A quick examination of factors contributing to the overall success of the UT HEP under the satellite format reveals characteristics that are consistent with the characteristics of effective adult basic education programs:

- The program is geared to empower students by increasing their success experiences, self confidence and feeling of self-worth and dignity.

- Class schedule is flexible and classes are accessible to potential students.

- A strong promotion and recruitment program.

- Coordinators, recruiters, counselors and instructors are culturally and ethnically representative of the student body.

- Bilingual counselors are available and an intensive counseling program is implemented.

- Student assessment is an integral part of the program.

- Tutors are utilized.

- An individually tailored plan is developed for each student.

- Staff training and development activities are provided.

- Teacher and program effectiveness are regularly evaluated.

- Placement plans start at enrollment, and placement activities are geared to end in post-secondary education or competitive employment.

Myles Horton, the founder of the Highlander Research and Education Center and an American pioneer of adult education, once said: "I look at a person with two eyes. One eye tells me what he is; the other tells me what he can become". The goals and objectives of our programs are geared toward the student overcoming the cycle of poverty and migrancy and becoming a productive member of society. The success of the program in meeting this overall goal was better expressed by a former student:

By attending the UT HEP I was really digging myself out of a mudhole.

The three years spent in implementing a residential program were not adequate training for the new format. However, the staff and administrators have learned a valuable lesson in program planning and implementation: to be flexible. The program has been recognized nationally as an effective dropout retrieval program because they have taken four important development steps:

1. Take the program to the student. Find where they are and locate the program there.

2. Make the program flexible enough to allow for family needs, work, etc.

3. Involve the other family members. Use family strengths for motivation and support. Keep the family unit intact.

4. Be familiar with and use other community resources to supplement services.

After four years following the non-resident/satellite format, the UT High School Equivalency Program is fully established. In order to better serve the population, the programs have become part of a net of programs and institutions in the community system. Each satellite is working in cooperation with a local community college. The program format has been recognized as a good example of interagency cooperation and coordination. Yet still, the sites' programs suffer from some of the problems experienced by other literacy programs:

- unstable attendance;

- enrollment drops if recruitment efforts are not maintained;

- the most needy student remains underserved since federal guidelines encourage serving those needing less instruction time.

The needs of migrant and seasonal farmworkers are many and complicated by their isolation. These needs include:

- Available and affordable housing.

- Comprehensive health benefits and services.

- Adult basic education, vocational education, and literacy programs.

- Enforced protection from work-related illness and injuries.

- Employers' compliance with legally established fair employment practices.

- Compliance with child labor laws, and other worker-protective laws.

The number of adult education programs serving the migrant population is very small and the information available about the culture of migrancy is minimal. The few programs available are under funded and traditionally designed. Creative and flexible programs like UT HEP are limited by lack of funds and federal guidelines.

EL CENTRO ARCOIRIS

The goals of UT HEP and most programs serving migrant and seasonal farmworkers are defined by the funding agency. In most cases there is a single goal: to provide better health services, to provide motivation to further education, or to provide higher education opportunities. Concerned and dedicated staff members try to connect clients with other agencies under the belief that as migrants become the recipients of multiple services, their lot in life will improve, community members will become more receptive to their needs and more acceptant of their existence. Experience has also proved this belief faulty. A UT HEP graduate explained this way:

> It was not until I realized that nobody was going to do it for me, that I had to become self-sufficient, that things started happening for me. I am not saying that I did not receive help here and there. I am grateful to so many people! But the best thing they did for me was to help me help myself, and that is what I want to do for other migrants coming to this area.

El Centro Arcoiris started as a dream for this UT HEP graduate. She had dropped out of high school to become a mother. With her migrant husband and child she moved through the migrant Eastern stream in search for work until they decided to settle in a farming town in Western North Carolina. Her husband became a crew leader, bringing migrant workers from Mexico and Texas to work at the many farm surrounding the town. She was working at a migrant store when the UT HEP recruiter came inside looking for recruits for the literacy class. She was expecting her second child and was reluctant to enroll but after her concerns were satisfied, (child care, flexible class hours, etc.) she started attending classes and graduated a few days before her son was born. Today she owns her own migrant store, El Mercado Mejicano, and with the assistance of other migrants and community members opened El Centro Arcoiris. The grassroots group that developed the idea of the centre listed the following as their goals:

1. To provide assistance with legal interpretation and advice.

2. To provide housing assistance. Part of the problem with workers coming to the area is that landlords will not rent their properties without a long term lease. Also there is a lack of communication because of the language barrier since most workers are hispanic. The centre will keep an updated list of landlords willing to rent to migrants and in this way eliminate much of the suffering that families experience when they arrive looking for housing.

3. To assist with agencies' document preparation and advise people on how to prepare their own official papers and to understand them.

4. To establish a food and clothes room for workers who arrive with very little.

5. To bring the experience of the hispanic culture to this area through art, music, dance and festivals to which the non-migrant community will be invited. In this way we will start bringing the worker in contact with the community.

6. To provide a place where literacy, English as a Second Language and other educational programs will be housed.

As the idea for the centre developed, the group faced a number of obstacles: securing a source of funding, finding a suitable location, getting community support, getting recently arrived migrants' participation. The UT HEP staff put the leaders in contact with The Highlander Research and Education Center where they received assistance on leadership training and researching funding sources. At the invitation of the migrant founders of the centre, and advisory committee of non-migrant community members has been formed and both groups are working together to develop the idea further. Through participatory research they have discovered the areas of greatest need among migrants, researched and secured some financial support, dealt with the court system and requested that a translator be hired to assist migrants having legal problems, convinced local merchants to use Spanish on store's signs and are diligently trying to secure enough funds to open a cultural centre. This group of migrant and seasonal farmworkers are determined not only to become self-reliant, but to make a contribution to the local community. They want the community to become familiar with their culture and their rich historical heritage.

The accomplishment of this grassroots group of migrant and seasonal farmworkers has no precedent in this Western North Carolina community. That some of the leaders are UT HEP graduates might not just be a coincidence. Although funded to provide high school equivalency education, the empowerment of this often invisible segment of the population has been the moving force behing most efforts. Yet of four satellite sites, only the migrants from this community are coming together in an empowered way. Undoubtedly a combination of factors have combined to provide fertile ground for the development of self assertion and a sense of empowerment. The most obvious are:

- The gathering of a group of young migrants with inborn leadership skills.

- The sense of accomplishment experienced after a successful experience (receiving the high school equivalency diploma).

- The sense of support received from group concerned about the plight of this segment of the population (Migrant Health, Migrant Headstart, Farmworkers Organizations, Highlander, UT HEP, Catholic Services and other religious organizations).

- The dependency of local farmers on the influx of migrants to harvest their crops.

- The developing awareness of local merchants of the migrant population as target clients.

- The innate sense of independence characteristic of migrants.

REFLECTIONS

Building self-directedness and a sense of empowerment is the overriding goal of adult education programs. The concept of praxis, that is, exploring, acting and reflecting on new ideas, skills and knowledge, stresses that learning does not take place in a vacuum. Understanding and describing the context is central to learning and literacy. The desire of adult migrant workers to improve their literacy is often overcome by the pressures of everyday life to simply survive and by a sense of powerlessness. Their life context, their need for survival and their sense of powerlessness, is not often acknowledged by programs trying to reach this group. Only programs that acknowledge and affirm the historical and existential experiences of migrants will be able to reach this population.

Although El Centro Arcoiris has given a voice to migrants in this Western North Carolina community, migrants all over the nation are silent and invisible. Traditionally designed adult education programs are unable to reach them. The future of the education of migrant adults depends on the development of programs that empower the local migrant population to help themselves. The future of programs such as UT HEP will depend on how well they listen to the migrant's voice.

Notes & References

1. Prewitt-Diaz, J.O., Trotter, R.T. & Rivera, V.A. (1990). *The Effects of Migration on Children: An Ethnographic Study*. PA: Center de Estudios Sobre la Migración

2. National Council of La Raza. (1990). *Hispanic Education A Statistical Portrait*. Washington, DC: National Council of La Raza Publications.

3. Hodgkinson, H.L. (1985). *All One System: Demographics of Education Through Graduate School*. Institute of Education Leadership, Inc.

4. King-Stoops, J.B. (1980). *Migrant Education: Teaching the Wandering Ones*. Bloomington,

Indiana: Phi Delta Kappa Educational Foundation.

5. Cranston-Gingras, A., & Anderson, D.J. (1986). Reducing the Migrant Student Drop-out Rate: The Role of School Counselors. *The School Counselor*, 38 (2), 95-104.

6. Apicella, R. (1985). *Perceptions of Why Migrant Students Drop Out of School and What Can be Done to Encourage Them to Graduate*. Oneonta NY: SUNY at Oneonta.

7. Nelken, I., & Gallo, K. (1978). *Factors influencing migrant high school students to dropout or graduate from high school*. Chico, CA: Nelken and Associates, Inc. (ERIC Document Reproduction Service No. ED 164 245.

8. Riley, G.L. (1985). HEP/CAMP national evaluation project research report #2, Fresno, CA: California State University.

9. Springstead, E. (1981). *Migrant drop-out study, 1980-1981: Final evaluation*. Austin, TX: Texas Education Agency, Division of Migrant Education.

10. Hispanic Policy Development Project. (1984). *Making Something Happen* (Vol. 5), Washington, D.C.: Hispanic National Development Project.

11. Freire, P. (1973). *Education for Critical Consciousness*. London: Sheed and Ward.

12. Young, W. E. (1968) *Educating Migrant Children*. Albany N.Y. The State Department of Education.

Chapter 19
APPALACHIAN COMMUNITIES: WORKING TO SURVIVE

Mary Beth Bingman and Connie White
Center for Literacy Studies
Knoxville, Tennessee, USA

POVERTY WITHIN A RICH CULTURAL HERITAGE

In Appalachia isolation and poverty are a reality for many, but so are a rich cultural heritage and a history of organizing. In this context adult education means more than academic degrees, more than straight literacy. But people's ideas of what education ought to look like are derived from years of acculturation and schooling. This may limit the degree to which community organizing and activism are integrated with formal basic skills education. While people understand the value of informal learning in their community organizing and development work, they may not apply this understanding to their education programs. Organizations may be a powerful voice for community development and social change, but still have very conventional literacy and adult classes. Even in organizations that are based on a vision of bringing about a more equal distribution of power in their communities, there are many barriers to realizing this vision in adult education programs.

Scattered throughout the mountains of Appalachia in the southeastern United States, a growing number of community-based organizations are practicing literacy and adult education work in a different way. These organizations, rooted in the region's rich history of organizing, are trying various ways to link their literacy and adult education work with the community development issues their groups also address.

Here we describe the region, its history, its strengths and its problems, and the organizations that have developed in communities to confront those problems. We offer examples of three rural organizations whose mission is the strengthening and empowering of communities as well as improving individual literacy skills. Finally, we will reflect on the ways those organizations have met some of their goals, and the distance that yet remains in understanding and implementing this literacy in a different way.

THE APPALACHIAN REGION

The Appalachian region of the United States is often portrayed by the media as a desolate region of "hills and hollers" and poor isolated communities of impoverished people. This current image of the region replaces an earlier version of a land of hardy mountaineers preserving a culture of ballads and quaint speech. There is some truth in both versions, but both are far too simplistic. Much of the area does remain isolated, but while a family may be far from hospitals and schools, they are close to neighbours and kin. Traditional music and food are still part of people's lives, but so are MTV and McDonald's. What is prevalent is an economy based on extractive industry, a pattern of outside ownership of land and natural resources, unemployment consistently above national levels, and access to services consistently below what is available to most Americans. Appalachia is a changing region, one which is becoming more and more connected to the "mainstream", but which remains distinct.

The Appalachian Mountains run down the length of the eastern United States from New York to Alabama. But the term Appalachia usually refers to the central part of the region — east Tennessee, eastern Kentucky, the far western part of Virginia, and most of West Virginia — the region most affected by coal mining. It is home to some five million people, most of whom live in small towns or in the rugged countryside. Flat land is limited and is mostly in river bottoms prone to flooding. Most of the mineral resources are owned and extracted by coal companies headquartered outside the region.

History & Economy

The southern mountains were home to Cherokee, Shawnee, and other Native American peoples who perfected many aspects of the art of living there. They passed these skills on to the European settlers who began arriving in the 18th century. The Europeans, calling themselves Americans, eliminated the native peoples, whom they called Indians, and took the land. In the days of Daniel Boone the mountains were at the cutting edge of the westward expansion of the United States, but soon the area was again isolated, a land of subsistence farming with little connection to the outside world. A part of the South, the mountains were nonetheless home to more abolitionists than slaves, and during the Civil War this region provided soldiers to both sides.

Around 1890 various outsiders began to observe that the mountains were a fabulous treasury of natural wealth. For the next 20 years agents of northern capital crisscrossed the region buying up mineral and timber rights until by 1910 substantially the entire stock of natural resources was in the hands of a few outsiders — where it remains today.

From that day to this, the story of Appalachia has been one of extractive industry. First to go were the trees; by 1920 the largest hardwood forest in North America was only a memory. Mining commenced in earnest around 1910, and for 80 years Central Appalachia has been home to a large part of the U.S. coal industry. This region has produced wealth by the untold billions. The mountains have also been home to numerous small and a few major manufacturing industries, particularly on the periphery of the coal region. Small sewing factories employing mostly women have been common. And while there was no major agriculture, subsistence farming continued to supplement many families' income. While the region has always been isolated and impoverished in comparison with much of the rest of the nation, many people lived reasonably well.

But today the region is in a state of economic crisis. A new round of mechanization in mining is reducing employment drastically, even as production sets new records. Real unemployment in the coal counties is running from 30-60%, and when we look into the future we see that the apparently inexhaustible reserves of coal are themselves coming to an end. Small manufacturing has diminished as many of the region's factories have been moved overseas. Many local governments today are pinning their hopes for the future on the construction of prisons. Some are tempted by the promise of jobs to allow their deep valleys to be turned into dumps for the trash of the nation's cities. The conventional economic development strategy of developing "growth centers", building highways and improving other infrastructure in an attempt to attract outside industry has for the most part been a failure.

Role of Education in Region

The chronic poverty and underdevelopment of the region is often blamed on poor schools and poor education, on a culture which does not value education. There have been and are problems with education in this region. Kraybill, Johnson and Deaton[2] compared the seven Appalachian coal counties of Virginia with state-wide educational accomplishments. Their findings give an indication of the situation of education in the region.

Educational indicator - 1980

	All of Virginia	Coal Countries
Adults with high school diploma	62.4%	38.3%
People with 4+ years college	19.1%	6.3%
Drop-out rate, grades 8 - 12	5.3%	6.3%
High school graduates going to college	52.8%	38.7%

Per pupil expenditure in the coal counties is about 85% of the average state rate in Virginia.

This substandard educational situation (worse in other central Appalachian states), is a symptom rather than a cause of Appalachia's problems. Schools are clearly underfunded. The county governments might have taken on the mineral companies and taxed the only valuable asset in their counties, but the realities of power distribution have made that nearly impossible. Some students stay in school and go on to achieve in American society; but for many of those, "success" has meant leaving the region. Much of what has been written about children of "minority" groups in the U.S. might also be true of mountain children. When finishing school has no clear benefits, when success means leaving family and home, perhaps dropping out makes sense. When schools devalue your language, fail to teach your history, disparage your music and culture and encourage a competition you reject, resistance may seem a healthy alternative. Education as historically practiced in mountain schools has often been education for getting out, not education for staying and confronting the problems of the region.

There is also a history of adult education in Appalachia. For the most part the goal of these programs has been to make mountain people more like the rest of the country. Church missionaries established settlement schools to "raise the spiritual, social, educational and economic standards of the mountain people".[3] *The Moonlight Schools*, adult literacy classes held in the evenings in mountain communities in the World War I era, aimed to "Americanize" Appalachians in the same way that immigrants to the United States were being Americanized in urban areas. A few efforts, notably those of the Highlander Folk School in Tennessee and the *Appalachian Folk Life Center* in West Virginia were based on the belief that education shoulc help adults make their own decisions about their lives and communities. These two organizations continue to work with communities working for change today.

But most current programs continue to provide education to help people better fit into the economy. The envelopes of the regional state-funded adult education program in southwest Virginia call for "Re-Tooling Workers in Virginia". Government operated programs, using federal and state funds and often referred to as ABE (*Adult Basic Education*), offer primarily individual instruction in literacy and preparation for taking the "GED" (*General Education Development*) test, a secondary school diploma equivalent. This instruction is usually offered in a classroom setting. In addition some private volunteer literacy groups provides one-on-one tutoring for adults at the lowest literacy levels. Published standardized materials are prevalent in both settings.

Organizing & Resistance

It would be a mistake to see the history of Appalachia as an unopposed series of expropriations. The region has a long history of resistance beginning with the *Whiskey Rebellion* against taxes imposed on small farmers by George Washington's administration and the battles by the Cherokee to preserve their land and culture in the Carolina mountains. The Mineworkers union has been one of the most militant in the U.S. labour movement, and union battles have also occurred in other Appalachian industries. Particularly in the last thirty years there has been an ôoutburst of community organizing across Appalachia"[4] around issues as diverse as education, welfare reform, tax reform, and opposition to stripmining and toxic dumps.

While most of these efforts have been organized around single issues there are also many community organizations which confront a broad range of local problems, and there are a few broad-based multi-issue regional organizations. The community groups are often started either to confront an immediate threat like poisoned water or to meet the community's basic needs, but have tended to evolve to also include both education and economic development as part of their mission. The groups are linked in informal networks and are often led by women.

The three groups described in this article are examples of community-based organizations working to confront problems of their members. Each organization is independent, democratically controlled and funded by piecing together small private and state grants as well as local fundraising efforts. Each group includes literacy instruction in their program and builds the literacy of its members in informal ways as well. And each is located in a rural area where access to educational programs and social services is very limited for many people.

While the organizations have much in common, they differ in their approach to literacy work. The *McClure River Valley Development Center* is involved in a wide variety of community issues and directly confronts injustice in innovative ways. But their literacy and basic adult education work is in many ways separate from other Center activities. In *Ivanhoe*, the Civic League has operated a traditional literacy program, but is now working to make both their education programs and their staff structure more democratic. *Appalachian Communities for Children* recognizes the importance of participatory education and tries to respond to many community needs, but has generally stopped short of collectively addressing the underlying causes of poverty and joblessness which are so pervasive in their students' lives.

THE McCLURE RIVER VALLEY COMMUNITY DEVELOPMENT CENTER

"Me and my wife have been in this a year and a half and never [found] anything bad in it." [This is how one man talked about the McClure River Valley Community Development Center.]

The Center is in one of the poorest and most isolated counties in Virginia. The terrain is rugged with long ridges and narrow valleys and hollows. Sixty per cent of the land is owned by the outside coal corporations which dominate the economy. Official unemployment was 17.4% in October,1992, down from 20.2% in 1985. The county seat and largest town has a population of 1,542 in a county with 17,620 people.

The Center is the location for many varied activities. Parties and baby showers are held by people who rent the Center for the occasion. Special events are sponsored by the Center, for example a vigil held on the eve of the war in the Persian Gulf and an effort of many months providing meals for miners active in a long strike. However, most of the activities are part of the Development Center's efforts to meet the needs of the people in their communities. These ongoing efforts include the food distribution program *SHARE*, GED classes, a pre-school, aerobics classes, Saturday dances and educational/volunteer activities for groups of college students.

Share

SHARE is a national effort to distribute low-cost food and encourage community service. The food is obtained and distributed regionally, but local distribution is organized and conducted by community groups. The Center takes part in *SHARE* and distributes food once a month. Anyone can buy a "share" for $13.40 for which they receive $30 - $40 worth of food. The Center is responsible for collecting the money or food stamps, ordering the shares, arranging for the food to be picked up at a warehouse, and handling distribution. This work is coordinated by volunteers. Fifteen to twenty people help each month, filling boxes for anyone who has bought a share. The *SHARE* distribution seems to help people stretch their food money, gives people a chance to visit, and is a way to involve people in the work of the Center. It is a fair amount of work, but the work is well-organized and "shared".

The Pre-School

Probably the most ambitious project run by the MRVDC is the preschool. It has been in operation for eight years. The program is run by one of the two paid Center staff people with the help of volunteers, primarily mothers of the children in the program. A van picks up the children each morning and brings them to the Center, the children arriving around 9:30 and staying until 12:30.

The preschool program is designed to prepare the children for school by teaching them academic skills including saying and recognizing the alphabet and the numbers from one to ten, naming and recognizing body parts and colours. They are taught to follow directions and behave in a structured class-room setting. The day is scheduled without a lot of free play. The children are encouraged to write the letters and their names and to use scissors, but there does not seem to be much art or science. The children's work which was displayed in the room were worksheets to match letters or numbers and pages from a Ninja Turtle colouring book which they had coloured. The children sing enthusiastically and know several songs.

Adult Education Classes

The basic skills classes at the Center are taught by an Adult Basic Education teacher hired by the county. She is assisted by one of the two Catholic nuns who work with the Center. The class meets twice a week for three hours and has seven or eight students. The class seems very much driven by the goal of obtaining a GED, or high school diploma equivalent. Each student works independently in a GED preparation book. Students who are not at that level work with the teachers in other texts. There is little group instruction. While several of the students are involved in Center activities, others only come to this class.

In addition to the GED class, adult reading instruction is provided by one of the nuns and other tutors trained in the *Laubach Way to Reading*. Tutoring is done privately in another building. Some students do both, having individual tutor-ing in reading and working in class on math. In neither of these programs does the curriculum seem integrated with the rest of the Center's work.

Other community centers in southwest Virginia hold community college classes, but McClure River has only done this once or twice, explaining that most people aren't ready for college classes yet, but that they will hold them when there is a demand.

The Center is involved in another kind of educational work through their student volunteer program. During summer and school holidays groups of high school and college students from outside the area come and stay at the Center and do volunteer work in the community, for example repairing houses. While this is helpful to the community, it is probably even more valuable to the students who get the opportunity to visit and learn from people in the com-munity.

Other Activities

On most Saturday nights the Center hosts dances to provide fundraising events and recreation. Local bands, both *bluegrass* and rock, play and the tables are set up like a club. Admission is around $5.00, depending on the band.

Aerobics classes for women meet on Thursday nights. Bible school is held in the summer. The Center also hosts many visitors interested in their work.

Responding to Special Times

While most of what happens at the Center is directly related to the immediate needs of the community, there is also involvement in issues beyond those on the River. In 1989 southwest Virginia was the scene of a long, bitter strike between the *United Mine Workers* and the Pittston Company. The struggle involved many people including miners and their families and other supporters, both local and from outside. The Center is located near many of the Pittston mines and became the site of a support center for the miners. The strikers used the Center as a place to meet and rest. Hundreds of meals were served every day and the Center was both a haven and a source of support for the strike. The effects of this involvement continued after the strike was over. This is discussed in the section on the women of the Center.

When the war in the Persian Gulf region began, the Center helped sponsor and was the site for a forum on the war and a prayer vigil. And while the events were far away the impact was quite local. A staff member's son was one of the many people from the mountains who were sent to the Gulf.

The vigil, held on a snowy evening in February was organized by several local organizations. The program began with a panel discussion on the reasons for the war and the effects both immediate and long term, ending with a vigil of prayer and songs held inside because of the weather.

The Board Meeting

The Development Commission is governed by a Board of Directors which meets monthly and is made up of local residents, who share the problems of the Valley's people. A few "resource" people, primarily religious workers, participate in the meetings, but do not have a vote. The meetings are well organized and productive. An agenda is written on newsprint and members receive copies of minutes and financial reports. Written materials are reviewed orally as well.

The Women & The Center

The Center is a community centre not a women's centre, yet women seem to be the most active members and do most of the work. And the programs seem to meet the needs of women more than men, although both are involved in the dances and *SHARE*. Women are clearly the strongest force in the organization.

Working at the Center has made a significant difference in the lives of the most active women. One woman who is very active described the impact of her work:

> Working with these people here in this center, they showed their love and their support and everybody, we're like brother and sister. My life is a complete turn-around from what it was before.... I learned things I never thought I would ever learn. It really made a difference in my life. It's a complete different world.... I'm really proud of the growth I've seen in the people that's got involved with me here.

The staff member who teaches in the pre-school spoke of all she had learned:

> Even though I finished school and I've taken night classes and I've been here and there, but actually the best education I've had was when I came to this center.... Communication with these people is the best education there is. I learned how to talk to people because I'm an outspoken person and I've learned who to talk to and who not to talk to, how their feelings are. I've learned that everybody's not the same as the other person. You've got to treat everybody different. There's some people that's more fragile than other people. I learned that just by working through this center.

Several of the women who first came to the centre when their husbands were on strike have continued to be actively involved.

Education & Change

For the women, the importance of the work and working together seems clear. Many of them spoke of how they felt changed and strengthened and how they had seen others change. Around a dozen people, most of them women, volunteer several hours a week to the Center's work. While they give, they also receive, possibly some material help, but primarily the satisfaction of making a change in their community. It also seems that the organization has developed ways for people to work together to get things accomplished. Conflicts seem to be confronted and settled. Both the *SHARE* distribution and the board meeting utilize carefully worked out organizational processes. The preschool and the dances both have procedures for involving people. The organization works.

When the group of women from the Center discussed their own education they were very clear about the value of informal learning and group support at the Center. But this understanding is not reflected in either the preschool or the adult education classes at the Center, both of which are highly structured around traditional curriculum, what school is "supposed" to be. Both also depend on volunteers, and there may be a belief that it is easier for volunteers to work in a highly structured program. Yet there is also a belief that drill in "readiness" activities — the letters, numbers, colors, shapes — is what the children need to succeed in school. The preschool teacher commented that at Head Start (a federally-funded preschool program) they "weren't allowed to teach them anything," and free play and unstructured creative activities were not a big part of her program. This is also true of at least some of the kindergarten classes in public schools in this area.

The *McClure River Valley Community Development Center* stands for more equitable power for ordinary people, such as supporting the striking miners, yet does not always extend that position to the classroom. McClure classes look in many ways like those of government-supported ABE programs. While the McClure group is not currently planning changes in its education program, the group is exploring ways to use participatory research in a project to improve water and sewer systems.

Despite the difficulties in integrating their shared-power approach into adult education classes, *McClure River Valley Community Development Center staff* and participants have made important, positive contributions to their community. The McClure group has created opportunities for people to become involved in solving problems together, getting child care and education services close to their homes, and participating in community life in ways that were not previously possible.

THE IVANHOE CIVIC LEAGUE

The town of Ivanhoe, population 800, is about 100 miles east of McClure. The mountains are not as steep, farming is more important, with some mining of zinc and lead. But the last mine closed in 1981 fifteen years after the carbide factory, the town's other large employer, shut down. In 1986 when the local county governments announced their plans to sell the industrial land — the last hope for bringing industry back to the community — people came together in the *Ivanhoe Civic League* to oppose the sale. They were able to stop the sale of the land and began to try to find an industry to locate there. This has not happened, but a lot else has.

The Civic League began a process of community building which has included the development of a park along the New River on some of the land slated for industrial development; an annual Jubilee Festival in the park which is a kind of community reunion with food, drama, music and a parade; a housing rehabilitation project with college volunteers; and a community newsletter. The Civic League also published a two volume history of the community based on extensive interviews.[5] and participated in the *SHARE* program and is developing a youth-run radio station. There has been an extensive education program including an economics discussion group, Biblical reflection, and the more formal GED classes, a literacy program, and community college classes taught in the community.

The Civic League education work currently is focused in three areas: the college volunteer program, the adult education project, and working with young people. The youth work includes an after-school tutoring program and support and educational counseling where they are advised about courses to take in secondary school for college preparation. When they are ready for college, Civic League staff offer advice on financial aide and help students prepare and apply for college. The Civic League also has a Youth Council working to develop a local radio station.

For many years college volunteers have come to the Appalachian region to help people. In Ivanhoe, too, college volunteers are used to help in the community. But while the community values what the volunteers can offer, the Civic League is aware that the community has much to offer the volunteers. The education of the college students by the community is deliberate and carefully planned. Groups of students come to Ivanhoe during their school holidays and spend a week or two repairing houses, helping with work at the Civic League, and visiting in the community. They also meet with Civic League staff to examine their preconceptions about poverty in the region.

Adult education has been an important part of the Civic League since the Oral History Project grew out of a community college history class. In 1990, 14 people graduated with GED certificates after attending adult basic education classes taught by a volunteer with the Civic League. Now the two staff educators are working to make their program more democratic and participatory and to more closely connect adult students with other work of the Civic League.

The League has recently received special funding from the state to develop an adult educaton program which integrates literacy, GED preparation and training in job specific skills. The project will be community based. Former students will be trained as tutors, and students will be involved in planning and governing the project. The staff also hopes to involve more adult students in the other work of the Civic League. A challenge has been to develop the program in a way that both meets the requirements of the state and is participatory and learner-centered. A student assessment and evaluation process based on student goals instead of standardized testing is being developed by the staff, with the hope of educating the state education people about this process.

The education staff is contending with the expectations of both the state education bureaucracy and some of their students to have traditional adult education classes which are teacher centered and focused on preparing individuals for the GED test. At the same time, the entire Civic League staff is also involved in changing to a more democratic work style after several years under the strong leadership of one person.

Despite the unmet challenges of economic development, Ivanhoe Civic League has managed to make important and lasting changes in the community. Housing has been rehabilitated, music, drama and cultural celebrations held, young people involved and educational goals met.

APPALACHIAN COMMUNITIES FOR CHILDREN

We have a different way of thinking about what education is. It's not just something that you learn within the school that somebody else tells you is important, but it's how you lead your life, what's going on around you. It's not just learning to do certain things and getting graded on it.

Judy Martin, Director
Appalachian Communities for Children

In 1974 a group of parents came together in Jackson County, Kentucky, to try to get a *Head Start* program for their children. In many ways, there was little reason to believe that they could accomplish such a feat. In the mountains of eastern Kentucky, grinding poverty was all around, illiteracy rates were among the highest in the nation. There was no hospital and few doctors and there were no colleges or vocational schools. Unemployment was high and training opportunities few. Perhaps the most immediate and difficult problem of all was the lack of a proper building. The federal government would not bring Head Start to the area without a structure that met extensive requirements.

Despite these obstacles, the group formed Appalachian Communities for Children (ACC) and began working for quality education and their right to involvement in schools.

Public School Programs

What we learned by working in our parents' group was the importance of acceptance of each child and the learning style they have, the value of that child. We're teaching math, but we're also teaching that each person is important...What's important is not just teaching subject matter, it's teaching children to believe in themselves in such a way that the expectation is there that the child will succeed. We've found that seven different kids can learn math seven different ways, but only one of them is thought to be right by teachers. Sometimes we forget to respect all the ways of learning.

Judy Martin

Throughout the 1980's and to the present, a very important part of ACC's work has been in the public schools. Every day, ACC volunteers teach in Jackson County schools, and parent volunteer efforts are growing in Clay County. The ACC parent volunteers work in classrooms to encourage alternative curriculum that is hands-on. Often based in community and family life, parent volunteers are busy helping children read and write books, experience math through the use of real-life manipulatives, and learn more about their communities. ACC workers don't look for parent volunteers that fit the stereotype of middle-class moms, but instead are often successful in helping rural parents of all economic levels participate in their children's education.

Funding of rural schools has been a serious problem in Kentucky as elsewhere in the United States. The Jackson and Clay county school systems are among the poorest in Kentucky. There are no art or music teachers in K - 8th grade in the most rural schools, so some children have never had a single art or music teacher in their first nine school years. There is one counselor in Jackson County who has to deal with over 1000 school children.

As a part of the ground-breaking school reform legislation enacted in 1990, Kentucky's schools now have ungraded primary sections, more emphasis on site-based management, and give parents more voice in decision-making. It is hoped that this will lead to schools resembling the Head Start programs which ACC developed long ago: activist parents and community people working with school professionals to create schools meeting the unique needs of families and children of the area.

The legislation also established Family Resource Centers, which may include early childhood development programs, inter-generational efforts, and parent involvement projects. For two years running, ACC has produced the top-rated plans for the development of Family Resource Centers in two Kentucky schools, through the use of extensive, participatory planning processes that involve a wide range of ACC parent volunteers, school personnel and others.

Adult & Community Education

When we first started our adult education program, other people were sure we would fail. Our idea was that we know a lot of things and we could teach one another and what we didn't know, we could learn... and now we are one of the few parent groups in Kentucky out of 120 counties that run the whole adult education program in the county. In almost all of the other counties, the school systems run the programs. In ours, the parents — low income parents — run the program. I want to bring you the good news that even though they said we were just a bunch of hillbillies... we won the Outstanding Adult Education award for having the best program in all of the South Central Kentucky counties.

Judy Martin

This different way of thinking about education is reflected in ACC's adult education work. ACC has developed literacy, adult basic education and GED preparation classes, as well as classes which are not academic in nature. The form each takes changes with the needs and wants of the participants.

One key to ACC's success is their staff who are very well-trained but are not certified teachers. In fact, several ACC teachers are graduates of the ACC GED programs themselves. ACC holds classes in their learning centers, in various communities in Jackson and Clay counties, in the jail, the prison, and other places. Last year over 500 people were a part of ACC's literacy and adult education program.

A barrier facing conventional programs is the isolation and separation of classes from the things that community people find familiar and comfortable. Adults are often asked to go to a strange place, and to engage in something they have failed at before — school. ACC has found ways to help overcome some of these barriers and one of the clearest examples is in their use of crafts.

The Crafts Class

Recently, ACC held a class in which participants made baskets. This community education class helped people feel comfortable with the organization and gave ACC workers the opportunity to talk a bit about other classes while offering people the opportunity to participate in them. ACC even held a series of adult basic education classes that built the curriculum on craft-making. As participants worked on their crafts, they read and wrote about craft-making, learned measuring and other mathematical operations by figuring materials or measurements needed for crafts. ACC gives coupons for attendance in any class (and double for bringing someone). People trade in the coupons for craft materials and kits which are often put together by volunteers.

The Men's Reading Class

In 1991, when state regulations changed and school bus drivers had to obtain a commercial driver's license (CDL) or lose their jobs, passing the CDL test became a pressing concern for many local people. ACC offered a preparation class for these drivers, and many completed the class and passed their test. Several enjoyed the experience so much they didn't want to stop going to class. The "men's reading class" has continued even though their original goal of passing the bus driver's test has been met. The teacher of the class feels that one of her responsibilities is to create a community within the class, an atmosphere of acceptance, one in which participants are respected for the experience and knowledge they already have. These adult learners visited various places in the community, took pictures, wrote, and generally sharpened their reading and writing skills in the context of their daily lives.

Family Life & Community Health

We saw that things were happening in different hollers, but people didn't know about each others' experiences. It was people coming together and saying "What happened to you — that happened to me too!"

Family life and community health efforts are an important part of ACC's work. In the *Mountain Scout* program, women visit other women to talk about and encourage screenings for breast and cervical cancer. The program is based on the idea that neighbours and friends have more access and influence with community people than "outsiders" do, so community women are employed and trained as the home visitors. A day care centre is being built in Clay County. ACC is active in the *East Kentucky Child Care Coalition*, and is helping develop a network of home day care providers both to give families better access to child care and to give local women an opportunity to create small businesses.

ACC has developed the *Resource Mothers* program, where workers visit pregnant and new teenage mothers and help them learn about nutrition and health issues. ACC also holds prenatal classes for women of any age who want to work with other expectant mothers to learn more about maternal and infant health.

Change Doesn't Come Easily

We don't want to make it sound like it was easy. we've had some failures. It hurts to work hard and then not get something. And it doesn't happen fast. We didn't spring up full-grown. We went through a long, hard process in terms of our confidence and ability to handle what we wanted to do....

Judy Martin

ACC has helped people have a voice in education, provided leadership development opportunities, and offered a way for people to support each other as they work toward social justice goals. They have acted on the belief that all adults have valuable knowledge and skills that can be shared in the community, including in schools, adult education, and health enhancement efforts. As ACC has tried to put these principles into action, they've found that change does not come easily. Embedded power structures do not bend quickly or act inclusively; there usually must be hard work, patience and a willingness to be confrontative on occasion.

REFLECTIONS

The three organizations we looked at are in different communities, but share the same culture and history. Much of the work they do is similar; some projects are unique to a particular community. Each group is working to improve life for people in the community both by meeting individual needs for better food, housing, and education and by trying to influence the decisions of government to serve their communities better. Each organization is made up of people from the community working together in a democratic fashion, recognizing that the distribution of power and resources in Appalachia must be changed for the needs of their communities to be truly met. And each organization has impressed the importance of literacy learning upon their members and the community, both through formal instruction of basic academic skills and through the skills learned and practiced in the ongoing work and special projects of the organization.

Formal adult education programs are a major part of the work of Appalachian Communities for Children, and both the Ivanhoe Civic League and the McClure River Center's programs include adult education. All their organizations provide basic literacy instruction as well as classes to help people prepare to take the GED test for a high school equivalency certificate. ACC has offered other classes including crafts and preparation for the Commercial Driver's License test, while Ivanhoe has brought community college classes to the community.

All three organizations have also provided many non-formal opportunities for learning and literacy use. and many staff and board members even with limited formal education and literacy skills, have learned and continue to learn both the skills needed for their particular jobs and the knowledge and skills involved in running an organization.

When we look at these three organizations we see groups which take clear stands for more equitable power for ordinary people and which have recognized the importance of people having a voice and control over their own lives, yet are perhaps not as strong or as supportive of the overall goals of the organizations as they might be. There is an emerging sense of the importance of long term organization building and leadership development and the role of adult education in this work, but this has not been included in programs systematically. Although the education programs of these organizations meet the individual educational needs of many people, the organizations themselves could benefit with more integrated programs.

State Adult Basic Education funding received affects the size of programs, administrative procedures, testing, and may tend to limit not only the issues raised but also serve to legitimize formal schooling. When adult education is practiced in a traditional, teacher-centred way and the people are involved only in education classes, they don't benefit from all the other kinds of learning resulting from active membership of the organization. People in these organizations have not had much experience being in situations where they are respected, thought of as leaders, share power. Democratically structured, student-centred classes focusing on community issues could be a place to gain such experiences.

Contradictions

Why, when these organizations are so committed to empowering the members of their community and to bringing about change, have the formal education programs been more traditional? The groups themselves recognize the contradictions and are exploring ways to change and democratize their classes, but the work is hard. Many factors may contribute to the difficulty.

Even when people recognize the value of experiential learning in their own lives, traditional schooling is a powerful cultural force in the United States. Programs are driven by students' desire for a GED, a diploma which is necessary to qualify for additional training or to get a job (though this result may be more perceived than real). And the cultural images associated with graduation are powerful. The opportunity to wear a cap and gown, to take part in a graduation ceremony, to have "finished" school are very important to many people.

It is of course true that classes which prepare people for the GED test can be conducted in ways which are student-centred, democratically run and focused on community issues. But it is hard to come up with ideas about doing school differently unless you have had experience with alternatives. Most people in community organizations have only experienced schooling which is quite conservative and there are few models or opportunities for learning alternative approaches. We have learned from our own experience that just reading about alternatives is not always enough to enable us to really change our practice. It takes time and support. And as one community activist and educator put it, "There are so many hoops. People get exhausted. To get the money and all the rest of it to come together is impossible."

Needed: A clear role for Adult Education

While there are some networks of community organizations, there is no political movement or a political agenda that would link these groups and efforts. For example the United Mine Workers union did not use the mobilization of people around the Pittston strike to move forward on broader goals. There is not a sense of adult education programs contributing to long term political mobilization and political change. In countries where people are part of a political movement, adult education happens in a different context. The methodology may not be particularly innovative, but the purposes are really different and the people involved, both teachers and students, understand the connections of their education work with a larger struggle.

This was the case with the Citizenship Schools during the civil rights movement in the U.S. south and in Nicaragua after the 1979 revolution. Despite all the disasters of the past ten or so years in Appalachia, people are not mobilized around a political agenda in which adult education has a clear role.

Even in difficult circumstances, people in McClure, Ivanhoe and Appalachian Communities for Children are bringing about change and empowering themselves and their communities. None of the three organizations we profile, nor others we know about and certainly not we ourselves, have all the answers. We are just beginning to understand how literacy and adult education work can be linked to help create skilled individuals and to strengthen and develop communities from within.

We want to acknowledge the staffs of the three organizations we profiled for their help with this paper, particularly Edna Gulley, Mary White, Claty Jonson from McClure; Mike Blackwell and Anita Armbrister from Ivanhoe; and Judy Martin from Appalachian Communities for Children. Community educator and activist Carol Honeycutt contributed to this last section.

Notes & References

1. This section draws heavily on Rich Kirby ("Radio and the Distribution of Power in Central Appalachia." Hamid Mowlana and Margaret Hardt Frondorf, Eds., *The Media as a Forum for Community Building*, School of Advanced International Studies, Johns Hopkins University, Washington, D.C. (1992)

2. Kraybill D., Johnston, T. and Deaton, B. *Income uncertainty and the quality of life: A socio-economic study of Virginia's coal counties*. Virginia Agricultural Experiement Station Bulletin 87-4, Virginia Polytechnic Institute and State University, Blacksburg, Virginia. (1987).

3. Lewis, H., Koback, S. and Johnson, T. *Growing Up Country*. Council of the Southern Mountains, Clintwood, Virginia. (1973).

4. Fisher, Steve. *Fighting Back: Resistance in Appalachia*. Temple University, Philadephia. (1992).

5. The Ivanhoe History Project. *Remembering our Past: Building our Future*, H. Lewis and S. O'Donnell, Ivanhoe Civic League, Ivanhoe, Virginia. (1990).

    The Ivanhoe History Project. *Telling our Stories: Sharing our Live*. H. Lewis and S. O'Donnell, Ivanhoe Civic League, Ivanhoe, Virginia. (1990).

Chapter 20
COMMUNITY IN THE CLASSROOM: LITERACY & DEVELOPMENT IN A RURAL INDUSTRIALIZED REGION

Juliet Merrifield, Connie White
and Mary Beth Bingman
Center for Literacy Studies
Knoxville, Tennessee, USA

CHANGING TIMES

Education has not necessarily been good for rural communities in the United States of America. Especially in poor rural areas, education has traditionally been the "ticket out" for individuals. If you get educated, the expectation is that you will leave. If you want to stay, education has little direct reward. While this has always been true to some extent, the trend seems to have accelerated in the 1980's when the U.S. Department of Agriculture has documented a substantial "brain drain" from rural communities, as more high-skill production jobs were developed in urban areas.[1]

Educators do not think much about education as the "ticket out," and the resulting decimation of rural communities. Our assumptions have been that education is an intrinsic good, always valuable. In these changing times we need to reassess the value of education and refocus on building communities, not just individuals. We need to create education programs in which people gain the skills and the sense of efficacy to become involved in their community's development.

In our work in Tennessee and in Appalachia, at the Center for Literacy

Studies we have been coordinating with ten Appalachian community based groups, a project called "Community in the Classroom".[2] Together we are exploring ways in which literacy education can build communities. But it has become clear that to contribute to the building of community, education must not only be in communities and by communities, but also for communities, and educational methodologies and approaches must be different from dominant (traditional) forms. The groups described in "Appalachian Communities: Working to Survive" are firmly rooted in their communities, and yet to varying degrees are trapped in dominant educational methods which make it hard to integrate education with community development. We knew we had to work together to design something new that must be rooted in the particular contexts in which we work. This paper explores some of the contexts of literacy in rural America, especially Appalachia, and describes the goals and some of the experiences of our Community in the Classroom project.

ECONOMIC CONTEXT

The dominant context for literacy education in the United States in the last decade or more has been the economic one. The ongoing "literacy crisis" in this country has focused primarily on jobs, sometimes expressed as, "if we only had an educated workforce, there would be good jobs for all".

Most rural people know from their own experience that the global economy is changing. During the 1980's, in the United States, jobs in the manufacturing sector declined in numbers, and employment in the service sector increased. Many of the traditional skilled and semi-skilled manufacturing jobs which have been the economic mainstay of much of southern Appalachia and the South are leaving for overseas (even lower wages) or changing (automating, reducing labour force). At the same time, there has been a considerable expansion in the service sector, ranging from low-paid, often temporary or part-time work to high-wage, high-skill occupations.

These changes are not taking place evenly. Urban and rural areas are changing in different ways, and different parts of the same state may also experience very different changes in job structure and opportunities. It is not easy to interpret what all that means for skills demands and education needs.

It is common wisdom that in this changing economic context, workers need higher skills in order to compete internationally. We are offered a choice between *High Skills or Low Wages*![3] The U.S. can become another low wage economy, or can invest in the skills of its workforce and therefore promote productivity growth, the key to a high standard of living. Pessimists note that 70 % of jobs projected for the U.S. by the year 2000 will not require higher education levels. Despite the growth rates in higher-skilled jobs, the greatest numbers of jobs are low wage and low skill.[4]

Education by itself does not create jobs, but many people have assumed that higher education levels can attract better jobs to a community. This is not necessarily true for rural areas. According to a recent U.S. Department of Agriculture report, there is no correlation between education levels in rural areas and economic growth.[5]

Rural areas were especially hard hit by the economic changes of the 1980's. They saw a small growth in numbers of low skill production jobs, and an actual decline in numbers of high education jobs and as a result, many rural areas are experiencing high unemployment levels. In many Appalachian counties, official unemployment rates hover around 20%. Actual unemployment rates are much higher, perhaps up to 60%, when you count those who have been unemployed so long that they have stopped looking for jobs, those whose benefits have expired and those who have dropped off the rolls.

As the gap between rich and poor increases, we may be seeing what John Gaventa of the Highlander Center has called the "Appalachianization" of the United States.(6) Some of the statistics from the 1980's are startling.[7]

- The Congressional Budget Office reports that 70% of the income gains generated in the 1980's accrued to the wealthiest one percent of families.

- The Federal Reserve Board reports that in 1989, that same one percent of families owned 37 % of everything that could be owned in America — as much as was owned by the bottom 90 % of families — and this was up from 31 % in 1983.

- The U.S. Census Bureau reports that in 1990, 13.5 % of the workforce worked 8 hours a day, 5 days a week, 52 weeks a year, and still was unable to earn more than $13,359 — the official poverty line. That is one in seven workers. The rate was up from 11.4 % in 1980.

The role of education in this context has become problematic. While there is some evidence that individuals with higher education do earn more, the translation from education to better pay is not so easy in rural communities. If you live in the coalfields of West Virginia or southwest Virginia, if you live in depressed rural areas of Tennessee and Virginia which have relied on shirt factories and furniture plants, only to see them leave for Mexico, Taiwan and the Philippines — the payoff in better jobs for better education may be possible only if you leave. Education simply enables more individuals to compete for the same limited number of not-very-good jobs.

What happens to our communities when those who get a good education must leave? And what is the role of adult education in supporting other "ends," not just better jobs? We need to look beyond the economic context to culture and community for an adult education that can have a broad impact on our communities and our society. Both of these are changing as much as the economy has changed in the last decade.

Cultural Context

Historically, culture has always been a very important aspect of education in this country. From instilling the "Protestant work ethic" to "Americanization" programs which were designed to assimilate wave after wave of immigrants, to the Moonlight Schools of Kentucky in the 1920's which were designed to bring Appalachian "hillbillies" into the mainstream, cultural aspects of literacy and education have been and continue to be important. Consistently, cultural aspects of education in this country have been rooted in a melting pot image — an attempt to change who people are, to bring them into "mainstream" culture, to devalue difference.

But times are changing, culturally as well as economically. Globally we have seen increasing, not decreasing, emphasis on diversity and difference and large nations and empires are collapsing into smaller ethnic identities. In this country we see increasing diversity, in which people are demanding to be affirmed and valued racially, ethnically and culturally, rather than diluted and dissipated into a "mainstream." It also means learning to "collaborate" in new ways — to learn to live with, work with and accept people who are not like themselves.

Adult literacy programs are attempting to meet this challenge. Telling our stories is not only a way of respecting and valuing difference, but also of finding common ground. Whatever the vehicle, good adult literacy programs say to participants that they are valued as they are; that who they are and where they came from matters in knowing where they are going; that people who do not read well have skills and experiences to share with others and to contribute to the community of the classroom. This is part of a process of building community in the classroom. Many literacy programs, especially English as a second language (ESL) programs in urban areas are doing quite well on this.

In rural areas of Appalachia, however, there are fewer examples of literacy programs using methods which respect and celebrate the local culture. Even some programs which are firmly rooted in their community may feel that in their education work they must use standard methods and materials, teach people mainstream ways, and minimize rather than celebrate difference.

COMMUNITY CONTEXT

Needed: An Expanding Focus

In this country, we have long defined literacy in terms of individual skills. We test individual skills, we measure advancement in individual terms, we count numbers and grade level gains. Issues like motivation, recruitment and retention dominate the discussions of adult basic educators.

In other parts of the world, most notably in the Third World, a very different conception of literacy is commonplace — literacy in a social and community role. We do recognize this viewpoint a little when we acknowledge that literacy has implications beyond individual outcomes, when we link a competitive economy with more literate workers. Literacy from a social perspective focuses on the capacity of individuals to transform themselves and their communities. Progress is measured not in individual skills, but in social impacts.

When Laubach Literacy International U.S. staff evaluate the programs of their partner groups in Africa, Latin America and Asia, for example, they may count the number of water wells drilled for a particular village, or the health clinics started, the income generating projects under way, improvements in infant mortality rates or family nutrition.

These differences in evaluation help us to focus not so much on the skills of literacy, but on its ends. While our primary focus in literacy education in this country has been on enhancing self — and that has been good for many people — we need to expand that to include the enhancement of our communities.

Many community based organizations have been asking, "what skills do we need to fight a toxic waste dump?" or "what skills do we need to operate a food bank?" They might be "what skills do we need to provide preschool or after-school programs for our children?" or "what skills do we need to make better housing, water and sewage systems in our community?" If these are the questions, then the evaluation of our success would be on the basis of reading gains and also on the basis of community actions.

Many community groups create jobs through respecting culture. Ivanhoe, Virginia, for example, is the town that died. When the mines closed, there were no jobs and many people had to leave. In an attempt to create new jobs, the Ivanhoe Civic League was formed to try to recruit industry to a newly formed industrial park. Now, four years later, the Ivanhoe Civic League has not attracted a single new employer to the town. But along the way it has sponsored a community festival each summer to celebrate community and culture. It has published a wonderful community history book. Youth of the community have produced plays using giant puppets, and now are developing a radio station. The Civic League has offered adult basic skills and literacy classes, as well as community college classes taught in the community. It has brought in young people to help renovate houses. And now the largest employer in town ... is the Ivanhoe Civic League.

Groups like these focus on how literacy is used for the community good. What would such programs look like? In some of their aspects, they simply put into practice what have long been regarded as good adult education principles. But the focus on building community takes them further, to bring the context of the community into the classroom, and to make connections for learners between the classroom and the real world of their communities.

Programs whose goals include building communities have some common characteristics in terms of teaching and learning. Such programs would:

- build their curriculum of reading, writing and math around people's real lives and concerns,
- model relationships within the classroom (teacher/student and student/student)

of respect, support and equality;

- provide opportunities for team work, for cooperation and collaboration;
- provide opportunities for people to develop leadership skills, through talking about what leadership is, and enabling students to be leaders in small groups, in the classroom and in the literacy program;
- affirm culture and community through texts and discussions, and through respect and understanding of difference. This does not preclude also teaching skills (including oral language, for example) to be used in dealing with the mainstream — a kind of cultural bilingualism;
- address diversity in our society, and provide opportunities to learn about other cultures and lives in real ways;
- address gender issues in the classroom and in people's lives;
- encourage critical thinking about what people read and hear;
- teach research skills — getting information about issues and concerns in people's lives, from jobs to health, from day care to further educational opportunities;
- prepare people for opportunities existing in the community for acting on problems and concerns by building links with community organizations of all kinds;
- support people wanting to initiate new community efforts, and teach the skills they need to work on these.

Such programs would build communities because they not only teach specific basic skills, but also provide opportunities for students to learn teamwork and cooperation, leadership and problem solving, critical thinking and decision making in a democratic environment. Students and teachers would know more about community needs and community organizations, and develop the sense of efficacy as well as the specific links to act on community issues. But we know that to do literacy in this way is hard, for many different reasons.

Barriers to Literacy for Building Community

Community-oriented literacy may be an enormous challenge to those adult literacy programs which have only concerned themselves with isolated, individual skills. For such programs, building links with the community context may be a logical next step.

But there are certainly barriers to community-oriented literacy, even for community based groups. In their educational work, community groups often forget the lessons they have learned from their own community organizing, and think they have to do education in the same way that schools do it.

One of the greatest barriers is our own and our students' ideas of what education is supposed to look like. If as teachers our definition of education centres on textbooks and workbooks, grade levels and credentials, it may be hard to do literacy in a different way. If as students we want to get our diploma in the shortest possible time, we may be impatient with anything that does not immediately appear to further that goal. Teachers feel pressured to get on with the "lessons," even though they don't have much to do with real life.

Individual vs. Community Relevancy

When community groups want to help people learn how to read, it seems they often replicate the dominant educational system which divides and individualizes instead of creating a community in the classroom which supports people acting on issues they care about in their lives. So programs issue individual workbooks, and congratulate themselves on people starting at their own level and moving at their own pace. They place an adult learner with a tutor, and congratulate themselves on protecting the learner's privacy. They forget that the way we get over shame is to talk about it with others in similar situations, the way we can feel powerful is to act with other people, the way we learn is by talking and acting.

The role of leaders and experts is often another barrier to community-oriented literacy. Community organizing groups often learn that a leader is not necessarily the person who knows the most, or is the most articulate, but may be the one who helps everybody contribute what they can to the effort, helping the group to get stronger. This kind of leader is one who believes and practices participatory decision-making and helps everyone have their say. But when community groups set up their adult basic education classes, they may forget this kind of leader, and look for a teacher who behaves as an "expert" and makes all the decisions about teaching and learning. With this kind of teacher, leadership in the classroom is neither shared nor learned.

When Funders Define the Standards

Another barrier is always resources. As long as adult literacy teachers are either volunteers or part-time and low-paid, with no paid planning time, and few rewards for excellence, we may not see sweeping changes in the way literacy education is carried out. As long as the demands of funders are for performance standards and competencies, as long as the funders define literacy in terms of individual skill gains, it may be difficult for a program to break the mold.

Professionalism vs. Paraprofessionalism

Another significant barrier may be that literacy teachers themselves may have limited knowledge and involvement in their communities. The increasing interest in "professionalism" among literacy teachers, while understandable and commendable, may also create additional distance between themselves and their students. Many of the community groups we work with employ "para-professional" staff, who are not certified teachers, who may themselves be graduates of the literacy program. For both paraprofessionals and professionals, little training is available to help them develop community-oriented approaches to their work. And there are few models in this country to show what community-oriented literacy would look like.

The Community in the Classroom project which we have been developing with ten Appalachian community based groups seeks to explore ways to overcome the barriers, to learn together and support each other as we do something we know is difficult, and to create models to show a kind of literacy that respects and values our culture and builds our communities.

COMMUNITY IN THE CLASSROOM

The Appalachian groups with whom we are working, including the three described in the paper entitled "Appalachian Communities: Working to Survive," are strong and effective groups. However, although their education work is "in" the community, it is not always directly connected to building the community. Most of the groups have been constrained to some extent by the methods which are dominant in adult education. The understanding which the groups have developed about how people learn and change are not always easily applied to the literacy work they do. The groups also have a wide range of experience in literacy education, from many years to a new start.

Whitley County Communities for Children, Williamsburg, Kentucky puts family and literacy work together in inter-generational approaches to education. They have run basic skills education programs for several years, along with parenting, children and youth programs.

For these groups, literacy connects with community issues in a variety of ways. In Dayhoit, Kentucky, for example, *Concerned Citizens Against Toxic Waste* has been working for the past two years to stop well water pollution from a nearby industrial site. As they have tried to organize their community, group members have found many people who lack the basic literacy skills to gain information about the environmental problem, and to be active in attempts to clean it up. *St. Charles Community Center* has offered literacy tutoring and basic adult education classes for several years. But as they open a new community-owned sewing factory they have discovered a need for a workers' education program which includes the history of the factory and analysis of the responsibilities of the board, management, and workers as well as instruction in reading and writing.

Such community-based approaches to education are very different from the traditional. These groups are saying that our communities need educated people who will stay, in order to develop the economic, social and political life of those communities. They see education as an investment in human capital which will pay dividends for their communities. In order to start local businesses, to create jobs, to market craft products, to staff a day care centre, people need better education. Education for them is not the "ticket out", but the "ticket in" — to develop the community and to develop leaders who care about their community and will work to resolve its problems.

Identifying the Key Needs

The challenge for our Community in the Classroom project is to help the community groups develop education to meet community needs. Each group has a different focus and approach. Each shares a common interest in developing their community, in participatory and community-based education. In order to revitalize their communities, they want to integrate education with community development activities. The groups identified key needs which gave rise to the Community in the Classroom project:

- **leadership development and training** for community-based tutors and teachers, especially in participatory education;

- **designing curriculum that incorporates real issues** confronting their communities, as themes for discussion, reading and writing;

- **channels for literacy students to contribute to their communities,** and for their concerns and issues to be connected with the organization's work; developing sensitivity in community-based organizations to the potential barriers to people with low literacy skills becoming closely involved;

- networking and support to strengthen community-based organizations with common concerns and similar programs.

The year-long project is now well underway. Three kinds of activities are taking place during the project year:

1. a series of **six workshops**, collaboratively planned and facilitated, which build knowledge, skills and leadership abilities of participants who are staff and volunteers in the groups;

2. a series of **special projects** developed by each community group to focus on a particular need of their organization;

3. a process of **program reflection** and development, designed to integrate literacy education with other community empowerment activities, and to address barriers to participation by adults with low literacy.

WORKSHOPS

Center for Literacy Studies staff and participants plan each workshop together, using : a variety of participatory activities that help people draw on their own experiences, opportunities to try things out, a chance to think critically and solve problems around community issues and linking them with literacy.

The first workshop was a time to get acquainted, talk about our organizations, our lives and the things that matter to us as individuals and groups; and the ways in which participating groups see adult education in their community work. Participants chose topics for the next five workshops: community participation, community-based teaching, building leadership, producing our own materials, and teaching methods.

One recent workshop gives a flavour of the experiences. The topic was *community-based teaching*. The morning began with participants introducing themselves and telling some challenge or celebration from their lives or work, or sharing a new teaching idea they had tried. After introducing the topic, the facilitator asked group members where each obtained water. (We knew that water is an active issue in several of the communities, and is of concern to all of us.) Those answers were recorded on newsprint, and the facilitator asked some other questions about what problems participants had with water, what they had tried to do about it, and what the results were. All of this was also recorded.

We then broke into small groups, depending on the student skill level participants usually worked with. The task for each group was to think about how to use this discussion with their students. Group members made lists and brought them back to report to the whole group. A wide variety of rich teaching ideas resulted, including:

- making a video tape or taking pictures of water problems;
- learning words associated with water pollution;
- counting number of wells or city water among the class and creating graphs;
- dictating language experience stories about our own water problems to each other;
- role playing a visit with water regulatory officials;
- writing a letter of complaint;
- using water bills to teach math;
- writing a pamphlet about our water rights under the law.

Workshop participants used these teaching ideas to reflect on ways that this approach differs from conventional adult education. Participants commented on the different purposes of education, the differences in the assumed roles of teachers and students, and the hoped-for outcomes of this approach. During all these lively discussions, there was also much information shared about water problems, exchange of strategy ideas, and celebrating of victories that communities have won in organizing on this issue. As in other workshops, one of the challenges was not to lose our focus on literacy methods among all the compelling discussion of community organizing and development.

PROJECTS

Each participating group has chosen a project, an area of focus for their work in their own program for the *Community in the Classroom* year. The projects are very diverse, as one might expect, and incorporate literacy in many different ways.

- *Mountain Women's Exchange* is working toward bringing GED graduates back as volunteers in their adult education program.
- *Dungannon Development Commission* participants are working through a process

which they hope will lead to an adult education class for members who are rehabilitating housing and want to learn reading and math skills related to that work.

- *Whitley County Communities for Children* staff are writing a curriculum for JOBS participants, the program for unemployed mothers receiving government aid. The curriculum contains participatory research and other activities that are community-based and provide opportunities for critical thinking and problem solving in groups.

- *Big Creek People in Action* are developing a literacy and adult education program in an isolated part of the county where none has been before.

- *Lonsdale Improvement Organization* members are writing a housing survey and a brochure about their community as a part of the group's neighborhood revitalization and development efforts.

REFLECTION

Some of the groups chose to engage in a process of Board reflection so that even more people from the organization could be involved in thinking through questions related to adult education.

- In Dungannon, Board and committees are holding a series of workshops in which members think through a broader definition of adult education and ways in which adult education can support their existing work.

- Participants from St. Charles hope to facilitate a process for their board to consider the mission of the community-owned sewing factory and the opportunity it can present for workers to be involved with the organization and its adult education classes.

While not all the groups have "boards," and not all those with boards wish to go through a reflection process, all of the participating groups have been and continue to go through a reflection process involving at least those individuals who are active in "Community in the Classroom".

LESSONS LEARNED

At this point, we have learned some lessons (some more than once) and can see more clearly some of the issues involved in using literacy to build communities.

A lot of learning is going on in communities throughout the Appalachian mountains, but sometimes it doesn't look like adult education as we usually conceive it. There are more efforts to link literacy and community development and organizing than we had imagined, although much of it does not fit a conventional image of adult education. One group which has discovered corruption in the local utility district is getting together to teach each other how to read their own water meters to avoid being victimized. This broadened view of literacy pushes back the boundaries of what we've thought of as adult education.

Working together is not always easy. It often takes longer to accomplish group work than we think, for many reasons. Participants are spread across the mountains. Getting together to plan, to have a workshop, to exchange ideas with each other can turn into a major undertaking. Some participants live far from main roads, secondary roads are not good, and driving, especially in winter, can be treacherous.

Lack of personal resources is also a barrier to working together. Even if people live only a few miles apart, if they don't have a car, that distance can still be insurmountable. The closer families are to poverty, the less back-up they have in times of crisis. One illness can totally sap family resources, and there is no time and no money for community work for a while. Even a few dollars for gas to get to a meeting or make a long-distance phone call is out of the question.

People's lives are unpredictable. Jobs must be attended to, families taken care of. Meetings are arranged and then cancelled. Deadlines get moved back. Participants can't commit their organizations to a piece of work, or a certain way of doing things, without discussing it with others. This accountability back to the group must be respected, and it takes time. All these things have a tremendous impact on ability to do work.

Our original intention to plan each workshop cooperatively with members of two participating groups has been much more difficult than we thought because of the logistical problems of bringing people together. A compromise, in which *Center for Literacy Studies* staff travelled first to one community to develop workshop plans, then to another for additional planning and input, finalizing the agenda with telephone calls, simply meant that the "planners" often could not recognize their contribution to the final agenda.

Relationships are critical to the process. Knowing each other as individuals, understanding each other's life situations, learning about each other's children and families, developing trust and an appreciation for each other's work has been vital. It is hard to tell "outsiders" about the problems you are experiencing, and it takes time to trust each other enough to do that.

This has been complicated in the project by the changing participants. It was the original plan that three people from each community would be active from beginning to end, come to all the workshops and spearhead the projects. But people's lives do not fit a plan. Illness, transportation problems, family and work crises have meant that the same people have not been able to come consistently to all the workshops. Time is needed at each workshop to rebuild the "group" feeling.

Changes come slowly, and learning is incremental. None of us hear ideas one time, immediately go back and try them, and integrate the new idea smoothly into our work. Instead, it takes a lot of listening and talking to understand how a particular experience might apply in your own situation. It takes a lot of courage and support to try out some new ways of teaching. It takes a lot of time for the change to feel comfortable. This is especially so because of the next lesson, which we learn over and over again.

The "schooling model" is hard to escape. We have found that even for those of us who want to do adult education in a different way, a way that respects people's culture and knowledge, a way that helps students share power with teachers, a way that builds communities as well as individuals, it is still very hard to do. It is hard to resist the pressure to "cover the material," to be driven by tests, to conform to conventional image of school that learners themselves often come with. To think about education in a different way, we need support, opportunities to try things out and then systematically reflect on them. We need the relationships with others that sustain us.

Tension Between Literacy Goals & Community Development Goals

What is "literacy?" In the communities involved in this project, literacy is only one of many things that the organizations do, and often not the most compelling. Sometimes in workshops and in projects, the "issues" themselves are so urgent, so important and so critical that literacy gets lost. Discussion of educational approaches, linking of community issues to literacy, methodologies and curricula easily get lost in the excitement of sharing organizing strategies, stories of victories and defeats. We have to remind ourselves that when we work with communities, we work with the whole. In the holistic view, we should respond, support and encourage what comes up, from the communities themselves. But that creates tensions for us, for we are a literacy organization, and the project is funded to work on literacy, not just community development.

Regardless of these challenges, the "Community in the Classroom" project has touched an important need and a compelling idea. Participants work on projects at home and gather for workshops. They participate eagerly, and write thoughtful, positive evaluations. They volunteer to host workshops and to help plan and facilitate them. They invite each other to visit programs and communities. They talk about the things they have learned, and what it has meant to them in their own lives and work. They are eager to continue after the project year is over, and determined to stay connected with each other.

The "Community in the Classroom" project demonstrates that literacy is an integral part of community development, and that meeting individuals' literacy needs can be done in a way that also supports and builds their involvement in community issues. We may not have all the answers about how it all works, and what should be done, but we are all clear that it can be done. The project confirms the ideas that participants held: that literacy can build communities.

We live in a world of limited resources. But we also know that many things can happen because enough people care about them, and can see where they are headed. We can think about and design literacy education in a different way. If we want education to be the "ticket in" rather than the "ticket out" for rural communities, then we *must* make education an integral part of community development rather than simply preparing people for their place in "business as usual." If we believe that it is not enough to educate people to compete for the same limited number of not-very-good jobs, then we *must* pay attention to what else education can do for our society. If we believe that diverse peoples can learn to live together, accept each other and work together toward common goals, then we *must* create opportunities for people to learn about each other, share common experiences and recognize commonalities as well as differences. If we want to hold on to our rural roots, then we *must* focus attention on building and rebuilding communities.

Notes & References

1. U.S. Department of Agriculture, Economic Research Service, Agriculture and Rural Economy Division, *Education and Rural Economic Development: Strategies for the 1990's*, ERS Staff Report No. AGES 9153, Sept. 1991. In 1988 and 1989, for example, nonmetro areas lost 3 % per year of their college educated adults. among young adults, age 25-34, the rate of loss was twice as large.

2. Funded in 1992-93 by The Public Welfare Foundation Inc., the Association for Community Based education and other sources.

3. National Center on Education and the Economy, *America's Choice: High Skills or Low Wages: The Report of the Commission on the Skills of the American Workforce*, June 1990.

4. Economic Policy Institute, 1991 report "The Myth of the Labor Shortage Study."

5. U.S. Department of Agriculture, Economic Research Service, Agriculture and Rural Economy Division, *Education and Rural Economic Development: Strategies for the 1990's*. ERS Staff Report No. 9153, Sept. 1991.

6. See, for example, the *New York Times* article "Appalachian Mirror" by Denise Giardina, October 31, 1992.

7. These statistics cited in a *Lear* magazine article, October, 1992.

Chapter 21
POPULAR EDUCATION FOR PEASANT COMMUNITIES IN CHILE

Isabel Infante R,
Eugenia Letelier G
Santiago, Chile

THE MARGINALIZATION OF THE RURAL AREAS OF CHILE

Although illiteracy rates are generally low in Chile owing to expanded education for children, the rural areas have a significant proportion of illiterate people. The overall illiteracy rate is 5.3% for adults.[1] In the urban areas, the adult illiteracy rate is only 3.3%, but in the rural areas it is 13.7%.

Illiteracy and lack of education are associated with poverty. The average level of education for the 15-24 age group is 10 years of schooling; in low-income sectors of the population, it is nine years in urban areas and seven years in rural areas. Among more affluent sectors, education levels for the same age group are nearly 13 years in urban areas and nearly 11 in rural areas.

The differences are particularly marked among older adults. For example, adults between 35 and 44 who have a high income have almost twice as much education as those who have a low income, especially in rural areas. In these areas, those with the lowest incomes have only 5.4 years of education and those with high incomes have almost 11 years.

Though there have been gradual improvements in the education system, rural schools do not have the capacity to provide adequate education to this sector of the population. Some of these schools have only one teacher, others do not give all courses. Their curriculum is that of Chilean basic primary schools and, while these schools are allowed to adjust course content to the situation of their pupils, most of the time they only curtail it. The result of all this is a school that cannot develop the same skills as urban schools, or meet the requirements of children in rural environments.

One of the most serious problems is certainly the way in which the education system ignores the characteristics of the rural population. The language, standards and curriculum are developed in the realm of symbolic representations that have been formalized into a specific code that is totally different from that of the neglected rural sectors. Not only is it different, it also originates with the dominant culture, which is usually that of the urban sectors.

This results in the serious inadequacy of teaching processes and learning strategies in the case of children from rural sectors, which stems from differences between these cultural codes. Schools thus communicate and foster social differentiation that influences the educational backwardness of the forgotten children of rural areas.

Illiteracy and low levels of education cause adults to have very poor self-esteem. The way in which education is associated with the transmission of codes validated in a certain way by society underlies this problem of low self-esteem. This negative self-image contributes to hindering the processes of education and organization for the purpose of improving living conditions in these sectors.

There is certainly more than one "rural culture" in Chile, and there is more than one form of peasant life. The rural population is in fact very diverse, owing to numerous factors, such as geographical location (which determines what is produced), the form of land ownership, and, in particular, the form of productive labour.

Political factors have, moreover, strongly influenced the structure of the countryside and its inhabitants. In the 1960s, there was an agrarian reform initiative in Chile, which was still incomplete when the military coup took place, leaving the peasants with no aid from the state. Worse yet, the organizations that grew out of this reform process were brutally repressed. As a result, they were dismantled and destroyed.

In the first years of the dictatorship, the military government hastened to allocate individual plots of land, without providing the peasants with ownership and administration assistance, which caused many peasants to eventually abandon the land because of indebtedness.

Moreover, the intrusion of large-scale capitalism into the countryside changed the existing systems of production. The technology of capitalism caused polarization among producers; some were able to acquire the technology (by heavily indebting themselves), while others remained marginalized with minimal means of subsistence. The large estates, mainly producing fruit and wood, employ a huge mass of seasonal labourers, relegating many peasants, in particular young people, to their former status as casual labourers and hired workers. Those marginalized by technology and capitalist methods of production have great difficulty getting out of the poverty trap.

Modernity has inexorably penetrated the rural world, although at an uneven pace. When the focus of modern values was restricted to the school, the traditional culture, with its customs and oral traditions, co-existed with it, perhaps because of the inefficiency of the education system. Now, however, the mass media, bringing a flood of foreign messages, are having an impact on rural areas, particularly among young people.

Moreover, peasants are in contact with several forms of government bureaucracy, from payment of taxes to special subsidies for rural areas. This increasingly complicated environment means, in ways that differ for each area, that peasants require increased writing skills.

The traditional culture, varying from region to region, is not sufficiently valued by young people, who suffer from a considerable degree of cultural rootlessness. Most young people no longer wish to be peasants. Their elders think that the rising generation has lost the spirit of initiative and sacrifice which they themselves had when they were young. Older people often stress the experience of beginning farm work at an early age, which caused them to leave school after only a few years. The fact that young people are receiving more education is seen as a cultural change that is alienating them from their elders and from the land.

All of this is contributing to the influx of young people into the cities, as they seek out better opportunities. However, young people are also migrating, although in smaller numbers, from the urban periphery to rural areas where seasonal work is available. The barriers between urban and rural life are tending to disappear, particularly among young people.

Young people who migrate to the cities have rather poor prospects, since they are unable to compete with those who have been educated in urban schools. Unemployment or low-income employment awaits them, since the labour market has become more demanding: more education is now needed for the same job.

In 1970, for example, 41.2% of heavy machinery operators and labourers had between four and six years of education, whereas all but 14.9% of workers in these categories had more education than this by 1980. The majority of operators and labourers had more education: between seven and ten years.

Occupational categories for those with little education are becoming increasingly rare, but they nonetheless are not disappearing. In 1970, 23.8% of the unemployed had between 4 and 6 years of education, whereas in 1980 only 13.6% of the unemployed had an incomplete education (between four and six years of primary school). The majority of the unemployed (50.9%) has 10 years of education or more.[2]

Young people who cannot migrate to the cities continue to work on the land. Often angry, they work at various temporary jobs, greatly overworked and without future prospects. They marry young, forming little clusters that survive with the whole family working, reproducing the conditions of rural marginalization.

THE MEANING OF POPULAR EDUCATION
IN A RURAL ENVIRONMENT

Faced with this situation, it is worth asking whether the population needs education. On what aspects of rural life should proper education focus?

Attempts have been made to answer this question through educational proposals and activities geared to the rural population. The state has persevered with the standardized system of formal education, adding a few agricultural schools. Some educators, acting individually, have carried out several valuable local projects with the support of an NGO or university.

Beyond the state, the most significant activity for just over the past decade has been popular education, which has attempted to educate people and put them in control of their destinies, with the ability to construct a more just social order.

Popular education projects, in the tradition of "liberation education", are based on popular culture, even when it incorporates major elements of the dominant ideology or when it can be considered a "culture of silence",[3] or a spontaneous and traditional culture.[4] It is assumed that, in a class society, culture is the expression and the embodiment of the social insertion of groups. Since there are many forms of insertion, there are also many cultures giving expression to them.[5]

Popular education proposes to save the core of popular culture and knowledge, through which popular groups identify themselves as such, communicate among each other and interpret their experiences. It should not be assumed that popular knowledge does not exist or that it merely reflects the dominant ideology, but neither is it possible to naively claim non-existent virtues for it. Since popular knowledge derives from life experience on the one hand and the influence of the ruling class on the other, it does not present itself as a systematic and orderly body of knowledge, but rather in a scattered and self-contradictory way.[6]

Popular education tries to make popular knowledge and culture coherent and to give them a critical orientation. It will also carry out activities to preserve specialized popular knowledge in the popular interest, freeing it from ideological distortions. In this way, it is claimed, the people will be able to reformulate humanity's knowledge and cultural heritage on the basis of its world view, thus achieving an authentic cultural synthesis.

Another task of popular education is to preserve history by and for the masses by helping to explain and systematize the collective memory (which already exists in a fragmentary and implicit form).

Using dialogue and participation, popular education projects deal with the main problems of the participants, as identified by investigation and thematic discussion techniques. Through a process of action and reflection, these projects promote the idea that the participants are able to confront and solve their own problems.

The real-life experiences of participants are always emphasized. Freire's notion of "becoming aware", seen as a first step toward action and organization with a view to solving concrete problems, is less emphasized than before.

In rural regions, numerous programs have been developed, some stressing culture and others farming. A smaller number deal with illiteracy, which is particularly difficult because of the dispersion of rural inhabitants, the age of illiterate people, the shame they feel about their problem, and the lack of written information reaching rural areas.

Literacy education, in the context of popular education, is rooted in the culture of groups and thus interrelates with other activities aimed at the rural population.

EDUCATION & SELF-EXPRESSION PROGRAM FOR PEASANT COMMUNITIES

The education and self-expression program for peasant communities originated between 1983 and 1987 on Isla Grande (Great Island) in Chiloé, 1100 kilometres south of Santiago.[7] Its general aim was to help peasant communities acquire a critical awareness of their experience, express their perceptions of their surroundings, confront their problems and organize to solve them.

From its inception, the program was closely related to the concept of communication. Its general concern was "the lack of expression and the undervaluing of popular culture in the region and its ongoing invasion by foreign cultural content propagated through the mass media."[8]

To confront this problem, the diocese of Ancud set up a radio transmitter, seeking to provide a means whereby popular groups could communicate and express their culture. Radio Estrella del Mar (starfish radio), as it was called, had a cultural focus, seeking to stimulate an "active and critical attitude, so that people are not taken in by false illusions or by various interests, and so that they can become agents of their own development and have their own organization."[9]

It should be noted that the inhabitants of Chiloé are Huilliches[10] are of mainly Huilliche descent, and have their own rich culture, which has remained more intact than elsewhere because of geographical isolation. The result is that culturally invasive media messages seem to contrast more sharply with aboriginal practices, which exemplify very different viewpoints, values and ideas. For example, several explanations of some social and natural phenomena call on mythological figures or specific customs such as the "minga"[11] (voluntary community labour) when moving house, planting or harvesting, "medan"[12] (sharing of goods), and "quelcun"[13] (hospitality), which show a concern for justice and the importance of solidarity among neighbours.

When the program was developed, the importance of the troika of education, communication and organization once more made itself clear. The groups (17 communities of small rural landholders) discussed concrete themes relating to everyday life, organized themselves to settle some of the problems identified and communicated aspects of this process of reflection, discussion and organization through a radio program and a bimonthly bulletin.

The "Voces Campesinas" (peasant voices) radio program, which is broadcast once a week and which is subsequently rebroadcast at the request of the peasants, has a large audience. Beginning as a half-hour program and subsequently expanding to an hour, it had a well-defined structure: first, it broadcast the discussion of a theme, often presented in the form of a radio play and/or interviews, both produced by the facilitators; then it usually presented an interview with an "important" member of the community; community news was then broadcast and, lastly, letters from listeners were read out over the air and answered.

The bulletin of the same name was sent to all the participating communities and circulated within the Red de Prensa Popular (popular press network) that was set up in Chile in the years of the dictatorship.

In this way the process grew through the mass media. It was thus not difficult for other peasants (listeners) to participate in thinking about and discussing a theme from remote locations. The many letters showed the importance of the radio program to peasant groups.

An average of over 30 letters was sent to the program each month in 1986. They mostly recounted community activities. In several cases they discussed or expanded on stories that were broadcast. They could also easily promote cultural expression: during the last months of 1986, a folklore competition was organized, which received 64 entries from various locations. It should be recalled that communication by letter was difficult in this region. Among the hindering factors were low levels of education, the fact that writing was not a habit, isolation and the burden of peasant work. Correspondence thus decreased markedly in the summer peak labour months.

On the basis of ongoing thematic research, materials were developed (simulation kits, helpful brochures) that discussed the community and its problems, health, communication within the family, crops, natural resources, alcoholism and animals. In discussing these topics, the program promoted the adoption of a critical outlook on reality and prompted people to organize themselves to meet various challenges, so as to improve the quality of life. For example, to remedy the lack of health care resources in the countryside, 11 community pharmacies were set up. Community sewing workshops were later set up to provide low-cost clothing. The construction of a greenhouse to provide vegetables during the winter was also important.

Seeking to discover their own identity, three communities researched their own history, noting the challenges they had confronted and the way in which some of their problems developed.

The program usually worked through facilitators drawn from the communities and elected by them, who had three functions: animation, education and communication. Facilitators were trained in group animation and recording techniques during periodic day-long training sessions. Since the training was of the "learn by doing" sort, the facilitators made recordings, several of them in the form of radio plays on themes they themselves chose; these were later broadcast on the radio program and appeared in the form of short stories in the "Boletin Voces Campesinas" (bulletin of peasant voices).[14]

The political and social context in which the project developed created enormous difficulties. In an era of dictatorship in which it was not safe to speak out, peasants were invited to "express themselves" and "make themselves heard" on local radio. Overcoming fear and urging others to do likewise was also an ongoing task of the project. Peasants living in isolated areas were the most easily intimidated.

The project got under way in 1983, a year in which nation-wide protests began in the cities, and especially in the capital, breaking silence in the face of the dictatorship. However, the rural populations in the most remote areas were far from involved in the turmoil. Worse yet, the sudden change in what had become to some extent "usual" circumstances, caused uncertainty and fear among the majority even while the first glimmers of hope were beginning to manifest themselves among the more politicized sectors.

Moreover, lack of communication and participation in the system had created a climate of scepticism and pessimism about accomplishing anything. The economy seemed to be a remote problem over which no control could be exercised.

In these circumstances, an invitation to become organized, to explore features of one's own environment and express them in recordings, could not meet with an enthusiastic reaction. Even so, the constant work with three communities during the pilot phase, the joint development of materials, and the climate of communication and confidence that was created, helped to calm fears and increase credibility, replacing the previous notion that "nothing can be done" with more optimistic sentiments.

EVALUATION OF THE PROGRAM

In order to expand on certain aspects of the educational process, it seems appropriate to consider the meaning and the possible effects of communication. The interrelatedness of communication and social structures should be emphasized, especially with respect to the goal of popular education, which is to change social relations and mobilize popular groups.

In general, in the interaction they develop, people will set up a given system of relations that can either reproduce (and thus reinforce) existing social structures, or else create small liberating zones, which in turn create the possibility of social change.[15]

The process of developing a critical consciousness, refining a world view and transforming it into a basis for action, develops through a dialogue within the group and with the educator. These horizontal relations are the beginning of the creation of new social structures. These new forms of interaction give rise to a specific language, community customs and new forms of organization of community groups. In several processes of popular education, as groups become more close-knit, it is possible to identify various elements that can be connected, resulting in communication that is more horizontal and multilateral. Here are a few examples:

Increased self-esteem

The process of confronting various specific problems in a community in a group discussion setting reinforces the perception that "we can", "we have worth", and "we are not afraid". The same horizontal interaction gradually lays the foundations for a greater degree of determination in personal projects that will be reinforced by the community.

> I think the peasant has not yet been granted enough recognition. What's more, he is a working person...and I think he should respect himself and understand that he is someone of importance. But I think that we the peasants, those in one group at least, are in the process of doing something. We have a program, Voces Campesinas, which is already going somewhere and which will mobilize other peasants.

Valuing the spoken word

It is not a matter of indifference to the group if someone "does not speak". It is important that everyone should "express themselves" on the problem or topic being discussed; everyone contributes in this way to "expressing the world view". This is built up collectively on the basis of each person's vision. Everyone becomes a participant in the situation around them by saying what they have to say.

In the case of the program, speech becomes of major importance, since it is reinforced and expanded by being broadcast over the radio. Expressing the reality of peasant life and being listened to, particularly by the authorities, can help to overcome fear of the dictatorship.

> Right now, I think we have a solution, because our complaints and problems are being listened to...Because we are able to do interviews ourselves and see the problems that we have, so that we can let the authorities know what is happening in the countryside, because they often don't know what is going on....

> What peasants are most afraid of is to speak out, to tell the truth....I welcome this program very much because in this way the peasant listens to others and our companions let go of fear.

Valuing personal experience & the distinctive culture

The way in which each person perceives or has experienced a particular problem or theme is important. Experience is accumulated and interpreted on the basis of one's own world view, through culture. A program that integrates the goals of publicizing and reinforcing specifically cultural themes is appreciated on both counts. This why the peasants identify deeply with the program.

Their recollection of their own vigorous cultural traditions puts them in touch with their own roots, with their identity as a people.

> This program has been very useful since it has listened to young people, adults and the elderly and it has compiled information about our cultural roots, because people must know how our ancestors lived if they wish to understand themselves.

Development of a group spirit

The totality of group phenomena (customs, language, actions), sustained by shared intentions and values, creates a certain mystique which works to reinforce the group. The individual places special value on his or her connection with the group, distinguishing it from others.

Therefore, what people say in the group or over the radio relates to them, and shows that they appreciate this and see and value it as something distinct, of an almost religious nature.

> Because you are part of us and we are part of you, because you unite us more each day, because you are the one we listen to most, because we were allowed to have a program which we needed; our program, where peasants express themselves and discuss their particular anxieties and problems, without neglecting our customs, legends and roots, expressed by mature people who have given their all, who have struggled and who continue to do so.... May friendship and recognition of the work of this broadcasting family be the symbol that lets us say: Thank you, thank you, Radio Estrella del Mar.

(greetings from a woman peasant participating in the 1985 anniversary celebrations of Radio Estrella del Mar)

Emphasis on collective learning

Through the sharing of experiences and the contribution of the outside educator, a certain knowledge is developed which is grasped collectively in a "natural" way, since these are aspects of the participants' own lives. The participants observe that this is a different kind of learning in which everyone progresses together.

> For me, I think this is a way of advancing by discovering several things which lagged in our communities and which at the same time were improving in different ways. This helps us in expressing ourselves and finding solutions in other fields, such as the

economic, cultural and education fields, and to many more problems which were hidden to us, so to speak, or which we were not aware of.

Bringing about collective projects & organization

The preceding elements reinforce the group in its collective action to settle, even if only partially, certain problems around it. The peasants perceive that communication is the first step in organizing to confront their problems and to put pressure on the authorities.

> The authorities should listen to the peasants more, so that between the authorities and the farmers, the solutions to the main problems can somehow be found, because if you try to do it alone, it will be very, very difficult to be listened to. This is why I repeat that organization must be the principal element so that peasants' voices can be heard.

> What we dealt with most was the family health theme. In discussing things, we began with the problem of the mail, because the mail was in a poor state at that time..., and from there the idea of pharmacies was born. Now, thankfully, we have pharmacies. Each associate helps out, one donates paint, another nails, another shelves, and this is how the pharmacy is born, and I think it is also very important for us, above all because we are so isolated from the rest of the people.

The radio programs also helped spur on communities or groups that had not participated in the program for organizing and carrying out collective projects. It thus affected more people than the original radio program, and it received requests from other groups that wished to participate. This is a path along which further progress is possible...

The effects of this type of educational process, stressing communication, which were observable both in the groups closely involved and in the radio program's audience, showed that this process is a path which should be followed, expanded and deepened.

The link between education , group and mass communication has been proven, even in the difficult conditions of a dictatorship, to be a good formula for educational work with peasant groups that need a great deal of support to mobilize themselves and confront concrete problems in a collective and organized manner, so as to improve their quality of life. Written material, including the bulletins published by the peasants and the support manuals developed with their participation, were of great value to those involved with the groups, since they recognized that the printed page remained to be reread in their families, as opposed to the radio program, which was in a way ephemeral.

Through the radio programs and the bulletins, it was possible to keep the process perpetually renewing itself. Radio, even more than television in these remote rural areas, proved to be an effective tool of horizontal communication that could give good results in other kinds of educational programs.

SOME REFLECTIONS ON EDUCATIONAL WORK IN RURAL AREAS

It is undoubtedly more difficult to work with rural groups than urban ones. Isolation (in most cases), the scattered population and apathy, which result in educational programs boycotted by the participants, are some of the problems encountered by educators attempting to work in these areas. Moreover, the diversity of the countryside makes it difficult to develop material that is easily propagated on a large scale. We can almost say that the diversity of the rural population is greater than that of the marginalized people of the cities, since the latter have more points in common.

The rural population varies in terms of geographical location, form of land ownership and type of production; also, the modern world has penetrated the countryside in varying degrees, without entirely destroying peasant roots and customs, which are differentiated at the same time by multiple factors, some of them ethnic. Alongside the "minifundistas" or small landowners, who make relatively good use of a certain level of technology, according to market requirements and their economic possibilities, there are agribusiness workers and seasonal workers who live in conditions similar to those of the "afuerinos"[16] (outsiders) in the first decade of the century.

For these reasons, educational activities in rural areas must take diversity into account and develop specific forms for different sectors of the rural population.

Another factor which must be taken into account is the pragmatism of the rural population. If an activity is to be successful, it must deal with the basic needs of popular groups and promote concrete actions in which these groups can become involved, not as recipients, but as agents of improvement of their own living conditions. Only thus will better participation and commitment to the developing process be obtained, which will convert it into something belonging to them.

Even when activities or themes involving agriculture, health, housing, or other concerns relating to the population's basic needs are being considered, any action must have a strong cultural component, so that the teaching-learning process respects the population's world view and develops on the basis of it. The language of literacy education texts must support and take into account the groups' culture.

Groups should continue to develop their own materials, not only to intensify participation, but also to make sure that groups "write and read their experience." It will therefore be very important to promote the development of texts that preserve customs, legends, stories and real-life accounts. By having these people read and write about what is specific to them, it will be possible to respect, promote and develop the cognitive processes inherent in their culture.

It will thus be possible to at least partially offset the social control that is an aspect of the modernization of the groups' culture.

The link between literacy education and basic necessities will be of major importance in ensuring that quality of life is improved by various means.

Any rural literacy education project must take into account the problem of scant and usually poor means of communication; isolation is a common problem. To do this, it is necessary to train the inhabitants of the communities themselves as educational action facilitators, by choosing those who have a particularly important role in setting up the process in the community and determining its links with the culture and basic necessities of the groups.

Isolation, the difficulty in reaching many places and the prevalence of oral culture make support to groups through such mass media as radio more effective. Undoubtedly, radio is the mass medium that can best integrate itself into an oral culture. This is probably one of the reasons why it is better accepted than television.

Notes & References

1. Encuesta de Caracterizacion Socio-Economica Nacional - CASEN (Data taken from the national socio-economic characterization survey) carried out in 1990 by the Department of Planning and Co-operation in co-operation with the University of Chile and supported by the UNDP.

2. Infante, Isabel: *Juventud, Analfabetismo, Alfabetizacion en América Latina* (Youth, illiteracy and literacy education in Latin America). Santiago, UNESCO/OREALC, 1985. Pp. 38-40.

3. P. Freire: *Acción cultural para la libertad* (Cultural action for freedom). Buenos Aires: Tierra Nueva, 1975.

4. Gramsci, A: *Il materialismo storico e la filosofia di Benedetto Croce* (Historical materialism and the philosophy of Benedetto Croce). Turin: Einaudi, 1972.

5. Garcia-Huidobro, J.E. and S. Martinic: *Educacion Popular en Chile: algunes proposiciones basicas* (Popular education in Chile: some basic concepts). Seminar on research-action and popular education in Chile (Seminario Investigacion-Accion y Educacion Popular en Chile). Santiago: Programa Interdisciplinario de Investigacion Educativa (Interdisciplinary educational research program), 1980.

6. CELADEC *Reflexiones en torno a la tarea de la educacion popular en América Latina* (Popular education and new hegemony: reflections on the work of popular education in Latin America). 1980 (mimeographed).

7. Chiloé is an archipelago made up of the main island surrounded by hundreds of smaller islands. The population of Chiloé is 111,000 people, of whom 80% inhabit rural areas.

8. *El Cide in 1985*. CIDE: Santiago, 1985, p 38.

9. Diocese of Ancud: *El Sentido de la Radio Estrella del Mar* (The path of Radio Estrella del Mar), 1984. (mimeographed).

10. Aboriginal inhabitants of southern Chile.

11. Collective voluntary labour among neighbours. The person needing special assistance provides only food for those helping out.

12. Assistance in cash to a newcomer in the community.

13. The custom of granting hospitality to any neighbour in case of bad weather, especially when on a sea voyage.

14. Over the past two years, some of them were used by the Department of Education in post-

literacy texts.

15.   In this vein, the contrast with K. Merten's analysis of the concept of communication is interesting. Based mainly on N. Luhman, it proposes the following definition: [Translation] "Communication is the smallest social system that has the possibility of temporal, objective and social reflection, which by means of the interaction of the persons communicating, enables the analysis of actions and differentiates social structures." In this definition, communication is placed inside a larger system, over which it has a great influence; communication is seen as a "core" social system, defining larger social systems. Of all the criteria that define the essence of communication, the most important is the concept of the possibility of reflection, which refers to the reflection of processes upon themselves, and generally implies an increase in their power.

Merten, in the proposed definition, endows communication with the capacity for reflection on three levels: temporal, objective and social. On the temporal level, the possibility of reflection implies that the consequences of communication processes affect communication itself, influencing the evolution of communicative and social structures. This means that, considered from this angle, communication can be seen as a process of generating structures. On the objective level, the possibility of reflection means that the content of communication sustains the process itself. In this sense, communication is a process that deals with facts and events; this is important in developing an objective principle to encompass it, and, because of this, in shaping cultural expression. On the social level, the possibility of reflection implies mutual support by the people communicating, in terms of perceptions, expectations, and actions. In this light, communication can be defined as a process of interaction. (Merten K., *Kommunication: Eine Begriffs und Prozessenanalyse* [Communication: Terms and Process Analysis]. Opladen: Westdeutcher Verlag, 1977).

16.   The name "afuerinos" is given to landless peasants working temporarily on one of the farms (haciendas) or estates, staying in one for a while and then moving on to another, depending on employment opportunities.

CLOSING REFLECTIONS
LITERACY & CULTURAL
DEVELOPMENT STRATEGIES

Jean-Paul Hautecoeur
Unesco Institute for Education

APPROACHES TO ILLITERACY

It was our good fortune to be able to conduct this study over a vast area, to address literacy issues in a dozen countries, to enter into highly diverse historical contexts, to work with associates from different disciplines and from a wide variety of professional and cultural backgrounds. The contributors do, however, have a number of shared characteristics: all are well-read, all are adult educators, all have worked in rural areas (either on-site or from a distance, in the case of university- based educators), all are involved in what may broadly be termed literacy, and all use a community- based approach. This volume tells a story of differences, similarities, intertwining paths, analogous objectives, contending discourses.

To start with, let us examine how each of these discourses addresses the subject which unites these contributors and their experiences. We take not a psychoanalytical but rather a topographical approach: charting the lay of the land, measuring the breadth of the range of meanings. We speak of "literacy strategies", so it is necessary to set out the differing positions.

General Cultural Deficiency

Q. Garcia has compiled a detailed list of underqualifications and deficiencies in a rural Spanish micro-population with which he was in daily contact over an extended period of time. He terms this set of negative traits "functional illiteracy," a culture of poverty which embraces 80% of the population. These traits may be summarized as follows: lack of participation in local social and educational activities, lack of schooling, little or no use of the written word or of the media, no habits of information and expression, low self-esteem regarding education and culture, poor vocational preparation, weak skills in the daily activities of modern life, obsolete habits with respect to basic needs, and inadequate preparation for family responsibilities.

This portrait reinforces the image of a backward, largely ignorant rural population, unskilled in the most common activities of daily life, victims of the crises which have ravaged rural societies, now in the grips of mass culture, secular habits and social assistance. It is an image of a passive, isolated population shunning available educational opportunities, a rural fourth world whose failings include passing the attitudes of forbearance and resignation on to the next generation. "Everything's gone" as they said in one of Daniel Seret's workshops.

A. Chacón and A. Polo, who set out to "create a school which would influence the behaviour of youths and adults and help them realize their full potential," present the population of the village on which they descended as equally depressed. They describe its full potential in the following terms:

> People in the area learn by imitation...people had almost no capacity for abstraction...their written and oral expression was very under-developed...they viewed the unknown and anything new with complete distrust...their thinking was wholly practical.

Was it at university or elsewhere that one learns to diagnose an "illiterate" population in these terms, before setting off on a literacy tour in the country? The description sounds like a diagnosis of mental disability rendered by a remedial teaching trainee. Were it not for the references to "viewing" and "thinking," it might come from clinicians at an experimental psychology lab discussing orangutans.

But this example drawn from the Spanish social context (which is in fact fairly typical of a widespread discourse found the world over) is still relatively respectful due to the fact that the target population is close to and of the same origin as the researchers. When writers deal with an outcast minority such as the Gypsies (Rom) in Central Europe or aboriginal peoples in North America, the disqualifying classifications quickly descend to terms of anomie, affliction, utter incompetence. No text illustrating this type of disparaging diagnosis couched in scientific rhetoric is included in this volume. But we did hear examples of it at the seminar we held in Bratislava (thanks to the participation of a Gypsy (Roma) Association). Outcast minorities are labelled with the radical discredit of illiteracy, while to their own kind writers attribute the lesser ill of "functional illiteracy," seen as a regrettable consequence of recent history, not a defect.

This discourse conceals (albeit poorly) a desire to subject the populations in question — referred to as "at risk" in the professional jargon — to radical treatment entailing total submission. Not so long ago, campaigns for literacy, religious conversion or political integration resorted to forced labour, compulsory sedentarization, displacement to isolated reserves or villages, residential schools for the children, military service for the men, etc. Today, there is compulsory enrolment and participation in vocational training courses for "idle" adults.

Low Education Levels, Failure in School, Exclusion

Another point of view, held by I. Infante and E. Letelier of Chile and by E. Fernández of Galicia, essentially attributes rural illiteracy and its systematic reproduction to the failings of the school system, "a school that cannot develop the same skills as urban schools, or meet the requirements of children in rural environments" (Infante, Letelier).

In traditional rural societies speaking a different tongue and beset by growing poverty and marginalization (the word "peripheralization" is also used in the case of outlying "land's end" regions such as Galicia), school is credited with mythical power to open the doors to modernity, the city, less poverty, more choices; to reduce discrepancies, to make changes possible, to give students added value which is marketable anywhere in the land. This rite of passage through the school system is supposed to accomplish in the real world what the mass media accomplish instantly in the realm of the imagination.

This rural school, impervious to history, represents a two-sided break for students: on the one hand, they are torn out of their native social environment, which is deprecated (reinforcing the rejection absorbed through contact with mass culture); on the other, they are disqualified by academic failure and by dropping out, symbolically closing off opportunities for advancement. These processes make their future exclusion all the more likely.

The family environment, embedded in local popular culture, does not support the transition to the school environment. The school, its staff, and its culture remain alien, distant from the "ignorant" populace. Parents and local associations confirm this distance, for the schools "make no concession to either their language or their cultural background" (Galicia). Their ambivalent relationship with the only institution which can enable advancement causes them to shun education and results in a deprecation of their cultural heritage and resigned acceptance of a fatalistic vision of the world, which those who have made the leap call ignorance and illiteracy.

> This type of illiteracy is common in rural areas, where people have a poor understanding of the changes brought on by progress. Rural regions also lack a vision of the future and fail to realize the importance of education in order to adapt to the complexities of modern life.
>
> H. Fernández

The importance of education and the unsuitable nature of the schools give rise to a search for local educational strategies which can effect the transition to modernity without a loss of identity.

This position is characteristic of educators who see ignorance as a blight upon rural societies, a cause of "backwardness, dependence, marginalization and injustice." It is therefore imperative to "raise education levels" (H. Fernández).

This vigorously interventionist approach is closely related to the first position, which posits a general cultural deficiency, but it differs in that it values regional identities and cultures and that cultural transformation projects are designed on the basis of the regional culture's social organization.

Loss of Literacy & Marginalization

This position, represented by H. Dionne and R. Horth of Quebec, shares the previous position's attachment to local culture, but also recognizes illiteracy as a "radical widening of the gulf between individuals living in marginalized rural communities and the social system," without interpreting this gulf as a deficiency or a shortcoming to be overcome. They do not attribute the gap to the schools or the education system but rather to "the social system which organizes this marginalization". This is a more complex schema. First, it speaks not of rural illiteracy but rather of a loss of literacy or the "illiterization" of rural culture driven by its alienation from modernity. People become illiterate. The cultural consequences of the induced decline of unproductive rural communities include loss of guide posts, exclusion from the orbit of knowledge, loss of control over one's daily environment: "Becoming illiterate means, first and foremost, losing control over one's environment." This loss is experienced as an attack and rural communities are fighting back: refusing to leave, refusing to accept the "destructive logic of a system gone haywire," searching for viable local solutions by recycling traditional practices and knowledge for use in a different developmental model.

There are indeed "illiterate" individuals in Quebec villages who attend literacy classes. These "traditional conceptions of training" are critiqued on the grounds that they are confined to the closed world of education, which is cut off from its sociocultural context and the dynamic of local social organizations. The socio-educational intervention Dionne and Horth advocate attempts to transform these isolated literacy education practices by linking them to community action in rural areas and changing their pedagogical approach.

Functional Illiteracy/Dysfunctional Literacy

We return to Spain, Portugal and Chile, to pre-modern rural societies where all communication is oral, except in school. Rural schools are unable to change social communication patterns because there is no use for writing outside of school. There is also a process of loss of literacy, in the sense of deterioration of reading and writing skills, which are learned at school (at least by the younger generations) but subsequently lost because they serve no function in local interchanges. According to J. Carrasco, "the ability to read and write becomes a cultural component in a sociological environment, or for a person, if it plays a *functional role....* It follows that the meaning of illiteracy refers to social expectations and social relations within a particular sociological environment."

At Santibáñez de Béjar, the written word is not used. Some professionals use it to communicate with the outside world but they communicate orally with villagers. Written material circulates only at the school. The books never leave the library; the few newspapers received do not circulate. This is a common situation in mountain regions, and also in Galicia, where contracts are verbal to this day. "At the Axantada livestock fair, all sales are made by verbal agreement, without paper. And it would never occur to anyone to challenge an agreement of this type; an unwritten covenant has the force of law."[1]

In these environments, there is no demand for literacy education, understood as **the process of changing the method of communication**; indeed, there is resistance to the introduction of new communication techniques, not only from the "illiterate" population but also from local educators. Among the populace, there are a number of reasons for this resistance: atavism, living in a closed microcosm, low self-esteem and defeatism, but also "low motivation for pursuing an education, since schooling offers no assurance of improved living conditions" (Portugal), resistance to a school and teachers identified with an alien culture, etc. The resistance of the schoolteachers of Santibáñez may be attributed to a corporatist desire to preserve their monopoly over education in the village.

But now the microcosm has been punctured. "Modernity has inexorably penetrated the rural world"; television is "bringing a flood of foreign messages" (Chile). The mixture of the two cultures remains oral until the arrival of literacy educators in the villages; they may break open the "static, closed world order" (J. Carrasco), or they may help lend legitimacy to the region's popular culture and its resistance to the "ongoing invasion by foreign cultural content propagated through the mass media" (Chile). In either case, literacy is presented as something necessary and inescapable, and the target populations are thereby classified as illiterate, as in the first three approaches we have described.

Dominant Literacy/Minority Illiteracy

The illiteracy of aboriginal minorities in Canada, who today are demanding official recognition as "First Nations" and the right to self-government, is the fruit of a long history of cultural eradication. Their illiteracy is a sign of the loss of their culture, their history, their legitimate life on the land. The loss of their language symbolizes this dispossession: "You took my talk."[2] Those who have suffered this fate refuse to view it in the same manner as those who are responsible for it. Illiteracy exists, to be sure, but it is a result of acculturation through literacy education in the country's official languages and in its schools, and through the dismantling of aboriginal social organizations.

The schooling system resulted in a loss of language and a loss of culture for several

generations of children.... The language and the culture was no longer passed from
elders to children.... Often they use neither their mother tongue nor English well....
They are called the "walk abouts" as they aimlessly pass their days.

L. Fogwill.

The leading demand, in legal terms, is for recognition of "First Nations
jurisdiction and their right to control their own lives" (P. George). But aboriginal
demands extend well beyond that: they seek to transform a social order built on
the oppressor/oppressed or national/foreigner dualism into a multi-faceted
order known as multiculturalism. This is a far-reaching change which opens the
door to a new order in every domain: culture, politics, law, educational standards and practices.

In the realities of a multicultural society, Aboriginal peoples must have the choice of
where and how they wish to live.... Literacy is an important first step in self-
government. P. George.

The article by the Tennessee contributors bears witness to the universal
nature of the indigenous demand for cultural emancipation: in the United
States, they note, cultural aspects of education "have been rooted in a melting
pot image — an attempt to change who people are, to bring them into "mainstream" culture, to devalue difference. But times are changing...In this country
we see an increasingly diverse society, in which people are demanding to be
affirmed and valued racially, ethnically and culturally.... Adult literacy programs can be and are being part of this challenge — the acceptance and
affirmation of difference" (Merrifield, White, Bingman). In the Appalachians,
this means fighting for survival at the village level and, to this end, transforming basic educational practices in local organizations — no easy task.

A similar process of change is evident among migrant workers in the U.S.
First, a remedial program was offered on a satellite basis in order to reach and
hold onto the fugitive migrant public. It met with mixed results. At the same
time, migrants opened a community centre; one of its main functions was to
open up channels of communication and cultural interchange in the locality.
They "convinced local merchants to use Spanish on store signs....They want
the community to become familiar with their culture and their rich historical
heritage" (L. Velásquez). "Illiterate" is not their own definition but rather a
cultural negation of their condition applied by the "host" society. In the current
reversal, the "foreigners" are attempting to take the initiative and transform the
dominant monologue into an intercultural dialogue.

C. Sauzier relates a similar experience in England, an attempt to open up
second language instruction to an intercultural exchange with the local community on the assumption that illiteracy cannot be reduced to the foreigner's
ignorance of the national idiom. On the contrary, illiteracy embraces the wider
organization of local communication processes and particularly of adult education, which closes off avenues of intercommunication and therefore of practical
use of the local language.

Totalitarian Literacy

Officially, socialist countries have drastically reduced the illiteracy which existed under past regimes through massive literacy campaigns and unprecedented development of cultural and educational facilities in the countryside. They have solved the social problems of capitalism, including illiteracy, through "ideological negation" and have created "an extensive institutional and organizational network within which adult education and social work were carried on" (S. Hubik). On the basis of this system and other techniques of ideological control, the most totalitarian regimes have rebuilt popular literacy education from scratch, with the goal of

> the materialization of...the myth of the 'new human being'....This 'evil rewriting of man' wanted all spiritual concerns to be repressed in favour of a dogmatic and ultra-pragmatic approach, intending to create a prototype of an animal-like person, with a dormant conscience and primal concerns.
> F. Anghel.

In a paradox of socialism or perhaps a populist tactic by the government, local popular culture has benefited in this situation from the development of cultural organizations and from the one-party state's tolerance — and sometimes even support — for its efforts to express itself, to renew traditional social ties and orally transmit vernacular knowledge and skills. We see anecdotal evidence of this "counter-literacy" in the example of the "cemetery of laughter" in rural Rumania. In the former Czechoslovakia, the movement was able to use the state television network to create a remarkably dynamic communication and education system to support local economic and sociocultural development. A second form of literacy education arose on the basis of systems for the distribution of commodities, folk knowledge (not so much in opposition to official propaganda as to fill a structural void) and cultural representations employing a living language (in contrast with the language of the technocrats or the party).

In Hungary, the village of Gyulaj was slated for destruction to make way for the forest. Villagers feared that "the whole village community could indeed end up as outcasts just like the Gyulaj Gypsies, tossed about by the vicissitudes of fate." In this case, an old "bourgeois (European, if you like) village" experienced a loss of literacy through geographic isolation, the fraying of the social fabric, removal from the traditional environment and exile: "Bird-song is all we got out of the forest." Soon, as with the Gypsies and the Amerindians, all would be lost of the old ties except in memory. But the subtext does not fade away as long as segments of the community continue to bear it within themselves. "There is now another culture in existence 'underneath' the circumstances forced upon them....They chose the common people's wise tactic of survival by outwitting authority. They strove to compensate for diminished freedom too by working harder" (F. Balipap).

Today, in Gyulaj, the energy of this quiet resistance is being channelled into opening up communications with the world and with the forest, and into a new multicultural and cooperative social contract with the Gypsies. This utopia is becoming a reality, in law, on the land, through community and solidarity, and now through increased competence to participate in new interchanges.

Women's Illiteracy

In Greece, female illiteracy is embedded in the traditional social structure: the lot of women is housework, limited and controlled contact with the outside, lack of participation in economic activities and social and political organizations, education and skills limited to traditional activities. Their communications are monitored. In Velvendos, the change was wrought by a women's cultural association set up for the purpose of "moving away from traditional activities such as embroidery and weaving and turning to activities tied to product processing and the cottage industry sector". According to an account in the local paper, where the women published a regular column as a way of taking part in the life of the community and changing their image and status in the village, "one of the reasons that led us to set up a co-operative was to give women an opportunity to get out of the home, considered their exclusive and sole domain, to become involved in participatory activities which until then had been unfamiliar to them and to interact and communicate on a daily basis with other women".

It may be worth recalling the dominant position in literacy circles at this point, since it represents a minority point of view in this volume: literacy education consists of transmitting recognized skills at the individual level and granting certification through the established institution of universal schooling. School is made compulsory for all citizens in the short and long terms for a variety of reasons: reasons of State, equal opportunity for all, maintaining competitiveness and camouflaging unemployment rates, fighting functional illiteracy. It could be said that on this score women have had the same opportunities as men in most countries of the northern hemisphere; indeed, women have generally received more schooling and earned higher grades. Moreover, the majority of teachers are women, at least in the lower grades, as are the majority of adult literacy educators. In the division of labour, domestic education and writing tasks are delegated to women. Is it fair to conclude that women are more literate and participate more in cultural life? The women of Velvendos are demanding participation of a different order.

To quote the Velvendos women's column again: "Some 'illiterate' women feel insecure and lack self-confidence because of their lack of education. Others, however, while illiterate, still manage to make their mark." The cooperative set up basic education courses for the first group and anyone else who was interested. But the main purpose of the cooperative, at the *collective* level, was to change the status of women in the village and eliminate *unequal relations of communication*. The literacy education activities (in the widest sense of the word "literacy") initiated by 75 Velvendos women from every social background were intended to work a comprehensive collective, sociopolitical change of this type. The result has been "a dynamic cultural spirit which has helped to broaden the written communication network and which has also enhanced the learning process for the population of Velvendos... [and] the personal growth of its members by providing a productive, commercial, educational and cultural framework for action".

Second-Level Illiteracy

I have included two different approaches under this heading to arbitrarily close this typology, without having exhausted all the texts.

The first is the article by H. Sánchez, who contends that illiteracy must be understood in relation to communications technology and data processing, the media of the post-modern age: "We may soon see a new 'class distinction' between an elite with unlimited access to the new information media and a very large sector of the population condemned to a kind of illiteracy."[3] Rural communities are particularly affected by this type of cultural lag for they are sorely lacking in modern information infrastructures, as well as stable information and exchange systems, research capabilities and professionalism on the part of local cultural agents. Development of this type was the mission adopted by the Peñaranda Cultural Centre, using facilities, social and cultural group activities, and professional services on a par with what is available in urban areas.

The second approach is represented by D. Seret and C. Mahy, from a Belgian cultural centre working to develop creative expression among the most underprivileged classes. The main medium used is the image, the visual aesthetic language they call second-level language. Activities are based on the experience of identity, which is traditionally expressed through form, colour, objects and the familiar montages of everyday life. The creative expression workshops are designed to foster "the discovery or rediscovery of the group's cultural identity, its acceptance of it, and its ability to communicate that identity to others." (The particular group in question here is a Turkish immigrant minority.)

The migratory condition (poverty, racism, exposure to mass culture, isolation) has a three-pronged effect on minority identity. It tends to rigidify or fetishize their cultural expression, which is placed on the defensive; it replaces some forms of expression which have lost their function or value with mass culture substitutes; it is conducive to fusions, to new unconscious arrangements which are not yet a language but do express a new fragmented identity. Here, illiteracy is the effect of the ossification, repression or rejection of an identity as expressed in a person's or community's aesthetic language. The image-based literacy therefore consists of decoding, recognizing and constructing a more conscious expression of the continuities and breaks in the group's history.

HOLDOVERS, DEFICIENCY, DOMINATION

To recapitulate, we did not begin this study with a normative definition of literacy but rather with methodological orientations broad enough to admit projects of all kinds. Different social and historical contexts, professional positions, theoretical priorities and action objectives justify this broadening of the object domain, which extends to texts which do not even mention the concept of literacy (F. Balipap, for example, and E. Fulkova, whose final text did not reach us).

Our libertarian and (multi) culturalist definition may be stated as follows: illiteracy is defined by each contributor with reference to an ideological and historical context. We attempted above to decode the various definitions and the social contexts in which they are embedded, to identify contributors' positions within these contexts, to group together similar positions and separate divergent positions (at the risk of schematizing complex arguments). The exercise led to the extrapolation of the above eight approaches.

It is possible to further reduce the range of positions to three categories, which might be called holdovers, deficiency, and domination. Each of these refers to an understanding of the relations of communication or cultural interchange among social groups in a regional, national and international system.

The "Holdovers" Model

The model which focuses on *holdovers* from traditional or "premodern" forms of oral communication in regions located far from the dominant exchange market (for goods, messages, values) is not reducible to the deficiency model. Oral communication performs specific functions which we may value, attempt to preserve or even recreate when they are threatened with extinction. A deal made on a handshake and a word in Axantada, Galicia may be more efficient, cost-effective and durable than a complex computerized transaction which may generate spin-offs in the information storage and legal advice markets.[4] In Quebec's Lower Saint Lawrence region and the U.S. Appalachians, there is opposition to neo-capitalist modes of communication and production aimed at preserving the village way of life and cultural continuity.

The holdover model must be understood as dynamic, not anachronistic. It seeks to reintroduce diachronic elements of culture, use value, continuity and difference into a totality extending beyond the synchronic system. For example, it attempts to find a role and active function for the older generations who enjoy immense respect in Canadian aboriginal cultures but have been allowed no place in the school system. It reincorporates the spoken word and oral tradition into what we call literacy, which school and literacy campaigns have taught us to reduce to individual reading and writing skills, obscuring the relationship between these skills and the social group's mode of communication as a whole:

> Placing education into culture rather than continuing the practice of placing culture into education.
>
> P. George

Jean-François Chausson has proposed the following conception of literacy, which emphasizes the fact that competence in cultural expression serves a knowledge transmission function (technical and scientific) and ensures the community's historical continuity:

> Functional illiteracy means…an inability to express oneself in one's national language so as to be recognized by the Other, to transmit one's cultural heritage, to integrate tradition into the adventure of modernity.[5]

While a systematic logic of communication seeks to achieve internal homogeneity by excluding alien and older elements, which are seen as undesirable, J.F. Chausson's historical vision rehabilitates these "relics" or elements of bygone modes of communication which serve to cement social and emotional bonds and to preserve meanings in a social system under constant threat of disintegration.

The Cultural "Deficiency" Model

The cultural deficiency model, which appears in various forms in a number of the texts, is a key element of the standard ideology of literacy. It serves to justify educational "interventions" in so-called deprived populations, with or without their consent. Defined from outside the mental categories and experience of the people it addresses, legitimated by scientific or institutional power, integrated into a positivist discourse which seeks development, independence, liberation or productivity, the diagnosis of lack serves first and foremost to impress upon the Other the reasons for his or her low social status, and to indicate the path to normalcy through education.

It therefore performs the primary ideological function of persuasion, opening the door to outside "professionals" and to sometimes far-reaching changes in the cultural and social fabric. Rural areas and working-class neighbourhoods in the cities have long been subjected to these literacy campaigns — brutal under socialist regimes, insidious in liberal regimes, inescapable in authoritarian democracies, charitable and paternalistic or maternalistic in the countryside, where they are conducted by local elites.

Another function of the application of the cultural deficiency model to a particular social environment and the individuals who make it up is to systematically adapt local modes of communication to a global market and to the state's planning, regulation and control mechanisms. The book market, for example, is very active in the "fight against functional illiteracy" in many countries. At the same time, state standardization of skills is promoted through legislated educational incentives and, more imperatively, through labour policies with respect to manpower training and unemployment.[6]

The introduction of cultural transformation projects in an environment which has been labelled deficient, needy and therefore "at risk" (hence subject to deviance and anomie) sparks resistance, which is interpreted by the professionals in "psychological" terms: lack of motivation, low self-esteem, lack of ambition, inability to cope with change — i.e., it is interpreted in terms of the original diagnosis of individual and cultural deficiency. Poor attendance and dropping out are attributed to the cultural deprivation of the students rather than to their rejection of unsuitable educational programs. Here is an example from a report on literacy in the rural U.S.:

> Cultural features common to many rural communities also create obstacles to literacy programs. Literacy directors report that it is not easy to convince small towns and rural communities to accept new ideas, nor is it easy to convince potential clients that they need more education. Perhaps this was why a director wrote: "Even people who are aware of their need will put you off." In contrast, another director attributes this resistance to an independent attitude and the need to be self-sufficient. One program director points out that "People are not used to asking for help". In all, directors wrote that many small towns do not yet believe that a problem exists. The widely given response is "We are OKAY".[7]

The reality is poor communication between the two sides, a different understanding and analysis of local "problems," different educational signs and values, and most importantly perhaps a desire by residents to deal with local questions in terms of their own rites of communication and shared references, to have their own knowledge, experience and skills recognized.

The suppliers of literacy education have viewed the process as a social service and used the discourse of deficit to describe their "clientele". The persuasive efforts of the suppliers were supposed to prompt a recognition of need by the target population and induce demand. But there is resistance to these intervention strategies, as the obsession with recruiting and holding on to "clients" in rural literacy programs attests:

> Overcoming what are often deeply established economic and cultural patterns in a community is extraordinarily difficult. Rarely did directors report effective methods that address the heart of these economic and cultural barriers. More frequently, directors talked about approaches to recruiting and retaining clients.[8]

We encounter passive, silent resistance from the community in the form of lack of response to the proffered service ("non participation"), polite refusals of the "We are okay" type when the community is indeed adequately structured to defend its independence, and also, as in Santibáñez, Spain, resistance to outside literacy workers by local teachers.

Located at the periphery of exchange systems and suffering from a relative shortage of goods, services and human resources, rural communities have developed values and skills in solidarity, independence, selection of inflows and outflows, self-defence, etc. In many areas, they have experienced major crises which have decimated their economic resources, populations and land, and curtailed their scope of action, protest and resistance. They are seeking ways to recover these powers, notably through suitable education.

> Scattered throughout the mountains of Appalachia in the southeastern United States, a growing number of community-based organizations are practicing literacy and adult education work in a different way. These organizations...are trying various ways to link their literacy and adult education work with the community development issues their groups also address.
>
> Merrifield, White, Bingman.

In some locales, active resistance has flared up in reaction to aggressive cultural interventions which have caused radical deculturation in the community and rents in the social fabric. This has occurred in the case of minorities which have been subjected to policies of assimilation. In some situations, active resistance has remained under the surface due to the risk of repression; this was true in eastern Europe. There are still situations in which resistance is being organized from within the community, as in the case of Greek women. The social organizing of these minorities (or majorities relegated to minority status) to resist cultural domination has generated the discourse of *domination* or *oppression*, which is our third category.

The Anti-Domination Model

The **anti-domination** model does recognize the existence of linguistic/cultural/structural **deficiency** but understands it as an effect of subordination to the dominant culture and society. It calls for a new identity to be rebuilt on the foundations of the **surviving vestiges** of precolonial times; these vestiges are viewed as a cultural asset which must be reclaimed and adapted to modernity. This then is a different version of modernity, what S. Hubik calls post-modernity: a heterogeneous system in which minorities are recognized, in which they can claim their rightful place, relative independence, and a new legitimate right to self-determination within a multicultural setting.

This last model, which advocates a counter-literacy in place of the former unitary order — be it "southern," patriarchal, or the one-party state — is explicitly political. It demands, first and foremost, a radical change in communications and refers to a new democratic order which must be community-based, cooperative, non-authoritarian. The account by Hungarian writer L. Harangi is an important example of this approach; it addresses the Gypsy community as an equal partner in the new local community order, although the Gypsies continue to be almost universally treated as pariahs under the new regime. For Harangi, illiteracy is not the other community's problem; it is bound up in the practices of exclusion which have governed majority/minority relations, under both the old regime and the new. The major obstacle to resolving the "Gypsy question" is, "in one word a lack of social conscience based on education and literacy" — on both sides, obviously.

The utopia which must be worked out at the local level in the village of

Gyulaj, where the two communities have long lived apart, is based on the premise that

> the gypsies' values, traditions and their special ability should be recognized, as should their right to their own way of life, which is based on their rich and unique cultural heritage. It is only in this spirit that this nation and its representatives can be considered as responsible and equal partners, and not just as the objects of a minority policy, no matter what amount of goodwill it reflects.[11]

Clearly, this "third road" must present literacy within its complex historical context, for it seeks to change the course of history by returning to the myth of Adamic language, to create new forms of social organization and test them pragmatically at the periphery of the major systems: the market, respected institutions, concentrations of cultural industries, urban areas, the centralized state. This attempt is necessarily political; instead of stretches of "no man's land," of burnt-earth policies and depopulation, it demands a legitimate living environment and a right to live on the land (often their ancestral lands). The environment for community survival is not given; it is coveted (by armies, waste management companies, the hospitality industry, electrical utilities, etc.). The residents of condemned regions must devote their energies to asserting their right of tenancy and their right to recourse if they are despoiled, and to claiming the basic services to which all citizens are entitled: "Not a single rural child without schooling: for a quality school in each village" (P. Marcos). Energies must be poured into demanding and creating autonomous zones for small and medium-sized associations in the face of large public and private organizations.[9] Much energy must still be devoted to seeking partners, information and various types of support in order to design and launch local projects.

This multitude of collective efforts at the outer limits of organized circuits of production, consumption and exchange must be recognized as a global workshop of lifelong education, independent learning, research and experimentation, in which the main capital consists of local human resources. They are learning work organization by practical experience, including how to select and obtain outside resources. We enter here into a different economic zone, a different political forum, a parallel system regenerated or driven by social values and techniques which no longer prevail at the centre — values of *solidarity, cooperation, participation,* "relics" of premodern eras which have been recycled virtually intact in postmodern contexts. They are learned (recognized) through action, which implies the use of adequate forms of communication in changed relationships. This is a practical and fundamental process of literacy education, in which there is no room for diagnoses of deficiency, recruitment campaigns or retention measures.

EDUCATIONAL & CULTURAL ACTION STRATEGIES

If we speak here of education instead of literacy, it is because one constant in all the contributions is a concern with the role of education in the community intervention process. While it is considered a priority everywhere and all agents acknowledge an educative role, education is understood by some writers as the **starting point** and precondition for change and development (Galicia, Canadian aboriginals, Portugal), by others as a **continuous** process embedded in a set of collective activities ("Action is in itself an educational method" — P. Marcos), and by still others as **subsequent** to certain types of action (Greece, Siete Pilas).

Adult Basic Education

On the first view, literacy is a specific educational intervention with particular forms of organization conducted by professional educators, who may take on local non-specialist assistants. Literacy initiatives, research, programs and partnerships serve to support the goal of raising the population's level of education, though they may also be related to broader local development objectives. In the Las Villas area, for example, an open, "integral" program model gave way to a literacy intervention focused on promoting reading.

We find various types of action in these adult basic education projects. Unlike the first three British experiments, they share a social organizing or empowerment approach, a community-based format and an explicit connection with local or regional culture:

- the traditional model of **offering a course** with sociocultural activities;
- the development of **cultural services**, especially book circulation (by changing the relationship between the library or media centre and its potential audience) or the creation of a community radio station;
- intervention in a community's **forms of communication** to develop a written culture, especially for communications between professionals and their clients;
- **cultural research**, expression and production in the oral tradition, in the aesthetic language, in the individual and collective memory.

These four types of action are not mutually exclusive; we have seen that in many cases they may be performed in conjunction. Neither is a focus on writing an absolute condition for a literacy intervention. It is possible to work primarily on oral expression (radio), pictorial or theatric expression, singing, music, popular arts. Unfortunately, there is only one article in this volume dealing with workshops of this type.

Community Education

There are examples from Appalachia, Huntington in the U.K., and migrant workers in the U.S. which stand at the transition point between the traditional approach to literacy and the second approach, which might be called the community education approach. In these three cases, we can observe a change in course: education in itself, a process conducted by professional educators, a process whose objectives and features are defined from the outside, for abstract purposes and not for local pragmatic applications, is being revised, indeed stood on its head. The process is leading, in Appalachia, from the "ticket out" to the "ticket in," placing education at the service of the community once again, at the risk of "shelving literacy" in favour of a community action strategy in which economic issues may be predominant; in Cambridgeshire, it is leading from a second language program isolated from its social context to a project aimed at refashioning communications between anglophone and allophone residents; in Tennessee, it is leading from a satellite high school equivalency program offered from the University of Tennessee to a community centre opened by migrant workers which provides emergency services and is working to open up channels of intercultural communication with local residents.

In all three cases, exogenous educational services are giving way to a dialogue which should facilitate the expression of local demands and reorient educational practices. The educators are becoming mediators instead of outside experts. Literacy now means changing the conditions of communication, the rules of interchange, the roles and status of the parties, setting new priorities. For example, instead of learning English immediately or submitting to academic qualification exercises, migrant workers are asking for a translator to be hired to help migrants with legal problems and raising money for a cultural centre. First and foremost, there is an assertion of independence, an expression of identity, and a refusal of oppressed status in daily life, not just in the isolation of the classroom (no matter how open it may be). It becomes the role of the teacher to facilitate these processes of empowerment, to perform a social education function which is central to the processes of communication.

Comprehensive Education

As we have seen, the community education approach, or education/research by and through action, implies a basic change in the teacher/student relationship and in social representations of education. Local educator/organizers can facilitate these changes or obstruct them. Their audience may accompany them down one path or another, but the dominance of the scholastic model in the prevailing ideology tends to confirm the status quo, without however increasing its impact on participation in adult educational services in rural areas.

Behind local initiatives there are of course programs and policies which may support or block these education projects, or force them to negotiate between two opposed sets of constraints (for example, a prescriptive manpower training policy and a regional development policy which emphasizes a comprehensive approach to existing problems, innovation and participatory research; or a literacy policy aimed at endowing students with qualifications and a cultural policy based on developing the region's economic potential through the expression of popular cultures, and so forth). For example, Q. Garciá's experience in Spain suggests that progressive education projects clash with national and supranational policies and with the structural forces which are imposing change on rural societies. On this view, the utopian nature of approaches based on comprehensive social change and the lack of public participation would justify a methodological change of course, returning to the more sectoral approach which we have called traditional literacy education.

However, many contributors refer to the comprehensive approach (or approaches?) even if they apply it only in part. At least two texts deal with it explicitly: Cáritas' action research and inductive teaching method in Spain and the television program "Receptar" in Czechoslovakia. Action is the priority: in the case of Cáritas, that means resistance to rural decline, strengthening the villages' ability to mobilize by organizing community-based vehicles, developing communications and applying a popular education method;[10] in the case of the "Receptar" program, it means creating and activating channels of communication and mutual assistance so as to generate the skills needed to produce goods locally and enable civil society to meet needs which the market and public services are failing to satisfy. In both cases, the priority is on economic issues; actions focus on communication and a process of education/research designed to increase participation, enhance effectiveness, train local leaders and more firmly entrench the process. These initiatives aim to convert popular experience and knowledge into a practical asset and activate this information-based asset by organizing communications and strengthening solidarity-based practices. The organization/communication/education triad also underlay the Chilean experiment in popular education be means of community radio, although this initiative had a cultural focus which places it nearer the first model than the comprehensive approach.

We must note the importance of *participatory research* within the comprehensive approach, not only to ensure the effectiveness of action initiatives but also because research is intrinsic to change, innovation and the methodical extension of the field of action. This cannot be achieved through mobilizing and developing solidarity alone (these have also been used as demagogic techniques in the past). It is therefore important for literacy initiatives to link up with a university or research centre or group, although this is seldom suggested when local agents seek partnerships.

In this connection, we may cite P. Federighi's conclusion, which applies to our work as a whole. It reunites the education and action models to yield a methodology we have called comprehensive education. The goal is "making students accountable for participation in organized community life":

> Developing abilities and opportunities for participating in organized community life is often the key to preparing people for management, teamwork and innovation...The model that is best suited to meet the objectives and yield the desired results is one which examines and creates a virtual future. The basic methods then consist of research...designed to give the end users of projects the conscious ability to control and change the educational process.

Local Development

In our last category, priority is assigned to economic initiatives and productive labour. Here, training is oriented towards the goal of developing local economic potential. Siete Pilas in Spain and Velvendos in Greece are examples of this model.

At Siete Pilas, the original project consisted of educating the population for change. This was transformed into a series of economic initiatives leading to a radical change in the educational process and in the Adult Education Centre's mission. An outside intervention by educators/group-leaders turned into a local economic development process with growing links to the outside. At Velvendos, a cultural association launched an economic initiative with the overall goal of changing living conditions — i.e. traditional modes of household production and communication.

The common point to these projects is that both set out to effect basic transformations; both shared a dynamic of economic change which yielded education, information and participation initiatives. Moreover, both were specifically targeted — at a limited audience of youths at Siete Pilas, after the adults were "abandoned," and at a group of women at Velvendos (we are not familiar with the history in this case). European Community directives supporting innovation in depressed rural areas are another common reference point and resource. Local autonomy is being constructed on the basis of existing systems with which it may be advantageous to link up in a particular situation.[11]

Both initiatives have been successful from an economic point of view, particularly since they subscribe to a cooperative model, not to capitalist growth targets. These successes cannot be attributed to the educational activities, which were added in mid-process; they were no more than an additional benefit. In the words of the president of the Velvendos cooperative, "The trick is to know how to organize and to ensure that all members have the desire to work and some community spirit."

The teachers who came to Siete Pilas to work on cultural development and literacy are now considered "promoters of work teams for youths...developers of projects...teachers responsible for work-study programs in cooperative management, seekers of subsidies, specialists in socioeconomic realities."

These projects also benefited from various types of support from local organizations and incentives; for example, professional teachers were loaned (on salary) and local lifelong education initiatives were welcomed and accepted (at least in Spain; this certainly is not the case everywhere, as the articles from Quebec and the U.K. indicate).[12] The expansion of local economic initiatives to other locales provided endogenous support, leading to the affirmation of local community empowerment through all the processes of change, especially in the fields of education, culture, and communications (methods and relationships).

In Velvendos, the result was

> the development of oral and written communication as well as the underlying processes...the change in the cultural status of women...the development on the local level of education and professional development strategies and policies for women...the fostering of the participation of the women of Velvendos in modern culture...the recognition of the traditional know-how of women...the preservation and promotion of local heritage and traditions.

Similarly, at Siete Pilas, education in solidarity was maintained throughout the project, leading in the final stage to the creation of an association to replace the "school," the inclusion in the projects of members of marginal groups, the creation of a fund to support other work projects for the youths and of an information centre on "alternative community service" for conscientious objectors.

These are impressive results, as were the results yielded by the Czech experiment in cooperative television, which as we have noted also had local economic development as its central objective. The authors' assessments should, however, be compared with those of other observers, and these successful projects should be compared with others which have been less so, such as the ones briefly reported by Q. Garcia in Las Villas.

CLOSING REFLECTIONS

In April 1993, most of the contributors to this volume met for a conference at the Germán Sánchez Ruipárez Foundation in Salamanca. The main purpose of the meeting was to pool our individual results and skills, produce an overview of our experiences, findings and questions, and draw conclusions for future action, research and international intellectual cooperation.

This part of our common effort has only just begun. For lack of a collective overview, I have presented in this final chapter elements of the personal overview I developed in the course of editing the texts. But I also wish to be faithful to the conclusions which emerged from the Salamanca conference, where the contributors split into three workshops (Spanish, English, French) and drafted joint proposals. These conclusions may be summarized as follows:

- Educational strategies in rural areas must approach problems **comprehensively** and not confine themselves to technical or technocratic initiatives.
- **Literacy** is political; it must be linked to general manpower training policies. We must resist the prevailing tendency to reduce literacy to a component of formal education.
- In the new international context, where the functions and responsibilities of the public sector are being reassessed, it is important for governments to **support** their most impoverished citizens by guaranteeing their right to accessible educational services.
- **Rural regions** have a special need for support. Principles of profitability cannot be applied to depressed rural regions which, in terms of a comprehensive vision of development, call for priority investments. The tendency for economic policies to abandon rural regions must be reversed and support must be extended to

human resource development.

- **Literacy** remains an essential stage in adult education, and the objectives of literacy being to fight social marginalization and underdevelopment, provide access to cultural products as well as to social services, adapt to technological change in the job market, and promote democratic participation.

- The development of lifelong education programs, which still relies too greatly on the work of volunteers, must meet professional **quality** standards, notably by adapting to new communication technologies, showing respect for local cultural traditions and improving the coordination of integrated development processes.

- In local literacy work, action must be guided **by four principles**:

  1. cultural diversity;
  2. sustainable development;
  3. the educator's role as mediator between the local community and the larger society;
  4. the educator's primary responsibility to listen to and understand his or her partners; we must speak of people's interests and potential, not their deficiencies.

- Educators are subject to certain constraints, such as the urgent need for job creation in rural areas, which limit their options. Solidarity with our partners can demand changes in our research topics and working methods. How then can new difficulties, such as obtaining research **funding**, be resolved?

- Three general subject areas deserve attention in the coming years within the Unesco Institute for Education's ALPHA research program:

  1. **communication** strategies — understood in the anthropological sense of the word and not reduced to the instruments of communication — which embrace literacy issues;
  2. **lifelong education** strategies in relation to **local democracy**, which is at the junction of today's major issues, including literacy and minority issues;
  3. strategies of cultural empowerment employing **artistic expression**, which plays a vital role in traditional cultures; sustainable development cannot forgo aesthetic language.

Notes & References

1. Margarita Rivière, "La Galice ne croit plus aux miracles," *Le Monde diplomatique*, July 1993: "À la foire aux bestiaux d'Axantada, les ventes se font exclusivement par accord verbal, aucun papier. Et nul n'aurait l'idée de contester une décision prise ainsi en commun; le pacte non écrit a valeur de loi."

2. Title of a report cited in Priscilla George's bibliography. See also Noëlla MacKenzie, "Those Indians Are Trouble," in *ALPHA 90*, Jean-Paul Hautecoeur, ed., Unesco Institute for Education/Ministère de l'Éducation du Québec, 1990.

3. Linda Shohet puts forward a similar argument in "Literacy and Technology: Changing New Concepts," in *Literacy Across the Curriculum*, The Centre for Literacy, Montréal, Summer 1993, Vol. 9, No. 2: "We mouth platitudes about living in an age when access to, and control over, information constitute a new form of capital. If the metaphor is viable, then we are in the process of creating a new underclass of the dispossessed and the exploited in all those adults who lack the skills to accept, choose and use the information that is multiplying faster than the most literate among us can comprehend..."

4. Serge Halimi, "Marée judiciaire aux États-Unis," *Le Monde diplomatique*, October 1993. Halimi quotes the following passage from Robert Reich, *L'économie mondialiste*, 1993). In the great international economic contest, where legal blows are also traded, "each ingenious legal argument is countered by a still more ingenious argument from the other party. The potential for escalation is unlimited: the case files grow thicker, the documents, depositions

and discoveries more numerous....The clients feel forced to spend more and more money to get an edge, or at least to avoid a costly defeat. From the point of view of society as a whole, this spending is wasteful."

5. Jean-François Chausson, "Formation en milieu rural et maitrise de la lecture-écriture", *Pour*, January-March 1989: "L'illettrisme désigne...l'incapacité à s'exprimer dans sa langue nationale pour se faire reconnaître d'autrui, transmettre son patrimoine culturel, intégrer la tradition dans l'aventure de la modernité."

6. In the new socioeconomic and ideological context, which in our field is characterized by a movement away from literacy education in the schools towards basic in-company training, the position of a research team at the Université de Lille, France (CUEEP) is representative: basic functional illiteracy is replaced by a "multidimensional phenomenon," inadaptation to change in the workplace, which is attributed to the workers' **cognitive deficiency**. Here are some examples from a study by E. Carlton, M. Lannoy, V. Robert and M.A. Sharma, "Entreprise et représentations de l'illetrisme," *Les Cahiers du CUEEP*, No. 20, June 1992:

    "...presenting functional illiteracy not as a handicap but as a multidimensional phenomenon...it draws attention to social difficulties in coping with this age of change in technology, industry and communications...[In the workplace] illiteracy appears as a lack of adaptation to change. Its definition therefore shifts from difficulty reading, writing and counting to difficulty understanding, analysing, and especially dealing with new situations, adapting."

7. *Literacy in Rural America: A Study of Current Needs and Practices*, Rural Clearinghouse for Life-long Education and Development, Kansas State University, 111 College Court, Manhattan KS66502, 1992, p. 41.

8. *Ibid.*, p. 41.

9. See Alpha 92 — Literacy Strategies in the Community Movement, Ministère de l'Éducation du Québec/Unesco Institute for Education, 1992.

10. See also the special issue of "El futuro del mundo rural," *Documentación social*, Cáritas, No. 87, April-June 1992; and Jean-François Chausson, "Pour une histoire de l'action culturelle en milieu rural," in Vaison, *Aujourd'hui la culture du monde rural*, Université rurale nationale/Universite de Toulouse-le-Mirail, Paris/Toulouse, 1987.

11. See the brief description of the Habitat and Leader programs in the "Rural Spain" chapter; also *Documentación social*, op. cit.

12. See the two texts on Portugal by Madalena Dias and Olivia Oliveira, who describe a similar transformation observed in literacy programs which have opened up to the community, in *ALPHA 92*, op. cit.

PREVIOUS TITLES IN THIS COLLECTION:
ALPHA 90 — Current Research in Literacy

ALPHA 92 — Literacy Strategies in the Community Movement

Orders for previous titles:
Unesco Institute for Education
Publication Unit
B.P. 131023
20110 Hamburg
Germany